HOW TO

GET INTO THE BIBLE

STEPHEN M. MILLER

Illustrated by
PAUL GROSS

Publishers Since 1798

Thomas Nelson Publishers

Nashville

Printed in Nashville, Tennessee, by Thomas Nelson, Inc.

Unless otherwise indicated, all Scripture quotations are from The Contemporary English Version (CEV), copyright © 1995 by the American Bible Society. Used by permission.

Verses marked "NKJV" are taken from the New King James Version, copyright © 1979, 1980, 1982 by Thomas Nelson, Inc.

The Scripture quotations contained herein from the New Revised Standard Version (NRSV) of the Bible are copyright © 1989 by the Division of Christian Education of the National Council of Churches of Christ in the United States of America, and are used by permission. All rights reserved.

Verses marked "RSV" are taken from the Holy Bible: Revised Standard Version, second edition, copyright © 1946, 1951, 1972 by the Division of Christian Education of the NCCCUSA.

Verses marked "NIV" are taken from the Holy Bible: New International Version, copyright © 1978 by the New York International Bible Society.

Scripture quotations marked "NLT" are taken from the Holy Bible, New Living Translation, copyright © 1996. Used by permission of Tyndale House Publishers, Inc., Wheaton, Illinois 60189. All rights reserved.

Library of Congress Cataloging-in-Publication Data

Miller, Steve, 1952–
    How to get into the Bible / Steve Miller
       p.   cm.
    ISBN 0-7852-1135-7
     1. Bible—Introductions.   I. Title
   BS475.2.M55   1997
    220.6'1—dc21   97-7843
                                                    CIP

Printed in the United States of America

13 14 15 16 – 08 07 06 05

CONTENTS

AUTHOR'S PREFACE

Welcome to *How to Get Into the Bible.*

When I have a choice, I don't venture into unfamiliar territory without taking some kind of guidebook or map—usually one or more of both. At the moment, my family is about ready to go on a two-week vacation to places we've never been. You'd need a yardstick to measure the pile of travel guides, brochures, maps, and travel articles we've collected in getting ready for the trip.

Why such bother? We want to get the most out of our experience. We want to see everything worth seeing and do everything worth doing—that is, everything within the energy level and bank account of a Ford-driving, middle-aged man.

For the masses of people who've never read the Bible, cracking it open and getting started can be a daunting challenge. It's one huge book. Where do you begin?

How about starting with the big picture? Scan the biggest scenes of the Bible. Introduce yourself to some of the starring characters. Familiarize yourself with the terrain. That done, turn to individual books within the Bible and do the same.

We've created *How to Get Into the Bible* to help Bible newcomers do just that. For the millions of people still unfamiliar with the world's all-time best-seller, we've provided a guidebook. Actually, it's perhaps more like the printed program you'd get before watching a play. It will help you get your bearings as you sit back and begin to enjoy one of the most wonderful journeys you'll ever take—a journey into the mind and heart of God.

A few friends.

I'd like to express my deep gratitude to the following people:

- Linda Annalisa Miller, my wife, frontline proofreader, articulate critic, persistent encourager.
- Joseph Coleson, gentle spirit, Old Testament professor at Nazarene Theological Seminary, and one of 90 scholars who produced the New Living Translation. He offered me his Old Testament insights. And I gladly, quickly snatched them up and included them in this book.
- Mark E. Roberts, editor, and a doctoral candidate in New Testament studies. He guided this project down its circuitous path to publication, and provided New Testament background that I would have otherwise missed.
- Dana Long, art coordinator, who handled more than 250 pieces of original art in helping produce this book. Her attention to detail gave the book its attractive appearance.
- Paul Gross, who created all of those drawings, ranging from Creation to the New Jerusalem, with just a few notes of guidance. His research into ancient cultures made each illustration more accurate.
- Lee Hollaway, contract editor turned reference editor, who handled the nuts and bolts of making the various elements of this book fit together.

God bless them, every one.
And God bless you as you read this book, and more importantly as you read His Book.

Steve Miller

HOW TO USE THIS BOOK

As you turn the pages of this book, here's what you'll find, and why.

• **How We Got Our Bible.** This is a fast-paced article that traces the story of the Bible from the days before it was written—when eyewitnesses told astonished listeners what they saw—to the computer age, when we can again see video recreations of the Bible events. It's astonishing to discover how God has preserved his message throughout the ages.

• **Highlights and Headliners.** Here you'll catch a sneak peak at the 30 biggest scenes in the Bible, and a concise biography of a dozen leading characters.

• **Genesis through Revelation.** From the first Bible book to the last, you'll get a thorough preview preparing you to read each book for all it's worth.

–**Famous Lines** from each book—quotes you've probably heard, but never knew where they came from.

–**Starring Roles,** briefly identifying each of the main characters in the book.

–**What to Look For,** pointing out insights you might otherwise zoom right past.

–**Timeline**, helping you picture where the book fits into other events going on in the Bible lands and beyond.

–**Did You Know?** intriguing nuggets of information about each book.

–**Author and Date,** evidence about who wrote the book and when. (Most Bible books were written anonymously, but clues in the text and in other ancient writings often suggest possible writers.)

–**On Location,** maps of key sites.

–**Big Scenes**—the heart of *How to Get Into the Bible*— quickly acquaints you with the main events and teachings in each book, using illustrations and captions.

–**Reviews,** a section that lets you listen in on what the critics are saying about the book. You encounter both affirmations and challenging perspectives.

–**Encore,** pointing you to related books in the Bible. If you like the book of Ruth, for example, you'll also enjoy the dramatic story of another heroine: Esther.

GETTING STARTED

You don't have to read this book from cover to cover before opening your Bible. Our hope is that you'll read the two together.

Here's one approach you might consider.

First, read How We Got Our Bible, then Highlights and Headliners. These will pique your curiosity, which you should follow as surely as you follow your nose. If you find yourself drawn to the story of Jesus, for example, you can turn to the Gospel of Mark— the shortest and most action-packed of the four Gospels. Read the overview of Mark that we offer in *How to Get Into the Bible*, then grab your Bible and read the complete story with enriched insight.

There are dozens of Bible translations you can choose from. Or you might select one of the paraphrases of the Bible, which seek to convey the key ideas in the Scripture without sticking to the Hebrew or Greek words used in the passage. A few versions deliberately choose to use only a limited vocabulary to tell the Bible's story. We especially like the Contemporary English Version because of its readability and accurate translation. In fact, unless we indicate otherwise, it's the version we use throughout *How to Get Into the Bible*.

One tip about looking up Bible references. If you see "John 3:16," for example, John is the name of the book, and 3:16 means chapter 3, verse 16.

One warning—but a happy one. It's a bit like the warning my wife and I got before we started our family. Our parents told us that having children would radically change the way we live, but that we would never regret the changes. They were ever so right. Our daily schedule is nothing like it once was, but our joy is rich beyond expression. There are times when I put my arms around each one of my children and tell them how happy I am that they have become a part of my life.

My warning to you about the Bible is much the same. Reading and learning about what God wants to say to you through the Bible can change your life forever, but you will never regret the changes. After living with them daily for many years, the words of God continue to change my life and fill it with joy. I believe they can do the same for you.

SNEAK PREVIEWS

How We Got Our Bible

There's a short version of how we got the Bible—and why.

It's summed up in a letter from the apostle Paul just before his execution: "All Scripture is inspired by God and is useful to teach us what is true and to make us realize what is wrong in our lives" (2 Timothy 3:16, New Living Translation).

Paul was talking about Jewish Scripture, which Christians call the Old Testament; the New Testament was not finished at that time. But Christians believe that Paul's words apply equally to the 27 books of the New Testament, which revolve around the life and teachings of God's Son.

Exactly how God "inspired" the many biblical writers is an intriguing mystery, and a source of sometimes hot debate. But all Christians who believe that the Bible is God's revelation to the human race agree on one rock-solid point: God guided the more than a millenium-long process, from beginning to end. He personally saw to it that humans got the message he wanted to deliver.

In the beginning, stories about God were probably passed on by word of mouth long before they were written onto clay slabs or tanned sheepskin. In ancient times, villagers and herders alike admired gifted storytellers who, with entertaining flair and evocative cadence, preserved and passed along the community's tradition and history. Listeners became familiar with the stories, and typically refused to allow storytellers to skip or add material—much like children today monitor and supervise the familiar stories that their parents read to them.

The Writing Begins

No one knows when the first Hebrew put pen to parchment, or stylus to clay. Moses is the first person the Bible identifies as a writer. Perhaps as early as the 1400s B.C. Moses wrote down the many laws God gave him—probably those preserved in the books of Exodus, Leviticus, Numbers, and Deuteronomy (Deuteronomy 31:9). But hundreds of years before Moses, Abraham, the father of the Jewish nation, may have written the dramatic stories about his life that are preserved in Genesis. He came from the Persian Gulf region where writing was already at least 1000 years old.

Most of the rest of the Old Testament—stories, poems, songs, genealogies, nuggets of wisdom, prophecies, and all the other genres of Hebrew tradition—was likely passed along orally, then eventually collected and recorded by scribes. The writing probably began in earnest after Israel established itself as a powerful nation, during the reigns of David and Solomon in about 1000 B.C. As scrolls began to wear out, scribes carefully duplicated the text onto fresh scrolls.

Exactly who wrote the Old Testament remains a mystery; most books don't say. The first five books of the Bible, for example, are anonymous. But ancient Jewish tradition says Moses wrote them. Some Bible authors, on the other hand, are clearly identified; many prophets wrote the books named after them.

All but a few sections of the Old Testament are written in Hebrew, the language of the Jews. A few passages are written in Aramaic, a similar language that the Jews picked up when they were exiled to Babylon. After twenty-some-year-old Alexander the

Great swept through the Middle East in the early 300s B.C., Greek became the prevailing language.

Within about a century, an Egyptian king decided to create a new holding for his renowned library in Alexandria. As legend has it, he asked the high priest in Jerusalem to loan him about 70 top scholars who would translate the five revered books of Moses into Greek. The result—the first Bible translation—became known as the Septuagint, meaning 70. Over the next hundred years or so, the rest of the Hebrew Bible was added. When New Testament writers later quoted the Old Testament, they quoted it from this Greek translation.

Rome destroyed Jerusalem in A.D. 70, leaving the Jews with no temple for offering animal sacrifices. So the Jews began to offer sacrifices of praise and prayer by reading from their sacred writings. The problem was that the Jews had a wide array of revered books, and many versions of some books. No one knows exactly how or when the

Jews settled on the books that make up their Bible, which Christians call the Old Testament. The five books of Moses, known as the books of Law, were probably among the first ones widely accepted. The books of the prophets likely came next, followed last by books known as the Writings: Psalms, Proverbs, and others. Eventually eliminated—partly because they were not originally written in Hebrew—were many books published in the popular Greek translation. They were called the Apocrypha, meaning "secondary" or "hidden" works, and would later reappear in Roman Catholic and Eastern Orthodox Bibles.

The Late-Breaking Good News

The story of how we got the New Testament is quite similar, though the time frame

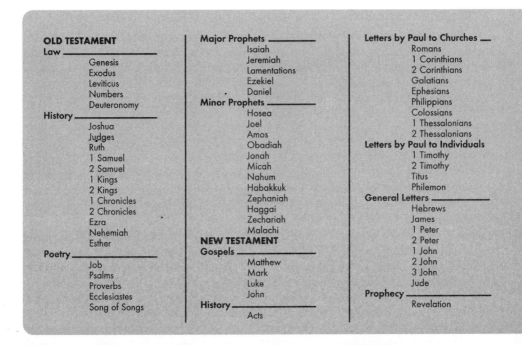

OLD TESTAMENT
Law
- Genesis
- Exodus
- Leviticus
- Numbers
- Deuteronomy

History
- Joshua
- Judges
- Ruth
- 1 Samuel
- 2 Samuel
- 1 Kings
- 2 Kings
- 1 Chronicles
- 2 Chronicles
- Ezra
- Nehemiah
- Esther

Poetry
- Job
- Psalms
- Proverbs
- Ecclesiastes
- Song of Songs

Major Prophets
- Isaiah
- Jeremiah
- Lamentations
- Ezekiel
- Daniel

Minor Prophets
- Hosea
- Joel
- Amos
- Obadiah
- Jonah
- Micah
- Nahum
- Habakkuk
- Zephaniah
- Haggai
- Zechariah
- Malachi

NEW TESTAMENT
Gospels
- Matthew
- Mark
- Luke
- John

History
- Acts

Letters by Paul to Churches
- Romans
- 1 Corinthians
- 2 Corinthians
- Galatians
- Ephesians
- Philippians
- Colossians
- 1 Thessalonians
- 2 Thessalonians

Letters by Paul to Individuals
- 1 Timothy
- 2 Timothy
- Titus
- Philemon

General Letters
- Hebrews
- James
- 1 Peter
- 2 Peter
- 1 John
- 2 John
- 3 John
- Jude

Prophecy
- Revelation

is compressed. Instead of taking a thousand years or more for spoken stories to give way to writing and then to widely revered status, the process takes about a century for Christians. The earliest followers of Jesus didn't immediately write their stories, apparently because they expected Jesus to return soon. They urgently spread his teachings in person, by speaking.

The first New Testament books were probably not written by Jesus' disciples, but by missionary-minded, circuit-preaching Paul. Scholars estimate that Paul's earliest letters of encouragement to young churches he had founded were written about 20 years after the death of Jesus. The rest of the New Testament was written throughout the remainder of the first century, roughly A.D. 50 to 100.

Christians had long respected the Jewish Scriptures as God's Word. But they also recognized that the message of Jesus, contained in the Gospels and other writings, was an essential part of God's revelation to human beings. Christians, however, didn't formally agree on which books to include in the New Testament until after Marcion, a Christian leader in the early A.D. 100s, proposed a short list: the letters of Paul and the Gospel of Luke—all of which he had edited to reflect his belief that Jesus was not human and could not really suffer.

Over the next two centuries, Christians debated which books should be included. Many had been written, including about 60 of questionable content and authorship. By 367, most church leaders agreed to accept as authoritative only the 27 books they believed were written by apostles—ministers who had actually seen Jesus, including the original disciples and Paul. The first known list of these books appears that year in the Easter letter that an Egyptian bishop, Athanasius, sent to his churches. He was the first on record to use the word canon—which originally meant "measure"—to describe the officially recognized books of the Bible. Church leaders decided that no other books should be added to the canon.

The Bible isn't one book, but a library of many books. Most Protestant Bibles have 66 books—39 in the Old Testament and 27 in the New—arranged in the order and categories shown here. Old Testament books by prophets, for example, appear together—starting with the Major Prophets (meaning the longer books), followed by the Minor Prophets.

This arrangement is different for some other Bible-believing faiths.

Roman Catholic and Eastern Orthodox Bibles include the Apocrypha, a collection of books that appeared in the Septuagint, a Greek translation made from the Hebrew Bible about 200 years before Christ. (See "The Apocrypha," page 459.) Jews, however, later decided against keeping these books in their Bible.

The Dangerous Art of Translation

Latin, the preferred language of Romans, eventually spread throughout the empire. Christian scholars began producing several Latin translations of the Jewish and Christian Scriptures. By 382, however, Pope Damasus decided the church needed a single, authoritative Latin translation. He assigned this arduous task to Jerome, leading Bible scholar of the time.

Jerome knew Latin and Greek, but not very much Hebrew. He was determined to translate the Old Testament from the original Hebrew language, not from the Greek Septuagint. So he moved to a monastery in Bethlehem and learned Hebrew from Jewish scholars. More than 20 years after he began, his monumental

TIMELINE	BIBLE EVENTS	Moses writes God's laws 1440 B.C.	David writes songs 1000 B.C.	Solomon writes wise sayings 950 B.C.	Jeremiah writes prophecy 600 B.C.	Old Testament translated into Greek 200 B.C.	New Testament written A.D. 100	New Testament accepted as Scripture 367
		1500 B.C.		**1000 B.C.**		**500 B.C.**		**A.D. 100**
	WORLD EVENTS	Canaanites create first alphabet (pictures used before) 1500 B.C.	Trojan War ends in sack of Troy 1190 B.C.	David becomes king of Israel 1010 B.C.	Solomon dedicates first Jewish temple 960 B.C.	Confucius born 551 B.C.	Jews win independence 164 B.C.	Paper invented in China A.D. 103	Pagan temples closed in Roman Empire 354

translation was complete. It became known as the Vulgate, meaning "common," since he wrote it in the common language of the day.

At first, his translation met stiff resistance. After one congregation heard his version of Jonah read to them, instead of worshiping, they rioted. They preferred the earlier version they were used to hearing and memorizing.

Because language changes, updated versions can sometimes sound dramatically different from previous versions. To further complicate the process, it's not always clear how to interpret the ancient text. For example, ancient Hebrew had no vowels and no lowercase letters. If we wrote English that way, "once upon a time" would look like this: NC PN TM. But those same letters could also read "Nice pun, Tom." Ancient readers

familiar with the story seemed to have little trouble reading it. Others had to look for context clues, which were plentiful. Solving the puzzle of one word gives you a clue about what the next word should be. When you put a lot of words together it's easier to figure out what the story is about.

At about the time Jerome was translating the Bible into Latin, a missionary named Ulfilas was inventing an alphabet for German tribes so he could translate the Bible into their Gothic language. This scene has been repeated throughout the world, throughout the ages.

ENGLISH BIBLES
A Sampler from Psalm 23

Readers today can choose from many Bible translations in modern English. To give you an idea of how they compare—and how they have changed over the centuries—here are excerpts from the most famous psalm in Scripture, a psalm often quoted in times of difficulty or read at funerals.

Wycliffe Bible, 1380s (first English Bible)	The Lord gouerneth [governs] me, and no thing shal faile to me; in the place of pasture there he hath set me.
King James Version, 1611	The Lord is my shepheard, I shall not want. He maketh me to lie down in greene pastures.

Jerome translates Bible into Latin 405	Caedmon, a monk puts parts of Bible to music 670	Wycliffe produces first English Bible 1384	Tyndale executed for translating Bible into English 1536	King James Version of Bible 1611	English Revised Version 1885	Dead Sea Scrolls discovered 1947	Revised Standard Version 1952	Contemporary English Version 1995
500		**1000**		**1500**		**1900**		
Muhammad has vision, recorded in Koran 610	Crusades begin 1095	Eyeglasses invented 1300	Bubonic plague kills one-third of Europe 1348	Columbus sails for new world 1492	Shakespeare becomes a London playwright 1592	Puritans land at Plymouth Rock 1620	Mark Twain writes Huckleberry Finn 1884	Israel becomes a nation again 1948

Dates are approximate

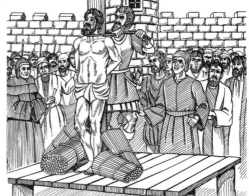

As Christianity grew, so did the number of Bible translations. Most Bibles were too expensive for common people, because it took months of work to copy them. In the 1300s a Bible could easily cost a priest a year's salary. This changed dramatically in about 1456, when the Bible was first printed with movable type. By the end of that century, printers were busy in more than 250 European towns, publishing a wide variety of Bible editions.

Surprisingly, Christian church leaders resisted the notion of translating God's Word into everyday language. The prevailing opinion was that people should get their teaching from ministers, not the Bible—because it was thought most people were not capable of traveling through God's Word without a spiritual guide. Oxford scholar John Wycliffe became viewed as a heretic for creating the first English Bible—which was banned in England. He died before anyone killed him, but 43 years later church leaders dug up his remains, burned them, and threw the ashes into a river. William Tyndale produced an improved English translation in the early 1500s. For this, he was publicly strangled with a rope and his body burned. His dying words were, "Lord, open the King of England's eyes." Within two years the king ordered English Bibles placed in every church.

New International Version, 1973	The Lord is my shepherd, I shall not be in want. He makes me lie down in green pastures.
New King James Version, 1982	The Lord is my shepherd; I shall not want. He makes me to lie down in green pastures.
Contemporary English Version, 1995	You, Lord, are my shepherd. I will never be in need. You let me rest in fields of green grass.
New Living Translation, 1996	The Lord is my shepherd; I have everything I need. He lets me rest in green meadows.

The most famous English Bible of all time is the King James Version, known in England as the Authorized Version. It remained the principal Bible of English-speaking Protestants for some 300 years, beginning with the time of Shakespeare. In 1611 the translation was presented to King James of England, who had commissioned about 50 of England's foremost scholars to produce it. Working at Oxford, Cambridge, and Westminister, they completed the task in about seven years.

Then, as now, people resisted change. It took 40 years for the public to warm up to this new version and accept it as a replacement for the Geneva Bible, which was translated 50 years earlier and was used by the American Puritans.

Bibles Today

Since King James commissioned his masterpiece translation, archaeologists have unearthed Bible manuscripts much older than the ones that his translators used—up to a thousand years older. For example, some Old Testament texts from the renowned Dead Sea Scrolls, a library cache preserved in dry caves near Israel's Dead Sea, date as far back as about 200 years before Christ. Variation in the Scripture is surprisingly minor—a tribute to the care taken by copyists.

So far, none of the original Bible manuscripts have surfaced. But translators today make good use of the ever-emerging ancient texts, linking them with cutting-edge technology. To piece together brittle and broken fragments of leather scrolls, for example, some scientists are using DNA testing to determine what sections belong together.

Today there are countless millions, perhaps a billion or more, Bibles in homes throughout the world. At the moment, at least parts of the Bible have been translated into about 2,200 languages from Abau in Papua New Guinea to Zulgo in the Cameroon. Surveys report that in the United States nine out of ten homes have at least one Bible—and the average home has about six. These are just the printed Bibles. People can now choose from a staggering array of ancient and new Bible translations on computer, via electronic disks, online services, and the Internet. People can also listen to narrated tapes of Scripture.

For children, there are Bible stories in comic book style and other age-tailored editions. And for kids who would never consider curling up with the Good Book, there are Bible story cartoons and dramas, and even interactive Bible video games.

Adults, too, can choose Bibles targeting their interests. There are storybook Bibles for parents to read to their children, and devotional Bibles with inspiring articles for singles. Readers interested in studying the cultural background of each Bible passage can buy thick volumes such as the *Nelson Study Bible*, with 15,000 expository study notes based on the latest scholarship. The less scholarly, yet equally inquiring, can turn to the *Word in Life Study Bible*, designed for today's media-smart reader. In addition to in-text maps and charts, this edition con-

---

SOME FAMILIAR VERSIONS

King James Version • 1611

American Standard Version • 1901

Revised Standard Version • 1952

Phillips: The New Testament
in Modern English • 1958

The Amplified Bible • 1965

The Living Bible • 1971

New American Standard Version • 1971

Today's English Version
(The Good News Bible) • 1976

New International Version • 1978

New King James Version • 1982

New Revised Standard Version • 1989

Contemporary English Version • 1995

tains hundreds of articles and features, including information on occupations in the Bible, geography and culture, and personality profiles.

The Bible has been the world's best-selling book since Johannes Gutenberg invented the printing press 550 years ago. With modern publishers producing niche editions that meet the spiritual needs of even the narrowest segments of the market, the Bible is likely one of the best-read as well.

Sayings from the Bible

Many frequently used sayings come directly from the Bible—especially from the King James Version. Here are just a few.

He'll go the second mile (Matthew 5:41).

I saw the handwriting on the wall (Daniel 5:5).

The leopard can't change its spots (Jeremiah 13:23).

She thinks she's holier-than-thou (Isaiah 65:5).

I escaped by the skin of my teeth (Job 19:20).

She's the apple of my eye (Deuteronomy 32:10).

He's a man after my own heart (1 Samuel 13:14).

It's a case of the blind leading the blind (Matthew 15:14).

This place is a den of thieves (Matthew 21:13).

That man is a thorn in my side (2 Corinthians 12:7).

Did You Know?

• Using the Bible at swearing-in ceremonies grows out of the ancient Jewish practice of making a promise and reminding each other that "God is watching" (Genesis 31:50). In the Middle Ages, Christians swore by kissing or touching a cross, a Bible, or a sacred object they believed once belonged to a holy person.

• The oldest Bible text is a Dead Sea Scroll fragment written in about 225 B.C. It's from one of the Old Testament books of Samuel.

• The oldest surviving New Testament text is a fragment of John 18:31-33, which includes Pilate's question to Jesus: "Are you the king of the Jews?" The fragment dates to about A.D. 125, roughly one generation after the original was written.

• Bible typos produced dubious nicknames for some editions. "The Adulterer's Bible," also called "the Wicked Bible," dropped an all-important "not" and commands "Thou shalt commit adultery." The printer was fined a hefty sum.

• Bizarre translations of key words spawned Bible nicknames. "The Bug Bible" (more respectfully known as Coverdale's Bible, 1535) encouraged its readers not to be afraid of "bugs by night." The King James Version later replaced "bugs" with "terror."

• The word "Bible" comes from a Greek word for papyrus (biblos), a plant used to make paper.

• "Gospel" comes from the old English word godspell. English scholars used it to translate the Greek word euangelion, which means "good news" and from which we get the word evangelist.

• The most widely translated Bible book is the Gospel of Mark—the shortest of the four Gospels about Jesus. It's available in about 900 languages.

• Christians were among the first people to discard the 3,000-year-old tradition of using scrolls. They adopted the codex, or book format. Every surviving fragment of Christian writing from the second century A.D. comes from books. But only 14 of 870 non-Christian works of that time are from books. Books, printed on front and back, were cheaper and easier to use.

• After Johannes Gutenberg of Germany invented the printing press in the mid-1400s, the first book printed was the Bible. The first press run, of about 180 copies, sold out before the presses started. Forty-eight copies of this masterpiece survive.

• The Bible didn't originally have chapters and verses. Scholars added chapters in A.D. 1231 and verses in 1551.

Highlights and Headliners

God the Father

Before the first star began to sparkle, there was God. That fact opens the Bible: "In the beginning God created the heavens and the earth" (Genesis 1:1).

When the last star fades, and creation gives way to a celestial realm, God will be there—with his people. That fact closes the Bible in John's vision of the future: "People will worship God and will see him face to face. . . . The Lord God will be their light, and they will rule forever" (Revelation 22:3–5).

Between Genesis and Revelation is a sacred library written over more than a millennium. It is the story of God revealed in history, biography, law, prayer, song, proverb, prophecy, parable, letter, and vision. Through this story we begin to understand God, though only in part. For as Job asks, who can understand "the mysteries surrounding God All-Powerful? They are higher than the heavens and deeper than the grave" (Job 11:7–8).

Why God reveals himself to humanity quickly becomes clear in Genesis. God created a good and idyllic world, and placed in it humans with whom he could fellowship. These humans chose to disobey him. Because of this, and in ways we can't fully grasp, sin contaminated God's creation and severed his intimate relationship with humanity. Since that moment, God has been working to restore his creation and his relationship with humans.

God begins by teaching humanity about himself through promises made and fulfilled in obedient people, like Noah, and through punishing evil people. Then through Abraham, God produces a race of people chosen to receive his special insights and laws, and to guide others in the ways of the Lord. He also sends prophets to remind these chosen people, the Jews, to obey him.

Finally, God sends Jesus onto the planet and the Holy Spirit into the human heart to further reveal what he is like. The Bible doesn't explain how three distinct entities can be united as one. It simply states this as fact, then reports a wide array of astonishing miracles and testimonies to prove it. Who but God, for example, could silence a storm (Mark 4:39)?

From beginning to end, the Bible paints a detailed and complex portrait of God. But all the descriptions are best expressed by John, a disciple of Jesus: "God is love" (1 John 4:8). Good news for humanity is that this love is offered to us, and when we accept it, it's ours forever.

God creates Adam (Genesis 1:27–31; 2:7).

After God creates the heavens and the earth, he finishes his creation with a finale: human beings. "The Lord God took a handful of soil and made a man. God breathed life into the man, and the man started breathing." Unlike all other creatures, humans are made in the image of God, "to be like himself."

Eve eats forbidden fruit (Genesis 3:1–24).

In the paradise garden of Eden, Adam and Eve are limited by only one rule: they are not to eat fruit from one particular tree because it will kill them. Eve eats it anyway, then convinces Adam to eat some, too. Sin enters God's creation and changes it for the worse.

The flood destroys life on earth (Genesis 6—9).

"Cruelty and violence have spread everywhere," God tells Noah, the only righteous man left. "Now I'm going to destroy the whole earth and all its people." God says he will flood the land, and that Noah should build a massive houseboat to preserve his family, along with pairs of "every kind of animal, tame and wild."

God makes a contract with Abraham (Genesis 15:1–21).

As a key part of God's plan to save sinful humans, he makes a contract, or covenant, with Abraham. It establishes Abraham as the father of the Jewish people. God's promise: "See if you can count the stars. That's how many descendants you will have." To seal the contract, Abraham offers animal sacrifices. He stands as the model for all who trust God.

Abraham

When Abraham was 75 years old, childless, and married to an infertile woman, God asked him to leave his homeland and move to Canaan, now Israel. In return, God said he would make Abraham into "a great nation" (Genesis 12:2). Because Abraham obeyed, he became father of the Jewish people, and is revered by Jews, Christians, and Muslims as the epitome of faith.

Abraham, a descendant of Noah's son Shem, was born and raised near the Persian Gulf in the culturally advanced city of Ur. This was a town where most people worshiped idols, yet Abraham worshiped only the Lord and trusted him explicitly. Once, God tested Abraham's loyalty by asking him to sacrifice his son, Isaac, who had been born when Abraham was 100 years old. Deeply saddened but steadfastly loyal, Abraham built an altar, then raised his knife to kill Isaac. An angel stopped Abraham, saying, "Now I know that you truly obey God, because you were willing to offer him your only son" (Genesis 22:12). Early Christians saw this episode as a foreshadowing of God's sacrifice of Jesus.

Abraham's flocks and family grew large in Canaan. His great-grandsons, the children of Jacob, produced the extended families that became known as the twelve tribes of Israel.

Jacob wrestles a heavenly being (Genesis 32:22–32).

One sleepless night, Jacob, Abraham's grandson, meets a mysterious man. Possibly recognizing him as a divine being, Jacob grabs him and says, "You can't go until you bless me." They wrestle until dawn, when the man blesses Jacob by giving him the new name of Israel. Jacob's twelve sons (the children of Israel) become the basis of a nation which later calls itself Israel.

Moses sees a burning bush that doesn't burn up (Exodus 3:1–10).

While grazing his flock near Mount Sinai, Moses sees a bush on fire—yet it is not burned. Out of the bush comes the voice of God, giving Moses a terrifying chore: Go to Egypt and order the king to free the Israelite slaves. Moses doesn't want to go, and says so. But God promises, "I will be with you."

Moses

No one in the Old Testament is more heroic and influential than the shy and humble Moses. He freed the Israelites from Egyptian slavery, organized them into a nation, gave them the Ten Commandments and other laws that still guide Jews and Christians, and is credited with writing the first five books of the Bible.

Moses was born in Egypt to an Israelite slave, some 400 years after Jacob's family emigrated to Egypt to escape a famine. As an infant, he was set adrift on the Nile in a waterproof basket to escape the king's order to kill all newborn Hebrew boys. The king's daughter found and raised him. But at age 40, Moses fled the country after killing an Egyptian he saw beating an Israelite. He settled east of Egypt, married, and became a shepherd. While he was grazing his flock one day, God spoke to him from a burning bush and asked him to go back to Egypt and demand the release of the Israelites. Reluctantly, Moses did as God asked.

Israel's deliverance, characterized by many spectacular miracles—ten plagues in Egypt, parting the waters of the Red Sea, manna from heaven, water from rocks—is the Exodus, the most celebrated event in Jewish history, still commemorated in religious holidays each year.

Israelites cross the Red Sea
(Exodus 14:1–31).

"Get your people out of my country and leave us alone!" the king tells Moses after a celestial being has killed the oldest child in each Egyptian family. But once the Israelites leave, the king changes his mind. His army traps the fugitives by the Red Sea. But God parts the water for the Israelites to escape and begin the journey to the land God promised to Abraham.

Moses destroys the Ten Commandments
(Exodus 20:1–17).

Moses leads the Israelites to Mount Sinai, where God gives him the Ten Commandments inscribed on two stone tablets. These laws are the constitution for the nation and its faith. Moses returns from the mountain and sees the people betraying God by worshiping a golden calf. Furious, he throws the tablets, shattering them.

The wilderness trek to the promised land (Numbers 10:11–36).

A pillar of cloud representing God's presence among the Israelites rises from the tent sanctuary and moves. This signals that it's time for Israel to break camp and follow. Priests lead, carrying the ark of the covenant, the chest containing the duplicated Ten Commandments. (Moses broke the first set.)

Jericho walls come tumbling down (Joshua 6:1–27).

Crossing the Jordan River into the promised land, the Israelites meet their first Canaanites, who are protected behind the walls of Jericho. Six days Israelite soldiers march once around the city. On the seventh day, they march around the city seven times. Then the priests blow trumpets, the soldiers shout, and the walls of Jericho collapse.

Samuel

Once settled in their new land, the Israelites lived in a loose federation led by judges. Perhaps the most important of these judges was Samuel. Though Samuel had a family, from early childhood he lived with the priest in Israel's worship center to fulfill a vow his mother made. Infertile, Hannah had promised that if God gave her a son, she would return this child to the Lord's service.

Samuel grew into a wise and righteous man who served God in many capacities. While he was still a boy, he received messages from God and delivered them to the people, as a prophet. He offered sacrifices, as a priest. And he traveled the countryside settling disputes, as a judge. In fact, Samuel was the last of the judges in the era before Israel crowned a king.

When Samuel grew old, the Israelites asked him to select their first king. Samuel believed that the people should continue thinking of God as their king. But God granted Israel's request, though he considered it a rejection of his kingship. Samuel chose Saul. Later, when Saul sinned and became an unworthy leader, Samuel secretly anointed David as the future king. When Samuel died of old age, the nation gathered to mourn him.

David kills Goliath
(1 Samuel 17:1–57).

Four centuries after the Israelites entered the promised land, they still have not captured the coastal area where the Philistines live. When Philistine champion Goliath challenges any Hebrew warrior to mortal combat, a shepherd boy steps forward and drops him with one stone from a slingshot. The shepherd, David, later becomes Israel's legendary king who forges a unified nation.

Solomon builds the temple
(1 Kings 6:1–38).

On a hilltop overlooking Jerusalem, Solomon, David's son, builds the first of only three temples the Jews have ever had. In seven years, a work force of about 150,000 builds one of the most beautiful and expensive temples in the ancient world—a worship center with gold ceilings, walls, and floors. It lasts for 400 years.

David

Israel's greatest king had a humble start in life. David was born into a Bethlehem shepherd's family, as the youngest of eight sons. But even as a lad he showed signs of greatness. He killed bears and lions that raided his flock. And with only a slingshot he defeated the Philistine champion, Goliath.

Invited to live in King Saul's palace, David calmed the moody ruler by playing a harp. When Saul erupted over David's growing popularity and tried to kill him, David fled and lived as a fugitive. David immediately began attracting an army of followers. After Saul died in a battle with the Philistines, Israel rallied around the still popular giant-slayer and crowned him king.

David chose Jerusalem as his capital, expanded the nation's borders, and launched Israel's Golden Age, which spanned his reign as well as Solomon's, his son. Yet David had failings: he committed adultery with Bathsheba and had her husband killed. And he raised an incredibly dysfunctional family—one son led a coup against him. Still, David never grew too proud to repent.

His dynasty began in 1000 B.C. and endured for nearly 500 years. Early Christians believed his dynasty was resurrected in Jesus, the Messiah promised from David's family and hometown.

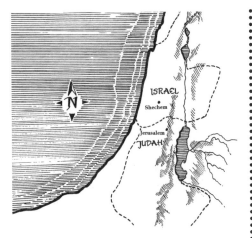

Israel splits into two kingdoms (1 Kings 12:1–33).

By the time Solomon dies, the people of Israel are tired of paying heavy taxes to build cities, forts, and palaces. They ask Solomon's son and successor for relief, but he refuses. The northern tribes secede and start their own nation: Israel. Only the tribe of Judah, in the south, remains loyal to David's descendant.

Elijah challenges prophets of Baal on Mount Carmel (1 Kings 18:1–46).

Idolatry becomes the biggest threat to both Hebrew nations. Queen Jezebel, of Israel, sponsors an association of 850 prophets devoted to Canaanite gods. Prophet Elijah, however, challenges the association to a contest. The god who sends fire from heaven to light a sacrificial altar will be the god of Israel. The Lord wins, and the false prophets are executed.

Isaiah

The prophet Isaiah lived 750 years before Christ, but his predictions about the Messiah—a deliverer who would save Israel—read as though he was an eyewitness to Jesus: "He was wounded and crushed because of our sins. . . . He was condemned to death without a fair trial" (Isaiah 53:5, 8).

Isaiah was an educated noble living in Jerusalem when, at age 20, he saw a phenomenal vision. In this vision God called him to become a prophet who would deliver messages of warning and hope to the Jewish people—a ministry Isaiah performed for 40 years. His style of delivery, preserved in the book of Isaiah, was dramatic and often symbolic. He even walked naked for three years to predict that the Egyptians would become slaves. This encouraged the Jews to trust in God rather than in an alliance with Egypt against Assyria.

During Isaiah's lifetime, Assyria crushed the northern Jewish nation of Israel. Isaiah warned his native Judah, in the south, that a similar fate awaited it. But he also offered hope, promising that God would one day send a messiah—promises the New Testament says were fulfilled in Jesus.

The sentence: 70 years in exile (Jeremiah 25:1–14).

Stubbornly the Jews break God's laws—for centuries. God sends prophets urging the people to repent, but few obey. So God invokes his rights under the covenant: "I'll scatter you among the nations" (Leviticus 26:33). Speaking through the prophet Jeremiah, God vows, "I will make all of you the slaves of the king of Babylonia for seventy years."

Jerusalem falls
(2 Kings 25:1–21).

Assyria invades the northern nation of Israel, deporting the Jewish survivors as slaves, and repopulating the land with their own settlers. One hundred fifty years later, Babylon defeats the southern nation of Judah, destroys Solomon's 400-year-old temple, levels Jerusalem, and exiles most of the survivors. Suddenly, there is no longer a Jewish nation.

Daniel

Hero of the prophetic book bearing his name, Daniel is most famous for surviving a night in a den of hungry lions. How he got there and what happened afterward enhance his fascinating story.

When Babylonians defeated the southern nation of Judah in 597 B.C., and before they destroyed the cities a decade later, they peeled away the top layer of society—the most educated and influential—taking them to Babylon to serve the empire. Daniel, a wise young noble, was among this group. He became the elite of the elite, chosen to work in the palace, as were his friends Shadrach, Meshach, and Abednego. They are remembered for surviving a fiery furnace after refusing to worship an idol.

Daniel was a gifted sage, and a visionary who interpreted dreams for King Nebuchadnezzar. The king became so impressed that he put Daniel in charge of all sages of the empire. Jealous rivals later tricked a subsequent king (of the conquering Persian Empire) into issuing a decree for all people to pray only to him for 30 days. When Daniel continued praying to God, he was punished by facing the lions. After surviving, Daniel was promoted to the number two position in the empire, second only to the king.

A time to cry (Psalm 137:1–9).

Exiled from their land and temple, the Jews endure bitter grief. Some of the most tender Hebrew songs are written during this time. In one such song, a Jewish exile paints a vivid and heartbreaking scene: "Beside the rivers of Babylon we thought about Jerusalem, and we sat down and cried. We hung our small harps on the willow trees."

Rebuilding Jerusalem (Ezra 1–6; Nehemiah 2–4; 6:15–16).

After the Persians defeat Babylon, exiled groups return home—Jews included. The first wave of returning Jews begins work on the temple, followed by later Jews who help finish the job. Rebuilding the walls comes next—a project bitterly opposed by non-Jewish locals. But the work is finished in just 52 days.

God promises to send a Messiah (Isaiah 11:1–16).

Isaiah, like other prophets, says that God will fulfill his covenant through a ruler from David's family who will lead the people into everlasting peace: "The wolf will live with the lamb . . . and a little child will lead them" (New International Version). Early Christians see these prophecies as describing Jesus and his kingdom.

Shepherds visit newborn Jesus (Luke 2:1–20).

Terrified shepherds watch the night sky burst into radiance, filling with angels. "Don't be afraid!" one angel says, "I have good news for you. . . . This very day in King David's hometown a Savior was born for you. He is Christ the Lord." The humble shepherds rush to nearby Bethlehem to see Baby Jesus, the promised ruler from David's family.

Jesus

Jesus, the Son of God, is a central figure of the Bible—from beginning to end.

He was with God when the world was created, says the Gospel of John. He was the hope that the prophets anticipated in the Messiah—a deliverer sent from God to save humanity from sin and to bring peace on earth. And he is the fulfillment of that hope, as reported in the New Testament, especially the remarkable Gospels of Matthew, Mark, Luke, and John. His title, Christ, comes from the Hebrew word for messiah, translated into the Greek language of his day as *christos*.

Jesus' mother was the virgin Mary, engaged to Joseph, a carpenter from Nazareth. When Joseph learned his fiancée was pregnant, he planned to leave her. But an angel assured him that the child was from God.

On orders from the Roman emperor, the couple traveled to the hometown of their ancestors to be counted in a census; for Mary and Joseph this was Bethlehem, birthplace of King David. It was there, in a Bethlehem stable, that Jesus was born. Many Old Testament prophets predicted that the Messiah would come from David's family; Micah added that the birthplace would be Bethlehem (Micah 5:2).

As a growing boy, Jesus worked with Joseph. When Jesus was twelve years old, he traveled with his family to the Jerusalem temple to celebrate Passover. There he astonished the scholars with his spiritual insights.

The Bible says nothing more about Jesus until he began his ministry at roughly thirty years of age. This was a ministry that spanned perhaps only three years, in the heart of a tiny Middle Eastern country. But this ministry has changed the values and lives of people throughout the ages and around the globe. Whether Jesus was healing illnesses, calming storms with a word, or teaching compassion, he gave humanity an intimate portrait of a God full of power and mercy.

Executed by crucifixion, Jesus also gave the world its greatest proof of both his deity and of life after death, for three days later he rose from the tomb. Over the next forty days he met many times with his followers, urging them to take his message to everyone. Then he ascended to heaven, but not before promising to return. The Bible concludes with the greatest hope of early Christians: "Lord Jesus, please come soon!" (Revelation 22:20).

Sermon on the Mount
(Matthew 5:1—7:29).

On a country hillside and surrounded by crowds, Jesus gives the Inaugural Address of his rule, the Sermon on the Mount. A concise summary of his main teachings, the Sermon is a call to life in his revolutionary kingdom: "Love your enemies," Jesus says, "and pray for anyone who mistreats you."

Jesus feeds 5,000
(Matthew 14:13-21).

Exhausted by their ministry, Jesus and his disciples sail away from the crowds for a rest. But the people follow along the shoreline. Though weary, Jesus is moved with compassion and heals all who are sick. Then, from one boy's lunch of bread and fish, Jesus feeds everyone. Dramatic miracles like these convince many that Jesus is the promised Messiah.

The crucifixion of Jesus
(Matthew 27:33-66).

Resisting Jesus' ministry, Jewish leaders condemn him of blasphemy for claiming to be God's Son, and Pilate bows to the pressure to execute him immediately. With this execution, Jewish leaders hope to prove that Jesus is no messiah, but is cursed of God. Yet the crucifixion fulfills the ancient prophecy: "He was wounded and crushed because of our sins" (Isaiah 53:5).

Women at the tomb of Jesus
(Mark 16:1-20).

Sunday morning, women who have followed Jesus walk to his tomb. Instead of finding a corpse, they find an angel announcing that Jesus is resurrected. In the following weeks Jesus appears to his disciples many times, then ascends to heaven. The apostle Paul later explains that Christians, too, will one day have resurrected bodies (1 Corinthians 15).

Holy Spirit

The Holy Spirit is one of three persons in what early Christians called the Trinity: God the Father, Son, and Holy Spirit. The Bible doesn't use the word "trinity," but it portrays all three divine persons as distinct yet equally God. For example, in Jesus' last words on earth he told his followers to make disciples all over the world and to baptize converts "in the name of the Father, the Son, and the Holy Spirit" (Matthew 28:19).

The Spirit's role on earth has changed over history. When the universe was yet dark and lifeless, "the Spirit of God was moving over the water" (Genesis 1:2), involved in the miracle of Creation. (Old Testament writers usually called him the Spirit of God, though occasionally the Holy Spirit.) Throughout Old Testament times the Spirit empowers the heroes and leaders of Israel. When, for instance, the prophet Samuel anointed David as Israel's future king, "at that moment, the Spirit of the Lord took control of David and stayed with him from then on" (1 Samuel 16:13).

In those days, the Spirit's work was apparently limited to unique leaders and special occasions. But the prophet Joel, speaking on God's behalf, promised that a time was coming when "I will give my Spirit to everyone" (Joel 2:28). That moment arrived in a dramatic miracle on the day of Pentecost, a springtime Jewish celebration. Jesus had warned his disciples that he needed to leave, "but the Holy Spirit will come and help you, because the Father will send the Spirit to take my place. The Spirit will teach you everything and will remind you of what I said while I was with you" (John 14:25). Jesus further instructed the disciples to stay in Jerusalem until the Spirit arrived. As the disciples waited, "suddenly there was a noise from heaven like the sound of a mighty wind!" (Acts 2:2). The Spirit had come, filling each disciple with spiritual vitality that gave them courage to preach about Jesus and to perform miracles proving that their message came from God.

Thousands began converting to Christianity and receiving the Holy Spirit. "You are God's temple," the apostle Paul later explained to believers. "His Spirit lives in you" (1 Corinthians 3:16). Christians guided by the Spirit, Paul added, will find themselves taking on the characteristics of godliness and rejecting sinful ways. "God's Spirit makes us loving, happy, peaceful, patient, kind, good, faithful, gentle, and self-controlled" (Galatians 5:22).

Peter

Lead disciple of Jesus, Peter is famous for trying to walk on water—and sinking. Ironically, his name was Simon until Jesus renamed him Peter, which means "rock." Jesus wasn't making a joke; the name change came later to emphasize Peter's rock-solid devotion to the Lord. Peter graphically demonstrated this allegiance when officials arrested Jesus: Peter cut off one man's ear.

Peter and his brother Andrew were fishermen when Jesus invited them to become his disciples. Bold and strong-minded, Peter established himself as the leader, often speaking to Jesus on behalf of the others, and vowing to defend Jesus to the death. Unfortunately, Peter is best known for his cowardice. While Jesus stood trial, Peter waited outside and three times denied knowing the Lord.

After the resurrected Jesus ascended to heaven, a re-energized Peter directed the emerging Christian church. He preached the first sermon, which produced 3,000 converts. And he defended Christians before the same Jewish leaders who tried Jesus.

Two New Testament letters bear Peter's name as author, and early Christian writers say that his sermons provided the source for Mark's Gospel. These writers add that Peter was crucified upside down on what is now Vatican Hill in Rome, when Nero persecuted Christians.

The Holy Spirit fills the disciples (Acts 2:1–13).

Before his ascension, Jesus tells the disciples to stay in Jerusalem until the Holy Spirit arrives to take his place. After about ten days the Spirit floods the room with the sound of a mighty wind and fills the disciples with courage. Boldly they preach about Jesus. On that day of Pentecost about 3,000 believe, and the Christian church is born.

Paul converts and becomes a missionary (Acts 9:1–19; 13–14; 16:16–40).

On his way to arrest Jewish "heretics" who believe in Christ, Paul encounters a blinding light and the voice of Jesus. The experience makes him a believer. Instead of traveling to suppress Christianity, he begins traveling as a missionary to expand it. Convinced that through Jesus God's promises to Abraham now apply to non-Jews also, he starts churches throughout the Roman Empire.

Paul argues against making non-Jews follow Jewish laws (Acts 15:1–21).

The church's first big controversy is over whether to make non-Jews observe the laws of Moses, especially laws about circumcision and diet. Paul and Peter convince assembled leaders that you don't have to be a Jew to be a Christian, because salvation comes through trusting Jesus, not through observing Jewish laws.

James leads the church to serve (James 1–5).

James, the brother of Jesus and leader of the church in Jerusalem, writes the letter bearing his name—a letter for Christian congregations, encouraging them toward holiness and compassion. "Religion that pleases God the Father must be pure and spotless. You must help needy orphans and widows." Jewish authorities executed James, said a first-century historian.

Paul

Next to Jesus, the person most responsible for Christianity was this fiery Jew who took the story of Jesus on the road for 10,000 miles and wrote over one-fourth of the New Testament.

More than any human being, it was Paul who turned a religion full of Jews into a religion made up mostly of non-Jews. In the earliest days of the church, if you wanted to be a Christian you had to be a Jew. If you hadn't been born Jewish, you had to convert and agree to keep all the Old Testament laws, including a painful one for grown men: circumcision.

Paul convinced church leaders that non-Jews should be granted full membership without having to obey Jewish laws. Old Testament laws, Paul argued, were part of God's old agreement with humanity. Jesus' death and resurrection marked the beginning of God's new covenant, prophesied by Jeremiah: "I will write my laws on their hearts and minds" (Jeremiah 31:33).

Paul was often assaulted and arrested. His final arrest, in Rome, led to his execution. As a Roman citizen, Paul had the right to a swift death and was probably beheaded.

Paul preaches, under house arrest, at Rome
(Acts 28: 17–31).

After Paul's last known arrest he is taken to Rome, where he waits two years for his trial. Constantly guarded, he freely teaches, preaches, and writes to his congregations. The Bible doesn't say what happened to Paul, but early Christian writers say he was beheaded in Rome.

John's vision of heaven
(Revelation).

Exiled on an island, John, the last of Christ's original disciples, writes his vision of the future. He sees the promised return of Jesus, the gathering of God's people into a celestial city, and a new heaven and earth free from sin or evil. "The city did not need the sun or the moon. The glory of God was shining on it, and the Lamb was its light."

John

When Jesus hung on the cross, dying, he looked down at his mother standing beside one of the first and dearest of his twelve disciples: an unidentified man that most scholars agree was John. "She is now your mother," Jesus said, entrusting Mary to John's care (John 20:27).

John and his brother James were fishermen whom Jesus nicknamed "Thunderbolts," perhaps because of their fiery personalities. Once they asked permission to punish some inhospitable Samaritans with fire from heaven—a request Jesus denied. Yet along with Peter, they were the closest friends of Jesus—the inner circle of disciples. They alone saw Jesus transfigured into his celestial form (Matthew 17:1–2) and witnessed his agonizing prayer just before his arrest (Mark 14:33).

Early Christian writers say that John outlived the other disciples and settled in Ephesus (western Turkey), where he wrote five New Testament books: the Gospel of John, 1, 2, and 3 John, and Revelation.

MAIN ATTRACTIONS

GENESIS

When It Happened

Adam 4000 B.C.   Abraham 2100 B.C.   Joseph dies   Moses 1500 B.C.   David 1000 B.C.   Ezra 450 B.C.   Jesus born 7/6 B.C.

When the World Begins

Genesis answers some of the most basic questions we'll ever face:

- **Who am I?**
  "God created humans to be like himself"(1:27).
- **Where did I come from?**
  "God took a handful of soil and made a man. God breathed life into the man" (2:7).
- **Why am I here?**
  "God said, We will let them rule the fish, the birds, and all other living creatures" (1:26).

We are caretakers of God's creation.

Genesis is an ancient Greek word that means *beginning*. That's what the book is about: the beginning of the universe, human beings, sin, the Jewish nation.

Here we watch God breathe life into Adam and Eve, sail with Noah during the Flood, marvel at the faith of Abraham, and travel with the families of Jacob as they escape a famine in Israel by migrating to Egypt where they will wind up as slaves making bricks for Pharaoh.

Without Genesis, the rest of the Bible makes no sense. The Bible talks about God's plan of salvation—his strategy for reaching out to human beings and saving them from sin and the destruction it causes. Genesis shows why salvation is necessary: God's good creation was invaded and contaminated by sin. And only the Creator can restore his creation. ❑

Famous Lines

- In the beginning God created the heavens and the earth (1:1).

- "Am I my brother's keeper?" (4:9, King James Version). *Cain's reply to God, when asked where Abel was, whom Cain had murdered.*

- Noah found grace in the eyes of the LORD (6:8, King James Version). *The reason Noah and his family weren't killed in the Flood.*

- "I will bless you and give you such a large family, that someday your descendants will be more numerous than the stars in the sky or the grains of sand along the beach" (22:17). *God's promise to Abraham, father of the Jewish nation.*

Behind the Scenes of Genesis

⭐ Starring Roles

Adam and Eve, the world's first human couple (3:20)
Noah, builder of the ark and survivor of the Flood (5:29)
Abraham, the man God chooses to become father of the Jews (17:4)
Isaac, the son God promises to Abraham; born when Abraham is 100 (17:19)
Jacob, father of the men whose descendants become the 12 tribes of Israel (25:26)
Joseph, Jacob's favorite son, who becomes a leader in Egypt (30:24)

📖 Plot

God makes a beautiful, sinless world, and human beings to take care of it. These first humans, Adam and Eve, enjoy a unique relationship with God and with each other, and are entrusted to manage a wondrous world teeming with life. Adam and Eve, however, decide to eat fruit that God had warned would kill them. God expels the couple from the Garden of Eden, explaining that they will reap the promised consequences: they will die. But first, the woman will "suffer terribly" when giving birth. And the man will have to "sweat to earn a living" (3:19).

Humanity and God become estranged. Apart from God, the world grows so evil that God purges it in a vast flood, saving only Noah and his family. Afterward, God launches a plan to reclaim humanity from the grip of sin.

God begins his plan by creating through Abraham a nation of Jews. This nation is to learn how to obey him and "do what is right and fair" (18:19). Later, God promises, he will broaden the scope of his salvation, making the Jews "a blessing to all other nations on earth" (18:18).

🎥 What to Look For

Truth in an ancient style. Don't read the creation story expecting it to be written like a modern laboratory report. What Genesis teaches about creation is true, and an increasing number of scientists think that the universe was born in a way startlingly similar to what Genesis has always said. But Genesis expresses this truth in the ways in which truth was expressed in ancient times, not in the technical, hyper-precise terms of modern science. It focuses on the *who* of creation much more than on the scientific *how*. Against all claims that creation happened on its own (through some unknown cause) or happened through the cavorting or clashing of any number of gods (according to many other

TIMELINE	BIBLE EVENTS	God creates the universe Before 2500 B.C.	Flood destroys the world Before 2500 B.C.		
		4500 B.C.	4000 B.C.	3500 B.C.	3000 B.C.
	WORLD EVENTS	First known Egyptian calendar 4230 B.C.		Floods devastate river basin of Iraq 3400 B.C.	Chinese develop acupuncture 2700 B.C.

ancient creation stories), Genesis says simply, *In the beginning God created the heavens and the earth.* Many of the details regarding *how* he did it remain a mystery. For example, Christians are divided over whether the days of creation were 24-hour periods or long stretches of time. (See "Six-day Creation" in Reviews.)

Reclaiming creation. Notice how the original sin of Adam and Eve grows to engulf the entire world, and how God sets out to correct the problem.

Adam and Eve disobey God. Cain becomes jealous of his younger brother and murders him. Lamech kills a younger man who wounded him and boasts that anyone seeking revenge will get punished ten times more than any trying to get even with Cain, whom God had given a special mark for protection. Meanness, violence, and murder cover the earth by the time of Noah, so God purges the world with a flood. A restored and sophisticated civilization repeats the spirit of the original sin, defying God, causing the Lord to scatter humanity to the four corners of the planet and to impose on them a variety of languages.

The very first sin corrupted God's "good" creation, with painful consequences not the least of which is a broken relationship between humanity and God. And from there sin spreads and infects the entire world.

God decides to reclaim his creation and make it good once again. He starts with one righteous man: Abraham. From Abraham he begins to grow a nation set apart to serve him and to become a model of godliness for the rest of the world.

Loving the underdog. Notice how God shows his love for people that society tends to look down on. Though ancient custom demands that the oldest son get the attention and glory, God shines the spotlight on younger sons like Isaac (instead of Ishmael), Jacob (instead of Esau) and Joseph (who had 10 older brothers).

Then there's the matter of childless women, ladies often treated as though they have done something to deserve infertility. God saves them from their agony by turning barrenness into fruitfulness with Sarah, Rebekah, and Rachel, as he will do later for the mothers of Samuel, Samson, and John the Baptist.

> **Did You Know?**
>
> • James Dean made his 1955 screen debut in *East of Eden,* a John Steinbeck tale of two quarrelsome brothers with similarities to Cain and Abel. The film's title comes from Genesis 4:16. East of Eden is where Cain fled after murdering his brother.
>
> • Genesis says God made Eve as a helper for Adam (2:18). This has led many people to argue that women are inferior to men. But the Hebrew word translated "helper" in some Bibles and "partner" in others is the same word that describes God's role in helping humans (Psalm 33:20).

God promises Abraham a nation 2100 B.C.	Joseph goes to Egypt, Hebrews follow 1800 B.C.		
2500 B.C.	2000 B.C.	1500 B.C.	1000 B.C.
Most pyramids completed 2200 B.C.	Stonehenge built in England 2000 B.C.	Astronomy starts in Babylon 1800 B.C.	Dates are approximate

Author and Date

The writer is never named. Many scholars say Genesis shows literary evidence of being a marvelously blended composite of several ancient sources. But Jewish tradition says Moses wrote the first five books of the Bible. Jesus agreed (John 7:19). If Moses wrote it, he may have received some of the information directly from God as he did the Ten Commandments. Other material may have come from stories passed on orally and in writing. Abraham, for example, came from the region where writing was invented; he may have recorded part of his story. Christians receive this book and the other books of the Bible as inspired by God, to reveal to human beings what he is like and what his will for us is.

It's uncertain when Genesis was written. It covers a time span from the birth of creation to the death of Joseph in Egypt, about 1800 B.C. Some Bible scholars say the book was compiled from several sources, perhaps as late as the 500s B.C., nearly a thousand years after Moses. But if Moses wrote the book, he probably did it during the 40 years he and the Israelites wandered in the Sinai Peninsula after leaving Egypt. It is uncertain, however, when this long journey took place; some scholars say the Exodus, as it is called, happened in the 1400s B.C. Others argue for the 1200s.

The book was written to show that God's creation was good, and that after it became spoiled by sin, God began his plan to reclaim it through the chosen people that come from Abraham.

On Location

Sites mentioned in the book cover a thousand-mile stretch from Abraham's hometown of Ur (in Iraq), to the land God promised him in Canaan (Israel), and

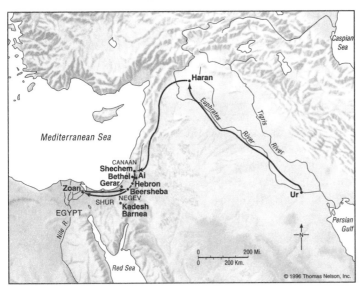

to Egypt. It's uncertain where the Garden of Eden was located. Most persistent theories put it somewhere in the Middle East, especially in the fertile strip of land between the Tigris and Euphrates rivers in Iraq, or along the Nile river in Egypt. ❏

Big Scenes from Genesis

After God creates the heavens and the earth, he finishes his creation with a finale: human beings. "The Lord God took a handful of soil and made a man. God breathed life into the man, and the man started breathing." God makes Eve from one of Adam's ribs.

Unlike all other creatures, humans are made in the image of God, "to be like himself." Their job is to rule over the earth, taking care of it.

God creates Adam
(1:26–31; 2:7)

In a paradise garden in Eden, Adam and Eve are limited by only one rule: they are not to eat fruit from one particular tree because it will kill them. Eve eats it anyway, then convinces Adam to eat some, too.

God expels both of them from the garden, and promises that they will die after experiencing a harsh existence unlike anything they have known before. Eve will suffer in childbirth. Adam will "struggle to grow enough food." The presence of sin radically changes creation, for the worse.

Eve eats forbidden fruit
(3:1–24)

Cain, a farmer, is the oldest son of Adam and Eve. Abel, a shepherd, is the younger son. Each man makes an offering to God; Cain gives crops and Abel gives livestock. God accepts Abel's offering but rejects Cain's, perhaps because Cain did not sacrifice the first and best of his crop (v.7).

Enraged by jealously, Cain commits the world's first recorded murder. He kills his brother.

As punishment, he can never again grow crops; if he tries, the ground will produce nothing. Also, Cain is doomed to become a fugitive, "wandering from place to place." But God protects him with an undescribed mark that somehow alerts others not to kill him.

Cain kills Abel
(4:1–16)

Cruelty and violence have spread everywhere," God tells Noah, the only righteous man left. "Now I'm going to destroy the whole earth and all its people."

God instructs Noah to build a massive, three-deck houseboat about 150 yards long, 15 yards wide, and 25 yards high. In this boat, God will preserve Noah and his family, along with pairs of "every kind of animal, wild and tame." Torrents of rain fall for 40 days, covering the mountains.

Only after five months do the waters recede enough that the boat comes to rest in the Ararat mountain range of Armenia, some 500 miles north of where many scholars believe civilization began.

The Flood destroys life on earth (6–9) ••

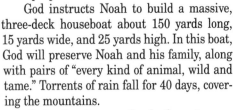

Noah's descendants speak one language, work together, and become arrogant because of their accomplishments. They decide to build a huge tower, perhaps as a staircase to heaven or in honor of pagan gods.

"This is just the beginning," God says.

God stops the tower project and puts human pride on pause by suddenly making the people speak different languages. As a result, they scatter all over the earth, apparently clustering by language groups.

People start building the Tower of Babel (11:1–9)
•••

Through Abraham, God launches his plan to restore creation to its original goodness. He tells Abraham to leave his homeland and go into what is now Israel. God says he will give this land to Abraham, and "make your descendants into a great nation." Abraham is 75 years old and childless at the time. But he obeys, and sets out for the promised land called Canaan.

Abraham goes to Canaan (12:1–9) ••

God makes a formal contract, or covenant, with Abraham. God's promise: "Look at the sky and see if you can count the stars. That's how many descendants you will have." To seal the contract, Abraham offers a sacrifice of a cow, a goat, a ram, a dove, and a pigeon.

God makes a contract with Abraham
(15:1 – 21)

Divine messengers, on their way to evaluate the situation in Sodom and Gomorrah, visit Abraham. They promise that he and Sarah will have a son. Sarah, listening from inside the tent, chuckles to herself. After all, Abraham is 99 and she 90. But within a year a star is born: Isaac. And the Jewish nation is begun.

Sarah laughs at the promise of a son
(18:1 – 2)

After delivering this happy news, the divine messengers move on to Sodom and Gomorrah, twin cities in a plain somewhere in Canaan. Their investigation finds such a depth of depravity that God decides to destroy them. In fact, the men of Sodom go so far as to try to gang rape the angelic messengers that God sends to warn Lot and his family to leave. The angels blind the would-be rapists.

With Lot and his family out of the city, "The Lord sent burning sulphur down like rain on Sodom and Gomorrah" (19:24). When Lot's wife looked back, she became a block of salt.

Sodom and Gomorrah are destroyed
(19:1 – 29)

To test Abraham's faith, God asks him to kill his son, Isaac, as a sacrifice. This is the son through whom God promised to produce the Jewish nation. Yet Abraham obeys.

Isaac doesn't know what is going on. As Abraham builds the sacrificial altar, Isaac asks where the lamb is. "God will provide the lamb," Abraham replies.

As Abraham raises his knife to kill Isaac, an angel suddenly appears and tells him to stop. "Now I know that you truly obey God," the angel says, "because you were willing to offer him your only son."

The New Testament portrays this story as a foreshadowing of Jesus. What Abraham was willing to do, God actually did, offering his only son as a sacrifice (see John 3:16; Romans 3:21–25). John the Baptist introduced Jesus to the world, saying: "Here is the Lamb of God who takes away the sin of the world!" (John 1:29).

Abraham prepares to sacrifice his son, Isaac (22:1 – 19) •

Isaac grows up, marries, and has two sons: Esau and Jacob. The two sons become estranged after Jacob, the younger son, tricks his father into giving him the deathbed blessing traditionally due the eldest son. The night before Jacob's tense reunion with his older brother Esau, who has vowed to kill him, Jacob meets a mysterious man. Jacob possibly recognizes him as a divine messenger, for he grabs hold of him and says, "You can't go until you bless me."

They wrestle until dawn, when the mysterious man throws Jacob's hip out of joint. This man then blesses Jacob by giving him the new name of Israel. Jacob becomes the father of 12 sons, whose descendants will become the tribes of Israel. The most famous son is Joseph.

Jacob wrestles a heavenly messenger • **(32:22 – 32)**

Joseph is Jacob's favorite child, born of his favorite wife. Joseph knows this, and flaunts it by bragging and tattling. His 10 older brothers are so fed up with him that they decide to get rid of him.

When Joseph goes to the pasture to check on his brothers, they grab him and throw him in a pit. As they argue over whether or not to kill him, a caravan of slave traders headed for Egypt happens by. Joseph's brothers sell him for 20 pieces of silver, in a scene that seems to foreshadow Judas betraying Jesus for 30 pieces of silver (Matthew 26:15).

In Egypt, Joseph lands in prison after he is falsely charged with trying to rape his master's wife. He remains in prison until summoned by the ruler of Egypt.

Joseph's brothers sell him into slavery (37:12 – 28) •

Pharaoh, the king of Egypt, has a dream that leaves him feeling troubled. He dreams of seven hungry, gaunt cows devouring seven fat cows, yet not becoming bigger. This dream is followed by one of seven blighted ears of corn consuming seven plump ears. Many people in ancient times believed that the gods communicated through dreams. Some kings consulted dream interpreters, as did Pharaoh. But when the king's wise men are unable to interpret the dream, he sends for Joseph, who has correctly interpreted the dreams of others.

Joseph tells Pharaoh that God is warning Egypt that the nation will enjoy seven years of good harvest, followed by seven years of drought. The grateful Pharaoh appoints Joseph as a top official, in charge of managing the grain reserves.

Joseph interprets Pharaoh's dream
(41:1–40)

Famine sweeps across Egypt, and Israel as well. Joseph's brothers make the several-hundred-mile trek down to Egypt in search of grain for sale. They don't recognize their younger brother, now a grown and married man. But he recognizes them.

At first, he keeps his identity secret. But eventually he can contain himself no longer. "I am Joseph," he says. Then he begins crying. When he is able to speak again, he asks if his father is still alive.

Indeed, Jacob is alive, but still depressed over losing Joseph.

To his frightened brothers, Joseph offers assurance that he has forgiven them. "Don't worry or blame yourselves," he explains. "God is the one who sent me ahead of you to save lives" (45:5).

At Joseph's request and with Pharaoh's approval, Jacob and his entire extended family move to Egypt to weather out the famine. But they are destined to suffer the fate of young Joseph; they will become an entire nation of slaves. And freeing them will take an act of God, working through a reluctant shepherd called Moses.

Joseph reveals his identity to his brothers
(45:1–15)

Reviews

Ancient lifestyles. Details in the story of Abraham and his descendants accurately reflect life in that era, according to records from Abraham's home region in what is now Iraq. For example, among the 282 laws inscribed on the seven-foot-high stone called the Code of Hammurabi is one stipulating that wives can use their slaves as surrogate mothers. In this case, the child legally belongs to the adopted mother. Sarah (wife of Abraham) and Rachel and Leah (wives of Jacob) all used surrogates to increase the size of their families. Prenuptial agreements inscribed on stone tablets at Nuzi, on the Tigris River, confirm this practice.

Sodom and Gomorrah. There's no trace of these cities that God destroyed in a firestorm of sulfur. But the region there is rich in underground gas, oil, and chemicals, sulfur included. The plain also sits on a major earthquake fault. One theory is that Sodom and Gomorrah were leveled when an earthquake opened a pocket of natural gas that rose, was later ignited by lightning or fire, and produced the effects described in Genesis.

Six-day Creation. The creation story reads like a myth, say many.

Specifically, the Bible account that the universe was created in six days does not jibe with current scientific theories that say creation took unimaginable eons. Christians are divided over whether *days* means 24-hour segments, or longer stretches of time; the original Hebrew word can mean either. Though Genesis doesn't answer our questions about the when and how of creation, it clearly delivers the main point it wants to make: God is the creator.

The Flood. Contrary to the story of Noah and his ark, there is no compelling archaeological evidence that a worldwide flood occurred on this planet. There is strong evidence, however, that at least one major flood swallowed up entire cities in the fertile region where human civilization possibly began: along the shores of the Tigris and Euphrates rivers in what is now Iraq. Traces of such a deluge date to about 3400 B.C. Babylonian epics also tell of a great flood there.

Some scholars wonder if the Flood covered just the known civilized world (the Hebrew term for *world* used in this story is not the most common term to describe the earth; it's a term that can also mean *land* or *country*).

Others wonder if the Flood covered the entire planet, and we simply haven't found the evidence yet. What we have turned up are flood stories from more than 100 cultures throughout the world: Egypt, Greece, North and South America, China, the South Pacific.

Repeatedly, Genesis shows that it was written in the ways and manners used to express truth in ancient times, not to satisfy modern scientific curiosity. It was written to reveal what God is like and how he began the long process of restoring his good creation and his relationship with the rebellious human race. ❏

Encore

- For more on the story of Abraham's ever-growing family, read Exodus. It starts where Genesis leaves off, with the Israelites in Egypt. Exodus tells of Moses leading the enslaved nation home to what is now Israel.

- For more about God's work in creation, read his reply to Job, who felt he had the intellectual savvy to argue with God (Job 38:4–40:2). Or try the prophet Isaiah's masterful poem about learning to trust in the God of creation (Isaiah 40:10-31).

- To learn more about why Abraham is so important to Jews and Christians, and how the New Testament presents him as a person who was saved through faith in God, read Romans 4:1-25 and James 2:14-26. ❏

EXODUS

When It Happened

(dates are approximate)

Adam 4000+ B.C. Abraham 2100 B.C. Moses 1500 B.C. Exodus 1440 B.C. David 1000 B.C. Ezra 450 B.C. Jesus born 7/6 B.C.

Moses Leads the Great Escape

Ask a Jewish friend to tell you about the greatest event in the 4,000-year history of their people.

They'll point you to their Great Escape, an epic adventure reported in Exodus.

This wasn't just a hair-raising chase scene, wrapped around some of the most spectacular miracles in the Bible. If you freeze this frame of history, you capture the moment of Israel's birth. For though God promised hundreds of years earlier to make Abraham into a nation, this was the moment for that promise to become a living, breathing reality.

Into Egypt had come one Hebrew family, seeking relief from a famine and led by Jacob. Out of Egypt came one Hebrew nation, seeking freedom from slavery and led by Moses.

During their trek home, to what is now Israel, they accepted their role as descendants of Abraham, and they vowed to obey God. So God, through Moses, set up the rules that would govern the people. At the heart of these rules are the Ten Commandments.

The story is a classic—not so much because of what it reveals about the Jewish people, but because of what it reveals about God. He is the great deliverer, who can and will invade the physical world to save those who call on him for help. ❏

Famous Lines

- "I Am" (3:14). God's name, as revealed to Moses at the burning bush.

- "Let my people go" (5:1). God's demand of Pharaoh, the Egyptian king.

- "Do not worship any god except me" (20:3). The first of the Ten Commandments.

- The payment will be . . . eye for eye, tooth for tooth (21:23-24).

Behind the Scenes of Exodus

⭐ Starring Roles

Moses, who leads the Israelites out of Egypt (2:10)
Egyptian king, known as Pharaoh, who uses the Israelites for slave labor (1:11)
Aaron, older brother of Moses and builder of the golden calf (4:14)

📖 Plot

To escape a famine in what is now Israel, Jacob moves his family to Egypt. They stay about 400 years. Sometime during this extended visit, Jacob's descendants grow so numerous that the Egyptians fear the Hebrews might take over. So an Egyptian king decides to turn them all into slaves. He forces them to make bricks for his massive building projects— including entire cities. The people ask God to free them. And God sends Moses to do just that.

🎥 What to Look For

God getting involved. Notice that God doesn't relax in the comfort of heaven, while expecting human beings to work out their own problems. He's a hands-on God. He produces a leader out of a man who wants to stay with the sheep. He generates breathtaking miracles to break the stubborn will of Pharaoh. And he blows a dry path through a standing body of water when the fleeing Israelites are trapped between a charging army and the deep blue sea.

Two sections. The first half of the book is the epic story about the Israelites escaping from Egypt. The last half, beginning with chapter 19, is made up of laws and worship instructions for the Israelites.

Did You Know?

• The 10 plagues probably aren't just attempts to twist Pharaoh's arm so he will let God's people go. Each plague seems to target and overpower an Egyptian god, to show that the Lord is the only true God. For example, when God covers the land in darkness (plague 9) he proves his power over Egypt's chief deity, Ra, the sun god.

• Israel captured the Sinai Peninsula from Egypt in the Six-Day War of 1967. But they returned it in 1979, under the terms of an Egyptian-Israeli peace treaty. ❑

TIMELINE

BIBLE EVENTS		Moses born 1530 B.C.*	The Exodus, Ten Commandments 1440 B.C.	Moses dies 1400 B.C.	*Many scholars say Moses lived about 200 years later, putting the Exodus at about 1275 B.C.
Dates are approximate					
3300 B.C.	2900 B.C.	2500 B.C.	2100 B.C.	1700 B.C.	1300 B.C.
WORLD EVENTS	Cuneiform (picture-style) writing begins 3300 B.C.		Thutmose I rules Egypt 1530 B.C.	People in Canaan (Israel) and Sinai use first known alphabet 1500 B.C.	Rameses II uses slave labor to build monuments 1292 B.C.

Author and Date

Probably Moses, though the book doesn't identify its writer. Other Bible books, however, speak of Moses as the author (Joshua 8:31; Mark 12:26). And Exodus 17:14 says Moses wrote at least part of the book. Critics once said Moses couldn't have written it, since the alphabet had not been invented. But archaeologists have uncovered many alphabetic writings from about 1500 B.C. in what is now Israel as well as the Sinai Peninsula, where the Israelites spent 40 years.

Like the others of the first five books of the Bible, Moses probably wrote Exodus during the Exodus. That would have been sometime during their 40-year trek to Israel, perhaps in the 1400s B.C.

He wrote the book to remind the Jews about how God delivered them from slavery.

On Location

The Hebrew captivity and the confrontation between Moses and Pharaoh take place in the Nile Delta of northern Egypt. The Exodus and 40 years of wandering in the wilderness take place in the Sinai Peninsula, a barren expanse between Egypt and Canaan, just north of the Red Sea. The map shows possible routes of the Exodus. ❏

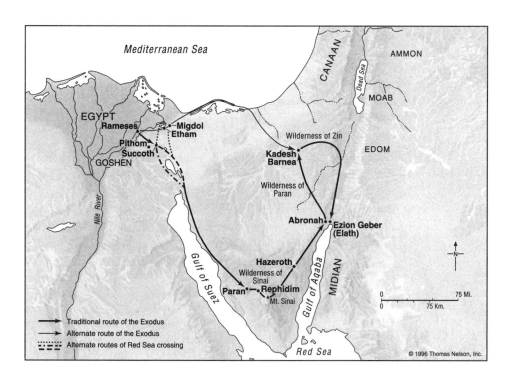

Big Scenes from Exodus

The Israelites migrate to Egypt during the days of Joseph, to escape a famine in Israel. They produce a lot of children there—so many that when a new pharaoh rises to power he complains that the Israelites pose a threat to national security. So he orders them enslaved to make mud bricks for massive projects such as the cities of Pithom and Rameses. They probably didn't build pyramids, since most of them were finished before 2200 B.C., nearly 1,000 years earlier.

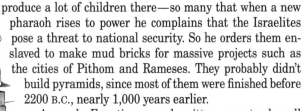

An early Egyptian record written on a tomb wall describes the slave brickmaker: "He is dirtier than vines or pigs from the treading under his mud. . . . He is simply wretched through and through."

**Israel becomes slaves
(1:1–22)** ••

To control the rapidly multiplying Israelite population, Pharaoh orders that all their newborn sons be killed at birth. But the mother of Moses puts her baby son in a watertight basket and sets him afloat near where the princess bathes. Big sister watches from among the reeds. When the princess finds the child and takes pity on him, Moses' sister walks over and asks if she needs someone to nurse him. When Pharaoh's daughter says yes, the child gets the mother of Moses, who serves as his nurse—and receives a salary as well.

Pharaoh's daughter finds baby Moses floating in a basket
•• **(2:1–10)**

Though Moses was raised in the king's palace, he knows he is an Israelite. And he feels a kinship to his people. When he witnesses an Egyptian foreman beating a Hebrew slave, Moses kills the Egyptian and quickly hides his body in the sand. When Pharaoh hears about this, he decides to execute Moses. So Moses runs away, east to Midian, which extends from the Sinai Peninsula to northern Arabia. There he marries into the family of a sheep herder.

**Moses murders an Egyptian slavedriver and runs away
(2:11–22)** •••

While grazing his flock near Mt. Sinai, Moses sees a bush on fire, yet it is not burned. Out of the bush comes the voice of God, calling Moses to come close. "Take off your sandals," God says, "the ground where you are standing is holy."

God then gives Moses a terrifying chore: return to Egypt and demand that the great pharaoh free the slaves. Moses doesn't want to go, and says so. But God promises, "I will be with you." So Moses goes to Egypt.

Moses sees a blazing bush that doesn't burn up
(3:1–10)

Let my people go" is the word of God that Moses delivers to Pharaoh. The king refuses.

Moses threatens—and delivers—plague upon plague to convince Pharaoh that the demand comes from none other than God. The Nile River turns to blood. Frogs invade the land, followed by

gnats, flies, then locusts. The livestock get sick. Lightning and hail destroy the crops. Darkness shrouds Egypt for three days. The people suffer from boils.

But only the last plague breaks Pharaoh's stubborn spirit. God kills the oldest child in each family, Pharaoh's included. But he passes over the homes of Israelites who have obeyed his directions to splash their front door posts with the blood of a sacrificial lamb they have eaten.

Since that fateful day, Jews annually commemorate their deliverance from Egypt by eating a Passover meal.

The angel of death visits Egypt
(12:1–32)

Get your people out of my country and leave us alone!" Pharaoh tells Moses that night. The Israelites leave the next morning, rushing east toward the Sinai Peninsula, nestled between the Gulf of Suez and the Gulf of Aqaba, which protrude up from the Red Sea like a couple of giant rabbit ears.

For Pharaoh, grief churns into seething anger. He assembles a massive chariot force that gives chase, trapping the Israelites on the banks of the Red Sea. God blocks the Egyptian advance with a pillar of smoke and fire. Then God sends a strong east wind to blow a path across the body of water. The Israelites walk across the sea floor.

When the Israelites safely reach the other side the Egyptians boldly—but foolishly—follow. The sea walls come splashing down, killing every Egyptian that enters the water.

Crossing the Red Sea
(14:1–31)

In the moment it takes two massive, opposing waves to crash together, the Egyptian threat is gone and the Israelites are free. Exhilarated, the entire nation joins Moses in a song of praise to God. Miriam, the sister of Moses, takes out a tambourine and leads the women in dancing.

The Israelites sing praise to God after the crossing (15:1–21) •

Moses returns to Mt. Sinai, where he earlier met God in the burning bush. Here God gives him the Ten Commandments, inscribed onto two stone tablets. And here, God outlines other laws that will govern Israel and make it clear to other nations that Israel is devoted to God.

The meeting takes 40 days—long enough for the Israelites to fear that Moses may not be coming back. So they talk his brother, Aaron, into building a golden calf, "an image of a god who will lead and protect us."

When Moses finally returns and sees many of the people dancing around the calf, he becomes so angry that he throws the stone tablets, shattering them. Already the people have broken the first and most important commandment: Do not worship any god except me.

Moses returns to Mt. Sinai, where God replaces the inscribed Commandments.

Moses destroys the Ten Commandments • (20:1–17; 31:18–32:35; 34:1)

On God's instruction, the Israelites build a portable worship center called the tabernacle. Wherever they go, they erect it in the center of their camp. The tabernacle courtyard—where people offer sacrifices to God to express gratitude or to atone for sins—measures 50 yards long by 25 yards wide. It is surrounded by a wall of curtains seven feet high. Inside the tent, 15 yards long and 5 yards wide, the Israelites keep the Ten Commandments, secured in a chest called the ark of the covenant. Only priests are allowed inside the sacred tent.

The presence of God, in the form of a cloud, settles on the tabernacle. Whenever the cloud moved from the tent, the people would break camp and follow.

The Israelites build a tent sanctuary (26:1–37) •

········· **Reviews** ·························

Golden calf. The Israelites made a golden calf to worship, when they feared Moses would not return from his 40-day meeting with God on Mt. Sinai. The story seems reliable since their choice of a young bull is not at all out of sync with the times.

Many countries in the ancient Middle East had bull cults. In fact, Egypt—where the Israelites had just spent the last 400 years—worshipped a bull god: Apis. People believed Apis provided fertile fields, flocks, and families. One Egyptian statue shows a king kneeling before a young bull.

When the Exodus took place. The Bible and archaeology seem to disagree about this.

First Kings 6:1 says the Exodus took place 480 years before Solomon's fourth year as king. His fourth year was 966 B.C., which means Moses led the Israelites out of Egypt in 1446 B.C. But many Bible scholars suggest the Exodus and conquest of Canaan (now Israel) took place in the 1200s. Their evidence? (1) Many Canaanite villages were destroyed during that century. (2) Exodus 1:11 says Israelite slaves built the city of Rameses, which Egyptian records say Rameses II built in his honor.

Some scholars in favor of the traditional date of 1446 B.C. say it is unknown who caused the destruction in Canaan two centuries later; it wasn't necessarily the army of Joshua. It could have been the Philistines. Regarding the mention of Rameses, scholars say that could have been a late editorial addition or a transcribing error (but the same argument could hold true for the 1 Kings verse that places the Exodus in 1446 B.C.).

Scholars remain divided on the issue. Many cling to the traditional date until stronger evidence compels them to do otherwise.

Parting of the Red Sea. Many find it unbelievable that God would miraculously create an escape path through the Red Sea—or that he would perform any miracle that would break the laws of nature.

The Hebrew term for "Red Sea" can mean "Sea of Reeds," suggesting the Israelites crossed a shallow marsh north of the Red Sea. For many people, it's easier to accept that a hot sirocco wind blowing in from the eastern desert quickly dried up the marsh. But whether the Israelites crossed a sea or a marsh, we seem confronted with a miracle. Either God parted a deep body of water, or he arranged for Pharaoh's chariot force to drown in a shallow marsh. ❏

·················· **Encore** ·························

- For the rest of the story, read about the end of the Exodus, when the Israelites reach the promised land. It's found in Joshua, a book named for the man who led the nation after Moses died.

- To see how Israel later celebrates the Exodus in song, read lyrics from their song book: Psalm 78, 105–106, 136.

- To discover how the New Testament portrays Jesus as the Passover lamb whose blood saves us from spiritual death, read John 1:29 and 1 Corinthians 5:1–8. ❏

LEVITICUS

When It Happened   (dates are approximate)

Adam 4000+ B.C.

Abraham 2100 B.C.

Moses 1500 B.C.
Exodus 1440 B.C.
Wandering Ends 1400 B.C.

David 1000 B.C.

Ezra 450 B.C.

Jesus born 7/6 B.C.

Israel's Spiritual How-to Manual

It's not what you'd call easy reading, but essential reading.

It was essential in ancient times, for Jews serious about honoring their commitment to obey God. And it's essential today, for an unobstructed look at God's take on sin and how he made a way for people to get rid of it.

Jews long ago called this book the Priest's Manual. The name *Leviticus* came later; it means "about the Levites." The book earned this later tag because Levites were worship leaders in Israel, and the book is full of detailed instructions about worship. Both titles are misleading, however, because the instructions—about sacrifices, religious holidays, and ritual cleanness—aren't just for priests. They're for everyone.

In many ancient nations, only priests were uniquely set apart to serve the gods and to live by a special code. But the Lord set apart an entire country. He told Israel, "You will be my holy nation and serve me as priests" (Exodus 19:6).

The book of Leviticus is their spiritual how-to manual. In a way, it's the volume preceding the new manual coming from Jesus, "the author and finisher of our faith" (Hebrews 12:2, King James Version).

To understand what Jesus did for us, we need to understand the Jewish faith on which he built. ❏

Famous Lines

- You must become holy, because I am holy (11:45).

- Love others as much as you love yourself (19:18). *A command later popularized by Jesus.*

- I will be your God, and you will be my people (26:12).

Behind the Scenes of Leviticus

⭐ Starring Roles

Moses, who receives detailed worship instructions from God (1:1)
Aaron, older brother of Moses and the chief priest in charge of implementing the instructions (6:8)

📖 Plot

There isn't really a story line to follow. After leaving Egypt, the Israelites camp at Mt. Sinai for a year. This is where they receive the Ten Commandments, build a tent worship center, and receive some 600 laws that will govern them—many laws of which are preserved in Leviticus.

🎥 What to Look For

Plan of salvation. It's easy to get sidetracked by all the details of the law, and by trying to figure out exactly why God orders the Israelites to perform all these rituals and obey these rules—some of which may seem bizarre and even unfair. Instead, read the book as God's first step in his plan of salvation—a step that dramatizes the seriousness of sin and the importance of obeying God.

Israel is unique. Notice that by laying out these rituals and rules for Israel, God is telling the people they are to be holy—a nation separated from sinful practices and devoted to him. In this way Israel becomes a witness to the world, testifying that God is holy and deserves our obedience.

Did You Know?

• The Liberty Bell is engraved with words that describe the trumpet blast signaling the release of slaves at the start of Jubilee, a celebration every half-century: "Proclaim liberty throughout all the land unto all the inhabitants thereof" (25:10, King James Version).

• The idea of a scapegoat—a person who takes the blame for others—comes from Leviticus. On Israel's national day of repentance, known as Yom Kippur or the Day of Atonement, the high priest puts his hands on the head of a goat, symbolically transferring the nation's sins to the animal. Then he has the goat led into the desert to die. As the goat departs, so does Israel's sin.

TIMELINE	BIBLE EVENTS	Jewish laws, sacrificial system begin 1440 B.C.					Dates are approximate
		1500 B.C.	1400 B.C.	1300 B.C.	1200 B.C.	1100 B.C.	1000 B.C.
	WORLD EVENTS	Hindu scriptures (Vedas) begin 1500 B.C.	People in Canaan (Israel) and Sinai use first known alphabet 1500 B.C.				Sacrificial altar used in northern Israel 1000 B.C.

Author and Date

The writer is unnamed, but traditionally considered to be Moses. Much of the book reports on the explicit worship instructions that God gives Moses at Mt. Sinai. In fact, nearly all of Leviticus is from the speeches of God; Moses likely provides the quotes.

Like the other books attributed to Moses (the first five in the Bible), Leviticus is probably written during the 40 years it takes Israel to reach the promised land. Perhaps some of Leviticus is written early in the trip, just after Moses receives the worship instructions from God. Moses would have wanted to implement the rules as quickly as possible, which means he had to teach the priests who would in turn teach the masses.

The book is written to give Israel directions on how to live in peace with God and with each other. Leviticus is not only a book of religious law, but civil law as well. That's because God presents himself as more than Lord at worship time, but as Lord all the time.

On Location

Israel is camped for a year at the foot of Mt. Sinai while God gives Moses the laws preserved in Leviticus. One mountain long associated with this event is Jebel Musa ("mountain of Moses"), a 7,500-foot-high peak near the southern tip of the Sinai Peninsula (approximate location marked with triangle on the map). In the fourth century A.D., Christians built a monastery there to commemorate the meeting between God and Moses. ❏

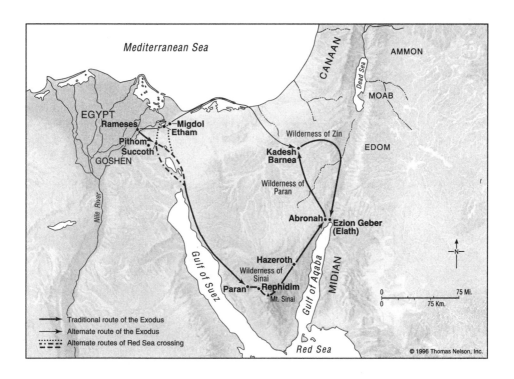

Big Scenes from Leviticus

God creates an intricate system of animal sacrifice. This gives the people a visible, tangible way of expressing their sorrow for sin and of being assured of God's forgiveness. Like a dramatic object lesson and visual aid, the sacrifice also reminds the people about the seriousness of sin: sin causes spiritual death. This is vividly illustrated by the death of the animal.

The ritual calls for the worshiper to lay a hand on the head of the animal, perhaps as a gesture recognizing that the animal is about to lose its life on his account—because of his sin. "Life is in the blood," God explains. "I have given you the blood of animals to sacrifice in place of your own" (17:11).

A lamb is sacrificed for sin committed (4:27–35) •

God tells the Jews they may eat animals that chew the cud and have a split hoof (such as cattle), fish that have fins and scales, and certain insects (such as locusts, crickets, and grasshoppers). But God bans a wide variety of animals, including pigs, camels, shellfish, lizards, and many birds as shown here.

God doesn't explain his reason.

Some have theorized God was protecting the Jews from health problems, or from idolatry, since some forbidden animals were used in pagan rituals—especially the pig. But it may be that God was simply providing a visible way of showing Israel and other nations that the Jews were set apart for special service to God.

People who eat non-kosher food become ritually unclean, and have to follow certain cleansing rituals before they can worship God.

The Jews can eat only select animals • **(11:1–47)**

The Day of Atonement, known also as Yom Kippur, becomes the holiest day on the Jewish calendar. On this day, each autumn, the high priest offers sacrifices for the sins of the entire nation. First, he sacrifices a bull to atone for the sins of his own family. Then he sacrifices a goat for the sins of the nation. Afterward, he lays his hands on the head of a second goat—called a "scapegoat"—and confesses the sins of Israel. This goat is led into the desert and released to die "so that it can take away their sins." In the New Testament, this image of the scapegoat becomes associated with Jesus "who died to take away the sins of many" (Hebrews 9:28).

The nation repents on the Day of Atonement (16:1–34) •

Reviews

Israel's unique laws. Though the 600-plus laws of God recorded in the first five books of the Bible are similar to the laws of other nations during this era, there are some important differences that reveal Israel wasn't simply borrowing from others.

For example, Hammurabi's Code, written several hundred years before Moses, favored the elite. If an upper-class man blinded the eye of another aristocrat, he paid with the loss of one of his eyes. But if he did the same to a commoner, he compensated the injured man only with "one mina [about a pound] of silver." In addition, if a builder constructed a house for a wealthy man and the house collapsed and killed the owner's son, the builder's son could be executed.

Biblical law, however, banned substitutionary punishment. And it treated all citizen offenders the same, regardless of status. Also, the law made special provisions for the disadvantaged. Farmers had to leave part of their crops in the field, as pickings for the poor, widows, orphans, and strangers in the land.

Half sister. One of the many rules God gave Israel was this: "Don't disgrace yourself by having sex with your . . . half sister" (18:11). Yet that's exactly how the Jewish nation began.

Abraham, father of the Jewish people, married his half sister Sarah and then had a son named Isaac. As Abraham explained to King Abimelech, "She is my half sister. We have the same father, but different mothers" (Genesis 20:12).

Jewish Bible scholars in the Middle Ages, and 16th-century Christian scholar John Calvin, were so uncomfortable with this apparent clash in Scripture that they argued that Abraham and Sarah were cousins. The Bible says they weren't.

The fact is, the marriage of Abraham and Sarah came first. The laws of Moses came later—several hundred years later. So the marriage doesn't show a disregard for the Law; it rather confirms that the story of Abraham comes earlier, as the Bible says. ❏

Encore

- To discover how New Testament writers build the Christian faith on Jewish traditions, read Hebrews. There, Jesus is shown replacing the sacrificial system, since he offers himself as the ultimate and final sacrifice for sin, "once for all" (Hebrews 7:27). ❏

NUMBERS

When It Happened

(dates are approximate)

Adam 4000+ B.C.   Abraham 2100 B.C.   Moses 1500 B.C.   Exodus 1440 B.C.   Wandering Ends 1400 B.C.   David 1000 B.C.   Ezra 450 B.C.   Jesus born 7/6 B.C.

Forty Years in the Desert

Don't be fooled by the title. Numbers is not just a report from census takers.

It does include two of these reports (which is how the book earned its name): one census at the beginning of the book, as the Israelites get ready to leave Mt. Sinai, and another at the end, as they camp near the border of what is now Israel. But the book is also full of dramatic stories that reveal a lot about what God is like and how he deals with ever-griping, rebellious human beings.

Jews in ancient times knew the book by the name "In the Wilderness." That's a more descriptive title, for that's what most of the book is about: what went on during the 40 years it took the Israelites to reach Israel, some 400 miles away—and why it took them so long.

The reason it took so long, in a word, is sin. In fact, one of the main points of the book, and a message for all generations, is that God punishes sin. He gives help when asked. He shows mercy unrequested. He offers love neverending. But when faced with sin, he knows it won't go away if he ignores it. So he doesn't.

Yet even when punishing citizens, leaders, and the entire nation, God gives encouragement and hope. As the apostle Paul noted: "The Scriptures were written to teach and encourage us by giving us hope" (Romans 15:4). ❏

Famous Line

- The Lord . . . by no means clears the guilty, visiting the iniquity of the fathers on the children to the third and fourth generation (14:18, New King James Version). *Sin can have long-lasting and painful consequences. The sin of parents can scar children for life.*

Behind the Scenes of Numbers

⭐ Starring Roles

Moses, leader of Israel's 40-year trek toward the promised land (1:1)
Aaron, high priest and older brother of Moses (1:2)
Miriam, sister of Moses (12:1)
Balaam, sorcerer hired to put a hex on Israel (22:5)
Eleazar, son of Aaron and successor as high priest (19:6)
Joshua, scout who explored promised land, successor of Moses (11:28)

📖 Plot

After about a year camped at the foot of Mt. Sinai, the Israelites set out for the promised land. Traveling through the Sinai desert they face many hardships, including hunger, thirst, and sickness. They are quick to complain but slow to ask for God's help. They don't seem to trust him for the future, though he has only recently come through for them in spectacular ways. Their lack of trust becomes shockingly apparent when they reach the boundary of Canaan, now Israel. They refuse to cross the border. They trust less in God than they do in the report of Israelite scouts who return with terrifying news of massive, fortified cities and of giants "so big that we felt as small as grasshoppers" (13:33).

Because the people refuse to trust that God who saved them from the powerful Egyptians could also save them from the Canaanites, God condemns them to wander in the desert until their generation dies.

Did You Know?

• The medical symbol of two snakes on a staff (caduceus) resembles the one described in Numbers. When poisonous snakes enter the Israelite camp, God tells Moses to make a bronze snake and put it on a pole. "Anyone who gets bitten," God says, "can look at the snake and won't die" (21:8).

• God sentenced Israel to 40 years in the desert, one year for every day the scouts explored the promised land. Ten of the 12 scouts advised against the invasion—advice that most of Israel accepted.

• The star of David, which has become the national emblem for modern Israel, comes from Balaam's prophecy of a future king of Israel who "will appear like a star" and conquer neighboring desert nations.

TIMELINE	BIBLE EVENTS				
		Exodus begins 1440 B.C.	Scouts explore promised land 1437 B.C.	Israelites prepare to enter promised land 1400 B.C.	Dates are approximate
		1500 B.C.	1450 B.C.	1400 B.C.	1350 B.C.	1300 B.C.
	WORLD EVENTS	Hittite empire begins 1460 B.C.	Babylonian creation story Enuma Elish written 1450 B.C.	India produces silk clothing 1400 B.C.	Nefertiti is queen of Egypt 1380 B.C.	Tutankhamen (King Tut), age 9, rules Egypt 1361 B.C.

What to Look For

Punishment for sin. Notice how quickly God punishes sin. But notice, too, how quickly he forgives this nation of repeat offenders. Time after time they gripe, harshly criticize, and outright rebel. But each time they repent, he forgives. The people do have to suffer the consequences of their actions, but they don't have to suffer alone. God is with them.

Author and Date

Moses is assumed to be the main writer. Numbers 33:2 says he wrote at least part of it. Others may have added to it. For example, it seems unlikely that Moses would write this: "Now the man Moses was very humble, more than all men who were on the face of the earth" (12:3, New King James Version).

Moses probably wrote most of Numbers during the nation's desert travels in the 1400s B.C. Other knowledgeable writers, such as priests, may have added material and compiled the work into final form after the Israelites settled in the land.

Perhaps the main reason Moses wrote the book is to show that God punishes sin. In fact, the reason the Israelites had to wait 40 years before they could go into the promised land is because they sinned.

On Location

Numbers is set in the Sinai Peninsula, east of Egypt and south of what is now Israel. This is the sun-parched, rugged land where God condemns the Israelites to spend 40 years before entering the promised land. The map shows only the first year of their journey. ❏

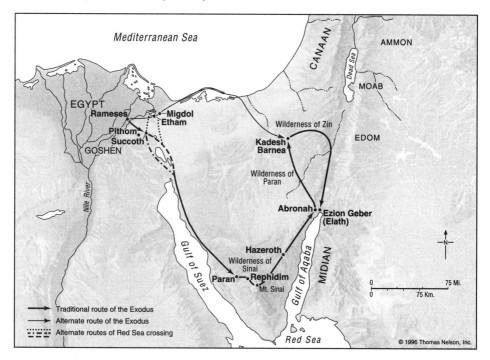

Traditional route of the Exodus
Alternate route of the Exodus
Alternate routes of Red Sea crossing

© 1996 Thomas Nelson, Inc.

Big Scenes from Numbers

After God gives Israel their governing laws during the year they camp at the foot of Mt. Sinai, he calls on Moses to get the people ready to leave. Since they will be invading an occupied land, God instructs Moses to take a census and determine how many fighting men he has. Among the 12 families descended from the sons of Jacob, there are 603,550 men of fighting age, 20 and older.

Moses takes a census of Israel's fighting men (1:1–54) •

A pillar of cloud representing God's presence among the people rises from the tent sanctuary and begins to move. This is the signal that it's time for Israel to break camp and follow. At the front of this migrating nation are priests carrying the ark of the covenant, the chest containing the Ten Commandments. As the ark sets out each day, followed by the long mass of people, Moses says this short prayer: "Our Lord, defeat your enemies and make them run!"

When the people travel by night, the pillar of cloud changes into a pillar of fire.

• **Ark leads the wilderness trek (10:11–36)**

When the dew covers the ground in the morning, so does manna, an unknown substance "like small whitish seeds" that tastes "like something baked with sweet olive oil." The Israelites eventually grow weary of this one-course meal.

"In Egypt we could eat all the fish we wanted," they complain, "and there were cucumbers, melons, onions, and garlic. But we're starving out here, and the only food we have is this manna."

God sends a wind that pushes quail in from the seacoast. The birds cover the ground "three feet high for miles in every direction." Each person gathers at least 50 bushels; then they begin a feast. What they can't eat right away, they dry in the sun for use later.

God provides manna and quail (11:4–32) •

With the Israelites camping on the southern boundary of Canaan, Moses sends 12 men—one from each family tribe—to scout the land. He wants to know if the towns are fortified with walls, if the soil is good, and if there are trees. The scouts return 40 days later. Two men, Joshua and Caleb, show off the grapes, pomegranates, and figs they bring, then urge the people to take the land.

But the other 10 scouts argue, "We won't be able to grow anything in that soil. And the people are like giants."

The Israelites refuse to go any further. For their lack of faith, God condemns the nation to wander in the desert for 40 years—until most of the adults who left Egypt are dead.

Twelve scouts investigate the promised land
(13:1–14:44)

The Israelites retreat south to Kadesh, an oasis where they apparently spend most of the 40 years. There, the water dries up and the people bitterly lament leaving Egypt. Moses and Aaron ask for God's help.

"Moses," God says, "you and Aaron call the people together and command that rock to give you water."

The two men assemble the nation and Moses angrily shouts, "Look, you rebellious people, and you will see water flow from this rock!" Then he strikes the rock twice with his staff.

Because Moses and Aaron do not speak to the rock as God commanded, so that God gets credit for the miracle, God is angry with them. He tells Moses that he and Aaron will not lead the Israelites into the promised land.

Water springs from solid rock
(20:1–13)

The nation of Edom, in what is now western Jordan, refuses to grant safe passage to Israel. This would have given the Israelites a direct path up to the Jordan River crossing into Canaan. So Israel turns south, deep into the desert, to go around Edom. There, again, the people harshly criticize God for making them endure such hunger and thirst.

God sends venomous snakes into the camp, which kill many people. The Israelites repent and ask for deliverance. God tells Moses to erect a pole with a bronze snake at the top. Anyone who gets bitten and looks at the pole will not die.

Centuries later, Jesus will compare this event to his crucifixion, which provides eternal salvation (John 3:14–15).

Poisonous snakes invade the camp
(21:4–9)

As Israel turns north and advances toward the eastern border of the promised land, they approach Moab in what is now the Dead Sea area of Jordan. The king of Moab becomes frantic. He sends messengers to what is possibly the region of Iraq to hire Balaam, an internationally known prophet and seer. The king wants Balaam to put a hex on Israel.

Balaam loads up his donkey and begins the journey. Somewhere along the way he encounters an angel with a sword. At first only Balaam's donkey can see the divine messenger, so the beast sits down and refuses to go further. The contrast is powerful: a lowly donkey can see what an acclaimed seer can't.

When Balaam beats the donkey, the Lord allows the beast to talk. "What have I done to you that made you beat me?" the animal asks.

Suddenly, Balaam is able to see the angel. This divine being permits Balaam to go to Moab on the condition that he speak only the word of God.

Instead of cursing the Israelites, Balaam blesses them and curses their enemies. Furthermore, he prophecies that "someday, a king of Israel will appear like a star. He will wipe out you Moabites and destroy those tribes who live in the desert." King David accomplished this in about 1000 B.C. (2 Samuel 8:2, 11–14).

Balaam's donkey talks
(22:1–24:25) •

Before Moses dies, God tells him to commission Joshua as successor. Moses takes Joshua before a massive assembly of the people, puts his hands on him, and appoints him Israel's leader.

Though God does not allow Moses to go into the promised land, he lets him see it. Moses climbs a mountain east of the Jordan River. There below him, just across the river, stretches the land "flowing with milk and honey."

There on the mountain, with this marvelous and moving vista before him, Moses dies (Deuteronomy 34:5–6).

Joshua is appointed leader when Moses dies
• **(27:12–23)**

Reviews

Balaam outside the Bible. The name of Balaam, son of Beor—as he is identified in Numbers—has shown up on a seventh-century B.C. plaster inscription found among ancient, non-Israelite ruins in Jordan. The words describe Balaam as a "seer of the gods" who received a divine message about a coming disaster.

Inflated population statistics. The census report suggests Israel had at least two million people—more than most nations of the day. This estimate is based on the report that Israel had more than 600,000 fighting men. If each man had, on average, a wife and two children, we're looking at a sea of 2.4 million people wandering around the desert for 40 years. And staying alive. We're also looking at 600,000 men only slowly capturing Canaan, a land of city-states with an estimated population of about 200,000. We're also looking at what Numbers says are only 22,273 firstborn sons (3:43). If there were also an equal number of firstborn daughters, each family would have needed more than 50 kids for Israel to have a population of 2.4 million.

Critics point to these unbelievable numbers as evidence that the Bible is not entirely reliable.

In fact, there may have been many fewer Israelites than seemingly reported.

The Hebrew word for "thousand" can also mean "group," "unit," or "family." So in this case, there might have been only 600 units of fighting men—units of unknown size.

Another theory is that scribes who preserved the book on new scrolls later got confused by various categories and merged the numbers. They may have not realized, for example, the difference between trained warriors and untrained militia, so they treated 44 warriors in Reuben's family as units of thousands, then added them to the 1,500 militiamen. The result: 45,500.

Whatever the population, Israel became large enough in Egypt that Pharaoh complained, "There are too many of those Israelites in our country, and they are becoming more powerful than we are" (Exodus 1:9).

The test of an adulteress. Women suspected of committing adultery had to drink a brew of water mixed with dirt from the floor of the tent worship center. If the woman got sick, she was guilty.

Critics ask, "Who wouldn't get sick?" The test conjures up images of the cruel, medieval trial by ordeal, in which accused people had to prove their innocence by enduring a fire or boiling water.

In Israel's case, however, God established the test, priests administered it, and the people believed that the God who created earth, water, and humans would control the outcome. ❏

Encore

- To find out what happens once the Israelites finally enter Canaan, read the book of Joshua.

- To see the fulfillment of God's promise to reward Joshua and Caleb for being the only two scouts to urge Israel to invade Canaan, read Joshua 14:6-15; 19:49-51. The other 10 scouts died from a "deadly disease" (14:37). ❏

DEUTERONOMY

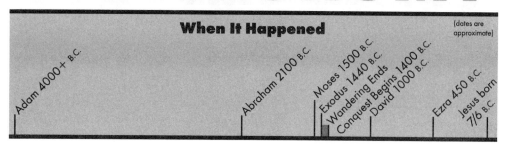

Adam 4000+ B.C.

Abraham 2100 B.C.

Moses 1500 B.C.
Exodus 1440 B.C.
Wandering Ends
Conquest Begins 1400 B.C.
David 1000 B.C.

Ezra 450 B.C.

Jesus born 7/6 B.C.

The Last Words of Moses

What do you say to the people you love when you're about to die? And how do you encourage them when you know they'll be facing the greatest challenge of their lives?

The entire nation of Israelites is camped just beyond the eastern border of Canaan, now called Israel. God has promised to give them the land, but they'll have to fight for it; the territory is full of city kingdoms, many protected by stone walls and seasoned warriors.

Moses won't be there to help anymore. He won't part the waters of the sea when they need to escape. He won't draw water from solid rock when they're thirsty. He won't call down quail when they need meat.

He'll be gone. But God won't.

"Stop worrying!" says Moses. "Just remember what the Lord your God did to Egypt and its king. . . . He will again work miracles for you" (7:18–19).

To bolster the people's faith, Moses tenderly reminds them of where they came from, where on the earth they stand, and how they got there. ❑

Famous Lines

• Hear, O Israel: The Lord is our God, the Lord alone (6:4). *The creedal statement of the Jewish religion.*

• Love the Lord your God with all your heart, soul, and strength (6:5). *The words Jesus quoted when asked to identify the most important commandment.*

• Apple of his eye (32:10, King James Version). *This is the first of several times that the familiar phrase shows up in the Bible. Here, it describes the love God has for Israel.*

Behind the Scenes of Deuteronomy

⭐ Starring Roles

Moses, who gives his farewell after leading Israel 40 years (1:1)

Joshua, appointed by God to succeed Moses (1:38)

📖 Plot

The Israelites are ready to cross the Jordan River and invade Canaan, the promised land. Most adults who escaped Egypt 40 years earlier have died. Moses, too, is about to die. The new generation assembled before him is one that grew up during the wilderness trek. They didn't witness the glorious escape. Nor did they stand at the foot of Mt. Sinai when their parents promised to obey God in return for guidance, protection, and blessing.

For this new generation, Moses prepares a series of sermons—history lessons that summarize the feats of God and the laws that Israel has vowed to obey. Israel's future, he warns, will be determined by how the people respond to God.

"Today I am giving you a choice," Moses says. "You can choose life and success or death and disaster. . . . Choose life! Be completely faithful to the Lord your God, love him, and do whatever he tells you . . . and he will let you live a long time in the land that he promised to your ancestors Abraham, Isaac, and Jacob" (30:15, 19–20).

The question is, will this new generation choose death, as their parents had done?

Did You Know?

• The concept of refuge for the fugitive starts in Deuteronomy, among a nation of former fugitives from Egypt. Moses orders that once the Israelites settle in Canaan, they are to establish six "cities of refuge" scattered around the country. These are cities where people can go after accidentally killing someone. Here they get a fair trial and protection from the victim's avenging relatives and friends. Other law codes from this era order the fugitive returned.

• The idea of a father/child relationship between God and Israel begins here: "The Lord has taken care of us the whole time we've been in the desert, just as you might carry one of your children" (1:31).

• Jesus quotes this book more than any of the other five books of Moses. There are nearly 100 quotes or references to Deuteronomy in the New Testament.

• The old saying, "The heavens are brass," which is a complaint that God doesn't seem to be listening, comes from Deuteronomy's list of warnings about what will happen if Israel breaks its contract with God. "The Lord will make the sky overhead seem like a bronze roof that keeps out the rain" (28:23).

TIMELINE	BIBLE EVENTS							
		Israelites leave Egypt 1440 B.C.	Moses dies, Israel ready to invade Canaan 1400 B.C.				Dates are approximate	
		1500 B.C. 1450 B.C.	1400 B.C. 1350 B.C.	1300 B.C.	1250 B.C. 1200 B.C.			
	WORLD EVENTS	Hittite empire begins 1460 B.C.			Canaanite civilization ends 1200 B.C.			

What to Look For

The book reads like a contract with God. Bible experts say the outline of Deuteronomy follows the format of ancient treaties between kings and their subjects.

In these treaties, such as those of the Hittites in the time of Moses, the king outlines what he expects of the people and what he will give them in return. The treaty also warns the people what will happen if they break their part of the bargain.

Here's the basic outline of ancient treaties, compared to the sections of Deuteronomy that seem to fit the pattern.

1. Preamble, which identifies the ruler (1:1–5).
2. Prologue, describing history of the relationship between ruler and servant (1:6—3:29).
3. Rules of the treaty (chapters 4—26).
4. Oath of allegiance, with benefits of keeping the treaty and consequences for breaking it (chapters 27—30).
5. Instructions for observing the treaty, such as periodically reading it in public (chapters 31—34).

The core of Israel's treaty with the King of kings is summed up in the Ten Commandments. Deuteronomy 28:1–14 explains the benefits of obeying God's law: fertile crops, big families, prosperity, protection against enemies, national fame. Deuteronomy 28:15–68 explains the warnings about disobedience: famines, plagues, and invasions ending with the people being uprooted and "scattered to every nation on earth." Some will even be loaded on boats and shipped back to Egypt.

Author and Date

Deuteronomy repeatedly says Moses wrote it. So do other Old Testament books and Jesus. The closing chapter, about the death of Moses, was probably added by Joshua or a priest.

Moses probably wrote the sermons that make up Deuteronomy shortly before he died, about 1400 B.C. He delivered these messages to remind the Israelites that they owed their very existence to God, and to urge them to remain faithful to him.

On Location

The Israelites move out of the wilderness and are camped in what is now Jordan, near where the Jordan River empties into the Dead Sea. Soon they will march west and cross the river into Canaan, the land God has promised them. From Mt. Nebo, Moses gets a view of the land. ❏

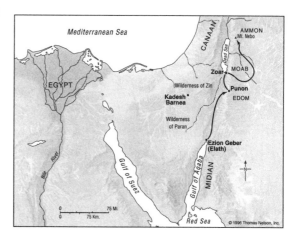

Big Scenes from Deuteronomy

In one of several farewell speeches before he dies, Moses reminds the Israelites of their rich heritage and of the laws that set them apart from other nations. "The Lord told me to give you these laws and teachings," Moses says, "so you can obey them in the land he is giving you."

At the center of the law is this: Israel is to worship God alone.

"Memorize his laws," Moses says, "and tell them to your children over and over again. Talk about them all the time, whether you're at home or walking along the road or going to bed at night, or getting up in the morning."

**Parents teach their children about God
(6:1–9)** ••

Some 40 years after God made a covenant with the Israelites at Mt. Sinai, Moses reminds the people about it. "The Lord has made an agreement with you," he says, "and if you keep your part, you will be successful in everything you do.

"We are at this place of worship to promise that we will keep our part of the agreement with the Lord our God," Moses adds. Israel's part is to obey the laws of God.

This contract isn't just for the assembled generation, any more than the contract at Mt. Sinai was for the previous generation. "It is also for your descendants," Moses reminds them.

**Renewing the contract with God
(29:1–29)**
•••

Moses is 120 years old. His sister and brother, Miriam and Aaron, have already died. So has most of the generation that he led out of slavery in Egypt. Now is the time for Moses to die.

He climbs Mt. Nebo, which rises high above the rich Jordan River valley and Jericho, the oasis "City of Palms." At the summit, Moses sees the land of promise. And then he dies.

He is buried nearby in an unmarked grave. For a month the people grieve their loss of the one prophet in the Bible who spoke "face to face" with God.

**Moses dies
(34:1–12)** ••

Reviews

Hills of iron and copper. Moses told the Israelites that the hills of the promised land are filled with iron ore and copper (8:9). The mountains east of the Sea of Galilee contain iron. And the rugged territory south of the Dead Sea has had rich deposits of both iron and copper. Some of the copper mines in the area date to before the time Israel had kings (starting about 1,000 B.C.), and were reopened when the Romans arrived. Copper mining has only recently been abandoned there.

Written long after Moses? Many Bible scholars say Deuteronomy was not written by Moses, or even in the time of Moses. They suggest it was compiled centuries later, in the 600s B.C., during the religious reform movements sparked by kings Hezekiah and Josiah.

Several clues lead them to believe this. Deuteronomy warns against worshiping sun, moon, and stars, a practice Assyria seems to have introduced to Israel in the 700s B.C. The book says God hates it when people "set up a sacred stone" (16:22), though this seemed acceptable as late as the time of Joshua (Joshua 24:26). Also, the phrasing and style of the speeches are not found in any Bible book written before the 600s B.C.

Scholars who argue that Moses did, in fact, write Deuteronomy counter with several points. Questions about the authorship have surfaced only in the last 200 years. But the earliest Jewish and Christian traditions accept the book's explicit claim that Moses wrote it. In addition, the historical setting seems accurate: the neighboring nations are correctly named, and the structure of the book seems based on treaties common in the time of Moses. ❏

Encore

- To see an elderly Joshua follow Moses' example of a farewell address and a covenant renewal ceremony, read Joshua 24.

- To follow Israel on its conquest of the promised land, read the book of Joshua.

- To discover how Israel repeatedly breaks its contract with God, read the book of Judges. ❏

JOSHUA

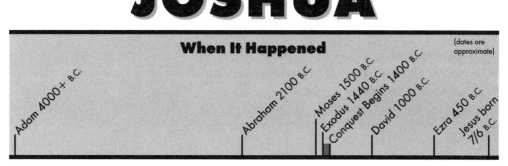

When It Happened

(dates are approximate)

Adam 4000+ B.C.

Abraham 2100 B.C.

Moses 1500 B.C.
Exodus 1440 B.C.
Conquest Begins 1400 B.C.

David 1000 B.C.

Ezra 450 B.C.
Jesus born 7/6 B.C.

Israel's Fight for a Homeland

This is the story of God delivering on a 700-year-old promise to an old man with no kids.

"Go to the land that I will show you," God told 75-year-old Abraham. "I will bless you and make your descendants into a great nation" (Genesis 12:1–2). When Abraham obeyed and arrived near the center of Canaan—now Israel—God said, "Look around to the north, south, east, and west. I will give you and your family all the land you can see. It will be theirs forever!" (Genesis 13:14–15).

Abraham's grandson, Jacob, led the family to Egypt to escape a famine. There they grew to such numbers that the Egyptians feared the Hebrews could overrun the country, so they enslaved them.

But under God's order, Moses freed them.

And now, under God's order, Joshua was taking them home.

Many scenes in this story are as dramatic as those of the great Exodus. The water of the Jordan River stops flowing so the Israelites can enter the promised land. The walls of Jericho spontaneously collapse before Joshua's army. The sun and moon stand still, so Joshua's soldiers can finish an important battle.

Famous Lines

- The priests blew their trumpets, . . . the soldiers shouted as loud as they could. The walls of Jericho fell flat (6:20).

- "Choose for yourselves this day whom you will serve. . . . As for me and my house, we will serve the Lord" (24:15, New King James Version). *Part of the elderly Joshua's farewell to Israel.*

The narrative makes it clear that the conquest of Canaan had little to do with Joshua's military savvy or the Israelite's bravery. It had everything to do with a promise God made to an old man with no kids. God delivers on his promises. ❏

Behind the Scenes of Joshua

⭐ Starring Roles

Joshua, leader and military commander of the Israelites (1:1)
Rahab, a Jericho prostitute who hid two Israelite spies (2:1)
Achan, Israelite whose greed cost his nation a battle (7:1)

📖 Plot

After escaping from about 400 years in Egypt—much of that in slavery—and wandering 40 years through the Sinai Desert east of Egypt, the Israelites finally arrive on the border of the land God has promised them. Their mission is to take the land by force and purge it of the idol-worshiping people who live there.

🎥 What to Look For

The land is God's gift, not spoils of war. Just before the invasion, when Joshua must have been plotting his war strategy, God assures his chosen leader that the victories are certain if the Israelites continue to trust him. "Wherever you go," God says, "I'll give you that land" (Joshua 1:2). And before the first trumpet is sounded at the battle of Jericho, God tells Joshua, "I have given Jericho into your hand" (Joshua 6:2, New King James Version). The battle is won before it starts.

> **Did You Know?**
>
> • Joshua and Jesus share the same name. The name Jesus is a Greek form of the Hebrew name for Joshua, much like Jacques is the French equivalent of James. Both "Joshua" and "Jesus" mean "God saves."

God rewards obedience, punishes disobedience. In times of obedience, Israelites watch God level the walls of Jericho, send hailstones to kill enemy soldiers, and stop the sun from setting perhaps to give Israel all the time it needs to defeat the enemy.

But when one man takes some possessions from the dead enemies, against God's order, the Israelites lose their next battle. And when they make a peace treaty without consulting God, they get tricked (see Joshua 9).

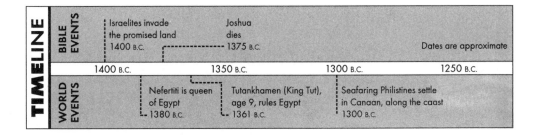

TIMELINE	**BIBLE EVENTS**	Israelites invade the promised land 1400 B.C.	Joshua dies 1375 B.C.	Dates are approximate

1400 B.C.	1350 B.C.	1300 B.C.	1250 B.C.

| **WORLD EVENTS** | Nefertiti is queen of Egypt 1380 B.C. | Tutankhamen (King Tut), age 9, rules Egypt 1361 B.C. | Seafaring Philistines settle in Canaan, along the coast 1300 B.C. |

Author and Date

The book doesn't identify its author. But because of Joshua's starring role in the book named after him, he has traditionally been considered the main writer. The report of his death may have been added by priests Eleazar (Aaron's son) or Phinehas (Aaron's grandson).

Joshua likely wrote the book during the final years of his life, about 1375 B.C., and reported on the 25 years it took Israel to conquer and begin to settle much of the land God promised them.

He wrote primarily to remind the Israelites, the book's first audience, that they didn't win their homeland through military genius and courage. The land was a gift from God.

On Location

Most of the story is set in what is now Israel. But the Israelites also conquered and claimed surrounding territory in what is now parts of Jordan, Syria, and Lebanon. After Jericho they moved west, then south (map at left). Only then did they attack the northern area, pressing past the Sea of Galilee (Chinnereth). ❑

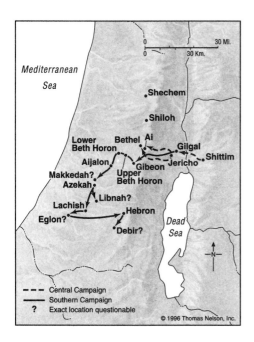

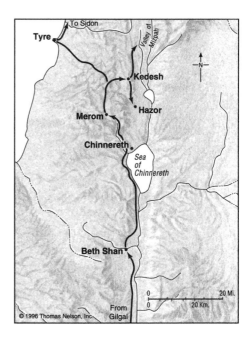

Big Scenes from Joshua

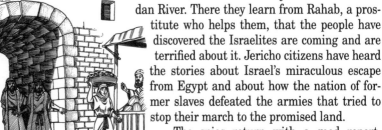

Before leading the Israelites into Canaan, Joshua sends two spies to scout the border town of Jericho just west of the Jordan River. There they learn from Rahab, a prostitute who helps them, that the people have discovered the Israelites are coming and are terrified about it. Jericho citizens have heard the stories about Israel's miraculous escape from Egypt and about how the nation of former slaves defeated the armies that tried to stop their march to the promised land.

The spies return with a good report. "We're sure the Lord has given us the whole country," they say. "The people there shake with fear every time they think of us."

Israelite spies investigate Jericho (2:1–24) •••

When the Israelites finally enter the promised land, after waiting 40 years, they do so in miraculous style. Leading the invasion are priests carrying the ark of the covenant, a sacred chest containing the Ten Commandments. When the priests step into the Jordan River, the eastern boundary of Canaan, the river stops flowing. The water begins "piling up at the town of Adam" some 20 miles north.

The Israelites enter the promised land much as they had left the land of enslavement: on a path that God makes by sweeping aside a river, as he earlier swept back the waters of the Red Sea.

Israel crosses the Jordan River
••• **(3:1–17)**

About five miles across the river the Israelites meet their first enemies, who are protected behind the walls of Jericho. For six days the soldiers march around the city, led by seven priests who continually blow ram-horn trumpets. On the seventh day, they march around the city seven times. Then the priests blow the trumpets, the soldiers give a unison shout, and the walls of Jericho collapse. The first of many enemies is defeated.

The Israelites lose the next battle, however. This is because one of their soldiers, Achan, disobeys God's order against taking spoils of war. Achan steals about five pounds of silver, a pound of gold, and a beautiful robe imported from what is now Iraq. For this he is executed. Afterward, the Israelites resume a successful campaign, sweeping south then turning north.

Jericho walls come tumbling down (6:1–27) ••

When Joshua learns that a coalition army from five cities, including Jerusalem and Hebron, is camped in the hills of Gibeon 15 miles to the west, he leads an all-night march uphill. As the battle is waged, Joshua asks God to extend the day, perhaps to give Israel time to finish off the enemy. As a result, "The sun stood still and didn't go down for about a whole day."

Eventually, the enemy turns and runs. But when they reach a mountain pass about five miles away, they die in a storm of huge hailstones. "More of the enemy soldiers died from the hail than from the Israelite weapons."

The sun and moon stop in the sky
(10:1–28)

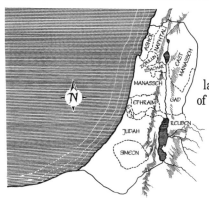

After Joshua's army conquers 31 cities in the highlands of Canaan, he divides the land among the 12 tribes of Israel and tells each tribe to finish securing their own territory. Yet to be captured are powerful cities in the coastal plains, such as those being settled by Philistines, who are also newcomers to Canaan.

Joshua divides the land among 12 tribes
(chapters 13—22)

Elderly Joshua calls together the leaders of Israel to bid them farewell. Like Moses before him, Joshua reminds the people of their agreement to worship God instead of the idols that had been so popular throughout Canaan.

At age 110, Joshua dies and is buried in the rugged hills north of Jerusalem.

Joshua's farewell and death
(chapters 23—24)

Reviews

Ruins of a city burned by Joshua. The Bible says Joshua's army captured the city of Hazor, north of the Sea of Galilee, "then set the town on fire" (11:11). Archaeological excavations confirm that the city was destroyed by fire during the era when the Israelites were capturing and settling the land.

The Jordan River stops flowing. When the Israelites crossed the Jordan into Canaan, God arranged for the water to be dammed up several miles to the north, at the city of Adam. Landslides have blocked the Jordan's flow several times in recorded history. An Arab historian writing in 1267 said that "a lofty mound" overlooking the river collapsed and fell into it, blocking the flow for 16 hours. Earthquakes produced the same effect in 1906 and 1927. The 1927 occurrence, remarkably, took place at Adam. Soil from the 150-foot cliffs tumbled into the river and blocked it for 21 hours.

No walls at Jericho? Archaeologists who have explored the ruins of Jericho confirm that the city did have mud brick walls that were violently destroyed. But the scholars don't agree on when the walls collapsed.

Kathleen Kenyon, a noted archaeologist who investigated the ruins in the 1950s, concluded that the city was completely destroyed in about 1550 B.C., long before Joshua arrived. But an earlier investigation, in the 1930s, led archaeologist John Garstang to say that the city died a fiery death during the time of Joshua in about 1400 B.C. More recently, scholars reviewing Kenyon's work say she misdated the city and that it did, indeed, fall in about 1400 B.C. The issue remains hotly contested among biblical scholars.

The sun and moon stood still? Critics argue that if the sun and moon froze in the sky, as the Bible says happened during the Israelite battle at Gibeon, humans would have been thrown off the planet as the rotation lurched to a sudden stop.

Biblical scholars don't know what happened. Perhaps the reference is figurative, and means that the day seemed longer because Israel accomplished so much, or that the sun remained cool and the sky overcast so the Israelites, weary from an all-night march, would not wither in the heat of the day. Some Bible students argue that if God could create the heavenly bodies of the universe, he could certainly put them in a pause mode for awhile.

Canaanite holocaust. Before Moses died, he left his people with this seemingly barbaric order: "Whenever you capture towns in the land the Lord your God is giving you, be sure to kill all the people and animals" (Deuteronomy 20:16). Beginning with Jericho, the Israelites "killed everyone, men and women, young and old. . . . They even killed every cow, sheep, and donkey" (Joshua 6:21).

What threat could a Canaanite baby pose to the invading Hebrews? And why kill perfectly useful animals, and leave their carcasses to rot?

The only explanation we get comes from Moses. "If you allow them to live, they will persuade you to worship their disgusting gods, and you will be unfaithful to the Lord" (Deuteronomy 20:18). Canaanite children adopted by Hebrews would grow up seeking their lost culture and religion. Animals bred for sacrifice to idols would serve as a constant reminder that other gods were available; as the Lord gave help in war, perhaps the rain god Baal would grant help in harvest.

What Moses warned is exactly what happened. Judges, the sequel to Joshua, reports that the Hebrews failed in their mission to rid the land of the Canaanites. Instead, they learned to live alongside them "and that's how they started worshiping foreign gods" (Judges 3:6). ❑

Encore

- The book of Judges continues where Joshua leaves off, with the Israelites getting settled in the land.

- If you enjoy the book of Joshua, read Deuteronomy. It, too, calls God's people to devote themselves to the Lord and to trust him for their needs. Among the last words of Moses are these: "The eternal God is our hiding place; he carries us in his arms" (Deuteronomy 33:27). Joshua's final speech, a generation later, offers evidence of that promise: "You have seen how the Lord your God fought for you. . . . Always love the Lord your God. Don't ever turn your backs on him" (Joshua 23:3, 11-12). ❑

JUDGES

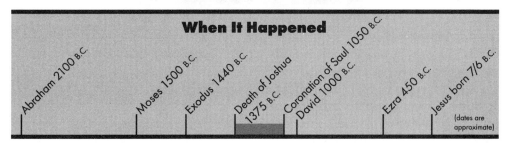

When It Happened

Abraham 2100 B.C. | Moses 1500 B.C. | Exodus 1440 B.C. | Death of Joshua 1375 B.C. | Coronation of Saul 1050 B.C. | David 1000 B.C. | Ezra 450 B.C. | Jesus born 7/6 B.C.

(dates are approximate)

Heroes Who Save Israel

Movie producers looking for blockbuster story lines packed with sexual escapades, gruesome violence, and larger-than-life heroes need look no further. The book of Judges has it all.

Among the riveting tales is one about the wife of a religious leader who is gang-raped to death by Israelite men from the tribe of Benjamin. What follows is a bloody civil war that nearly annihilates the tribe of Benjamin.

Then there's Samson, Israel's strongman with a weakness for immoral women. He winds up with an unwanted haircut, strength sapped, eyes gouged out, and dead in a suicide.

These are gut-wrenching, distressing stories of what happened to Israel after Joshua died. What happened, in a word, is sin—followed by rerun after rerun of more sin. Readers often react to these stories in anger. They want to grab Israel by the collective throat and yell into their face, "Don't you remember all God has done for you? Don't you remember your contract to obey him, and what the penalty is if you don't?"

The fact is that they didn't remember.

But God did. He punished them for their sins. Yet no matter what they did, he refused to stop loving them. And whenever they got themselves into deep trouble and called on him for help, he was there. ❏

Famous Lines

- "I shall put [out] a fleece" (6:37, New King James Version). *What Gideon did to prove that God would help him.*

- "Delilah had lulled Samson to sleep with his head resting in her lap. She signaled to one of the Philistine men as she began cutting off Samson's seven braids" (16:19).

Behind the Scenes of Judges

⭐ Starring Roles

Samson, strongman and last of Israel's 12 judges (13:24)
Delilah, Samson's fatal attraction (16:4)
Gideon, a farmer turned commander of 300 militiamen (6:11)
Deborah, the only female judge (4:4)

📖 Plot

The Israelites have captured and se-cured most of the highlands in Canaan, now Israel. Joshua has died, leaving them with the charge to continue serving God and to finish the job they started: conquer the land and get rid of all the idol-worship-ing Canaanites.

The Israelites do none of the above. They settle into the highlands, learn to live as neighbors with the Canaanites, and be-gin adopting their religion and way of life. Before long, the lines of distinction between Canaanite and Israelite start to blur.

God punishes the Israelites by sending invaders. Israel endures the suffering for awhile, then asks God for deliverance. God sends a leader—called a judge—who saves the people. This plot is rerun over and over twelve times.

🎥 What to Look For

Repetition. Judges has one basic pat-tern or plot repeated throughout the book. The Israelites prosper, then they stop wor-shiping God, face the consequences of pun-ishment, cry out for God's help, and get that help in the form of a leader chosen by God. Notice that by the end of the book, Israel sinks to a new, all-time low.

Did You Know?

- The phrase "missed it by a hair" could have come from Judges. The tribe of Benjamin had 700 left-handed warriors "who could sling a rock at a target the size of a hair and hit it every time" (20:16).

- Most of the twelve judges of Israel weren't legal experts who settled disputes, like judges today. The Hebrew word that best describes these judges means "savior" or "deliverer." Most Israelite judges were military leaders. God chose them to lead regional campaigns against enemies. Samson was the exception; he was a one-man army who led no one. Yet, like the other judges, he is remembered as a mili-tary hero. The twelve judges, in the order they appear, are Othniel, Ehud, Shamgar, Deborah, Gideon, Tola, Jair, Jephthah, Ibzan, Elon, Abdon, and Samson.

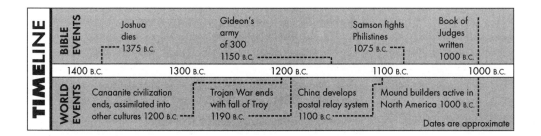

		Joshua dies	Gideon's army of 300		Samson fights Philistines	Book of Judges written
TIMELINE	**BIBLE EVENTS**	1375 B.C.	1150 B.C.		1075 B.C.	1000 B.C.
		1400 B.C.	1300 B.C.	1200 B.C.	1100 B.C.	1000 B.C.
	WORLD EVENTS	Canaanite civilization ends, assimilated into other cultures 1200 B.C.	Trojan War ends with fall of Troy 1190 B.C.	China develops postal relay system 1100 B.C.	Mound builders active in North America 1000 B.C.	
						Dates are approximate

God's mercy and unrelenting love. Israel breaks its contract, or covenant, with God. For this, they suffer some of the consequences Moses warned about. One in particular: "Your enemies will eat the crops you plant, and I will turn from you and let you be destroyed by your attackers" (Leviticus 26:16–17).

For repeated breach of contract, God has every right to do more: "You shall perish among the nations, and the land of your enemies shall eat you up" (Leviticus 26:38, New King James Version). But God stops short of allowing this. For as he had explained through Moses, "No matter what you have done, I am still the Lord your God, and I will never completely reject you" (Leviticus 26:44).

Author and Date

The writer is not named. Samuel the prophet has traditionally been considered the writer. He was Israel's religious leader a few decades after the judges, when many believe that the stories were compiled into a book.

The book covers roughly 300 years, just after Joshua dies in about 1375 B.C. until just before Saul is crowned the first king of Israel in about 1050 B.C. The stories spanning these centuries were probably compiled and preserved in writing sometime after Israel had a king. One strong clue is that the writer repeatedly says the stories take place "before kings ruled Israel" (17:6). The book may have been compiled during the reign of Saul or David, the first two kings. Samuel, the possible author, anointed both men king.

The book was written to preserve an important—though horribly unflattering—slice of Israel's history. The stories vividly show the consequences of disobedience, as well as the never-ending love of God.

On Location

The stories take place in what is now Israel. The map shows locations where the twelve tribes of Israel settled. ❏

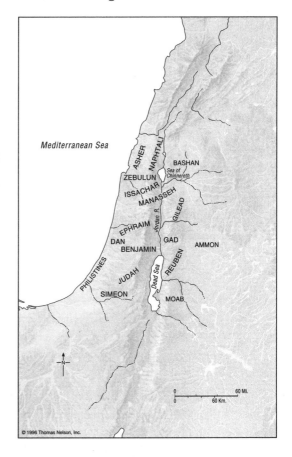

Mediterranean Sea

ASHER
NAPHTALI
BASHAN
Sea of Chinnereth
ZEBULUN
ISSACHAR
MANASSEH
GILEAD
Jordan R.
EPHRAIM
DAN
BENJAMIN
GAD
AMMON
PHILISTINES
JUDAH
REUBEN
Dead Sea
SIMEON
MOAB

0   60 MI.
0   60 Km.

© 1996 Thomas Nelson, Inc.

Big Scenes from Judges

The people of Joshua's generation do a poor job of passing along the faith to their kids: "The next generation did not know the Lord or any of the things he had done for Israel." So the people stop worshiping the Lord and begin worshiping the gods of Canaan.

"The Lord was so angry at the Israelites that he let other nations raid Israel and steal their crops and other possessions."

From time to time, however, the oppression becomes so unbearable for the Israelites that they call on the God of their parents. He answers by sending leaders who rescue Israel from their enemies. "The Lord would be kind to Israel as long as that judge lived. But afterward, the Israelites would become even more sinful than their ancestors had been."

**Israel starts worshiping idols
(2:6–23)** ••

For 25 years the people in northern Israel suffer from a nearby, hostile king further north. When Israel finally calls on God for help, he responds through the prophet Deborah. She tells the people to assemble an army. The odds seem to favor the enemy, for they have a corps of 900 chariots, manned by seasoned professionals. Israel has untrained militia, hastily called to defend themselves.

The Israelites gather at Mount Tabor, a steep hill on which no charioteer would care to fight a battle. But the mountain quickly becomes the least of their worries. Rain suddenly pours from the sky, transforming the valley into a huge mud field that clamps onto the iron wheels of the chariots. The enemies dart from their chariots and run for their lives, but none escape.

Deborah starts the battle of Mount Tabor
•• **(4:1–24)**

The Israelites return to their sinful ways. So at harvesttime each year, God allows desert raiders on camelback to invade Israel. When the people ask God for help, he calls on Gideon who replies, "How can I rescue Israel? My clan is the weakest one in Manasseh, and everyone else in my family is more important than I am."

The reluctant Gideon raises an army of about 32,000, but God tells him to reduce the size to a mere 300. In the dark of night Gideon's men secretly surround the enemy camp filled with tens of thousands of invaders. Each Israelite carries a burning torch hidden inside a clay jar. On Gideon's signal they smash the jars, raise the torches, and blow trumpets. The horrified marauders turn for home and run.

**Gideon's army of 300 routs thousands
(7:1–25)** ••

Samson is like none of the other judges. He doesn't settle disputes among his people, and he leads no one into battle. He's a one-man army who hates the Philistines, for they have killed his new bride and burned her body. So he burns their crops, then slaughters a thousand of their soldiers by using nothing but the jawbone of a donkey.

Samson has incredible strength given by God. He also has a vow to keep—he is never to allow his hair to be cut.

When Samson falls in love with Delilah, the Philistines offer her nearly 30 pounds of silver to find his weakness. After two failed attempts, she succeeds. While he is sleeping, she clips the hair she had earlier woven into seven braids. Then she calls in the waiting Philistines.

Soldiers rush in, capture Samson, gouge out his eyes, then put him to work at a grinding mill. By the time they decide to parade him as a war trophy in front of crowds gathered for a religious festival, his hair has grown. Standing between two pillars, probably made of wooden or stone blocks, Samson prays for strength once more so he can kill more Philistines and die with them. In a powerful surge he breaks the pillars. The roof collapses, killing at least 3,000 Philistines. Samson dies, too, the last of Israel's 12 judges.

Samson meets his match: Delilah
•• **(16:4–31)**

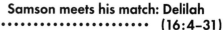

The book of Judges draws to a close with stories showing that life in Israel can't get much worse. An Israelite man hires a silversmith to craft him an idol. Then he hires a priest to live with him, thinking, "Now I know that the Lord will be kind to me." Apparently he didn't know the first of the Ten Commandments: "Do not worship any god except me" (Exodus 20:3).

In a more disturbing—even sickening—story, an Israelite religious leader traveling with his wife to the nation's worship center in Shiloh is attacked by a mob. The mob surrounds a house in which the couple is spending the night in the territory owned by the tribe of Benjamin. They demand that the man come out so they can have sex with him. Instead, the man pushes his wife outside. She is gang-raped all night, and is dead by morning. The husband cuts her into pieces and sends the body parts to the 12 tribes of Israel, with a plea for revenge. The result is a civil war in which 11 of the tribes nearly exterminate the tribe of Benjamin.

The book ends with this unsettling portrait of anarchy: "In those days there was no king in Israel; everyone did what was right in his own eyes" (New King James Version).

Israelites worship God and idols
(17:1–13) ••

Reviews

Accurate picture of Israel. The stories in Judges match what has been uncovered about Israelite history during this era. Israel was not yet a united nation, led by a central leader. It was a collection of independent tribes, or extended family groups, that occasionally worked together to fight off invaders. The earliest known nonbiblical reference to the Israelites is inscribed on a stone from the 1200s B.C. The inscription tells of an Egyptian raid into Canaan.

Why would God choose the likes of Samson? For a hero chosen by God, Samson was surprisingly unrighteous and earthy.

Endowed with incredible strength, he had a pitiful weakness for immoral women. In fact, all of his run-ins with the Philistines started over women: first his bride, then a prostitute, then Delilah.

Samson had also taken vows, since childhood, to avoid anything ritually unclean, to refrain from drinking wine, and to protect his hair from being cut. He apparently broke all these vows. He ate honey from a lion's carcass, knowing that touching this dead animal would render him ritually unclean. Wine flowed freely at his wedding feast. And he allowed himself to be tricked into a haircut.

The book of Judges portrays Samson as a selfish man, driven by his appetites. Even the few prayers he prayed were selfish. His final prayer was for revenge: "Please remember me, Lord God. The Philistines poked out my eyes, but make me strong one last time, so I can take revenge for at least one of my eyes!" (16:28).

Yet as flawed as Samson was, God used him to drive a wedge between the Philistines and the Israelites. This was important because at that time the two nations were getting along pretty well, allowing intermarriage and business dealings. Philistia, however, was the stronger power, and Israel was in danger of becoming assimilated into their culture. Samson made peaceful coexistence much more difficult, helping preserve Israel as a distinct people. About 50 years later, King David finished what Samson started, ending the Philistine dominance in the region. ❏

Encore

- To continue the flow of Israel's story, read 1 Samuel. It picks up where Judges leaves off.

- Hebrews 11 names several of the judges, calling them models of faith. ❏

RUTH

When It Happened

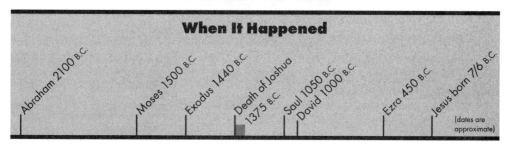

Abraham 2100 B.C.   Moses 1500 B.C.   Exodus 1440 B.C.   Death of Joshua 1375 B.C.   Saul 1050 B.C.   David 1000 B.C.   Ezra 450 B.C.   Jesus born 7/6 B.C.   (dates are approximate)

Mother of Israel's Best Kings

The touching story of King David's great-grandmother is one of the most masterfully crafted in all of Hebrew literature. The suspense begins in the first sentence, with a famine driving a family from their home. By the end of the next paragraph, all three men in the family are dead and their widows are destitute.

The suspense doesn't stop until the story reaches its jaw-dropping, surprise conclusion: Ruth—a foreigner—gave birth to Israel's most famous family of kings. Not only is she related to King David, born in Bethlehem; she is an ancestor of the King of kings also born there (Matthew 1:5).

But until the reader reaches this surprise conclusion, Ruth looks cursed of God. In those days, a woman's greatest accomplishment was to have children. Ruth had none. And nearly all of a woman's legal rights depended on her husband—including the right to own property. Ruth had no husband. Also, in the tiny village of Bethlehem, people found acceptance and support in being part of the close-knit Israelite family, the chosen people of God. Ruth was no Israelite.

Ruth was an outsider, but she chose God. And he brought her inside, to the very heart of Israel's faith, transforming her into a model of love and the mother of Israel's most respected kings. ❏

Famous Line

- "I will go where you go, I will live where you live; your people will be my people, your God will be my God" (1:16). *What Ruth told Naomi after both became widowed.*

Behind the Scenes of Ruth

⭐ Starring Roles

Ruth, young widow from Moab and great-grandmother of David (1:4)
Naomi, Ruth's mother-in-law, an elderly widow from Bethlehem (1:2)
Boaz, second husband of Ruth (2:1)

📖 Plot

To escape a famine in Israel, a Bethlehem man moves with his wife and two sons to a neighboring country. There, his sons marry local women. Then all three men die, leaving their widows destitute. The matron, Naomi, decides to return to her extended family in Bethlehem. She urges her daughters-in-law to go back to their families as well. One does, but Ruth refuses to abandon the elderly Naomi.

The two widows arrive in Bethlehem in time for the spring harvest of barley and wheat. A kind farmer lets Ruth pick some grain for her and Naomi. Ruth later discovers this man is related to Naomi. Ruth proposes marriage to him, he accepts, and they have a son: Obed, the grandfather of King David.

Did You Know?

• Television and film personality Oprah Winfrey was named after Orpah, the daughter-in-law who chose not to stay with Naomi and Ruth. The letters "r" and "p" were switched in Oprah's name.

• The mother of Boaz was Rahab, probably the prostitute who helped the Israelite spies in Jericho. That would make Rahab the great, great-grandmother of King David, as well as an ancestor of Jesus (Matthew 1:5).

• Jews today honor Ruth by reading her story during an annual religious festival at the end of the grain harvest.

🎥 What to Look For

Salvation. This is the theme of the book. Ruth's life takes one about-face after another, from hardship to blessing. She is saved from poverty to wealth, widow to wife, childless to mother, and foreigner to Israelite. Her savior is Boaz, a "kinsman-redeemer." According to ancient custom, the closest relative of a widow could agree to redeem her from a life of poverty by marrying her, taking care of her, and giving her children to inherit the dead father's land. Boaz doesn't marry Naomi because she is too old to have children. So he agrees to marry Ruth and take care of both women.

TIMELINE	BIBLE EVENTS					
	Judges lead Israel in Ruth's era 1375 B.C.			Saul becomes first king of Israel 1050 B.C. -------	David crowned king of Israel 1000 B.C. Dates are approximate	
	1400 B.C.	1300 B.C.	1200 B.C.	1100 B.C.	1000 B.C.	0900 B.C.
	WORLD EVENTS					
	Nefertiti is queen of Egypt 1380 B.C.		Iron tools, weapons used in Israel 1200 B.C.		China develops refrigeration, using winter ice 1000 B.C.	

Many Bible scholars see in Boaz an example of God redeeming Israel from slavery and of Jesus later redeeming the world from sin.

Spoken blessings. In every chapter you'll find one person speaking a word of blessing to another. Naomi blesses her widowed daughters-in-law with a prayer that God will treat them kindly and give them new husbands and homes. And when Boaz greets the workers harvesting his grain he says, "The Lord bless you" (2:4). To which the workers reply, "And may the Lord bless you."

The frequency of these blessings suggests that people who believe in God have a right to speak blessings in God's name—and that God hears and responds to those prayers.

Author and Date

The writer is unknown. Jewish tradition says Samuel wrote it. But this seems unlikely since the climax of the book identifies Ruth as the great-grandmother of David, who is crowned king only after the death of Samuel. (Before the people accepted David as king, however, Samuel anointed him as God's choice to succeed King Saul.)

The story takes place in the time of the judges, "before Israel was ruled by kings" (1:1). The story was then likely passed on by word of mouth for several generations, before being written down sometime during or after the time of David, who began his reign about 1,000 B.C.

It's unclear why someone decided to preserve this story. One theory is that it was written to trace the family tree of David, Israel's most popular king. But perhaps there were other reasons as well: to encourage the Israelites to embrace God-loving foreigners (as God embraces Ruth), and to allow future generations to learn from Ruth's example of love for Naomi.

On Location

The story begins in Bethlehem, then briefly shifts to Moab, Israel's neighbor east of the Dead Sea in what is now Jordan. Within a few paragraphs, the scene switches back to Bethlehem where the rest of the story unfolds. More than a thousand years later, Luke calls this Bethlehem "the city of David" (Luke 2:4) because of family ties going back to Boaz and Ruth. ❏

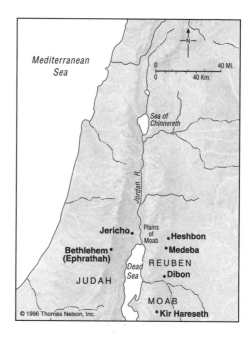

© 1996 Thomas Nelson, Inc.

Big Scenes from Ruth

A famine in Bethlehem drives an Israelite man out of his country. He takes his wife and two sons east of the Jordan River into Moab, part of what is now Jordan. There his sons marry Moabite women. But within 10 years, all three men die.

Naomi, matron of the family, decides to return to her homeland, perhaps hoping that some family members will take her in. But she urges her two daughters-in-law not to follow. If they return to their own families they might be able to remarry. But for elderly Naomi, it's too late. In a time and culture where women depend on a husband or a son to take care of them, Naomi has neither.

One daughter-in-law leaves, but Ruth adamantly refuses to abandon Naomi. "Please don't tell me to leave you," Ruth implores, "I will go where you go, I will live where you live; your people will be my people, your God will be my God. I will die where you die and be buried beside you."

**Ruth stays with Naomi
(1:1–22)** •

Naomi and Ruth arrive at Bethlehem in the spring, as the barley is being harvested. This is fortunate for them, because the Israelite system of welfare requires farmers to leave some of their crop for the poor, "including foreigners, orphans, and widows" (Deuteronomy 24:19).

Ruth goes to the field of a man named Boaz and gets permission from the harvesting foreman to glean behind the harvesters. When Boaz finds out that Ruth is the woman who helped Naomi, he instructs his workers to leave extra grain for her. He also invites Ruth to share meals with the group.

Ruth gleans leftovers in a harvested grain field
• **(2:1–23)**

When Naomi finds out that Boaz—a relative of hers—treated Ruth so kindly, she counsels Ruth on the custom of "kinsman-redeemer." Perhaps Boaz will marry Ruth, and redeem her and Naomi from poverty.

"Take a bath and put on some perfume, then dress in your best clothes," Naomi instructs. "Watch where he goes to spend the night, then when he is asleep, lift the cover and lie down at his feet. He will tell you what to do."

Ruth does as she is told, crawling under the covers after Boaz goes to sleep. Later in the night Boaz awakens to find someone curled up at this feet.

"Who are you?" he asks.

"Sir, I am Ruth," she answers, "and you are the relative who is supposed to take care of me. So spread the edge of your cover over me."

Boaz is impressed with Ruth's loyalty to her family and to the Jewish traditions. She could marry someone outside the family, and abandon Naomi as a troublesome burden. But she doesn't. Boaz agrees to marry her.

**Ruth asks Boaz to marry her
(3:1–18)** •

Boaz marries Ruth, and takes Naomi into his care as well. The couple has a son, to the delight of parents and grandmother.

The child is named Obed. He will grow to become the father of Jesse, grandfather of King David, great-grandfather of King Solomon, and an ancestor of Jesus.

Ruth and Boaz have a son
(4:13-22)

Reviews

Protecting the crops from thieves. The book of Ruth is set in the rough-and-tumble times of the judges, when many Israelites lost sight of God's laws. This setting seems confirmed by the fact that Boaz, a landowner wealthy enough to use hired help, chooses to sleep outdoors beside his grain—apparently to protect it from thieves.

Sneaky Ruth. When Ruth bathes, sprinkles on the perfume, slips into her prettiest robe, then quietly crawls under the covers of Boaz, it looks like she has something other than matrimony on her mind.

But her first words to Boaz when he awakens, and his response, suggest she is following an accepted custom of the day. As a childless widow, she has a right to ask a relative to marry her, take care of her, and help her produce children who can inherit their dead father's property. Women in this culture are not permitted to own property.

Ruth's proposal uses a play on words. She asks Boaz to spread the edge of his "cover" over her. The Hebrew word for "cover" is the same for "wing." When the couple first met, Boaz had said he hoped Ruth would find reward from "the Lord God of Israel, under whose wings you have come for refuge" (2:12, New King James Version). Ruth was calling on Boaz to serve as God's wing of protection.

As soon as Ruth is finished speaking, Boaz reveals his respect for her. "The Lord bless you" he says. "This shows how truly loyal you are to your family. You could have looked for a younger man, either rich or poor, but you didn't. Don't worry, I'll do what you have asked. You are respected by everyone in town" (3:10-11). ❑

- For stories of other women who win their way into Israel through their own initiative, read about the Canaanite woman Tamar (Genesis 38) and the Jericho prostitute Rahab (Joshua 2; 5:13–6:25).

- Esther is the only other Bible book named after a woman. Like Ruth, she is portrayed as a brave heroine loyal to her family.

- The New Testament story of Mary and Joseph has similarities to the story of Ruth and Boaz. Ruth was an outsider, and that's how Mary would have been treated once her neighbors discovered she had an early baby. Boaz showed compassion for Ruth by agreeing to marry her. Joseph did the same for Mary, though he knew he was not the father of the divine child. Ruth and Boaz raised a family of kings. Mary and Joseph raised the King of kings. You can read the story of Mary and Joseph in Matthew 1–2 and Luke 1–2. ❏

1 SAMUEL

When It Happened

Abraham 2100 B.C.   Moses 1500 B.C.   Exodus 1440 B.C.   Death of Joshua 1375 B.C.   Birth of Samuel 1150 B.C.   Death of Saul 1010 B.C.   Ezra 450 B.C.   Jesus born 7/6 B.C.

(dates are approximate)

Israel Gets a King—and His Baggage

There's a lot more here than the history of how Israel made the switch from a loosely connected group of tribes into a united nation led by a king. There's humanity, flawed to the bone. And there's God, accomplishing his plans in spite of it.

You'll see major personality flaws in all the starring characters, as well as in many of the supporting cast.

Priest Eli didn't seem to have strong parenting skills. His two sons grew up crooked.

Samuel had a similar problem with his boys. Yet he tried to appoint them as the next generation of spiritual leaders. He was deeply hurt when Israel's elders said they'd really rather have a king.

Saul, Israel's first king, seemed clinically depressed much of the time. And when David tried to calm him with the gentle song of a lyre, Saul threw a spear at him. Twice.

And David, the man who would later become Israel's most respected king of all, had a life-size idol in his house. His wife dressed it in a robe, put goat hair on its head, and slipped it under the bed covers one night to fool Saul's soldiers who were coming to kill David.

These are colorful people, living and learning at a critical moment in Israel's history. What they're learning is the depth of God's love for his people, and the breadth of his resources for proving it. ❏

Famous Lines

• "Long live the king!" (10:24). *An Israelite crowd's response to Samuel introducing Saul as the nation's first king.*

• "To obey is better than sacrifice" (15:22, New King James Version). *Samuel's criticism of Saul after Saul disobeys God by keeping livestock as spoils of war so he can use them as sacrifices.*

Behind the Scenes of 1 Samuel

⭐ Starring Roles

Samuel, prophet and spiritual leader of Israel (1:20)
Saul, Israel's first king (9:2)
David, Saul's successor (16:1)

📖 Plot

The prophet Samuel becomes the spiritual leader of the nation, serving primarily as a prophet who delivers God's messages to the people and as a judge who settles disputes. When he grows old, the people decide they want a king "just like all the other nations."

But they are not like other nations. That is the point of God's covenant with them. They are God's people, and he is their king. Yet God honors their request. He chooses Saul as their first king. But after Saul repeatedly disobeys, God rejects him as king. God chooses a successor—a shepherd boy named David.

🎥 What to Look For

Samuel's birth. Notice that the book tells the story of Samuel's birth, but not the birth of Israel's first king, or even of Israel's most revered king of all time. This is a clue about how important Samuel is to the story. He plays the key role in Israel's shift from a loose coalition of families to a nation ruled by a king. Not since Moses, whose birth story is reported in Exodus, has Israel seen such a charismatic and dynamic leader.

Traits that God admires. You'll encounter plenty of human foibles in this book. But notice, too, the character traits that God admires and rewards—Hannah's heartfelt prayer; Eli's confidence in God even when faced with painful news; David's life-on-the-line assurance that God will help him slay a giant.

> ### Did You Know?
>
> • Ichabod Crane, the vain and cowardly man who is terrorized by a man disguised as a headless horseman in "The Legend of Sleepy Hollow," gets his name from a grandson of Eli. When Eli's daughter-in-law gives birth shortly after the Philistines defeat the Israelites, steal the ark of the covenant, and kill her husband, she names the boy Ichabod, which means "the glory is gone."
>
> • The old saying "stay by the stuff" comes from 30:24, "tarrieth by the stuff" (King James Version). David was arguing that soldiers who stayed behind to guard the camp deserve a share of the booty taken in battle.

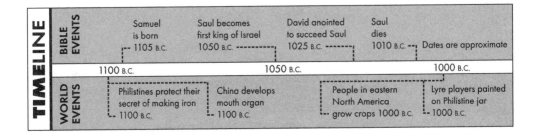

TIMELINE	BIBLE EVENTS	Samuel is born 1105 B.C.	Saul becomes first king of Israel 1050 B.C.	David anointed to succeed Saul 1025 B.C.	Saul dies 1010 B.C.	Dates are approximate
		1100 B.C.	1050 B.C.		1000 B.C.	
	WORLD EVENTS	Philistines protect their secret of making iron 1100 B.C.	China develops mouth organ 1100 B.C.	People in eastern North America grow crops 1000 B.C.	Lyre players painted on Philistine jar 1000 B.C.	

Author and Date

The two books of Samuel were originally written as one book, by an unknown writer. Because the books give detailed and personal information about Samuel, Saul, and David, it seems likely that the writer had access to records from national leaders. The Bible says such records did exist: "Everything David did while he was king is included in the history written by the prophets Samuel, Nathan, and Gad" (1 Chronicles 29:29).

The book was written sometime after Solomon died and Israel split into two nations, in about 930 B.C. The writer speaks of the two nations, Israel in the northland and Judah in the south (17:52).

The reason the book exists is to preserve the history of the Israelite nation when they made the change from an association of 12 independent tribes to a unified nation led by a king.

On Location

The stories take place in Israel. When Saul becomes king, he establishes his capital in Gibeah (identified on this map with the alternate spelling of Geba), the village where he was born, a few miles north of Jerusalem. At this time Jerusalem was still held by the Jebusites; this mountain stronghold had not yet been conquered (see Judges 1:21). ❏

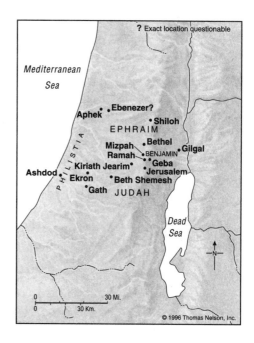

Big Scenes from 1 Samuel

When Hannah, an infertile woman, asks God to let her have a son, Hannah promises she will let the boy serve God all of his life. Within the year, Samuel is born. As soon as he is old enough to feed himself, perhaps around age three, Hannah takes him to the nation's worship center at Shiloh.

"A few years ago I stood here beside you and asked the Lord to give me a child," Hannah reminds Priest Eli. "Here he is! The Lord gave me just what I asked for. Now I am giving him to the Lord, and he will be the Lord's servant for as long as he lives."

Hannah later has other children, but she never forgets her firstborn. Whenever she comes to Shiloh to worship God, she always brings her boy a new robe.

**Young Samuel goes to live with the priest
(1:21–28)** ••

While sleeping one night, young Samuel hears his name and assumes Eli is calling him. But when he goes to find out what the aged and nearly blind priest wants, Eli says he did not call Samuel. When this happens again, Eli realizes it must be the Lord. So he tells Samuel, "If someone speaks to you again, answer, 'I'm listening, Lord. What do you want me to do?'"

God does, indeed, call again. He tells Samuel that because Eli's two sons are selfish and evil, he will not allow them to become the spiritual leaders of Israel.

The next morning, when Eli hears the disappointing prophecy, he responds with resignation and faith: "He is the Lord, and he will do what's right."

Young Samuel hears God's voice in the tabernacle
•• **(3:1–21)**

When Israelite soldiers begin losing a battle to the Philistines, they send a patrol 20 miles back to Shiloh to get the ark of the covenant, Israel's most sacred object—a gold-covered chest that holds the Ten Commandments. The warriors think it will work as a magical charm, to help them defeat the enemy.

The warriors are dead wrong. The battle is lost, Eli's sons are killed in the fight, and the ark is stolen. When Eli hears what happens, he falls backward off his chair, breaks his neck, and dies.

The Philistines put the trophy in their temple, at the feet of a statue of their god. Seven months later they return the ark to Israel, after discovering that it seems to cause diseases.

Samuel becomes the spiritual leader of the people.

**Philistines capture the ark of the covenant
(4:1–10)** ••

When Samuel grows old, he appoints his sons to serve as spiritual leaders and judges. But they are as corrupt as Eli's sons were, for they accept bribes. The tribal elders realize this and tell Samuel, "You set a good example for your sons, but they haven't followed it. Now we want a king to be our leader, just like all the other nations."

Samuel feels rejected, but agrees to take the matter to God.

"Samuel," God says, "do everything they want you to do. I am really the one they have rejected as their king."

God chooses Saul, whom Samuel presents to a crowd that responds with the cheer, "Long live the king!"

Saul becomes the first king of Israel
•• **(9:1–10:26)**

Every morning and evening during a 40-day standoff between the armies of Israel and Philistia, a Philistine champion named Goliath taunts his enemies: "Choose your best soldier to come out and fight me! If he can kill me, our people will be your slaves."

No Israelites take him up on the offer, for he stands more than nine feet tall and wears 150 pounds of body armor. The sword he carries can easily slice off a man's head.

When shepherd boy David arrives, bringing food for his brothers in the militia, he hears the challenge and accepts. Using the weapon with which he has driven predators away from his flock—a sling loaded with a stone—David hits Goliath in the forehead. The giants falls facedown in the dirt, and David uses Goliath's own sword to cut off his head.

The Philistines run, chased by the Israelites.

David kills Goliath
(17:1–52) ••

David's popularity soars. People even write songs about him. One song that enrages Saul includes these lyrics: "Saul has killed a thousand enemies; David has killed ten thousand enemies!"

Jealous, brooding, and deeply depressed, Saul "began acting like a crazy man inside his house." While David is trying to calm him with the gentle music of a lyre—a technique that has worked in the past—Saul raises the spear he is holding and hurls it toward David. Twice he throws it, and twice David dodges it.

Saul tries to pin David to the wall
•• **(18:1–11)**

Fearing that David will steal his kingdom, Saul issues the order that David be killed on sight. David becomes a fugitive, with a growing band of followers.

Once, Saul pursues David and his men into an oasis area honeycombed with caves. Saul, unfortunately, chooses to relieve himself in the very cave where David is hiding. A single thrust of a knife may have ended David's problems. Instead, David sneaks up behind Saul and silently cuts off a corner of the royal robe.

After Saul leaves, David bursts out of the cave, raising the cloth like a flag. "I will not harm the Lord's chosen king," David shouts. "Yet you keep trying to ambush and kill me."

Humiliated, Saul calls off his soldiers and returns home. But he later renews his irrational quest to kill the giant killer.

**David and his men hide from Saul
(24:1–22)** •

When the Philistine army advances deep into Israelite territory, Saul rushes to engage them, but he is filled with terror. He wants to know what God wants him to do, but there is no one to tell him. Samuel has died of old age. Other prophets have no news. And Saul's own prayers to God go unanswered because of Saul's previous disobedience.

In desperation, Saul visits a nearby medium, asking her to conjure up the spirit of Samuel. To the horror of everyone present, including the medium, the spirit of Samuel appears.

"The Philistines are about to attack me," Saul tells Samuel. "What should I do?"

"If the Lord has turned away from you and is now your enemy, don't ask me what to do," Samuel replies. "Tomorrow the Lord will let the Philistines defeat Israel's army."

**Saul consults a medium
(28:1–25)**

• •

Saul returns to camp before daybreak. As Samuel predicted, the Philistines press through the Israelite defenses and begin to close in on Saul and his three sons. One by one the princes fall: Jonathan, Abinadab, Malchishua. Then enemy archers critically wound Saul.

The king asks his weapons bearer to finish him before the Philistines have a chance to capture and torture him. But the soldier can't do it. Saul props the handle of his sword into the ground and falls on the blade.

The first king of Israel is dead.

**Saul kills himself when the battle is lost
(31:1–13)** •

Reviews

Philistine temple of Dagon. When Philistines captured the ark of the covenant, a golden chest containing the Ten Commandments, they brought it to "the temple of their god Dagon and put it next to the statue of Dagon" (5:2). Archaeologists have found the name of this mysterious deity at several places in the region. One document from the 1300s B.C. says Dagon is the father of Baal, the Canaanite god of rain and fertility.

Engedi. David and his men hid from Saul in a cave "in the desert around Engedi" (24:1). The oasis of Engedi would have been a perfect place to hide, for it is concealed in a narrow ravine. Rocky ledges and mounds—pocketed with caves—surround the oasis on three sides. The fourth side opens onto the shore of the Dead Sea. In Bible times Engedi was famous for its vineyards, white henna flowers, and palm trees. *Engedi,* in Hebrew, means "spring of the kid," named after a freshwater spring that plummets from a 300-foot cliff into a refreshing pool.

Why does God pick a loser like Saul? God chose a shy and humble man to become Israel's first king. Saul was out looking for some of his father's donkeys that had run off when he first came upon Samuel. That's when Samuel broke the news that Saul was about to become Israel's first king. Saul was dumbfounded. "I'm from Benjamin, the smallest tribe in Israel," Saul said, "and my clan is the least important in the tribe" (9:21).

Later, when Samuel was about to introduce Saul to the people, no one could find the reluctant monarch. He was hiding among the pack animals.

Saul had both the potential and the opportunity to faithfully serve God. But like others before and after him, he let power make him into a new and lesser creature. As Samuel later explained to him, "You didn't obey the Lord your God. If you had obeyed him, someone from your family would always have been king of Israel" (13:13). ❏

Encore

- To read the rest of the story, turn to 2 Samuel. The two books were originally one, but were separated when they were translated from Hebrew into Greek, in about 300 B.C. This apparently made the size more manageable, allowing each volume to fit onto a single scroll.

- For the story of another infertile woman who has a son and who promises to let him serve the Lord, read about the mother of Samson. It's in Judges 13.

- For a song in the spirit of Hannah's in 2:1-10, read Mary's song in Luke 1:46-56. ❏

2 SAMUEL

When It Happened

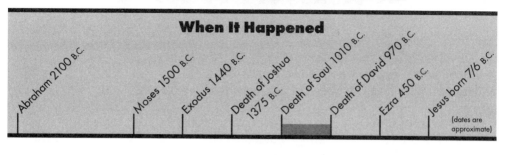

Abraham 2100 B.C.

Moses 1500 B.C.

Exodus 1440 B.C.

Death of Joshua 1375 B.C.

Death of Saul 1010 B.C.

Death of David 970 B.C.

Ezra 450 B.C.

Jesus born 7/6 B.C.

(dates are approximate)

David: Super King, Sorry Family Man

A prince falls in love with his half sister, seduces her, rapes her, then hates her. Enter prince number two, the sister's full brother. He kills prince number one, then flees the country and remains an outcast of the family for five years.

These are King David's kids.

Like father, like son. For when David catches a glimpse of a married woman taking a bath, he invites her to the palace, gets her pregnant, kills her husband, and marries the woman.

This is David, whom God described as "a man after His own heart" (1 Samuel 13:14, New King James Version).

The stories are heart-wrenching, the theology perplexing. These alone make 2 Samuel a captivating book for both casual readers and devoted Bible scholars.

Yet there's more to draw us: a lasting message for everyone who has ever made such a miserable mess of their life that they wondered if God could ever forgive them.

Time and again God forgave David—whenever David asked, no matter what David had done.

This mercy, as irrational as the love of a father for a rebellious child, is available to everyone. As David put it in a song, "Give thanks to the Lord, for He is good! For His mercy endures forever" (1 Chronicles 16:34, New King James Version). ❏

Famous Lines

- "I have sinned" (12:13, New King James Version). *David's response when Nathan accuses him of committing adultery with Bathsheba and killing her husband.*

- "My son, my son. . . . I wish I could have died instead of you!" (18:33). *David's reaction to hearing that his son Absalom has been killed while trying to overthrow him.*

Behind the Scenes of 2 Samuel

⭐ Starring Roles
David, king of Israel (1:1)
Absalom, crown prince who leads a rebellion (3:3)
Nathan, prophet and David's chief advisor (5:14)

📖 Plot
David becomes the new king, replacing Saul. During the 40 years of David's reign, he expands the borders of Israel as far north as the Euphrates River into what is now Iraq, and eastward into Jordan. The taxes he gets from these conquered neighbors help lower taxes for the Israelites. But David's reign is not just a success story. Though he secures his borders and throne, thrusting Israel to the top of the heap among Middle Eastern nations, his family lies at the bottom of the barrel. A big chunk of the book is a surprisingly frank set of stories about David's domestic problems—not the least of which is his adultery with Bathsheba, the rape of one of his daughters by one of his sons, and another son's attempted revolution.

> **Did you know?**
> • William Faulkner's novel, *Absalom, Absalom*—the tale of a southern aristocrat who returns from the Civil War to find that his son has disappeared and his plantation is nearly ruined—was inspired by the tragic story of King David and his son.

🎥 What to Look For
No sugar-coating. The writer tells it like it is. He doesn't try to make flawless heroes out of flawed human beings. In all of Israel's history, the king most revered is David. And for good reason. He is a godly man who never becomes so brain-damaged by power and prestige that he refuses to acknowledge his sins and repent. But sin he does. His most famous is the adultery with Bathsheba, which he tries to cover up by having her husband killed. But David repents. And God forgives.

David's everlasting dynasty. "I will make sure that one of your descendants will always be king," God promises David (7:16).
The kings that rule in Jerusalem are descendants of David—part of a dynasty that reigns for nearly half a millennium, until Israel is defeated in 586 B.C.

TIMELINE	BIBLE EVENTS				
	David secretly anointed king 1025 B.C.	David becomes king 1010 B.C.	Absalom's revolt 975 B.C.	End of David's reign 970 B.C.	Dates are approximate
	1050 B.C.	1000 B.C.		950 B.C.	900 B.C.
WORLD EVENTS	Calendar of farming cycles, oldest example of Hebrew writing 1000 B.C.		Greeks worship Zeus, Aphrodite, and other gods 1000 B.C.	Wigs worn by Egyptian aristocrats 950 B.C.	

and much of the population is taken away in exile. Afterward, God's promise to David becomes a springboard for the Jewish anticipation of a messiah—a new king from the dynasty of kings.

The New Testament presents Jesus as that messiah. When he rides into Jerusalem on the day that becomes known as Palm Sunday, the people acknowledge this by shouting, "God bless the coming kingdom of our ancestor David" (Mark 11:10).

Author and Date

The unnamed writer is the same person who wrote 1 Samuel. Both books were originally a single volume, but were separated into two books when the Hebrew text was translated for Greek-speaking Jews in about 300 B.C. The two books could fit onto a single scroll written in Hebrew because the ancient Hebrew language used no vowels. But Greek used vowels, and required about twice as much space.

Like 1 Samuel, the story was written sometime after Solomon died and Israel split into two nations, in about 930 B.C. The book was written to preserve the history of David's 40-year rule over Israel.

On Location

Most of the stories take place in Israel. But some, such as battles, occur in surrounding nations that include Jordan and Syria. The shaded area shows the extent of David's kingdom. After he made Jerusalem his capital, it became known as the city of David. ❏

© 1996 Thomas Nelson, Inc.

Big Scenes from 2 Samuel

The disastrous defeat of King Saul and his army leaves Israel in danger of being overrun by the Philistines. Tribal leaders unite behind David, a proven warrior, and install him as the new king. This fulfills the prophecy of Samuel years earlier, and his secret anointing of the shepherd boy.

David rules out of Hebron for seven and a half years. But that's a city within his own family's territory, in the southern part of Israel. David apparently decides that to fully unite the 12 tribes, and to eliminate any hint of favoritism, he needs a neutral capital. He chooses Jerusalem for several reasons. It lies on the border of two tribes, near the center of the nation. And the Israelites haven't yet taken it from the Jebusites who live there.

When David's men capture it, in a daring attack through an underground water shaft, the village becomes known as the City of David, later called Jerusalem.

Tribes gather to confirm David as king (5:1–5) ••

Since the time of Priest Eli, decades earlier, when the Philistines captured the ark of the covenant, the ark has been out of the spotlight. Though the Philistines returned this chest that holds the Ten Commandments, it sat neglected in a private shrine. David, however, recognizes it as the most sacred object in all of Israel—a symbol of God's presence among his people. He decides to bring it to Jerusalem, in a move that will unite in one location the king's throne and the symbolic throne of God.

In a joyful procession, filled with music and shouts of glee, David dances as he accompanies the ark. His enthusiasm is so unrestrained that his wife, a daughter of King Saul, later criticizes him for acting undignified and "dancing around half-naked." But David says he doesn't care what she thinks, he was celebrating in honor of the Lord.

David temporarily puts the ark in a tent, but wants to build a temple. "I live in a palace made of cedar," he says, "but the sacred chest has to stay in a tent."

The Lord, however, says that a tent is good enough for now. "I didn't live in a temple when I brought my people out of Egypt," God says, through the prophet Nathan. "A tent has always been my home wherever I have gone with them." The temple, God says, will come later. It will be built by the next king, one of David's sons.

David brings the ark to Jerusalem
•• **(6:1–23)**

One spring evening when David is apparently having trouble sleeping, he gets out of bed and takes a walk on the roof of his palace. Below he sees a beautiful woman bathing; she's Bathsheba, wife of a soldier away at war. David invites her to the palace, has sex with her, and she leaves. She discovers later that she's carrying his child.

David calls her husband home, hoping the soldier will sleep with Bathsheba and think the child is his. The soldier sleeps outside, since his comrades are suffering on the battlefield. David then arranges for him to fight on the front line, while the troops are pulled back. The soldier dies and David marries Bathsheba.

The prophet Nathan later confronts David about this sin. Though David repents, Bathsheba's son dies. Bathsheba later gives birth to Solomon.

David watches Bathsheba bathe
(11:1–26)

Resentment between David and Absalom begins when David fails to punish another of his sons, Absalom's half brother, for raping Absalom's sister. Absalom takes revenge by murdering his half brother then fleeing the country. Three years later David calls his estranged son home, but refuses to meet with him for another two years.

By then, Absalom has decided to overthrow his father. Absalom travels around the country stirring up resentment, then declares himself king. His following is strong enough that David flees the capital.

The armies of father and son clash in a dense forest. There, Absalom gets yanked off his mule when his long hair becomes tangled in tree branches. The mule runs off, leaving Absalom dangling. Some of David's soldiers surround him and, against the king's order, kill him.

Absalom is killed in a rebellion against his father, David
(18:1–33)

David has turned Israel into a powerful fighting nation. He expands his kingdom into an empire that engulfs the Philistines on the Mediterranean coast, and extends eastward into what is now Jordan and northward all the way into Iraq.

In the process, David commits an unspecified sin that God feels obligated to punish. Perhaps David trusts too much on his military might and too little on God. Whatever the sin, God lets David choose the punishment: three years of famine, three months of being chased by enemies, or three days of plague. David chooses the plague, which kills thousands.

When the plague ends, God instructs David to buy the threshing floor on the hilltop overlooking his capital. There, David builds an altar. Later, his son Solomon will build Israel's first temple on that site.

David builds an altar
(24:18–25)

Reviews

City of David. On the crest of a ridge just outside the walls of Jerusalem, archaeologists have found the remains of David's capital. The walled fortress that David captured lies between the temple mount, which overlooked his city, and the Kidron valley below.

The city covered about 15 acres—about half as big as the inside of a large shopping mall—with an estimated population of roughly 2,000. David's son, Solomon, more than doubled the size and population of the city by adding the hilltop on which he built a magnificent temple.

Were David and Jonathan gay lovers? When David heard that Jonathan, his best friend and Saul's son, had died in battle he sang a lament that included these words: "Your love to me was wonderful, surpassing the love of women" (1:26, New King James Version). This has led many to speculate that the two men were more than best friends, they were homosexual lovers.

This, however, doesn't fit with the Old Testament's repeated condemnation of homosexuality or with David's many heterosexual relationships. The Bible names eight of his wives, and he had many others.

When David spoke of Jonathan's love, he was likely referring to Jonathan's selfless loyalty to him, and to the deep friendship the two men shared.

Why does God kill someone trying to keep the ark from falling? When David decides to move the ark of the covenant to Jerusalem, he suffers a major setback. While transporting it by oxcart, one of the oxen stumbles and the ark begins to fall. Uzzah, son of the man who has been taking care of the ark for the past 20 years, stops the ark from falling.

"God was very angry at Uzzah" for touching the ark, the Bible says, "and he killed Uzzah right there beside the chest" (6:7). David immediately changes his plans, and stores the chest in someone's home for three months before trying again—successfully.

God's slaying of Uzzah seems more like the kind of capricious behavior we would expect from one of the mean-spirited gods of Greek mythology.

Why did God kill the man? The Bible doesn't say. Even David didn't understand, and "got angry at God for killing Uzzah." It is clear, however, that the ark was not carried as God directed in Numbers 4:4–20.

The ark was the most sacred object in Israel. It represented the presence of God among his people. Only the Kohathites, one branch in the tribe of Levi, were allowed to carry the ark—even then, the ark and other sacred objects of the tabernacle had to be covered "so the Kohathites won't touch them and die" (Numbers 4:15). Once, when some Israelites tried to sneak a peak inside, God killed them.

Perhaps God killed Uzzah for the flagrant disobedience of transporting the ark improperly and to dramatically remind the onlookers that they should take seriously the warnings of the agreement that their ancestors had made with him. ❑

Encore

- The story of Israel's history continues in 1 Kings. There, the dying David names his surprise successor: passing over his oldest surviving son, David appoints Solomon, his son with Bathsheba.

- To get a feel for the kind of intimate relationship David has with God, read some of the psalms he wrote. Psalm 51 seems to express the kind of sorrow he felt after committing adultery with Bathsheba.

- Psalm 18 conveys the kind of feelings David may have experienced when his son led a coup against him. ❏

1 KINGS

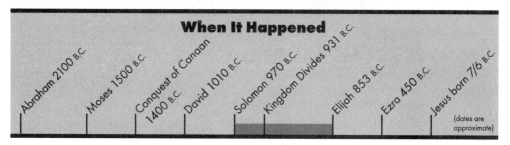

When It Happened

Abraham 2100 B.C. Moses 1500 B.C. Conquest of Canaan 1400 B.C. David 1010 B.C. Solomon 970 B.C. Kingdom Divides 931 B.C. Elijah 853 B.C. Ezra 450 B.C. Jesus born 7/6 B.C.

(dates are approximate)

The Rise and Fall of Israel

King Solomon orders a baby cut in half, so he can watch the reaction of two women who claim to be the mother.

The prophet Elijah challenges 450 prophets of Baal to a contest on Mount Carmel. The deity who sends fire from heaven to consume the sacrifice will be treated by Israel as the only true God.

That's gripping drama. And there's plenty more, thanks in part to the infamous Queen Jezebel. (She executes a farmer who refuses to sell his family's vineyard so the king can turn it into a vegetable garden for his summer palace.)

But there's take-away value in the book as well. You reap what you sow—this message comes through more clearly here, perhaps, than anywhere else in the Bible. Kings who obey God's law reap the benefits listed in the covenant that God made with Israel: rain for the crops, peace in the land, power over invaders. Kings who disobey reap the disasters, which are also listed: disease, famine, overpowering enemies.

Time and again the writer names godly kings, and the blessings they reap. And time and again the writer names ungodly kings, and the disasters they reap. God, like a loving and savvy father, is consistent in his discipline. But the Israelites, like stubborn and self-willed children, are persistent in their rebellion.

Yet one thing remains certain: "No matter what you have done," God has promised their ancestors, "I will never completely reject you" (Leviticus 26:44).

> ### Famous Lines
>
> - "Cut the baby in half" (3:25). *King Solomon's decision when two women each claim a baby boy belongs to her.*
>
> - "The Lord, He is God!" (18:39, New King James Version). *The response of the Israelites after fire from heaven burns up the sacrifice Elijah offers on Mount Carmel.*

❏

Behind the Scenes of 1 Kings

⭐ Starring Roles

David, elderly and dying king of Israel (1:1)
Solomon, David's son and successor, builder of the temple (1:10)
Elijah, prophet who challenges prophets of Baal on Mount Carmel (17:1)
Ahab and Jezebel, Baal-worshiping king and queen of the northern kingdom (16: 28, 31)

📖 Plot

Solomon becomes king after his father David dies of old age. Solomon stretches the wealth and boundaries of Israel to levels never before attained. With the wars of David's reign behind, the Israelites enjoy peace and prosperity as they enter into business deals with surrounding nations. But when Solomon grows old, he begins yielding to pressure from his foreign wives to worship the gods of their homeland. The peace begins to collapse as enemies rise up. When Solomon dies, the nation splits in two and the troubles escalate.

🎥 What to Look For

The lesson behind the history. This isn't your typical history lesson, for the writer doesn't focus on the most accomplished kings. If he did, he'd be giving more attention to kings like Omri, Ahab's father. Omri was one of the most powerful rulers of the northern nation of Israel—a fact illustrated by ancient records from other nations. But Omri nets a mere six verses in the book.

Did You Know?

• The derogatory phrase "she's a Jezebel," meaning a shameless and immoral woman, comes from 1, 2 Kings. Jezebel was the Phoenician princess who lived in what is now Lebanon and who married King Ahab. She executed many of God's prophets, and imposed on the nation her own religion. She worshiped Baal, a fertility god. Worship included having sex with cult prostitutes—male and female—as a way of persuading Baal to grant fertility to family, flock, and field.

• Legend says the queen of Sheba gave birth to a son by Solomon, and that this child became king of Ethiopia. Falashas are a group of Ethiopian Jews who trace their roots to this king. Before the Ethiopian emperor was overthrown in 1974, the nation's constitution said that the royal line descended from the son of "the queen of Sheba and King Solomon of Jerusalem."

		Solomon becomes king 970 B.C.	The temple is finished 960 B.C.	Israel splits into two nations 930 B.C.	Ahab begins his reign 874 B.C.	Dates are approximate
TIMELINE	**BIBLE EVENTS**					
		1100 B.C. — 1050 B.C. — 1000 B.C. — 950 B.C. — 900 B.C. — 850 B.C. — 800 B.C.				
	WORLD EVENTS	Egypt splits in two 1085 B.C.	Celts of central Europe migrate to France 900 B.C.	The city of Canton, China is founded 887 B.C.	Assyrian empire begins expanding 883 B.C.	Homer writes the Iliad and the Odyssey 800 B.C.

The writer focuses on kings who are most obedient to God, or least obedient. He's interested in showing what happens when rulers honor the covenant with God, and what happens when they don't.

Author and Date

Like the two books of Samuel and Chronicles, the two books of Kings were originally written as one book, by an unknown writer. They were separated into two books when the Hebrew text was translated for Greek-speaking Jews in about 300 B.C. This allowed each book to fit onto one scroll.

The writer drew from a variety of ancient sources, including three that are named: a book about Solomon (11:41), and two books about the many other kings (14:19, 29). The writer may also have had access to records kept by court historians or the prophets: "Everything David did while he was king is included in the history written by the prophets Samuel, Nathan, and Gad" (1 Chronicles 29:29).

It's uncertain exactly when the stories were compiled into a single book. Many scholars suspect it was in the mid-500s B.C., after the Babylonians had destroyed Jerusalem and dragged off much of the Jewish population into exile. The history recorded in 1, 2 Kings—which spans the 400 years from the final days of David's reign through the fall of Jerusalem—seems targeted to Jewish readers in exile. The history vividly explains that the Jews got where they are because generation after generation disobeyed God. So the Jews suffered the consequences God had been warning them about since the time of Moses.

On Location

Israel is the center of the action. But other areas in the Middle East add to the setting. To build the temple in Jerusalem, Solomon sends loggers to cut cedar from the forests of Lebanon (Phoenicia on this map). Visiting Solomon, to investigate rumors of his incredible wisdom, is the queen of Sheba, coming from what may have been southern Arabia. The shaded area shows Solomon's kingdom. Trade and transportation routes through the kingdom added to Solomon's influence. ❑

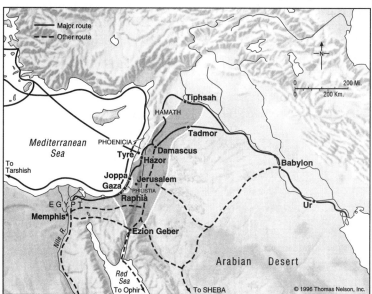

Big Scenes from 1 Kings

Before David dies an old man, he appoints the new king. To everyone's surprise, he does not select his eldest surviving son, Adonijah. The new king is Solomon, David's son with Bathsheba.

Early in Solomon's reign, he asks God for wisdom. What follows is astonishing proof that God has granted his request.

Two young women come to him, each claiming to be the mother of a newborn son. There are no witnesses to call, so Solomon gives a frightful order:

"Cut the baby in half!" he says. "That way each of you can have part of him."

One woman quickly agrees; the other pleads for him to spare the child.

Solomon points to the pleading woman and says, "She is his real mother. Give the baby to her."

**Solomon decides to cut a baby in half
(3:16–28)** •

On a hilltop overlooking Jerusalem, Solomon builds the first of only three temples the Jews have ever had. Stonecutters quarry massive, limestone blocks. Craftsmen from throughout the Middle East design furnishings of gold and ivory. Lumberjacks travel to Lebanon to harvest the finest wood available: bug-proof, rot-resistant cedar.

Seven years later, the job is done. Israel has one of the most beautiful and expensive temples in the ancient world—a worship center with golden ceilings, walls, and floors. This white limestone temple is 30 yards long, 10 yards wide, and 15 yards high, shimmering on the Jerusalem hilltop.

Here Jews will offer sacrifices to God for 400 years—until Babylonian soldiers invade the city, strip away the gold, then destroy the building.

**Solomon builds the temple
(6:1–38)**
• •

The queen of Sheba, from an Arabian trade nation probably 1,000 miles away, hears about the wisdom and wealth of Solomon. So she assembles a large caravan and goes to investigate.

She is amazed. "Solomon," she says, "I had heard about your wisdom and all you've done. But I didn't believe it until I saw it with my own eyes."

She showers him with expensive gifts: nearly five tons of gold, along with jewels and rare spices. He returns the favor, giving her anything she wants.

**The queen of Sheba visits Solomon
(10:1–13)** •

Solomon makes one big mistake. He grows a harem of 700 wives of royal birth and 300 concubines, or secondary wives. These are mainly political marriages, to secure peace and trade agreements with neighboring kingdoms. But these marriages break a rule that Moses gave several hundred years earlier: a ruler "must not have a lot of wives—they might tempt him to be unfaithful to the Lord" (Deuteronomy 17:17).

That's exactly what happens to King Solomon. "As Solomon grew old, his wives turned his heart after other gods, and his heart was not fully devoted to the Lord his God, as the heart of David his father had been" (11:4, New International Version).

To punish the king, God raises up enemies who shatter the decades of peace that Israel has enjoyed.

Solomon's harem of a thousand
(11:1–13)

By the time Solomon dies, the people of Israel are tired of paying heavy taxes to support the king's enormous household and administration. They're weary, too, of being drafted to build cities, forts, and palaces.

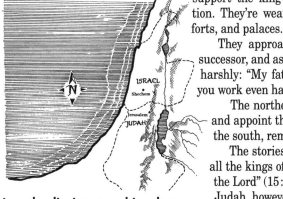

They approach King Rehoboam, Solomon's son and successor, and ask for relief. The rookie monarch responds harshly: "My father made you work hard, but I'll make you work even harder."

The northern tribes secede, start their own nation, and appoint their own king. Only the tribe of Judah, in the south, remains loyal to the descendant of David.

The stories that follow in 1 and 2 Kings reveal that all the kings of the northern nation of Israel "disobeyed the Lord" (15:26). Most kings in the southern nation of Judah, however, are good—with notable exceptions.

Israel splits into two kingdoms
(12:1–33)

Ahab is one of the ungodly kings that blemishes the history of the northern nation. He marries Jezebel, a princess from what is now Lebanon. She kills most of the prophets of God, and imports her own prophets of Baal, god of rain.

God punishes Israel with a three-year drought. Then he orders the prophet Elijah to challenge Jezebel's 450 prophets to a contest, while crowds of Israelites watch. Baal's prophets and Elijah are each to offer a sacrificed bull, laid on a pile of wood. The deity that starts the fire on the altar will become the god of Israel.

Baal's prophets pray for hours, but nothing happens. Elijah prays one short prayer, and the fire falls from heaven. The Israelites kill the prophets of Baal, and the drought ends that day.

Elijah challenges prophets
of Baal on Mount Carmel
(18:1–46)

Reviews

Ivory from Solomon's temple. In 1988 the Israel Museum paid a Jerusalem antiquities dealer $550,000 for a 1.68-inch-high ivory decoration shaped like a pomegranate. They paid this hefty sum for a tiny object because they believed the decoration was the head of a scepter used by priests in Solomon's temple.

What led them to this conclusion is a Hebrew inscription written during the 700s B.C. It reads: "Belonging to the Temp[le of Yahwe]h, holy to the priests." The letters in brackets represent a guess by scholars, since that part of the ivory is broken off. *Yahweh* is the Hebrew name for God.

Ahab and his father, etched in stone. The Bible doesn't mention the battle of Qarqar in which Ahab led Israel in a multi-national force against King Shalmaneser III of Assyria. But Shalmaneser did, in a document called the Monolith Inscription of Shalmaneser. The Bible confirms that Ahab was a warrior king.

The name of King Ahab's father, Omri, shows up in the ancient records of both Moabites and Assyrians. Inscriptions on what has become known as the Moabite Stone, written during the time of Omri in the mid-800s B.C., credit him with capturing Moabite territory in what is now Jordan. And long after Omri's death, Assyrian documents continue referring to Israel as "the Land of Omri," in recognition that he was one of Israel's most influential rulers.

King Jehu's portrait. A stone carving from the Assyrian capital of Nimrud shows Jehu bowing before the Assyrian king. Jehu ruled Israel in the early 800s B.C. The caption reads: "The tribute of Jehu, son of Omri; I received from him silver, gold, a golden bowl, a golden vase with pointed bottom, golden tumblers, golden buckets, tin, and a staff for a king."

Statues of Baal. The Bible portrays Baal as a fertility god, responsible for the rain that gives life to crops and animals. Ancient statues of Baal show him holding a lightning rod in his hand.

Jereboam's sanctuary for a golden calf. To keep northern Jews from worshiping in Jerusalem, the king of the northern tribes set up two worship centers in the north. The most important was at Dan, where he set up a golden calf. Archaeologists have uncovered the remains of this sanctuary and an altar during excavations that began in 1966.

If Solomon was so wise, why did he marry a thousand women? It was common in ancient times for kings to seal trade and peace agreements with a marriage. The kings would give and receive royal daughters in marriage, hoping this would discourage other parties from breaking the agreement and putting their own daughters in jeopardy.

These marriages, however, chipped away at Solomon's faith. By the time he was an old man, he was worshiping the gods of his foreign wives. Suddenly, the luster of Israel's Golden Age began to fade. ❑

Encore

- To read the rest of the story, turn to 2 Kings. The two books were originally one.
- Ecclesiastes, a book that says it was written by a son of David—perhaps Solomon—may reflect the despair Solomon felt after abandoning God. If so, it spotlights the wise conclusion he reached after suffering the consequences of his disobedience: "Respect and obey God! This is what life is all about" (Ecclesiastes 12:13).
- To read about the return of an Elijah-like prophet who will come just before the Messiah, turn to Malachi 4:5-6 and to the words of Jesus in Matthew 11:7-14, where he identifies John the Baptist as that prophet. ❑

2 KINGS

When It Happened

Abraham 2100 B.C.   Moses 1500 B.C.   David 1010 B.C.   Kingdom Divides 931 B.C.   Elijah/Elisha 850 B.C.   Fall of Israel 722 B.C.   Fall of Judah 586 B.C.   Ezra 450 B.C.   Jesus born 7/6 B.C.

(dates are approximate)

Israel Dies, the People Scatter

The most tragic event in the history of Israel is vividly, painfully reported in this book.

As a nation, Israel dies.

It's a bit like the Garden of Eden revisited. Adam and Eve are given one rule, and are told what will happen if they break it: they'll die. They break it anyhow, and sure enough they die.

Much later, God enters into a contract, or covenant, with Israel promising to take care of them in return for their obedience. He explains what will happen if they break the covenant: the nation will be scattered abroad. They break the contract anyhow, and sure enough the Jews of Israel become the Jews of the *Diaspora* (dispersion).

The negative slant is not the only slant in 2 Kings. There's disobedience and punishment—and plenty of each. But there's obedience and reward, too. There are godly prophets accomplishing tremendous miracles. And there are godly kings, whose prayers and righteous living become the difference between life and death for them and the people they govern.

Religion, 2 Kings reveals, is not merely a matter of the heart. It affects history, for better or worse. ❏

Famous Lines

- "You baldhead!" (2:23, New King James Version). *How some young people taunt the prophet Elisha. Two bears immediately charge out of the woods and maul the youths.*

- "He drives like a madman" (9:20, New International Version). *A watchman on a city wall identifies charioteer Jehu by his driving style.*

- "Is your heart right? . . . If it is, give me your hand" (10:15, New King James Version). *Jehu asking a man if he is on Jehu's side. When the man replies he is, Jehu gives him a hand up into the chariot he is driving. Apparently the pedestrian doesn't know what the watchman knows about Jehu's driving.*

Behind the Scenes of 2 Kings

⭐ Starring Roles

Elijah, prophet who rides to heaven in a fiery chariot (1:3)
Elisha, Elijah's successor (2:1)
Naaman, Syrian commander cured of leprosy (5:1)
Jezebel, an evil queen who is murdered (9:7)

📖 Plot

The story of the two Jewish nations of Israel and Judah picks up where 1 Kings leaves off. Elisha becomes Israel's most influential prophet, after his mentor, Elijah, is taken to heaven in a whirlwind. Elisha performs many miracles, even raising a child from the dead and curing an enemy soldier of leprosy. But his efforts to turn the nation's heart back to God seem futile. Assyria destroys Israel in 722 B.C. The southern Jewish nation of Judah enjoys more godly leadership and survives 150 years longer. But in 586 B.C. it, too, collapses. Jerusalem with its magnificent temple is torn to the ground.

🎥 What to Look For

The connection between sin and punishment. The Jews have seen it before, with individuals enduring the consequences of sin, and with the entire nation suffering because of disobedience. But they've never seen punishment as intense as they're about to witness. After generation upon

Did You Know?

• The 1981 Oscar-winning movie "Chariots of Fire," about an Olympic marathon runner who is a Christian who refuses to run on Sunday, gets its title from 2 Kings 6:17. The verse says that when the prophet Elisha's hometown was surrounded by enemy invaders, God sent his own army to protect his people. "The mountain was full of horses and chariots of fire" (New King James Version).

• The phrase "thrown to the dogs" comes from 2 Kings 9:10, 33–34. It describes what happens to Queen Jezebel after she is thrown from her palace window.

• The Lost Tribes of Israel refers to the 10 Jewish tribes, descended from 10 of Jacob's 12 sons, who seceded from the Jewish union and were later destroyed by Assyria. Survivors of the invasion were deported to what is now Iraq, and eventually lost track of what tribes they belonged to.

• The only woman to rule Judah was Athaliah. After her son, the king, died, she killed all the heirs she could find, then assumed the throne. She was executed several years later when an heir she missed suddenly showed up.

TIMELINE	BIBLE EVENTS	Elijah's ministry ends, Elisha's begins ┌---850 B.C.			Northern nation of Israel destroyed ┌--722 B.C.		Southern nation of Judah falls, with Jerusalem 586 B.C. ----------┐	Dates are approximate	
		850 B.C.	800 B.C.	750 B.C.	700 B.C.	650 B.C.	600 B.C.	550 B.C.	
	WORLD EVENTS		Ohio River people build earth burial mounds 800 B.C.	First recorded Olympic games in Greece 776 B.C.	Rome founded by King Romulus 753 B.C.		Chinese philosopher Confucius is born 551 B.C.		

generation heaps disobedience upon disobedience, God invokes the full measure of punishment, according to the terms of his covenant with the Jews. Their nations—first Israel in the north, then Judah in the south—cease to exist.

Author and Date

The two books of Kings were originally written as one book, by an unknown writer. They were separated into two books when the Hebrew text was translated for Greek-speaking Jews in about 300 B.C. This allowed each book to fit onto one scroll.

The writer drew from a variety of sources including a book about Solomon, a book about the kings of Israel, and a book about the kings of Judah. The writer may also have had access to records kept by royal historians and prophets.

No one knows for sure when the stories of 1, 2 Kings were compiled into a single book. Many scholars suspect it was in the mid-500s B.C., after Israel and Judah were conquered. They suspect this because the two books seem to target exiled Jewish readers who want to know what they did to deserve such a horrible punishment.

On Location

The main events take place in the Jewish nations of Israel, in the north, and Judah, in the south. Neighboring empires play important roles. Egypt allies itself with the Jews, while the Assyrians and Babylonians invade and defeat the Jewish nations in spite of the Egyptian alliance. By 650 B.C. Assyria has overrun Israel and dominates the entire fertile crescent (see map). Less than 100 years later, Babylon is the major power in the area and defeats Judah. ❏

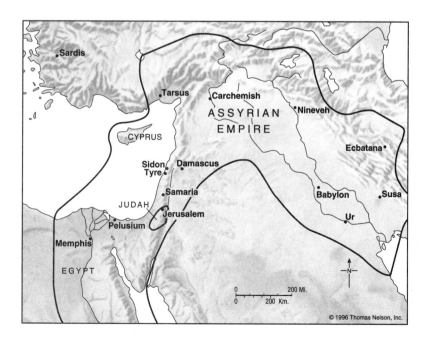

Big Scenes from 2 Kings

At the end of Elijah's 25-year ministry as a prophet, he is walking with his young associate, Elisha. At the Jordan River Elijah rolls up his cloak and strikes the water. "At once a path opened up through the river, and the two of them walked across."

"The Lord will soon take me away," Elijah says. "What can I do for you before that happens?"

Elisha asks to take Elijah's place as the leading prophet. Elijah replies, "It can happen only if you see me as I am being taken away." Suddenly a flaming chariot pulled by fiery horses takes Elijah up into heaven.

Elisha picks up Elijah's cloak, which has fallen, and returns to the Jordan River. There, he rolls up the cloak, strikes the water, and a path opens—a sign that God has granted his request.

**Elijah's whirlwind ride to heaven
(2:1–18)** •

A childless woman and her elderly husband provide Elisha with a guest room to use whenever he's in their area. In return, Elisha promises that the couple will have a child. The following year, a son arrives.

Years later the young boy begins to complain of a terrible headache. By noon he is dead.

The woman immediately gets on a donkey and rides to Mount Carmel to find Elisha. She tells him her son has died and convinces him to return with her.

When Elisha arrives, he walks into the boy's room, shuts the door, and prays.

"Then he got on the bed and stretched out over the dead body, with his mouth on the boy's mouth."

The boy sneezes seven times and opens his eyes.

**Elisha raises a child from the dead
(4:8–37)**

• •

Naaman, commander of the Syrian army that God is using to punish Israel for its sin, is a valiant warrior but a man with a dreaded disease—leprosy. A servant girl in his house, captured from Israel, tells Naaman's wife that he could be cured if he would ask Elisha for help.

Naaman goes to Elisha. The prophet gives the commander these simple instructions: "Wash seven times in the Jordan River. Then you'll be completely cured."

The commander is furious. He has been expecting some mysterious ritual, not a bath. But with a little encouragement from his servants he obeys and is cured.

"Sir," Naaman says as he reports back to Elisha, "from now on I will offer sacrifices only to the Lord."

**A Syrian commander is cured of leprosy
(5:1–27)** •

After King Ahab dies in a battle, his son becomes king. Jezebel still wields great influence and "has caused everyone to worship idols." Elisha tells Jehu, an Israelite soldier, that Ahab's family must die and that Jehu is to become king.

Jehu assembles some men and rides to the king's summer palace in the hills of Jezreel. Outside the city he meets the king and kills him. As Jehu continues toward the city, Jezebel learns that he's coming. "She put on eye shadow and brushed her hair. Then she stood at the window, waiting for him to arrive."

Once he does, she yells out, "Why did you come here, you murderer?"

Jehu looks up and asks, "Is anyone up there on my side?" Some palace workers catch his eye. "Throw her out the window!" Jehu orders. They do, and Jezebel falls to her death.

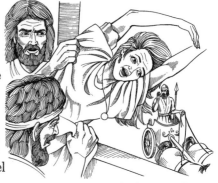

Jezebel is murdered
(9:30–37)

Solomon's magnificent temple, built about 150 years earlier, has suffered from neglect. Baal worship that had grown popular in the northern nation of Israel has also become popular in the

southern nation of Judah. The reason is because Ahab of Israel had made a peace treaty with Judah, and sealed the treaty by giving one of his daughters in marriage to the crown prince of Judah. When the prince becomes king, Ahab's Baal-worshiping daughter becomes queen.

After her husband dies, she orders the execution of all of David's dynasty, then declares herself queen. One heir survives: her infant grandson Joash, who is secretly raised by a temple priest. About six years later, young Joash is presented as the rightful ruler. The queen is executed. When Joash comes of age, he orders that the temple be renovated.

Solomon's temple is repaired
(12:1–21)

Assyria, in what is now Iraq, emerges as one of the most powerful forces in the Middle East. Many nations, including Israel, pay taxes to stay on the good side of the Assyrian rulers. Hoshea, king of Israel, decides to stop payment.

Shalmaneser, king of Assyria, marches into Israel. He surrounds the capital of Samaria for three years and starves the people into submission. The citizens are deported as slaves to several cities in Assyria. Israel is then resettled with Assyrian homesteaders. The 10 Israelite tribes that once made up the nation eventually lose track of their tribal identity forever.

"All of this happened," the Bible says, "because the people of Israel had sinned against the Lord their God."

The northern nation
of Israel falls
(17:1–41)

Judah has been paying taxes to Assyria, but when the Assyrian king dies, Judah decides to rebel. Judah's King Hezekiah enters into a treaty of mutual support with Egypt, Assyria's rival power.

The army of Sennacherib, the new Assyrian king, captures one Judean city after another before laying siege to Jerusalem.

Standing near the city walls, the Assyrian commander yells out his warnings. "Hezekiah claims the Lord will save you," he shouts. "Were any other gods able to defend their land against the king of Assyria? . . . Do you think the Lord your God can do any better?"

"The Lord sent an angel to the camp of the Assyrians. . . . The next morning, the camp was full of dead bodies. After this King Sennacherib went back to Assyria." Jerusalem is spared—for now.

Sennacherib lays siege to Jerusalem, but suffers disaster (18:1—19:37) •

Hezekiah, one of Judah's most godly kings, raises a godless son named Manasseh.

This son assumes the throne at age 12, after his father dies. He rebuilds pagan shrines his father had torn down. And he worships the gods of Baal, Asherah, as well as the sun, moon, and stars. He practices witchcraft, consults fortunetellers, and even sacrifices his own son—all in blatant defiance of God's law.

Manasseh sacrifices a son
• **(21:1–18)**

The horror that befell Israel 150 years earlier now comes to Judah—but in the form of Babylon, which has conquered Assyria.

Jerusalem suffers a siege that lasts a year and a half, starving many of the people to death. When soldiers of Babylonian King Nebuchadnezzar finally break through the city walls, they make an example of Jerusalem and tear it to the ground. Utterly destroyed is Solomon's temple, the symbol of Jewish national and religious identity.

Many Jewish citizens who survive the battle are deported to Babylon as captives.

The great nation that God promised to make of Abraham's descendants no longer exists.

Jerusalem falls (25:1–26) •

Reviews

Hezekiah's tunnel. To provide Jerusalem with water during a siege, Hezekiah tapped into an underground spring by commissioning the construction of "a pool and tunnel" (20:20). This tunnel still exists, cut through nearly 600 yards of solid rock. Miners started at each end and met in the middle, preserving the accomplishment with a brief inscription describing how they did it. The inscription was written shortly before 701 B.C., when Assyria invaded Judah and surrounded Jerusalem.

Sennacherib's record. The Bible says Sennacherib led the Assyrians in a siege against Jerusalem, but that he retreated after an unspecified disaster struck his camp and killed many of his soldiers. Sennacherib's own records add credence to the story. He writes about his invasion, and of conquering numerous cities. But he stops short of saying he conquered Jerusalem. "As for Hezekiah, the Judean who did not submit to my yoke. . . . I made a prisoner in Jerusalem, his royal residence, like a bird in a cage. I surrounded him with earthwork."

Why did God change his mind about killing Hezekiah? When King Hezekiah became critically ill, the prophet Isaiah arrived with a message from God: "You won't ever get well. You are going to die" (20:1).

As Isaiah walked away, Hezekiah turned his face to the wall and prayed, "Don't forget that I have been faithful to you, Lord. I have obeyed you with all my heart." Then he cried hard.

Before Isaiah reached the middle of the palace court, God stopped him with a new message for Hezekiah: "I heard you pray, and I saw you cry. I will heal you, so that three days from now you will be able to worship in my temple. I will let you live fifteen years more, while I protect you and your city from the king of Assyria."

The Bible doesn't explain why God changed his mind. But it certainly shows that prayer makes a difference. ❏

Encore

• The two books of Chronicles cover the same period of history as 1, 2 Kings. Chronicles was apparently written later to Jews who had returned from exile wondering if they were still God's people, or if the covenant was irreparably broken.

• To read a detailed, eye-witness account of the fall of Jerusalem, turn to Jeremiah 52. And for more background on this era in history, read the story sections throughout Jeremiah. You can skip the prophecy sections, which in many Bible translations are easily recognizable because they are indented like poetry.

• For another view of Hezekiah, read Isaiah 36–39; this section parallels 2 Kings 18–20.

❏

1 CHRONICLES

When It Happened

Abraham 2100 B.C.

Moses 1500 B.C.

Exodus 1440 B.C.

Era of Judges 1375 B.C.

David becomes King 1010 B.C.

Death of David 970 B.C.

Ezra 450 B.C.

Jesus born 7/6 B.C.

(dates are approximate)

The Jews Come Home

The chosen people needed to know if they had become the unchosen.

The Israelite nation was born when Abraham entered into an agreement with God, promising to serve him alone. The nation died after Abraham's descendants shattered the agreement by serving a gallery of gods. Babylon crushed the Jewish defenders in 586 B.C., set the cities on fire, and led the masses into exile nearly a thousand miles away.

Decades later, some Jews were allowed to return home. But to what?

Was this still the promised land? Was the covenant still valid? Were the Jews still the chosen people?

The books of 1, 2 Chronicles answer these questions. Yes, this is still the promised land. Yes, the covenant is still in force. And yes, the Jews are still the people chosen by God—though a people who have suffered terribly for their sin.

Evidence of God's favor? The Jews are back in Israel. The temple is rebuilt. The legacy of the priesthood remains intact, with priestly leaders clearly identified. And David's family has been preserved. All of this is God's doing.

He just doesn't give up. That's the good news of Chronicles. ❏

Famous Line

- "Give thanks to the Lord, for He is good! For His mercy endures forever" (1 Chronicles 16:34, New King James Version).

Behind the Scenes of 1 Chronicles

⭐ Starring Role

David, king of Israel who makes plans for the temple (2:9)

📖 Plot

The first nine chapters of the book trace the Israelite family tree from Adam, at creation, to Zerubbabel and beyond, after the captivity in Babylon. Then Israel's story picks up with the death of Saul, followed by the crowning of David as king. David secures the nation by defeating Israel's enemies and establishing the capital in Jerusalem. Then he brings into Jerusalem the ark of the covenant, Israel's most sacred relic, which contains the Ten Commandments. Though David is not permitted to build a temple, he receives from God the temple plans that he passes on to his son, Solomon. David also begins gathering the construction supplies that Solomon will need later.

🎥 What to Look For

What's missing. Notice what the writer leaves out, because this is a clue about the purpose of the book. In telling the story of David, the writer doesn't mention: the conflict with Saul, the adultery with Bathsheba and the murder of her husband, the troubles in the royal family after a prince rapes his half sister, or the attempted coup led by the crown prince.

It's not that the writer is trying to sugarcoat history. He's drawing from a painful history that is already well-known and recorded.

Did You Know?

• Years ago, some scholars thought that the genealogy in this book was mostly fictional, until archaeologists began discovering that towns were named after many people listed among the tribes of Israel.

• Asaph, author of many of the songs in the book of Psalms, is appointed by David to lead musicians who "play music and sing praises to the Lord God of Israel" (16:4). To read the kind of songs they sang, see Psalm 105.

• There's only one time in the Old Testament that a person is reported to pray to God while seated. It happens when David thanks God for blessing his family and nation: "You have chosen Israel to be your people forever," David prays, "and you have become their God" (17:22). A typical posture for prayer in the Old Testament is kneeling. Some people, however, prayed while lying on the ground. Solomon prayed standing, with his hands raised to the sky.

TIMELINE	BIBLE EVENTS									
		Adam is created Before 2500 B.C.					David becomes king 1010 B.C.		David dies 970 B.C.	Dates are approximate
		2500 B.C.	2300 B.C.	2100 B.C.	1900 B.C.	1700 B.C.	1500 B.C.	1300 B.C.	1100 B.C.	900 B.C.
	WORLD EVENTS			Egypt splits in two 1085 B.C.		China develops refrigeration, using winter ice 1000 B.C.		Wigs worn by Egyptian aristocrats 950 B.C.		

Nor is the writer trying to fill in the missing gaps, to preserve an exhaustive history of Israel. He's trying, instead, to preserve Israel's connection to their ancient covenant with God.

For this reason, he focuses on excerpts of history that show God at work on Israel's behalf.

Author and Date

Ancient Jewish tradition says Ezra wrote 1, 2 Chronicles along with the books of Ezra and Nehemiah. Ezra was a priest and teacher of Jewish law who returned to Israel after the exile and who led in the rebuilding of the temple. Genealogies listed in 1 Chronicles, and the point at which they end, suggest the book was written about the time Ezra lived.

Whoever the writer was, he apparently used a wide variety of sources. From the Bible, the books of Samuel and Kings provided about half of his material. He also drew from the books of Moses (the first five in the Bible), along with several books of prophets, as well as Psalms. Sources outside the Bible included history books about the kings and records by various prophets.

Like the books of Samuel and Kings, the two volumes of Chronicles were originally one book, later separated so each could fit onto a single scroll.

Chronicles was probably written in the early 400s B.C., roughly a hundred years after many of the Jews returned home from exile and rebuilt the temple.

Though the Chronicles repeat some of the same history as the books of Samuel and Kings, the motive is radically different. The earlier books are written for Jews in exile, to show them how they got there. So Samuel and Kings spend a lot of time talking about the sins of Israel. The two books of Chronicles, however, are written for Jews who have returned from the exile wondering if their covenant with God is still in force. Chronicles focuses less on the sinful history of Israel, and more on the godly heritage on which the nation should build.

On Location

Most of the story takes place in what is now Israel. David's military victories extend the boundaries of the kingdom (see shaded area on map). ❏

Big Scenes from 1 Chronicles

Beginning with Adam, and continuing all the way through the Jewish exile in Babylon, the writer identifies notable people of God—highlights of the Hebrew family tree.

Nine chapters of names may not seem like a compelling way to draw in readers today. But for the Jews recently back in Israel after decades of exile in Babylon, the list communicates a powerful message: God has not given up on them. Because they have a past with God, they also have a future as the newly restored community of faith.

This genealogy also has the practical value of clarifying who the new leaders are. Among the names of David's descendants, for example, is Zerubbabel. He is the leader who rebuilds the temple so the Jews can reestablish their system of worship. The genealogy also identifies the descendants of Levi, who are to serve as temple priests and assistants.

**The Israelite family tree
(chapters 1—9)** •

After listing the relatively short genealogy of Saul, the writer reports on the final moments of King Saul's life. This becomes a prelude to the many chapters about the accomplishments of King David.

Saul dies during a fierce battle, with Philistine invaders pressing through the Israelite defenses. One by one the princes fall: Jonathan, Abinadab, Malchishua. Then enemy archers critically wound Saul.

The king asks his weapons bearer to finish him before the Philistines have a chance to capture and torture him. Terrified, the soldier can't do it. Saul props the handle of his sword into the ground and falls on the blade.

**Saul kills himself when the battle is lost
(10:1–14)**
• •

David becomes the new king of Israel, establishing his capital in Jerusalem. Since the time of Priest Eli, decades earlier, when the Philistines captured the ark of the covenant, the ark has been out of the spotlight. Though the Philistines returned this chest that holds the Ten Commandments, it sat neglected in a private shrine. David, however, recognizes it as the most sacred object in all of Israel—a symbol of God's presence among his people. He decides to bring it to Jerusalem, in a move that unites in one location the king's throne and the symbolic throne of God.

In a joyful procession, filled with music and shouts of glee, David dances as he accompanies the ark.

He temporarily puts the ark in a tent, but wants to build a temple. "Here I am, living in a palace of cedar," he says, "while the ark of the covenant of the Lord is under a tent" (17:1, New International Version).

The Lord, however, says that a tent is good enough for now. "You have killed too many people and have fought too many battles. That's why you are not the one to build my temple. But when your son becomes king, I will give him peace during his rule. . . . Solomon will build my temple" (22:8–10).

David brings the ark to Jerusalem
(13:1–14; 15:1—16:6)

David continues to secure his nation so he can establish for his son an era of peace. He does this by defeating the surrounding enemies, including the Philistines who have harassed Israel for several hundred years.

Though David is not permitted to build the temple, God entrusts him with the construction plan. David not only passes this along to his son, he begins stockpiling the supplies that Solomon will need: cedar logs imported from Lebanon, 4,000 tons of gold, 40,000 tons of silver, iron for nails and gateways, precious gems, turquoise, onyx, and marble. David even develops a strategy for managing the work of the priests and the temple support staff, and carefully assigns job responsibilities. Among the temple associates are musicians who sing or play instruments, judges, guards, accountants, and custodians.

With the plans safely in the hands of Solomon, David dies of old age.

David prepares building materials for the future temple
(chapters 22, 28—29)

Reviews

The family trade. The genealogies speak of clans, or extended families, that work together in a shared trade. It mentions, for example, one family of "experts in weaving cloth" and another of "potters" (4:21-22). This practice of joining the family business was common in the ancient Middle Eastern world.

Why 70,000 innocent people die, while the sinner lives. Chronicles and Samuel each report a perplexing story about King David sinning in some unknown way by counting his fighting men (2 Samuel 24; 1 Chronicles 21). How he sinned is unknown. Perhaps the census was for bragging rights, to highlight his military prowess instead of giving God the credit for Israel's victories.

Whatever the sin, God sent a plague on Israel. David, the sinner, lived. But 70,000 others died.

The Bible doesn't explain why it worked out this way.

But ancient Middle Eastern culture understood better than Western culture today that families and nations share the reward and punishment of their leaders. Ancient societies weren't as individualistic as we are. We see ourselves as responsible for no one but us. The ancients saw things differently. When a family man did something that pleased a king, for example, the man's entire family benefited. But if the man did something wrong, his sons or even his entire family could be executed. ❏

Encore

- Read 2 Chronicles to continue the rest of the story that was originally one book.

- Read 2 Samuel to fill in the details of David's story. ❏

2 CHRONICLES

When It Happened

Abraham 2100 B.C. · Moses 1500 B.C. · Era of Judges 1375 B.C. · David 1010 B.C. · Kingdom Divides 931 B.C. · Fall of Israel 722 B.C. · Fall of Judah 586 B.C. · Ezra 450 B.C. · Jesus born 7/6 B.C.

(dates are approximate)

Searching for God in a History Lesson

This is a book about hope.

To people standing beside ash and stone piles that were once their nation, their city, their home, hope is a critical commodity.

After half a century of exile in what is now Iraq, the Jews were given permission to return to their homeland. Many didn't, for they had gotten used to their new life. Many of the Jews who were young and fit enough to make the nearly thousand-mile journey to Israel had never even seen the place. It was not home to them.

But many other Jews, young and old, had preserved the stories of their past. They knew God had promised them the land. So they went back. But they desperately needed to know if this was part of God's plan. Perhaps God had abandoned the Jewish people for their disobedience. Perhaps by now he had found another chosen people.

For Jews struggling with doubts such as these, the writer of Chronicles has a history lesson mingled with a sermon of assurance. He shows them their long history with God. And he implies that they will have a long future, too.

What makes Chronicles a classic, however, is its timeless message—if there is hope from above for a people who came as unraveled as the Jews, then there's hope for the likes of us. ❏

Famous Line

- If my people, who are called by my name, will humble themselves and pray and seek my face and turn from their wicked ways, then will I hear from heaven and will forgive their sin and will heal their land (7:14, New International Version). *God's promise to Solomon in the event that God has to punish Israel for sin.*

Behind the Scenes of 2 Chronicles

⭐ Starring Roles

Solomon, Israel's king and builder of the temple (1:1)
Hezekiah, a godly king who helps Judah survive Assyria (28:27)
Josiah, king and religious reformer (33:25)

📖 Plot

Solomon is crowned king after his father, David, dies. He builds the temple and rules the nation during a golden era of peace and prosperity. After Solomon dies, the northern tribes reject his son as king when the young ruler threatens to rule harshly. These tribes form a separate nation that is later wiped out by the Assyrians. Survivors are deported, and never return. After about 150 years, the southern nation of Judah is also destroyed, the people deported. These Jews, however, are eventually allowed to return home and rebuild their ruined nation.

🎥 What to Look For

The moral behind the history. As in 1 Chronicles, notice that the book is not just a reporting of the history. After all, the history books covering this era have already been written. Chronicles is history from a priest's point of view; it's an attempt to interpret what this history means to Jews who have come back from the exile in Babylon. The moral behind the history is that the Jewish people have a future with God.

> **Did You Know?**
>
> • The cedar wood that Solomon imported from Lebanon and used in constructing the temple was valued by ancient builders above all other trees. Its warm red wood was slow to decay, free of knots, and filled with a fragrance that pleased humans but repelled insects. Cedar trees can live 3,000 years. But because of widespread demand for Lebanon's cedar, only remnants of the once-great forest remain.

Dearth of material about the northern nation. The writer almost totally ignores the northern Jewish nation of Israel, except to acknowledge the monumental events: their seceding from the union and their annihilation.

As far as the writer of Chronicles is concerned, the Lost Tribes of Israel, as they became known, no longer represent the true Israel. Their connection to the covenant of God has been severed. From the beginning of their secession, they

TIMELINE	BIBLE EVENTS						
		Solomon becomes king 970 B.C.	The temple is finished 960 B.C.	Israel splits into two nations 930 B.C.	Northern nation of Israel destroyed 722 B.C.		Southern nation of Judah falls, with Jerusalem 586 B.C. Dates are approximate
		1100 B.C.	1000 B.C.	900 B.C.	800 B.C.	700 B.C.	600 B.C.	500 B.C.
	WORLD EVENTS	Egypt splits into two 1085 B.C.	Assyrian empire begins expanding 883 B.C.	First recorded Olympic games in Greece 776 B.C.	Rome founded by King Romulus 753 B.C.		Chinese philosopher Confucius is born 551 B.C.

worshiped idols. As a result, their nation is destroyed and their surviving citizens dragged into exile—never to return. Those left behind become assimilated into foreign cultures when they intermarry with Assyrian pioneers.

Author and Date

The writer is unnamed. Ancient Jewish tradition says Ezra wrote 1, 2 Chronicles along with the books of Ezra and Nehemiah. Like the books of Samuel and Kings, the two books of Chronicles were originally one volume that was later separated so each could fit onto a single scroll.

Chronicles was probably written in the early 400s B.C., roughly a hundred years after many of the Jews returned home from exile and rebuilt the temple.

The stories are carefully chosen to assure the Jews that they have a godly heritage and that their covenant with God is still in force. But the stories also warn them not to repeat the mistakes of the past.

On Location

Most of the story takes place in what is now Israel. The "golden age" of Solomon's reign ends with his death, and the nation quickly divides in two—Israel in the north and Judah in the south. ❑

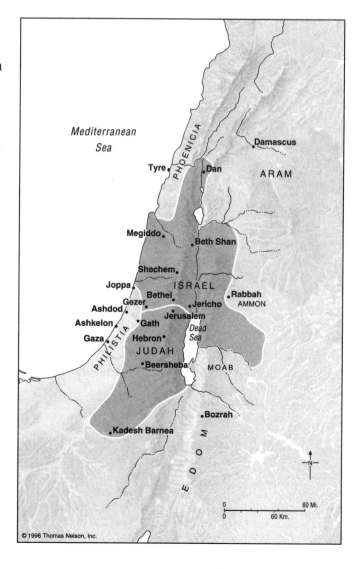

© 1996 Thomas Nelson, Inc.

Big Scenes from 2 Chronicles

Shortly after Solomon is crowned king of Israel, God speaks to him in a dream, as God has done to Abraham, Jacob, and Joseph in years past.

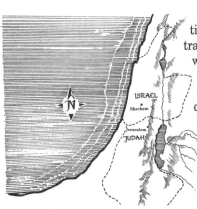

"Ask for anything you want," God says, "and I will give it to you."

"Give me the knowledge I'll need," Solomon replies, "to be the king of this great nation of yours."

"You could have asked me to make you rich or famous or to let you live a long time," God says. "Instead you asked for wisdom." For that, God decides to give Solomon the whole package. "I will make you wise and intelligent. But I will also make you richer and more famous than any king before or after you."

**Solomon asks God for wisdom
(1:1–17)** •

On a hilltop overlooking Jerusalem, Solomon builds the first of only three temples the Jews have ever had. He assembles a monumental work force of about 150,000.

Seven years later, the job is done. Israel has one of the most beautiful and expensive temples in the ancient world—a white limestone worship center adorned with golden ceilings, walls, and floors. This elegant temple is 30 yards long, 10 yards wide, and 15 yards high.

Only priests are allowed inside. In the back room, where only the high priest can go one day a year, sits the Ten Commandments inside a gold-covered chest—the ark of the covenant.

In this temple, Jews will offer sacrifices to God for 400 years—until Babylonian invaders destroy the building.

Solomon builds the temple
• **(3:1–17)**

By the time Solomon dies, the people of Israel are tired of paying heavy taxes to support the king's administration and his enormous household (he has a thousand wives). They're weary, too, of being drafted to build cities, forts, and palaces.

They ask King Rehoboam, Solomon's son and successor, for relief. The rookie monarch responds harshly: "My father made you work hard, but I'll make you work even harder. He punished you with whips, but I'll use whips with pieces of sharp metal!"

The northern tribes secede, start their own nation that they call Israel, and appoint their own king. Only the tribe of Judah, in the south, remains loyal to the descendant of David.

**Israel splits into two nations
(10:1–19)** •

The northern nation suffers under godless kings for about 200 years. In 722 B.C., Assyria invades and annihilates the kingdom, taking the survivors away as captives.

Like other countries in the region, Judah has been paying taxes to Assyria. But when the Assyrian king dies many years later, Judah decides to rebel.

The army of Sennacherib, the new Assyrian king, captures one Judean city after another before laying siege to Jerusalem. Standing near the city walls, the Assyrian commander yells out his warnings. "No god of any nation has ever been able to stand up to Assyria. Believe me, your God cannot keep you safe!"

The Lord sends an angel to the camp of the Assyrians. The next morning the camp is full of dead bodies. Sennacherib returns to Assyria, disgraced.

Sennacherib lays siege to Jerusalem but suffers disaster
•• **(32:1–23)**

The southern nation of Judah outlasts its northern brother by about 150 years. This is because Judah has many godly rulers. But some kings lead the people astray.

"The Lord God sent prophets who warned the people over and over about their sins. But the people only laughed and insulted these prophets." God decides to punish Judah (36:15–16).

Judah's capital city of Jerusalem suffers a siege that lasts a year and a half, starving many to death. When soldiers of Babylonian King Nebuchadnezzar break through the city walls, they tear the city to the ground. Solomon's glorious temple, the symbol of Jewish national and religious identity, is looted and then destroyed.

Jewish citizens who survive the assault are deported to Babylon as captives.

The nation of Abraham and David no longer exists.

Jerusalem falls to Babylon
(36:9–21) ••

About 50 years later, the Persian empire swallows up Babylon, just as Babylon had earlier overpowered Assyria. The new ruler is Cyrus who, prompted of God, issues the following decree: "The Lord God of heaven has made me the ruler of every nation on earth. He has also chosen me to build a temple for him in Jerusalem, which is in Judah. The Lord God will watch over any of his people who want to go back to Judah."

With this promise, many Jews begin their long trek home.

The king of Persia frees the Jews
••• **(36:22–23)**

Reviews

Cyrus' policy of releasing captives. Second Chronicles and Ezra both say that Persian King Cyrus let the conquered Jewish people return home to Judah so they could rebuild the temple. A 10-inch-long clay cylinder inscribed with cuneiform writing confirms that Cyrus had a policy of allowing defeated people to return to their homeland.

Known as the Cyrus Cylinder, the document quotes the king as saying he ordered the rebuilding of sacred sanctuaries in holy cities "on the other side of the Tigris. . . . I also gathered all their former inhabitants and returned them to their homes."

No 70-year exile. Jeremiah, the prophet who witnessed the fall of Jerusalem in 586 B.C., said the exile would last "seventy years" (Jeremiah 29:10). It lasted only about 50, because Persian King Cyrus released the Jews to return home in about 538 B.C., just after Persia defeated the Babylonians (2 Chronicles 36:22).

The 20-year difference remains a puzzle. But there are several possible solutions.

1. Jeremiah had in mind the first deportation of Judeans to Babylon. This happened in about 605 B.C., nearly 70 years before Cyrus' decree.

2. The exile extended from the destruction of the temple in 586 B.C. until its rededication in 516 B.C., 70 years.

3. Jeremiah didn't mean 70 literal years. He simply meant a long time. This number was used in this manner on other occasions in the Bible (2 Chronicles 36:21; Daniel 9:24). ❏

Encore

- The book of Ezra continues Israel's story, with the Jews returning from exile and starting the job of rebuilding the temple.

- For more details about the era covered in the book, read 1, 2 Kings.

- To catch a glimpse of what Jesus had in mind when he spoke of "Solomon in all his glory" (Matthew 6:29), review chapter nine, about the queen of Sheba's reaction to Solomon. ❏

EZRA

When It Happened

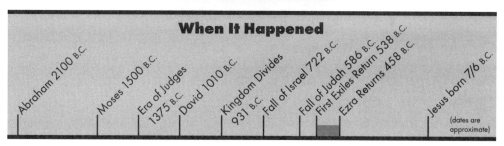

Abraham 2100 B.C.
Moses 1500 B.C.
Era of Judges 1375 B.C.
David 1010 B.C.
Kingdom Divides 931 B.C.
Fall of Israel 722 B.C.
Fall of Judah 586 B.C.
First Exiles Return 538 B.C.
Ezra Returns 458 B.C.
Jesus born 7/6 B.C.

(dates are approximate)

A Second Great Escape

Out of the ashes and rock piles of the annihilated Jewish nation emerges a restored Israel.

It's a miracle, reminiscent of the Exodus. But instead of confronting a resistant, stubborn pharaoh who absolutely refuses to let the Jews go—as happened in the days of Moses—we read of three Persian kings who encourage the exiled Jews to return home—and give them gifts and tax breaks as added incentive.

So, nearly a thousand years after the great Exodus, the Jewish nation begins a second exodus. It takes place over several decades, as wave after wave of exiles pack up the families they raised in a foreign land and begin the long, nearly thousand-mile walk northward along the fertile Euphrates River valley in what is now Iraq, then south along the Mediterranean coast, through Lebanon and into Israel.

Pioneers had settled into the land during the Jewish exile. As far as they were concerned, the Jewish homecoming was an unwelcome intrusion.

But with the support of pagan kings, whom the Jews believed were instruments of God himself, they prevailed.

The result is a story that inspires courage and perseverance in anyone facing the intimidating challenge of rebuilding their life, their home, or their faith from the ground up. ❑

Famous Lines

- "Let the temple be rebuilt" (6:3, New International Version).
  The Persian king's declaration about the Jewish temple that the Babylonians had destroyed.

- Praise the Lord God of our ancestors! He made sure that the king [of Persia] honored the Lord's temple in Jerusalem (7:27).
  Priest Ezra's reaction to news that the king was authorizing royal treasurers to contribute silver and other gifts for the rebuilding of the temple. In addition, temple workers would not have to pay taxes.

Behind the Scenes of Ezra

⭐ Starring Roles

Ezra, priest who preaches against Jews marrying non-Jews (7:1)
Cyrus, Persian king who frees Jewish exiles (1:1)

📖 Plot

After 50 years of living in exile, the Jews are free to go home. Persia has defeated Babylon, and Persian King Cyrus has decreed that all Jewish captives may return to their homeland. Furthermore, the king encourages the Jews to rebuild their temple. He even returns the temple furnishings that the Babylonians had taken from Solomon's temple before they leveled it.

Many Jews return and begin to rebuild the temple in Jerusalem. The job grinds to a halt because of local opposition. But the work begins again, at the urging of the prophets Haggai and Zechariah who arrive later. Jerusalem's second temple is completed in 516 B.C., 70 years after Solomon's temple was destroyed.

> ### Did You Know?
>
> • Though Ezra preaches a stern sermon against Jews marrying non-Jews, including people from Moab in what is now Jordan, King David's great-grandmother was Ruth, a Moabite. Though foreigners tended to lead Israel away from God and into idolatry, God accepted non-Jews who worshiped him, as Ruth did.

Priest Ezra arrives and begins teaching the people from the laws of Moses. His sermons generate nationwide repentance, and abruptly end the marriages of many Jewish men to non-Jewish women.

🎥 What to Look For

🎬 **God working through people who don't worship him.** Notice that the writer says the temple is rebuilt because of the support of three pagan kings. (1) Persian King Cyrus issues a formal decree inviting the Jews to return to Jerusalem and rebuild the temple. (2) Decades later, Persian King Darius brushes aside non-Jewish opposition to the continued rebuilding project and tells the Jews to finish their work. (3) Yet another Persian king, Artaxerxes, encourages Jews who have remained in Babylon to return home. He gives money and supplies to any who wish to go.

TIMELINE

BIBLE EVENTS	Jews exiled in Babylon	Persia defeats Babylon	First wave of exiles return to Jerusalem	Temple rebuilt	Ezra arrives in Jerusalem	Dates are approximate
	586 B.C.	539 B.C.	538 B.C.	516 B.C.	458 B.C.	
	600 B.C.	550 B.C.	500 B.C.		450 B.C.	400 B.C.
WORLD EVENTS	Chinese philosopher Confucius is born 551 B.C.	Cyrus Cylinder confirms return of Jews 539 B.C.	Persia conquers Egypt 525 B.C.	Buddha, in India, preaches first sermon 521 B.C.	Roman republic founded 509 B.C.	Greek Parthenon in Athens dedicated to goddess Athena 432 B.C.

Copies of official letters. Most of the book, like most of the Old Testament, is written in Hebrew. But Ezra includes some official Persian messages written in Aramaic, the language used in the exile. One example is the memorandum by King Darius in 6:3–12. These are included to give evidence that the Jews had the king's approval to do what they were doing. Some Bible scholars a few decades ago thought these letters were made up. But recently discovered Persian documents reveal that the letters track with Persian policies, and are written in the language of the region, using the formal tone of royal decrees.

Author and Date

The writer is not named. Ancient Jewish tradition says the book was written by Ezra, a priest and teacher who returned from exile about 60 years after the temple was rebuilt. Many believe that the author of Ezra also wrote 1, 2 Chronicles as well as Nehemiah.

In the earliest editions of the Bible, Ezra and Nehemiah were one book. The first known writer to speak of them as separate was Christian scholar Origen, who lived in the A.D. 200s. He called them 1, 2 Ezra.

Like the two books of Chronicles, Ezra was probably written in the early 400s B.C., roughly a hundred years after many of the Jews returned home from exile and rebuilt the temple.

The author wrote the book to preserve the good news about what happened when the Jewish exiles were finally freed to return home. What happened is that they began rebuilding their nation by rebuilding their temple. They also made a serious attempt to distance themselves from idol-worshiping foreigners, who could undermine their faith in God.

On Location

The story takes place in two locations: first in Babylon (modern Iraq), where exiled Jews prepare to return home, then in Jerusalem, where they begin rebuilding the temple. Zerubbabel and the first group of exiles returned to Jerusalem in 538–537 B.C. The city walls were not rebuilt until Ezra and Nehemiah led a second wave of Jews back eighty years later. ❏

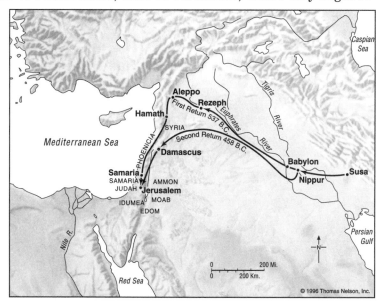

Big Scenes from Ezra

After Persia conquers the Babylonian Empire, Persian King Cyrus issues a magnanimous decree allowing the exiled Jews to return home. He is also encouraging them to rebuild their temple, and is ordering others to donate supplies. He's even returning the sacred furnishings of the temple, stolen by the Babylonians 50 years earlier.

Some 42,000 Jews decide to return, though perhaps most had been born in exile and had never seen the land God promised them.

Once they arrive in Jerusalem, they take up a collection among themselves to begin rebuilding the temple. They produce about half a ton of gold and nearly three tons of silver—a fraction of the nearly 4,000 tons of gold and 40,000 tons of silver that David set aside for the temple built by his son, Solomon.

The Jews begin by rebuilding the altar, so they can quickly renew their practice of worshiping God by offering animal and crop sacrifices.

The Jews return from exile (chapters 1–2)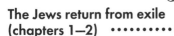

With the sacrificial system back in place, the Jews begin the arduous task of clearing away the rubble of the previous temple and laying the foundation for a new one. When the foundation is complete the people assemble for a service of praise to God. Many are shouting with glee and singing songs that King David had written hundreds of years earlier.

But woven in among the celebrants are disappointed old-timers crying out loud "because they remembered seeing the first temple years before." Apparently they realize there's no hope of the new temple matching the glory of the first one. What they don't realize, however, is that though the new temple will be smaller and less elegant than Solomon's, it will last nearly a century longer—about 500 years.

Rebuilding the temple (3:7–13; 6:13–18)

Pioneers who had settled in the land while the Jews were away had started worshiping God, but only as the local god of the land, not as the one and only God of creation. They offer to help rebuild the temple, but the Jews reject the offer.

Insulted, the locals begin causing trouble, threatening the workers and trying to sabotage their efforts. Then, when a new king comes to the Persian throne, they write him a letter and say the Jews are nearly done rebuilding the city. When that happens, the letter charges, "the Jews won't pay any kind of taxes, and there will be less money in your treasury." Furthermore, they add, the Jews have a history of rebelling—a fact they say the king can confirm by checking the records of his ancestors.

The king does check the records and finds that the Jews do have a long record of rebelling. So he orders the work stopped.

For about a decade, the Jews do nothing to rebuild the temple. Then, prodded by newly arrived prophets, they resume their work. When the locals again file their complaint to what has become yet another Persian king—Darius—the king digs out the original decree of Cyrus and allows the rebuilding to continue. About four years later, in 516 B.C., the temple is completed and dedicated.

The locals manage to get the work halted
•• **(4:1–24)**

Upon arriving in Jerusalem, Ezra discovers that many of the Jewish men have ignored the law against marrying non-Jewish women. Even some of the priests and temple workers have broken this law. Ezra goes to the temple courtyard and begins praying and weeping on behalf of the people. He knows that it was Israel's association with non-Jews that led to idolatry, which brought on the exile. And he fears that God will punish the new nation, just as he had punished Judah.

One by one, a crowd of worshipers gathers around him. When they hear his prayers, they begin weeping, too. Within three days a vast assembly has gathered there. As rain pours onto the courtyard, Ezra stands to speak.

"You have broken God's Law by marrying foreign women," he says. "Now you must confess your sins to the Lord God of your ancestors and obey him. Divorce your foreign wives and don't have anything to do with the rest of the foreigners who live around here."

The assembly agrees.

Ezra condemns the marriage of Jews to non-Jews
(9:1—10:17) ••

······················· **Reviews** ·······················

Cyrus on the record. Inscriptions from the time of Persian King Cyrus confirm that he was tolerant of the religion of conquered people and that he had a policy of allowing the captives to return home and resume their faith. He apparently hoped this would endear him both to the people and to their gods.

In one of his inscriptions he asks, "May all the gods whom I have resettled in their sacred cities ask daily Bel and Nebo [two Babylonian gods] for a long life for me and may they recommend me to Marduk [chief Babylonian god]."

Later Persian kings followed the same policy.

The numbers don't add up. Ezra 2 lists the exiles who returned, as does Nehemiah 7. Both say the total number of people is 42,360. But Ezra's list adds up to 29,818 and Nehemiah's list adds up to 31,089.

There's no clear explanation for the apparent discrepancy.

Perhaps they each took the time to record just a partial list, and added unnamed women to reach the total.

Many Bible scholars, however, think that scribes who preserved the book century after century by copying it from worn-out scrolls onto new scrolls made some mistakes with the numbers. Perhaps some of the numbers on the old scrolls were too hard to read.

Why abandon non-Jewish wives? At what appears to be the insistence of the people, Ezra preached a blunt sermon against Jews marrying non-Jews, then instructed all Jewish men with non-Jewish wives to divorce them and "send them away, together with their children" (10:3).

The Jews decided on this painful course of action because Ezra reminded them that God's law prohibited such marriages. The law, referring to the Canaanites, said, "don't let your sons and daughters marry any of them. If you do, those people will lead your descendants to worship other gods and to turn their backs on the Lord. That will make him very angry, and he will quickly destroy Israel" (Deuteronomy 7:4).

Ezra reminded the former exiles that this is exactly what happened. And the Jews apparently concluded it could happen again. So rather than simply change in the future, they tried to undo the past.

This may not have been how God wanted them to handle it, but it certainly seems to be what they thought God expected of them. Perhaps they believed it was too risky to do anything less. After all, disobedience had recently wiped out their country. They didn't want any chance of a repeat performance. ❏

······················· **Encore** ·······················

- To continue the next stage of the story, read Nehemiah, which was originally the second half of the book of Ezra.

- To compare the second and less-magnificent temple of Ezra's day with the first one of Solomon's day, read 1 Chronicles 28–29 and 2 Chronicles 2–7.

- To read the words of prophets who inspired the exiles to rebuild the temple and recommit themselves to God, turn to the books of Haggai and Zechariah. ❏

NEHEMIAH

When It Happened

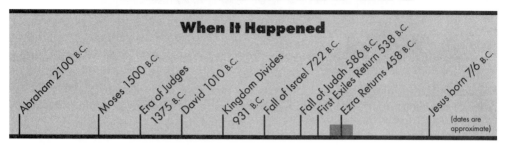

Abraham 2100 B.C.
Moses 1500 B.C.
Era of Judges 1375 B.C.
David 1010 B.C.
Kingdom Divides 931 B.C.
Fall of Israel 722 B.C.
Fall of Judah 586 B.C.
First Exiles Return 538 B.C.
Ezra Returns 458 B.C.
Jesus born 7/6 B.C.

(dates are approximate)

Rebuilding Jerusalem's Walls in 52 Days

Sometimes, faith and prayer are not enough to get the job done. Sometimes it takes brains, muscle, and courage. Nehemiah needed it all.

He was a palace servant in Persia when he got word that the former Jewish exiles who had returned to Jerusalem were in trouble. They were both defenseless and disgraced because the city walls were broken and gates burned. Jerusalem held a sacred place in the heart of Jewish people because, since the time of King David nearly 600 years earlier, it had been the spiritual and political center of their nation. Jews without Jerusalem would have been like Americans without America, a congregation without a church, or a family without a home.

The very thought of the city remaining in disrepair plunged Nehemiah into four months of deep depression, which prayer and fasting could not cure. His only remedy was to tackle the insurmountable: to see to it that the walls and gates got repaired. Nehemiah, a palace cupbearer, was going to do this.

The reason the book is a classic is because Nehemiah, the cupbearer, actually did it, with God's help. Nehemiah talked the Persian king into supporting the project, convinced the apathetic Jews to embrace the work, and outsmarted the local opposition.

In accomplishing this, Nehemiah wrote himself into history as a model for tackling God's tough assignments. ❏

Famous Lines

- "Come, let us rebuild the wall of Jerusalem" (2:17, New International Version). *Nehemiah's invitation to Jerusalem-area Jews.*

- The people had a mind to work (4:6, New King James Version).

- "The people shouted, 'Amen! Amen!'" (8:6). *How the Jews responded to hearing Ezra reading the laws God had given them through Moses.*

- The joy of the Lord is your strength (8:10, New King James Version).

Behind the Scenes of Nehemiah

⭐ Starring Roles

Nehemiah, Persian palace servant who oversees repair of Jerusalem's walls (1:1)
Sanballat, leader of opposition and possibly governor of Samaria (2:10)
Artaxerxes, Persian king who gives Nehemiah permission to repair the walls (1:1)
Ezra, priest who reads God's Law to the assembled people (8:1)

📖 Plot

Nehemiah, a palace servant who guarantees that the Persian king's wine is not poisoned, is granted a leave of absence so he can oversee the repair of Jerusalem's walls. Despite opposition, and apparent plans to attack the workers and kill Nehemiah, the work is completed in stunningly short order: 52 days. Afterward, the priest Ezra reads from God's Law given through Moses, while the Jews listen. Ezra then leads the people in confessing their sins and pledging their allegiance to God.

🎥 What to Look For

Faith coupled with action. Notice that Nehemiah "puts feet to his prayers," as the old saying goes. When he hears that Jerusalem's walls need repair, he prays *and* asks the king for a leave of absence and supplies to do the work. Later, when Nehemiah hears of a possible attack against his workers at the walls, he reports "We kept on praying to our God, and we also stationed guards day and night" (4:9).

Did You Know?

• The Persian city of Susa, where Nehemiah got the disheartening news that Jerusalem's walls were broken, is the same setting for the story of Esther, the next book in the Bible.

• Women helped rebuild the wall (3:12).

• Once Nehemiah repaired the walls of Jerusalem, people apparently didn't want to live there. They had to "cast lots," an ancient version of drawing straws, to see who would be uprooted from the neighboring villages to live inside the city. One in ten drew the short straw and had to move to town. Perhaps one reason for their reluctance to move is that the walls had apparently been torn down only recently, in a previous attack. Maybe they feared an encore attack. Or perhaps they feared the regional leaders who had resisted the renovation project and threatened the workers.

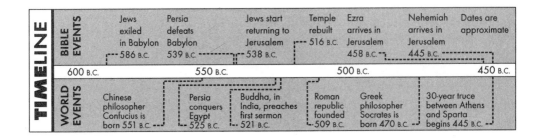

		Jews exiled in Babylon	Persia defeats Babylon	Jews start returning to Jerusalem	Temple rebuilt	Ezra arrives in Jerusalem	Nehemiah arrives in Jerusalem	Dates are approximate
TIMELINE	BIBLE EVENTS	586 B.C.	539 B.C.	538 B.C.	516 B.C.	458 B.C.	445 B.C.	
		600 B.C.	550 B.C.		500 B.C.			450 B.C.
	WORLD EVENTS	Chinese philosopher Confucius is born 551 B.C.	Persia conquers Egypt 525 B.C.	Buddha, in India, preaches first sermon 521 B.C.	Roman republic founded 509 B.C.	Greek philosopher Socrates is born 470 B.C.	30-year truce between Athens and Sparta begins 445 B.C.	

Leadership qualities. Notice the leadership skills of Nehemiah. He seeks the help of God. Once he realizes what he needs to do, he becomes strong-minded and decisive in pursuing his goal. He uses sound judgment to deal with the sly tactics of his enemies.

Author and Date

The story is compiled from the memoirs of Nehemiah, a Jewish servant in the palace of the Persian king. The book was originally combined with Ezra, so both books were likely written by the same person. Jewish tradition says the author was Ezra, a priest and teacher who returned from exile after the temple was rebuilt. Many believe that the author, whoever he was, also wrote 1, 2 Chronicles, partly because all these books are set in the time just after the Jewish exile.

Like Ezra and the two books of Chronicles, Nehemiah was probably written in the early 400s B.C., shortly after the incidents in the book occurred. This was roughly a hundred years after many of the Jews returned home from exile and rebuilt the temple.

The author preserved the memoirs of Nehemiah to show how this man of action and hero of the faith turned to God in times of need. The book also reminds the Jews not to become careless about honoring their commitment to God.

On Location

The story begins in Susa, winter capital of the Persian Empire, located along the border of Iraq and Iran. Here, the palace servant Nehemiah is granted a leave of absence to go to Jerusalem, where the rest of the story unfolds. By 500 B.C. the Persians completely dominate the region (see map). ❑

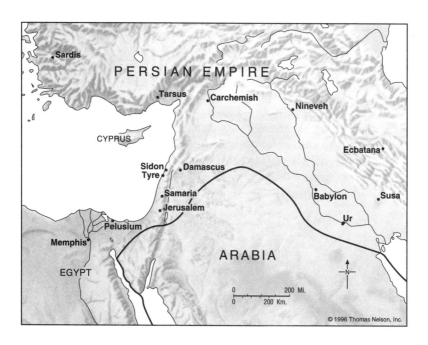

© 1996 Thomas Nelson, Inc.

Big Scenes from Nehemiah

Nehemiah, a Jew living in Persia and working as a palace servant, is paid a visit by his brother, Hanani, from Judah. Nehemiah asks how things are going back in Jerusalem. He's not prepared for what he hears.

"Jerusalem's walls are broken down, and its gates have been burned," Hanani replies.

This is apparently the result of recent attacks, not of the Babylonian destruction about 150 years earlier. But whatever the cause, the word leaves Nehemiah deeply distressed.

"I sat down and cried," he says. Then for several days he goes without food and prays.

Nehemiah works as the king's cupbearer, the person responsible for making sure the wine is not poisoned. One day when he delivers some wine, the king notices how depressed Nehemiah looks. The king asks what's wrong.

"I feel sad," Nehemiah says, "because the city where my ancestors are buried is in ruins, and its gates have been burned down."

The king asks how he can help.

Nehemiah has had about four months to think about this, since that's when he first got the news. He promptly asks for a leave of absence so he can rebuild the walls, and for letters to Persian governors in the west ordering that they supply him with timber for the job. The king grants these requests, and gives Nehemiah an armed escort of soldiers and cavalrymen.

Nehemiah asks permission to rebuild the walls of Jerusalem (1:1—2:10) ••

Several non-Jewish leaders in the area bitterly oppose the renovation project. Perhaps they feel threatened by the proposed fortification. One man, Sanballat, openly ridicules the effort. "What is this feeble bunch of Jews trying to do?" he asks. "Look at the wall they are building! Why, even a fox could knock over this pile of stones."

When Nehemiah hears that an attack may be in the works, he posts armed guards around the wall and tells all the haulers to keep one hand free to grab a weapon.

As the work speeds on, Sanballat and some of his associates apparently try to set a trap for Nehemiah. They try to schedule a meeting with him. Four times. Each time he refuses.

"I knew they were planning to harm me," Nehemiah says. "So I sent messengers to tell them, 'My work is too important to stop now'" (6:2–3).

Fifty-two days after the repair work begins, it ends—completed. The people in the surrounding nations are astounded. They're also afraid because they realize that since the job got done so quickly, God must be on their side.

Rebuilding the walls in 52 days
•• **(chapters 3—4; 6:15–16)**

After the walls are repaired, the Jews meet by one of the city gates and listen to Ezra read some of the laws God gave through Moses. He reads from dawn until noon.

What he reads are possibly selections from the first five books in the Bible, or perhaps Deuteronomy, which is a summary of the Law.

During or after this reading, teachers of the Law walk among the crowd, "explaining the meaning of what Ezra had read." Perhaps they are translating the Law from Hebrew, in which it is written, to Aramaic, the language the Jews learned in exile. Or maybe they are explaining how the people need to apply the Law in their present circumstances, much like Bible teachers and ministers do today.

Ezra reads the Law
(8:1–18)

After the people have heard the Law, Nehemiah begins making changes to bring the community in line with the Law. He notices that merchants are selling their produce on the Sabbath, so he orders the newly built gates closed each Sabbath day—from sundown on Friday until sundown on Saturday.

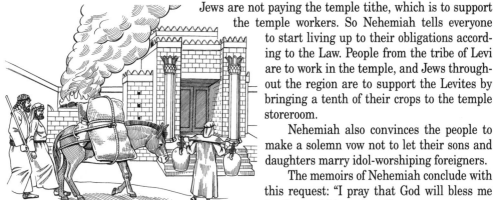

Nehemiah also observes that the temple is being neglected because temple assistants are working on farms instead. They're at their farms because Jews are not paying the temple tithe, which is to support the temple workers. So Nehemiah tells everyone to start living up to their obligations according to the Law. People from the tribe of Levi are to work in the temple, and Jews throughout the region are to support the Levites by bringing a tenth of their crops to the temple storeroom.

Nehemiah also convinces the people to make a solemn vow not to let their sons and daughters marry idol-worshiping foreigners.

The memoirs of Nehemiah conclude with this request: "I pray that God will bless me for the good I have done."

Religious reform begins
(13:4–22)

Reviews

Three people on record. Ancient records outside of the Bible identify two of Nehemiah's opponents—Sanballat and Tobiah—as well as Nehemiah's brother, Hanani.

A letter to the Persian-appointed governor of Judah in the 400s B.C. says Sanballat was governor of Samaria, north of Jerusalem. He led the opposition to the rebuilding of Jerusalem's walls.

Another reference in the same group of documents speak of Hananiah, probably Nehemiah's brother whom Nehemiah called by the shortened nickname Hanani. Hananiah is described as head of Jewish affairs in Jerusalem. The book of Nehemiah says that Hanani of Judah visited the Persian winter capital of Susa and brought news of Jerusalem's broken walls. Perhaps he was there on official business instead of simply visiting his brother.

Several records tell about an important Tobiah family with a genealogy that extends from perhaps 590 B.C. to 200 B.C. One record, written in the 500s B.C. and found about 25 miles from Jerusalem, speaks of a Tobiah as the servant of a king. Other records place some Tobiahs in what is now Jordan, where the Tobiah of Nehemiah's day lived (2:10).

Why did the king give so much help to a mere "cupbearer"? The Bible describes Nehemiah as a cupbearer, the person who brings the king his wine. Yet the king quickly agrees to give Nehemiah: an extended leave of absence, supplies to rebuild the Jerusalem walls and gates, timber to build Nehemiah a house in Jerusalem, and an armed entourage of soldiers and cavalry.

Cupbearers in ancient times often did more than bring the king his wine and taste it to make sure it wasn't poisoned. Many became trusted confidants of the king, and wielded considerable influence. Some held other jobs as well. According to Tobit, part of an ancient collection of books known as the Apocrypha, the cupbearer for Esarhaddon, a king of Assyria, was the number two man in the empire: "chief cupbearer, keeper of the signet [royal seal to stamp official documents], and in charge of administrations of the accounts" (Tobit 1:22, New Revised Standard Version). ❏

Encore

- For the other half of what was originally one book, read Ezra.

- For another book that speaks of faith in action, read James. He says, "Faith that doesn't lead us to do good deeds is all alone and dead!" (James 2:17). ❏

ESTHER

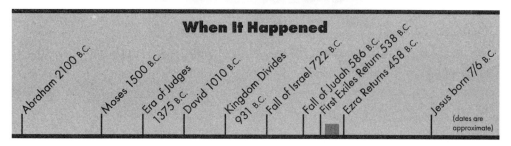

When It Happened

Abraham 2100 B.C. | Moses 1500 B.C. | Era of Judges 1375 B.C. | David 1010 B.C. | Kingdom Divides 931 B.C. | Fall of Israel 722 B.C. | Fall of Judah 586 B.C. | First Exiles Return 538 B.C. | Ezra Returns 458 B.C. | Jesus born 7/6 B.C.

(dates are approximate)

The Queen Who Stops a Holocaust

Esther is one of the best-written short stories in all of Hebrew literature. In fact, it's so well written that some people think it's fiction—just too good to be true.

You've got a queen who refuses to make a command appearance before the king, so the king commands her never to appear before him again. Divorce, Persian style.

You've got a beautiful Jewish maiden who becomes queen and puts her life on the line to save her race from a holocaust.

And you've got a deliciously evil villain, Haman, a high Persian official who seethes with vengeance when a lower official, Mordecai, refuses to bow before him. Haman plots to hang Mordecai on 75-foot-high gallows and slaughter his entire race: the Jews. Instead, Haman winds up paying homage to Mordecai by holding the reins of his horse and walking him through the capital while Mordecai wears the king's robe and Haman shouts, "This is how the king honors a man!" (6:11). If Esther had a laugh track, the volume would be turned up full during this scene.

Famous Line

• "It could be that you were made queen for a time like this!" (4:14). Mordecai's urging of Esther to take the life-threatening risk of asking the king to show mercy on the Jews.

Later, Haman is hanged from the gallows he built for Mordecai. Happy ending.

Behind this powerful story, which churns up a full platter of emotions from glee to fear, there's an equally powerful message: God looks after his people. ❏

Behind the Scenes of Esther

⭐ Starring Roles

Esther, Jewish queen of Persia who saves the Jews from slaughter (2:7)
Mordecai, Esther's cousin, Persian official who prods her to risk helping the Jews (2:5)
Haman, Persian high official who plots to kill the Jews (3:1)
Xerxes, king of Persia (1:1)

📖 Plot

Persian King Xerxes divorces his queen. To replace her, he chooses a young Jewish orphan named Esther, raised by her cousin Mordecai, a palace official. Mordecai refuses to bow in honor of a higher official, Haman. In retaliation, Haman hatches a scheme to kill all the Jews in the empire. Without identifying who the "troublesome" people are, Haman manages to talk the king into signing an irrevocable order permitting the citizens to slaughter the Jews on a set day. Esther appeals to the king, who is surprised to hear that Haman has targeted the Jews and that Esther is a Jew. He executes Haman, then issues a second order allowing the Jews to defend themselves. The Jews unite, and with the help of Persian nobles defeat their enemies.

🎥 What to Look For

God. You'll not find him mentioned by name. But if you look closely, you'll see him standing in the wings directing the action. You'll recognize his work in several places, including in the long string of "coincidences" that end up saving the Jews from mass slaughter.

Did You Know?

• Each spring, usually about a month before Passover, Jews celebrate Esther saving the Jews from a massacre. They do this in the joyous spirit of a Mardi Gras, and call the event Purim (POR-im). Many dress in costumes (especially the children), put on plays, share large meals with family and friends, and give gifts to friends and the poor. *Purim* is an ancient word for the lots, or dice, that Haman used to select which day he would slaughter the Jews.

• When the Jews read aloud the story of Esther during Purim, they boo Haman by stomping, jeering, and rattling noisemakers every time his name appears. This drowns out the sound of his name.

TIMELINE	BIBLE EVENTS					
		Xerxes begins 21-year reign as Persian king 486 B.C.	Esther becomes queen of Persia 479 B.C.	Slaughter of Jews scheduled to take place 473 B.C.		Dates are approximate
		500 B.C.	450 B.C.	400 B.C.	350 B.C.	300 B.C.
	WORLD EVENTS	Persian King Darius builds a canal between the Nile and Gulf of Suez 500 B.C.	Greeks defeat Persian fleet 480 B.C.	Hippocrates, the father of medicine, is born 460 B.C.	Persia falls to Alexander the Great, of Greece 332 B.C.	

Author and Date

The writer is unnamed. But the writer's familiarity with the Jewish festival of Purim and with the fact that the Jews had a sense of national identity suggests he was a Jew. His insight into Persian customs, along with the absence of any reference to the Jewish homeland, suggests he lived in Persia—perhaps in the city of Susa, where the story takes place. Among the many possible authors are Mordecai, Ezra, and Nehemiah.

King Xerxes, known also by the Hebrew version of his name, Ahasuerus, ruled Persia from 486 to 465 B.C., after his father, Darius. Esther was written sometime during or after this, perhaps near the end of his reign, in the waning years of the Persian Empire.

The book of Esther preserves the marvelous story of how the Jews are delivered from an empire-wide slaughter. It also reveals the reason behind the Jewish celebration of Purim, which Jews still observe.

On Location

The story takes place in the Persian city of Susa, along today's border of Iraq and Iran, about 100 miles north of the Persian Gulf. The map shows the Persian Empire in 500 B.C., when it included Israel. ❑

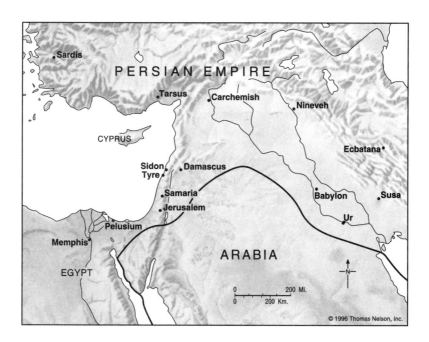

Big Scenes from Esther

At the end of a week-long banquet, when Persian King Xerxes is "feeling happy because of so much wine," he sends for his queen. He wants her to wear her crown and parade before the male guests, so they can all see how beautiful she is.

Queen Vashti, however, is entertaining the female guests at a dinner party. She refuses the command appearance. The king becomes so angry that he strips Vashti of her title and forbids her to ever show her face before him again.

Next, he assigns officials in each of his provinces to search for "beautiful young women" and bring them to the royal harem. Among these women is a young Jew named Esther. She is an orphan raised by her cousin Mordecai, a Persian official. Like other candidates for the grand title of queen, Esther is led through a one-year regimen of beauty treatments to prepare her to meet King Xerxes. Each woman who spends the night with the king becomes one of his concubines, or secondary wives. But only one will be favored with the title of queen.

Four years after the search began, it is Esther's turn to appear before the king. He falls in love with her. At a dinner party in her honor, and before the leaders of the empire, Xerxes places a crown on her head.

**Esther, a Jew, becomes queen of Persia
(1:10—2:20)** •

Sometime later, the king appoints as his second-in-command, Haman, a descendant of the Amalakites, who were bitter enemies of Israelite settlers in the promised land. Though the king orders everyone to bow when Haman walks by, Mordecai refuses. And when Mordecai's colleagues ask why, he responds simply, "Because I am a Jew."

Some officials report this to Haman. He becomes incensed and decides to wipe out all the Jews in the empire. He meets with the king and tells him, "There are some people who live all over your kingdom and won't have a thing to do with anyone else. They have customs that are different from everyone else's, and they refuse to obey your laws. We would be better off to get rid of them!" To prod the king in the right direction, Haman reminds him that property confiscated from the victims will boost the royal treasury.

Apparently without even asking who these people are, the king approves the plan.

Haman sets the date for the slaughter—11 months ahead. Meanwhile, he sends couriers throughout the empire to deliver a message translated into every known language. The message says that on the 13th day of Adar (March 7, 473 B.C.) "all Jewish men, women, and children are to be killed. And their property is to be taken."

**Mordecai won't bow to Haman
(3:1–15)**

• •

When Mordecai hears about the letter, he asks Esther to go to the king and beg him to have mercy on her people. At this point, the king doesn't seem to know that his ruling is against the Jews, or that Esther is a Jew.

Esther refuses, reminding her cousin of the Persian law that allows the king to execute anyone who visits him uninvited.

Mordecai's reply is blunt. "Don't think that you will escape being killed with the rest of the Jews, just because you live in the king's palace. If you don't speak up now, we will somehow get help, but you and your family will be killed. It could be that you were made queen for a time like this!" (4:13–14).

Esther agrees to intercede, on the condition that Mordecai has all the Jews in the city go without eating and drinking for three days, on her behalf. Afterward, Esther goes to the king. Fortunately, he greets her warmly. She invites him to bring Haman to a dinner that evening. There, building the king's anticipation for what she *really* wants, she invites the men to dinner the following day.

By the second meal, Haman is feeling higher and mightier than usual—proud that he has caught the queen's eye. Then Esther tells the king that Haman's plot is against the Jews, which means that both she and Mordecai could die in the slaughter. The king is furious. Adding to his anger is that the night before he had been reminded that Mordecai once had warned him of an assassination plot and was never rewarded.

The king orders Haman hanged, and promotes Mordecai to fill the vacancy.

Esther asks king to spare her people from a holocaust
•• **(4:8–5:8; 7:1–10)**

King Xerxes says that his decree against the Jews, like any other decree bearing his seal, cannot be revoked. But he writes a second irrevocable decree allowing the Jews to assemble into a fighting force and defend themselves. These orders are delivered throughout the empire on swift horses, bred for the king.

When the day of fighting arrives, on the thirteenth of the Jewish month of Adar, Persian nobles and governors lend their support to the Jews. The fighting extends into a second day, with the Jewish forces killing 75,000 throughout the empire. On the third day, the fifteenth day of Adar, the Jews celebrate their survival and victory with a feast.

Every springtime, Jews memorialize the event in a joyful celebration called Purim.

The Jews celebrate a holocaust missed
(9:1–32) ••

The Persian palace uncovered. The Persian palace of Susa, where Esther lived, has been unearthed by archaeologists. It covered more than 12 acres—nearly as big as Jerusalem in King David's day, and about half as big as the inside of a large shopping mall today. The palace had living quarters, along with a smaller section for the king and other officials to conduct the business of the empire. The palace included courtyard gardens, like the one that the Bible says King Xerxes stormed off to when he learned of Haman's plot against the Jews.

No mention of God. Like the Song of Solomon, there is absolutely no mention of God in the book of Esther. Nor is there any mention of prayer, sacrifice, or any other worship practices. The book seems thoroughly secular, and not at all religious.

For this reason, it was one of the last books approved into Hebrew and Christian Bibles. In fact, the most ancient library of Old Testament books, the Dead Sea Scrolls, which date back to the third century B.C., contains at least fragments from every book of the Old Testament *except* Esther.

Yet the book was eventually added to the Bible because on closer examination it was judged as thoroughly religious. Though God does not get the spotlight or his name added to the credits, he is directing the events through an incredible string of "coincidences." Esther, a Jew, finds herself catapulted into a position to help the Jews. Mordecai overhears an assassination plot against the king and reports it, endearing himself to the king. The king reads of this, and learns he never rewarded Mordecai—and he discovers this the very night before he finds out that Haman has plotted to kill Mordecai and all other Jews.

There are other clues to the religious nature of the book. For example, though Esther doesn't ask the people to pray for her, she does ask them to fast. And Mordecai tells Esther that if she doesn't take a stand for her people "we will somehow get help" (4:14)—an apparent reference to the way God has helped the Jews in the past.

Why the writer disguises the religious nature of the book remains a mystery. Perhaps he wanted to draw in secular readers, and help them reach their own conclusion that the Jews had help from above.

Fact or Fiction. Some critics charge that Esther is a fictional story. The captivating writing technique seems to portray a story too good to be true. There's the exotic setting, fast-paced action, humor, and sudden reversals with the high and mighty ending up down and dead. There's also the scrumptious irony, balanced events (feasts mingled with fasting), and the happy ending.

In addition, ancient records say nothing of a Queen Esther or Vashti. Historians of Greece, the nation that defeated Xerxes' forces in battle and later conquered Persia, say his queen was Amestris. But Amestris may have been but one of several queens.

The story's accurate reporting of customs and careful attention to names—even of the supporting characters—suggests that the events really did happen. The book also starts the way most ancient histories start, and ends the way they end—even citing sources. ❏

- For insight into what happens to people like Haman, who "make useless plans" against God and his people, read Psalm 2.

- For another story about a strong-minded woman who did the right thing, read the short book of Ruth, another excellent example of the best in Hebrew literature. ❏

JOB

Adam 4000 B.C.   Abraham 2100 B.C.   Job 2000 B.C.   Moses 1500 B.C.   David 1000 B.C.   Ezra 450 B.C.   Jesus born 7/6 B.C. (dates are approximate)

Why Good People Suffer

This is not the story of a man suffering silently, patiently in the night. This is the story of a man yelling at God—a man who wants answers now.

This man is Job. And he has just lost nearly everything he has spent his life working for: his riches, his children, his health.

He has just one quick question for the Creator and Sustainer of the universe.

It's the same question a mother asks after watching her kindergarten son get crushed beneath the wheels of a school bus. It's the question an aging grandfather asks when he finds out he has cancer. It's the question a middle-aged father asks after learning he's been laid off from the company he has dedicated himself to for the past 25 years.

Why?

For Job, self-perceived wise men answer the question. But they answer it wrong.

Then for Job, and for us, God answers the question. It's not a complete answer. But it was complete enough for Job. ❑

Famous Lines

- "Naked I came from my mother's womb, and naked I shall return" (1:21, New King James Version). *Job's reaction after hearing his children have been killed in a windstorm and his vast flocks stolen by raiders.*

- "I have escaped by the skin of my teeth" (19:20, New Revised Standard Version). *Job's analysis of how close he has come to dying.*

Behind the Scenes of Job

⭐ Starring Roles

Job, a wealthy man who loses his riches, children, and health (1:1)
Eliphaz, the first of three of Job's friends who try to convince him that he sinned (2:11)
Bildad, the second of Job's friends to speak (2:11)
Zophar, the third friend to speak (2:11)
Elihu, a bystander who argues with Job and his friends (32:2)
Job's wife, who tells her husband to curse God and die, so the suffering will end (2:9)

📖 Plot

Job is a rich man who owns thousands of sheep, camels, cattle, and donkeys. He's also blessed with a large family of 10 children. But he loses them all one tragic day. Raiders take his herds and kill his servants. A windstorm crushes a house where his children are eating. Then Job breaks out with skin ulcers all over his body. Friends come to comfort him, but add to his misery by insisting he must have committed some horrible sin for which God is punishing him. God sets the record straight and ends Job's torment.

🎥 What to Look For

The format. As a kind of road map to the book, notice the three cycles of debates between Job and his three friends. Each cycle runs like this: friend #1 talks, Job replies, friend #2, Job, friend #3, Job. (The one exception comes at the end of the third

Did You Know?

• Aunt Jemima owes her name to Job's oldest daughter, of his second-chance family (42:14).

• "Patient as Job" is a phrase that comes from the story of Job's suffering. Actually, he isn't all that patient. "How I wish that God would answer my prayer," he moans, "Why should I patiently hope when my strength is gone?" (6:8, 11). "Tenacious as Job" is a better match. In spite of the catastrophes that hit him, and his three nagging friends who insist he's to blame, Job won't budge from his plea of innocence or his faith in God.

• There aren't a lot of references to life after death in the Old Testament. But Job speaks so clearly of a resurrection that he sounds like a New Testament apostle: "I know that my Savior lives, and at the end he will stand on this earth. My flesh may be destroyed, yet from this body I will see God. Yes, I will see him for myself, and I long for that moment" (19:25-27).

• The book of Job contains more rare and archaic words than any other book in the Bible. This suggests it was written a long time ago. It has also made the book hard to translate.

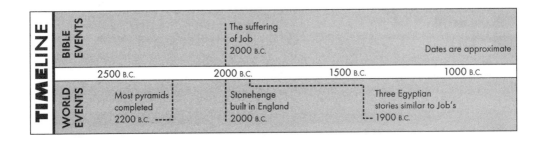

TIMELINE	BIBLE EVENTS		The suffering of Job 2000 B.C.		Dates are approximate
		2500 B.C.	2000 B.C.	1500 B.C.	1000 B.C.
	WORLD EVENTS	Most pyramids completed 2200 B.C.	Stonehenge built in England 2000 B.C.	Three Egyptian stories similar to Job's 1900 B.C.	

cycle, when friend #3 doesn't speak. Instead, a bystander adds his thoughts about the matter.) This routine takes up most of the book.

Job's persistence that he is innocent. Like many others in his day, Job believes that health and wealth are signs of God's blessing—disease and poverty are signs of sin. Because Job knows he has done nothing to deserve the horror that has invaded his life, he is left wondering why God is putting him through all this. Bitterness begins to engulf him as he sarcastically complains, "God destroys the innocent along with the guilty. When a good person dies a sudden death, God sits back and laughs" (9:22–23).

Author and Date

The writer is unknown, though he was probably an Israelite. The writer used the Hebrew name for God, *Yahweh*, a term sometimes translated Jehovah or the Lord.

The story seems to be set sometime in the era of Israel's founding fathers: Abraham, Isaac, and Jacob. Several clues suggest this. As was common in Abraham's day, his wealth was measured by his herds, and he acted as the priest for his family by offering sacrifices to God. In addition, he was raided by Sabeans and Chaldeans, who lived in patriarchal times.

It's uncertain when the story was written. It may have been passed down by word of mouth for generations before being committed to writing in the 900s B.C. That was the golden age of Israel's wisdom literature, which grew out of the wisdom of King Solomon. Jewish writings from the second century B.C. speak about the book of Job, showing that it was well respected by then.

Though the writer and the date of the writing remain a mystery, the purpose of the book is clear. It corrects the ancient misunderstanding that suffering is God's punishment. The fact is, as the book of Job dramatically shows, good people are not exempt from suffering.

On Location

The story takes place in the mysterious homeland of Job, "the land of Uz" (1:1). No one knows where that is. Some guess it was in Edom, a region southeast of Canaan, along the border of what is now Israel and Jordan. Two clues suggest this: one of Job's friends comes from Teman, an Edomite city; also, Edomites were famous in ancient times for their wisdom—and the book of Job is considered wisdom literature, which seeks answers to practical and philosophical questions of life. ❏

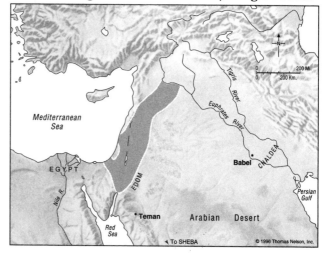

Big Scenes from Job

Job is a godly man who lives near the desert, perhaps east of what is now Israel. He is rich in herds—and servants to tend them. He is also rich in children, with seven sons and three daughters.

Satan, however, decides to test Job's loyalty to God. And God allows the test.

Marauders kill the herdsmen and then steal Job's cattle, donkeys, and camels. A mysterious fire kills the sheep and their shepherds. And a windstorm crushes the home of his oldest son, where all the children have gathered for a meal.

Grief-stricken at the news, Job tears his robe and shaves his head: "The Lord gave, and the Lord hath taken away; blessed be the name of the LORD" (1:21, King James Version).

**A desert windstorm kills Job's children
(1:13–22)** •

With his wealth and children gone, Job now suffers a third great loss: his health. He becomes infected with a painful skin disease that covers his body with open, festering sores. We can only guess what kind of disease it is: smallpox, chronic eczema, ulcerous boils. Whatever it is, it's agonizing.

Job's wife can't stand to see him suffer. "Why do you still trust God?" she asks. "Why don't you curse him and die?" (2:9).

Job absolutely refuses. "Don't talk like a fool!" he replies. "If we accept blessings from God, we must accept trouble as well."

Job suffers with a painful skin disease
• **(2:1–10)**

Three of Job's friends come and sit silently with him for seven days. Finally Job breaks the silence: "I wish I had been born dead and then buried" (3:16).

One by one, his friends respond. They are certain Job has sinned, and he won't find relief until he repents.

"In my experience," Eliphas says, "only those who plant seeds of evil harvest trouble" (4:8).

Bildad asks Job, "Why don't you turn to him and start living right? Then he will decide to rescue and restore you" (8:5). Zophar then says to this tormented man who has lost nearly everything, "God has punished you less than you deserve" (11:6).

In the grueling debate that follows, Job maintains his innocence and retaliates, "Miserable comforters are you all!" (16:2, New King James Version). Eventually he turns his attack heavenward: "You, God, are the reason I am insulted and spit on" (17:6).

**Three friends come to comfort Job
(2:11–13)** •

A fourth and younger man named Elihu joins the gathering. He takes on the whole group. He's angry with Job for blaming God instead of himself. And he's angry at the three men for not being able to prove Job wrong.

As the youngster drones on, a storm begins rolling in. Suddenly, from out of this storm, God speaks to Job, raising questions no human can answer.

"How did I lay the foundation for the earth?" (38:4).

"Where is the home of light, and where does darkness live?" (38:19).

God's point is clear: there are some things that human beings can't understand. And—sometimes—suffering is one of them.

"I am the Lord All-Powerful, but you have argued that I am wrong," God accuses Job. "Are you trying to prove that you are innocent by accusing me of injustice?" (40:2, 8).

Job cowers, thoroughly embarrassed. "I have talked about things that are far beyond my understanding," he admits (42:3).

The Lord answers Job (chapters 38:1—42:6)

God now turns his attention to Job's friends. "I am angry at you," God says, "for not telling the truth." Then he orders these men to go to Job—the man they had been wrongly accusing—and ask him to pray for them. Otherwise, God warns, he will punish them for their foolishness.

Each man expresses his sorrow to Job, and gives him gifts of gold and silver.

In time, Job raises 10 more children and produces herds double the size of those he had before. He lives long enough to see his great-grandchildren have children of their own.

Job receives a new family and doubled wealth (42:7–17)

Reviews

Ancient stories much like Job's. There are many ancient stories similar to Job's, some written in the time of Abraham, about 2000 B.C. But one story is especially similar: *Man and His God,* written in the 1700s B.C. It tells of a Job-like man who complains to a god called the "righteous shepherd." The man laments that the god has become angry with him, and has allowed enemies to harass him. Then, appealing to the god like son to father, the suffering man asks how long the god will let this go on. Eventually, the man is delivered from his torment and praises his god.

This story is so much like Job's that the man, who lived in Sumer in what is now southern Iraq, is known as the Sumerian Job.

Stories such as these, along with the mention of Job in other ancient Middle Eastern documents, suggest that Job and his story were widely known.

Surprising scientific insights. Though Job was written perhaps 2,500 years before Columbus sailed the ocean blue, the book doesn't speak of a flat earth. It says God "suspended the earth on empty space" (26:6).

The book also shows that the writer knows a thing or two about the hydrological cycle. "God gathers moisture into the clouds and supplies us with rain" (36:27-28).

It's a fictional collection of poetry. The book begins and ends with material written in story form. Sandwiched in between is poetry. This has led many to conclude that the events described in the book never happened—that Job is a collection of poems that deal with suffering and that were tied together by the prose introduction and conclusion.

Furthermore, they argue, the prose makes Job out to be a man patiently enduring his calamities, while the poetry shows him challenging God. So the fit seems artificial.

The writing structure, however—poetry surrounded by prose—has shown up in other ancient accounts. And elsewhere the Bible mixes poetry and prose, as when Moses and Miriam sing after the crossing of the Red Sea.

As for the prose and poetry sections revealing a split-personality Job, these two sections present Job at different stages in his struggle. ❏

Encore

- For more evidence that people in Bible times associated suffering with sin, read the story of Jesus healing a blind beggar. The disciples asked Jesus if the beggar was suffering because of his own sins or the sins of his parents. "Neither," said Jesus, "this happened so that the work of God might be displayed in his life" (John 9:3, New International Version).

- To read about another man confronting God with tough questions about suffering, read the short book of Habakkuk. There, the prophet Habakkuk asked God why he was going to punish the unrighteous Jews by sending an invasion of the even more unrighteous Babylonians.

- For songs lamenting that God seems to be hiding, read Psalms 10 and 22. ❏

PSALMS

When It Happened

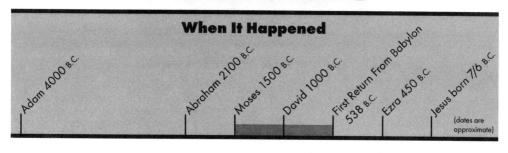

Adam 4000 B.C.　　Abraham 2100 B.C.　Moses 1500 B.C.　David 1000 B.C.　First Return From Babylon 538 B.C.　Ezra 450 B.C.　Jesus born 7/6 B.C. (dates are approximate)

Songs the Israelites Sing

You hear the words as someone reads to a dying loved one, or perhaps as a minister comforts the family beside the grave:

The Lord is my shepherd; I shall not want.

He maketh me to lie down in green pastures: he leadeth me beside the still waters.

He restoreth my soul: he leadeth me in the paths of righteousness for his name's sake.

Yea, though I walk through the valley of the shadow of death, I will fear no evil: for thou art with me (Psalm 23:1–4, King James Version).

Famous Lines

- Make a joyful noise unto the Lord, all ye lands (100:1, King James Version).

- Thy word is a lamp unto my feet, and a light unto my path (119:105, King James Version).

The choice of words, the images conveyed, even the steady rhythmic pace, seem to generate a consoling, healing power.

Psalms is a songbook, direct from the heart of poets who experience the full range of life's sorrow and joy. These inspired writers express in words what the rest of us can only feel. Yet when we read these words of anger, sadness, hope, and praise, they become our own, for they reflect our deepest, and sometimes most private, emotions. ❏

Behind the Scenes of Psalms

★ Starring Role

David, the source or inspiration behind nearly half the 150 psalms (18:50)

Plot

This is a collection of songs written over many centuries. There is no plot. There are, however, themes within each song. Surprisingly, the most common songs are those you'd have to file under "complaint." But there are many songs about praise as well, which is why ancient Jews called the book *Tehillim*, meaning "praises."

What to Look For

Repeated thoughts, not sounds. Hebrew poetry doesn't have rhyme or rhythm. Its unique characteristic is repetition of thought, called parallelism. The poet will make a statement in one line, then in a second and perhaps a third line he'll repeat the thought, extend it, or contrast it with an opposite idea. In some Bible translations, the second and third ideas are indented from the first one.

From David's prayer of confession after committing adultery with Bathsheba, here's an example of the second line repeating the thought of the first one:

Cleanse me with hyssop, and I will be clean;
wash me, and I will be whiter than snow (51:7, New International Version).

Radically different topics. If someone today published a collection of favorite

---

Did You Know?

• The shortest chapter in the Bible, also the middle chapter, is Psalm 117. It has only two verses.

• The longest chapter in the Bible is Psalm 119, with a whopping 176 verses. This poem is so long because it's an acrostic built on the 22 letters of the Hebrew alphabet. The poem has 22 eight-verse sections. The first section starts with the first Hebrew letter, *Aleph*. The second section starts with the next letter, *Beth*. And on it goes, clear through the alphabet. Twenty-two times 8 equals 176.

• The middle verse in the Bible is this one:
It is better to take refuge in the Lord than to trust in man (118:8, New International Version).

• "The Bug Bible," as it became known, was an early English translation of Scripture. It earned its nickname because of a peculiar translation from Psalms. Instead of telling people there's no need to fear the "terror by night" (King James Version), it calmed them regarding "bugs by night" (91:5).

(continued on next page)

TIMELINE

BIBLE EVENTS					
Moses writes Psalm 90 ---1440 B.C.		David writes many songs later preserved in Psalms 1000 B.C. ---		Psalm 137 written in Babylon 550 B.C. ---	Compilation of Psalms is completed 300 B.C. ----
1500 B.C.	1300 B.C.	1100 B.C.	900 B.C.	700 B.C. 500 B.C.	300 B.C.

WORLD EVENTS				
Hindu scriptures (Vedas) begin -1500 B.C.	China develops mouth organ 1100 B.C. ----	Lyre players painted on Philistine jar ---1000 B.C.	Plato starts the Academy at Athens, later becoming world's first university 387 B.C.----------------	Dates are approximate

Christian songs, you could expect that the songs would cover a wide range of topics. So does the ancient collection known as Psalms. You'll find songs praising God for his gorgeous universe. And you'll find songs for weddings, worship services, pilgrimages to Jerusalem, the crowning of a king, and soldiers on the march—to name a few.

Author and Date

The book attributes 73 songs to David. But the original Hebrew phrase can mean "by David," "dedicated to David," or "in the style of David." Other songs are attributed to Solomon, Moses, and Asaph, chief musician during the reign of David and perhaps Solomon. Some songs remain anonymous.

> **Did You Know?** (continued)
>
> • "The Printer's Bible," another early English translation, incorrectly reads, "Printers have persecuted me without a cause." Actually, "princes" were doing the persecuting (119:161).
>
> • Psalms is not only a collection of songs, it's a collection of five collections. There are five songbooks in Psalms: Book 1 (chapters 1–41), Book 2 (42–72), Book 3 (73–89), Book 4 (90–106), Book 5 (107–150)

The psalms were written throughout Israel's history, some from the time of Moses in about 1440 B.C., others from the time of King David in about 1000 B.C., and others after Babylon defeated the Jewish nation and exiled many of the citizens in 586 B.C.

The book exists to give people the words to express their deepest spiritual feelings, privately or in group worship.

On Location

The songs are set throughout the Middle East, from the Sinai desert where Moses leads the Hebrews, to Israel where David builds a powerful Jewish nation, to Babylon where the defeated Jews spend 50 years in exile. The composition of the psalms stretched over 1,000 miles (from Egypt to Babylon) and 1,000 years (from the Exodus to the Exile). ❏

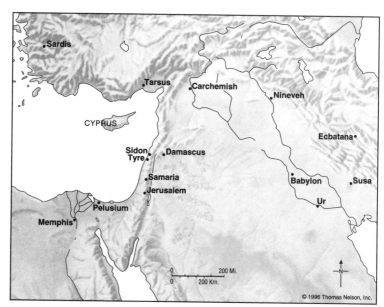

Big Scenes from Psalms

In a song attributed to David, the onetime shepherd boy who spent a lot of time outdoors, Psalm 8 praises God for creation and expresses dismay that he would entrust such majesty to human beings.

> I often think of the heavens your hands have made,
>   and of the moon and stars you put in place.
> Then I ask, "Why do you care about us humans?
>   Why are you concerned for us weaklings?"
>
> Our Lord and Ruler,
>   your name is wonderful everywhere on earth!
>   (8:3–4, 9).

**The majesty of God's creation
(8:1–9)** •

In a song expressing deep trust in God—a song that is perhaps the most loved in all of literature—David compares God to a shepherd who protects his flock.

> The Lord is my shepherd, I shall not be in want.
>   He makes me lie down in green pastures,
> he leads me beside quiet waters,
>   he restores my soul.
> He guides me in paths of righteousness
>   for his name's sake.
> Even though I walk through the valley of the shadow
>   of death,
>   I will fear no evil,
> for you are with me;
>   your rod and your staff, they comfort me.
> (New International Version).

**The Lord, our shepherd and protector
(23:1–6)**
• •

When the Jews assemble to worship God, professional musicians add their support by filling the temple courtyard with the sounds of harps, lyres, horns, flutes, tambourines, bells, cymbals, and metal rattles.

Some psalms are written to be accompanied by certain kinds of instruments. Psalm 4, for example, says it is written for stringed accompaniment. The very name *psalms* comes from the Hebrew word *psalmos,* which means "twanging of strings."

In an anonymous song of thanks, written for public worship, the writer invites worshipers to praise the Lord with music.

> Praise the Lord with harps!
> Use harps with ten strings to make music for him.
>   Sing a new song. Shout! Play beautiful music.

**Musicians leading worship
(33:1–3)** •

In a private, passionate prayer for help, the song-writer expresses deep sorrow because he feels cut off from God. Perhaps he is among the thousands of Jewish exiles forced to live in Babylon, far from home.

As a deer gets thirsty for streams of water,
  I truly am thirsty for you, my God (1).

Why am I discouraged? Why am I restless?
I trust you! And I will praise you again
  because you help me, and you are my
  God (11).

Thirsting for God
(42:1–11)

In an uninhibited show of praise to God, or an unre-strained plea for help, the Jews sometimes address him with arms raised.

David, not yet a king and still living in the desert as a fugitive hunted by Saul, expresses his confidence in God:

I will praise you as long as I live,
  and in your name I will lift up my hands (63:4,
  New International Version).

Raising hands in praise and prayer
(63:4; 134:1–2)

Though sacrifices and prayer are an important part of worshiping God, so is singing. The people sing about God when they're alone, and when they gather at the temple or synagogue. Sometimes, gathered for worship, they take turns singing to each other. One group will take the first line of a song, and the second group will respond with the second line.

In a song for public worship, the writer encourages the whole world to sing to God.

Tell everyone on this earth to shout praises to God!
  Sing about his glorious name. Honor him with
  praises.

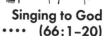

Singing to God
(66:1–20)

Three times a year—spring, summer, and fall—every Jew who is able travels to Jerusalem to celebrate important Jewish holidays: Passover and two harvest festivals.

Fifteen songs, Psalm 120—134, are written especially for pilgrims. The songs are called "songs of ascent," perhaps because no matter which way you approach Jerusalem—north, south, east, or west—you have to climb. The city is on a hill, surrounded by hills. Travelers likely sing these songs as they walk to the Holy City. And when they arrive in Jerusalem they may sing one song on each of the 15 steps leading up to the temple.

Traveling to Jerusalem
(84:5) ••

The Jews sing of God's ability to protect them, no matter what the odds. This doesn't mean God will always keep them from harm, but it means he has the power to protect. Yet when suffering comes, he is still in control and will help in ways that human beings can't fully understand.

He who dwells in the shelter of the Most High
    will rest in the shadow of the Almighty.
I will say of the Lord, "He is my refuge and
    my fortress (1–2, New International Version).

Protected by God
•• **(91:1–16)**

Just like sacrifices, prayer, and music, studying the laws of God is an important feature of worship. At home and in groups, the Jews read aloud their scripture and memorize parts of it.

Psalm 119, the longest chapter in the Bible, has 176 verses—every one of which speaks about God's law. Set to music, it becomes a song urging people to nurture their faith by thinking about God's word.

You have ordered us always to obey your teachings;
    I don't ever want to stray from your laws (4–5).

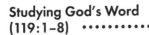

Studying God's Word
(119:1–8) ••

The largest group of psalms are those of people crying to God out of pain or sorrow.

In one such song, written anonymously, a Jewish exile in Babylon paints a vivid and heart-breaking scene about the day the music died.

Beside the rivers of Babylon we thought about
    Jerusalem,
       and we sat down and cried.
We hung our small harps on the willow trees.
Our enemies had brought us here as their
       prisoners, and now they wanted us to sing
       and entertain them.
They insulted us and shouted, "Sing about
    Zion!"
Here in a foreign land,
how can we sing about the Lord? (1–4).

A time to cry
(137:1–9)

Reviews

Golden oldies. In the early 20th century some Bible and history experts were claiming that the psalms were written only about 200 to 400 years before Jesus, even those allegedly written by David and Solomon during Israel's golden age.

Recent archaeological discoveries, however, reveal that the Canaanites, Babylonians, and Assyrians all produced poetry that's incredibly similar to the poetry of the Jews. In fact, scholars today wonder if the Jews of David's time adopted the poetic forms of neighboring cultures to express their unique faith in God.

Songs of hatred. Not all the psalms praise God. Some give him advice. Consider Psalm 140, attributed to David.

Don't let the wicked succeed in doing what they want (8).

Dump flaming coals on them and throw them into pits
    where they can't climb out.
Chase those cruel liars away!
    Let trouble hunt them down (10-11).

That certainly doesn't sound like a song Jesus would sing. He said, "Love your enemies and pray for anyone who mistreats you" (Matthew 5:44).

Psalms, however, is brimming with the poetry of honest human emotion. It stands as enduring proof that it's okay to tell God how we feel, even when we haven't gotten over the hurt and anger of something that has happened. Admitting the pain is the first step to recovery. ❑

Encore

- To see how New Testament writers use Psalms to identify Jesus as the promised messiah, compare Psalm 22:1, 6-8, 12-13, 28 with Matthew 27:36-46, Luke 23:35-36, and 1 Corinthians 15:23-24.

- For another Hebrew song, read Habakkuk 3. ❑

PROVERBS

When It Happened

(dates are approximate)

Adam 4000+ B.C.　　Abraham 2100 B.C.　　Moses 1500 B.C.　　David 1000 B.C.　Solomon 971 B.C.　Hezekiah 700 B.C.　Ezra 450 B.C.　Jesus born 7/6 B.C.

Snappy Advice from Wise Old Men

It's certainly not the seamless, fluid writing style that keeps people coming back to Proverbs. The book reads like a lifetime collection of someone's Chinese fortune-cookie messages, scribbled down in the order they came out of the bag.

However disjointed these snappy one-liners and two-liners are, they contain the wisdom of the ages, condensed for the quickly bored.

In the time it takes to read one sentence, we're dished up a life-tested insight on any one of a thick menu of everyday topics: good women, bad women, spoiled kids, lazy slugs, etiquette at dinner meetings, co-signing loans (the advice is "don't"), controlling that temper, avoiding the wrong crowd.

Lots of great topics. But if you've ever gone to a convention you probably discovered pretty quickly that you don't choose workshops by their titles. You choose them by who's doing the talking. The primary source for Proverbs is Solomon—the Israelite king about whom God said, "I'll make you wiser than anyone who has ever lived or ever will live" (1 Kings 3:12).

He's worth a listen. ❏

Famous Lines

- Those who spare the rod hate their children (13:24, New Revised Standard Version). *Source of the old saying, "Spare the rod, spoil the child." This isn't necessarily a command to spank children; it's an encouragement to discipline them in some way. Shepherds carry a long staff, or rod, to reach out and nudge sheep in the right direction—not to club them.*

- Pride goes before destruction (16:18, New King James Version).

- Trust in the Lord with all your heart, and lean not on your own understanding (3:5, New King James Version).

- Train up a child in the way he should go: and when he is old, he will not depart from it (22:6, King James Version).

Behind the Scenes of Proverbs

⭐ Starring Role

Solomon, reputed to be the wisest king of Israel and author of most of the proverbs (1:1)

📖 Plot

There is none. Most proverbs are two-liners, not arranged according to any noticeable pattern or theme.

Consider these two that follow one another, but have nothing in common:

All crooks are liars,
but anyone who is innocent will do right.
It's better to stay outside on the roof of your house
than to live inside with a nagging wife (21:8–9).

🎥 What to Look For

General truths, not promises. The proverbs state general principles, not promises from God. For example, it's often true that "A gentle answer turns away wrath" (15:1, New International Version). But don't count on it every time.

A nine-chapter introduction. Notice that the first nine chapters are different from the rest of the book. They form a poetic essay contrasting wisdom with foolishness. Afterward comes a long string of one-line and two-line maxims, each of which sums up a truth gleaned from life. These truths are universal, not just for God's people. Any person who follows the advice will likely live a better, happier life.

Poetry. The proverbs follow the characteristics of Hebrew poetry. They don't have rhyme or rhythm, but they have

Did You Know?

• The 1960 film "Inherit the Wind," starring Spencer Tracy as a lawyer who argues to let public educators teach the theory of evolution, takes its title from Proverbs. "He who brings trouble on his family will inherit only wind" (11:29, New International Version).

• "God helps those who help themselves" is not in Proverbs, or anywhere else in the Bible. Neither is "Cleanliness is next to godliness," or "Early to bed and early to rise make a man healthy, wealthy, and wise." These are proverbs that Benjamin Franklin published in *Poor Richard's Almanack* during the mid-1700s.

TIMELINE						
BIBLE EVENTS		Solomon writes most of Proverbs 950 B.C.		King Hezekiah's scribes compile proverbs 700 B.C.		
	1000 B.C.		900 B.C.	800 B.C.		700 B.C.
WORLD EVENTS		Calendar of farming cycles, oldest example of Hebrew writing 1000 B.C.		Homer writes the *Iliad* and the *Odyssey* 800 B.C.		Dates are approximate

parallel thoughts. The second half of the proverb might repeat the idea in the first, or expand it, or perhaps contrast it. A contrasting proverb:

A dry crust of bread eaten in peace and quiet
    is better than a feast eaten where everyone argues (17:1).

Author and Date

Proverbs is a collection of pithy sayings from several wise men. Most are attributed to King Solomon, who is reported to have composed 3,000 proverbs (1 Kings 4:32).

Two otherwise unknown contributors are Agur (30:1) and a king named Lemuel (31:1), who says he is passing along the advice of his mother. Additional proverbs come from a group of sages simply identified as "people with wisdom" (22:17).

Sages were an important part of Jewish society. They served as consultants to kings, and as teachers to young men. These sages grappled with practical and philosophical problems, while priests and prophets specialized in religious matters.

Many of the proverbs come from Solomon, who reigned from about 970–930 B.C. Other proverbs, however, were added as the centuries went by. Some 250 years later, scribes working for King Hezekiah began compiling the proverbs of Solomon (25:1). Still more proverbs were likely added later. It's uncertain when the book was completed, but Bible experts speculate the work may have continued until as late as the 300s B.C.

The purpose of Proverbs is clearly stated in the first chapter. The book exists so "young people can gain knowledge and good sense" (1:4). The sayings, in fact, were probably part of the curriculum that sages taught to young sons of aristocrats.

On Location

Most proverbs were apparently written by Solomon in Israel (shaded area). But some of the other proverbs could have come from anywhere throughout the Middle East. Similar collections of wise sayings from about Solomon's time have been uncovered in both Egypt and Iraq. ❑

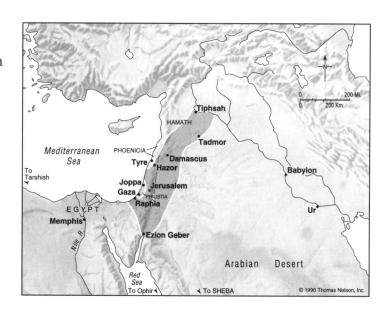

Big Scenes from Proverbs

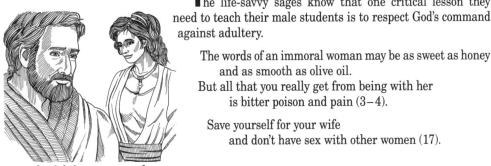

The life-savvy sages know that one critical lesson they need to teach their male students is to respect God's command against adultery.

The words of an immoral woman may be as sweet as honey
    and as smooth as olive oil.
But all that you really get from being with her
    is bitter poison and pain (3–4).

Save yourself for your wife
    and don't have sex with other women (17).

Stay faithful to your wife
(5:1–23) •

Like sex, money is the cause of many troubles in life. So Proverbs is full of advice about money matters. One persistent piece of advice is to avoid debt—especially another person's debt—like a deer avoids the hunter.

My child, suppose you agree to pay the debt of someone,
    who cannot repay a loan.
Then you are trapped by your own words,
    and you are now in the power of someone else.
Here is what you should do:
    Go and beg for permission to call off the agreement (1–3).

Don't co-sign a loan
• **(6:1–5)**

In the long run, say the sages, honesty pays off.

The Lord hates anyone who cheats,
    but he likes everyone who is honest (1).

If you do the right thing, honesty will be your guide.
    But if you are crooked,
        you will be trapped by your own dishonesty (3).

Treat people with honesty
(11:1–3) •

Teaching children to behave themselves is a theme that
shows up throughout Proverbs.

Teach your children right from wrong,
and when they are grown they will still do right.

Teach your children well
(22:6)

Some of the most biting words of the wise men are reserved for lazy people.

I once walked by the field and the vineyard of a lazy fool.
Thorns and weeds were everywhere,
and the stone wall had fallen down.
When I saw this, it taught me a lesson:
Sleep a little. Doze a little.
Fold your hands and twiddle your thumbs.
Suddenly poverty hits you and everything is gone!

Don't be lazy
(24:30–34)

The book of Proverbs ends with a poetic tribute to a
good wife. These are the words of a queen mother, passed
along to her son King Lemuel, unknown outside of this
one reference to him.

A truly good wife is the most precious treasure
a man can find (10).

She takes good care of her family and is never lazy.
Her children praise her,
and with great pride her husband says,
"There are many good women, but you are the best!"
(27–29).

Treasure your wife
(31:10–31)

Reviews

Proverbs from Egypt. The old age of Proverbs is confirmed by similar teachings from ancient times. In fact, the 30 sayings of the wise men (22:17–24:22) have striking parallels to 30 sections of an Egyptian collection called "The Wisdom of Amenemope," a sage who taught sometime between 1200-1000 B.C.

Here, for example, is the first proverb from the wise men:

Don't take advantage of the poor
　　or cheat them in court (22:22).

Here is a similar saying from the beginning of the Egyptian book:

Do not steal from the poor
　　nor cheat the cripple.

The fine art of manipulating others. Some proverbs seem better suited to a self-help book on getting ahead than to the Bible. Proverbs 23:1-3, for example, shows how to make an impression when dining with a king (don't eat like a pig). And Proverbs 22:1 praises the value of making a good name for yourself.

Advice like this can, in fact, be misdirected and used as a way to gain power and prestige for selfish reasons. But you can also use it to place yourself in a position of service to others. ❏

Encore

- Jesus used proverbial sayings throughout his ministry. For a taste of them, read the Sermon on the Mount in Matthew 5–7, especially the Beatitudes in Matthew 5:3-10.

- Proverbs is practical advice for young men. To read practical advice to young pastors, turn to 1, 2 Timothy and Titus. ❏

ECCLESIASTES

When It Happened

(dates are approximate)

Adam 4000+ B.C.

Abraham 2100 B.C.

Moses 1500 B.C.

David 1000 B.C.
Solomon 971 B.C.

Ezra 450 B.C.
Jesus born 7/6 B.C.

Life: What's the Point?

"What is the meaning of life?" That seems like an ethereal, boring question—unless, of course, you've reached mid-life and it suddenly dawns on you that someday in the not-distant-enough future when people talk about "ashes to ashes, dust to dust," they'll be talking about you.

When we stand eyeball to dustball with our own mortality—when we suddenly know and feel the full awareness that we will someday die—we begin asking this question that was tackled long ago by the writer of Ecclesiastes.

The first words out of the writer's mouth don't leave us with a great sense of his ability to answer the question.

Nothing makes sense! Everything is nonsense.

I have seen it all—nothing makes sense! (1:2).

But don't take this as his final word. The final word comes later, after he lays out and analyzes what he has seen in life.

Famous Lines

- Eat, drink, and be merry (8:15, New King James Version).

- To everything there is a season, a time for every purpose under heaven (3:1, New King James Version).

- Cast your bread upon the waters (11:1, New King James Version). *Which means "be generous."*

- There is nothing new under the sun (1:9, New King James Version).

In the end, he answers the question by pointing directly to heaven. Life, he concludes, is a mysterious gift from God. We should learn to enjoy the gift, and to show our gratitude to the Giver. ❏

Behind the Scenes of Ecclesiastes

★ Starring Role

Solomon, reputed to be the wisest king of Israel and possible author of Ecclesiastes (1:1)

Plot

The writer seems to be performing an experiment—he's analyzing life. He examines the cycles of life, the chores we run ourselves ragged on, the pleasures we pursue. And he reaches the bleak conclusion that everything "under the sun" is meaningless. Bible experts debate what he means by this phrase, but some say he means "all human endeavor apart from God." That is, without God no one can find lasting satisfaction and meaning in their work, their diversions, or their life.

What to Look For

One man's search for meaning. This will seem like one incredibly convoluted, contradictory book if you read it like a typical essay or a sermon. One minute the writer's saying life is unfair, unfulfilling, and makes no sense whatsoever. The next minute he's saying we should enjoy life, work hard, and obey God.

> **Did You Know?**
>
> • The name of the book comes from the word the writer uses to describe himself: Teacher or Assembly Leader. In Greek, this word is *ekklesiastes*.
>
> • The Ernest Hemingway novel *The Sun Also Rises* takes its name from Ecclesiastes 1:5, New King James Version.

What you're reading are the honest confessions of a man struggling with doubt, disillusionment, and despair. Fortunately, he works his way through the struggle and finds a sense of comfort worth sharing.

Author and Date

In the first verse, the writer identifies himself as "the son of David," "king in Jerusalem," and "known to be very wise." Certainly sounds like Solomon, especially when you add a bunch of other clues from chapter 2—such as foreign rulers bringing him "silver, gold, and precious treasures" (as the queen of Sheba did) and his "many wives" (he had a thousand).

Many Bible experts, however, say the style of Hebrew words suggests it was written many centuries later, maybe as late as 300 B.C., perhaps by someone

TIMELINE	BIBLE EVENTS	Solomon begins his 40-year reign 970 B.C.		Dates are approximate
		1000 B.C.	900 B.C.	800 B.C.
	WORLD EVENTS	Eastern North Americans grow crops 1000 B.C.		Greek city of Corinth is founded 800 B.C.

trying to approach a vexing issue in the manner that wise King Solomon would. Some passages, in fact, don't sound like something we would expect Solomon to say: 5:8–9 blames the king for overtaxing the poor.

Fragments of the book found among the Dead Sea Scrolls were copied in about 150 B.C., suggesting Ecclesiastes was revered at least by then.

If Solomon wrote this book, he may have done so late in his reign, after he had allowed his foreign wives to coax him away from God and into worshiping their gods. Perhaps Solomon got to the point in his life where he realized that even with all his wealth, power, and wisdom, he was empty without God.

The point of the book—the conclusion the writer reaches after analyzing life—is something he says "can be put into a few words:"

Respect and obey God!
This is what life is all about (12:13).

On Location

If Solomon wrote the book, the setting takes place in his capital city of Jerusalem. The numbered areas are the administrative districts in Solomon's kingdom. ❑

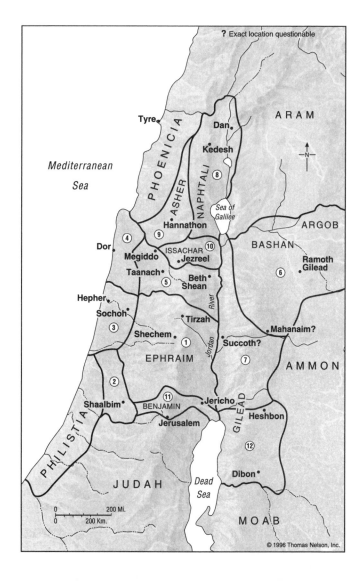

? Exact location questionable

Tyre
Dan
Kedesh
ARAM
Mediterranean Sea
PHOENICIA
ASHER
NAPHTALI
⑧
Sea of Galilee
Hannathon
ARGOB
Dor
④
⑨
BASHAN
Megiddo
ISSACHAR
⑩
Jezreel
Ramoth Gilead
Taanach
⑥
Beth Shean
⑤
Hepher
Sochoh
③
Tirzah
Mahanaim?
Shechem
①
Succoth?
EPHRAIM
⑦
AMMON
②
⑪
Jericho
Shaalbim
BENJAMIN
Heshbon
Jerusalem
GILEAD
⑫
Dibon
JUDAH
Dead Sea
Jordan River
0   200 Mi.
0   200 Km.
MOAB
© 1996 Thomas Nelson, Inc.

Big Scenes from Ecclesiastes

Solomon takes a long, hard look at life. And he doesn't like what he sees.

I have seen it all—nothing makes sense!
What is there to show for all of our hard work
here on this earth?
People come, and people go,
but still the world never changes (2–4).

What good is hard work?
(1:1–18) ••

God is in control of the life cycle, Solomon says. And there is no amount of hard work we can do to change this.

Everything on earth has its own time and its own season.
There is a time for birth and death, planting and reaping,
for killing and healing, destroying and building,
for crying and laughing, weeping and dancing,
for throwing stones and gathering stones,
embracing and parting (1–5).

Everything that happens has happened before,
and all that will be has already been—
God does everything over and over again (15).

The cycle of life rolls on
•• **(3:1–22)**

If you love money and wealth, you will never be satisfied," Solomon says. "The more you have, the more everyone expects from you. Your money won't do you any good—others will just spend it for you" (10–11).

In the end, Solomon says, wealth is worthless to human beings. "They came into this world naked, and when they die, they will be just as naked. They can't take anything with them" (15).

Wealth is unsatisfying
(5:10–17) •••

After living a long and luxurious life, Solomon concludes that it's the simple things that matter most.

"What is the best thing to do in the short life that God has given us?" Solomon asks. "I think we should enjoy eating, drinking, and working hard. This is what God intends for us to do" (5:18).

When Solomon's analysis of life is complete, the main conclusion he reaches—the core of everything he has ever been taught—is this:

Respect and obey God!
This is what life is all about. (12:13)

Life is short. Enjoy!
(5:18–20; 9:7–9; 12:13)

······························· **Reviews** ·······················

Words at least as old as Solomon. Many scholars suspect Ecclesiastes was written hundreds of years after Solomon. Yet a short excerpt, 9:7-9, is remarkably similar to advice that shows up in the Babylonian *Epic of Gilgamesh,* which had been circulating for hundreds of years before Solomon. Parts of this story have survived in several documents, one dating about 300 years before the king, and another about 700 years before him.

Perhaps Solomon, widely known for his international contacts, read the story and drew from it while reflecting on the meaning of life.

Here's a comparison of the two:

Ecclesiastes	*Epic of Gilgamesh*
Be happy and enjoy eating and drinking! God decided long ago that this is what you should do.	Day and night enjoy yourself, eating and dancing.
Dress up, comb your hair, and look your best.	Wear sparkling fresh clothes. Wash your hair and bathe.
Life is short, and you love your wife, so enjoy being with her.	Pay attention to the child who holds your hand. Make sure your wife enjoys being with you.
This is what you are supposed to do as you struggle through life on this earth.	This is what you are supposed to do.

Almost not in the Bible. Ancient Jewish writings say that Ecclesiastes was one of the last books admitted into the canon of scripture. Many people didn't like it because it seemed so pessimistic.

Why it was eventually added is uncertain. One reason may be because many Jewish leaders believed Solomon wrote it. And another is because it was written in Hebrew, which indicated it was an old book (Greek was the prevailing language when the Hebrew Bible was agreed upon, in the first century A.D.).

For whatever reasons it found its way into the Old Testament, Ecclesiastes serves up a dramatic reminder that as much as we human beings like to think we're in control, we're not. God is. ❏

······························· **Encore** ·······························

- To discover more on fulfillment in life, read the parables of Jesus about the kingdom of heaven. Matthew 13 has several. They help put life on earth in the context of eternal life, and encourage us to give our attention to things of greatest value.

- For still more practical advice about living, read James, often described as the Wisdom book of the New Testament. ❏

SONG OF SONGS

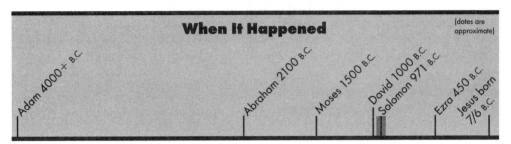

When It Happened   (dates are approximate)

Adam 4000+ B.C.   Abraham 2100 B.C.   Moses 1500 B.C.   David 1000 B.C.   Solomon 971 B.C.   Ezra 450 B.C.   Jesus born 7/6 B.C.

An Intimate Love Song

You can rate this book PG-30. Jews in ancient times did. They wouldn't let a man read it until he was 30 years old. Jewish elders didn't worry about the women because, unfortunately, most of them couldn't read.

This is an erotic poem. The theme is for adults only. As a result, you're not going to hear many sermons from this book because, frankly, it's too frank for kids. You've got a man and woman in love, graphically and explicitly praising the physical features of each other and disclosing their shared fantasy about making love.

Their words are not vulgar or obscene, yet they are unapologetically sensual and intimate.

This is not like any other book in the Bible—not even close. Many godly people, in fact, have argued that it never should have been added in the first place.

> **Famous Lines**
>
> • I am the rose of Sharon, and the lily of the valleys (2:1, King James Version).
>
> • I am my beloved's (7:10, King James Version).

But because it's here, we have a beautiful reminder that human sexuality is a gift of God. We also have a model for romance—a reminder that true love feeds on tender words of endearment, whether poetic or plain, spoken straight from the heart. ❑

Behind the Scenes of Song of Songs

★ Starring Roles

An unnamed woman, from the countryside of Israel (1:2)
An unnamed man, the woman's true love (1:8)
Solomon, king of Israel (1:1)

Plot

This is a poem, full of highly symbolic language. So Bible experts don't agree on the story behind the poem.

There is a host of proposed plots. Here's a sampling.

Solomon chooses a country girl for his bride, but the young lady refuses the king in favor of her country lover. Or, Solomon and the country lover are the same man. Or, the unnamed country lover is the only man in the story, and when he comes to the woman, she looks upon him as a glorious king—a kind of knight in shining armor.

In ancient times, many Jewish and Christian scholars didn't take the poem literally. Jews saw the poem symbolizing God's love for the Jewish people. Christians later saw it as Christ's love for the church.

Did You Know?

• Like the book of Esther, the Song of Songs doesn't mention God.

• The title of the book comes from the introduction, "Solomon's most beautiful song" (1:1). So it's called the Song of Songs just as Jesus is called the "King of kings."

What to Look For

Unrestrained passion. This is a passionate, erotic celebration of love between a man and a woman. Neither the man nor the woman feels the least bit inhibited about expressing their most intimate feelings and desires. The man lovingly, poetically compares the body of his beloved to a garden filled with sweet aroma and brimming with delicious fruit. "Let the north wind blow, the south wind too!" the woman replies. "Let them spread the aroma of my garden, so the one I love may enter and taste its delicious fruits" (4:16). Remember, this was PG–30. ❏

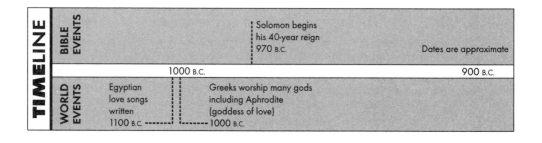

		Solomon begins his 40-year reign 970 B.C.	Dates are approximate
	1000 B.C.		900 B.C.
	Egyptian love songs written 1100 B.C.	Greeks worship many gods including Aphrodite (goddess of love) 1000 B.C.	

TIMELINE — BIBLE EVENTS / WORLD EVENTS

Author and Date

It's uncertain who wrote the book. The Hebrew phrase in verse one that attributes the poem to Solomon can mean it was written by him, for him, or dedicated to him. It is possible Solomon did write it, for he wrote some of the psalms. And he is said to have written 1,005 songs altogether (1 Kings 4:32). But it's also possible that a professional musician wrote the song for one of Solomon's weddings. Or, it may have been written for weddings in general, and dedicated to the memory of the king with a thousand wives.

It's uncertain when the poem was written. If it was composed by or for Solomon, it was probably written sometime during his reign: 970–940 B.C.

Though ancient Bible scholars felt strongly that the song was a symbolic expression of either God's love for Israel or Christ's love for the church, modern experts are nearly unanimous in arguing that the poem is a celebration of God's gift of love and sexuality.

On Location

The setting is Israel. The young woman addresses the "women of Jerusalem." And the two lovers occasionally compare one another to landmarks in Israel. The man says of his beloved: "Your head is held high like Mount Carmel" (7:5). ❏

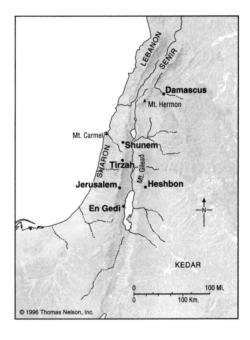

Big Scenes from Song of Songs

Kiss me tenderly!" a young and beautiful peasant woman tells the man of her dreams. "Your love is better than wine, and you smell so sweet."

These are the captivating, opening lines of a passionate song about sexual intimacy. What follows is an exchange of compliments, in which each lover boldly praises the physical attributes of the other.

"My darling, you are so lovely, so very lovely—your eyes are those of a dove," the man says. "You move as gracefully as the pony that leads the chariot of the king."

"My darling," the young woman replies, "you are handsome, truly handsome—the fresh green grass will be our wedding bed."

**Beauty, in the eyes of the beloved beholder
(1:1–17)** •

On the day of the wedding, friends of the bride are the first to notice a dust cloud rolling in from the desert. It is the groom, arriving with his procession. This man may actually be Solomon, coming to marry the young woman. Or the poetic description may be a way of saying the young peasant couple is so deeply in love that their humble wedding feels to them like the majestic ceremony of a king and a queen.

**The wedding day
(3:6–11)**
• •

After the wedding, the groom praises the beauty of his bride by comparing her to some of the most natural beauty he has ever seen. Her hair flows gracefully upon her shoulders, like a flock of goats moving in rhythmic union down a mountainside. Her teeth shine as white as freshly washed wool.

"Your breasts are perfect;
    they are twin deer feeding among the lilies.
I will hasten to those hills sprinkled with sweet perfume
    and stay there till sunrise."

The bride is just as daring in praise of her husband. She, too, compares him to the natural beauty she has seen: hair wavy and "black as a raven," legs strong as "columns of marble on feet of gold."

**The words of love
(4:1—5:16)** •

The passionate compliments continue flowing, as husband and wife praise each other and even more boldly describe their physical desires. The intensity of their expression heats up, crossing the border into sensuality that is neither obscene nor ashamed.

"You are tall and slender like a palm tree," the husband says. "I will climb that tree and cling to its branches."

"My darling," his wife replies, "I am yours."

In what Bible scholars describe as the high point of the poem, the wife gives her husband a bracelet to remember her by. Then she shares with him a remarkable insight into the very nature of love.

It is "more powerful than death, stronger than the grave. . . . It cannot be bought, no matter what is offered" (8:6–7).

The honeymoon
(7:1–8:14)

Reviews

Other ancient love songs. It's not at all impossible that the Song of Songs was written in the time of Solomon. Older, similar songs have been recovered from the Middle East. Collections of Egyptian love songs from 1100-1300 B.C. share similarities with the Song of Songs. Both, for example, were set to music. In both, the lovers refer to one another as "brother" and "sister." And in both, the lovers lavishly praise the beauty of one another and boldly express their shared desires.

Where's God? If you look for any explicit mention of God or religion in the Song of Songs, you won't find it. This is a song about the love between a man and a woman—not just spiritual love that exists within the heart, but physical love as well.

Early on, godly Jews and Christians asked what such a book was doing in the Bible.

How and why the Song made it into the canon of scripture is uncertain. Perhaps the ancients began revering the poem because they believed Solomon wrote it. Eventually, many felt so uncomfortable treating the poem as a love song between a man and a woman that they began interpreting it symbolically. For the Jews, the husband symbolized God and the wife symbolized Israel. For Christians, the husband was Jesus, and the wife was the church.

More recently, however, Bible experts interpret the song more literally—as a celebration of romantic love that is God's gift to humanity. ❏

Encore

• To read about the prophet Hosea wooing back his unfaithful wife, as a symbol of God trying to win back the affection of Israel, turn to Hosea 1–3.

• To see how the New Testament writers speak of the church as the bride of Christ, read Matthew 9:15; 25:1-13; Revelation 19. ❏

ISAIAH

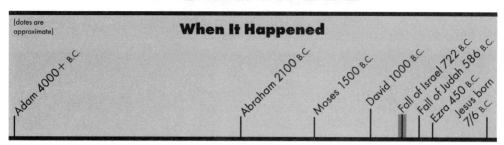

(dates are approximate)

When It Happened

Adam 4000+ B.C.

Abraham 2100 B.C.

Moses 1500 B.C.

David 1000 B.C.

Fall of Israel 722 B.C.

Fall of Judah 586 B.C.

Ezra 450 B.C.

Jesus born 7/6 B.C.

He Wrote Like He Knew Jesus

It's not just because of the prophet's bizarre escapades—like walking around naked for three years—that his book has become a classic, at the top of the heap among the Bible's 17 prophetic books. And it's not just because it's one of the thickest books of the lot, nor that its dramatic prophecies came true.

It's a classic because, though Isaiah lived 700 years before Christ, he wrote like he knew him. Scattered throughout Isaiah's oracles are vivid descriptions and graphic scenes that read as if they flowed from the pen of a poet who saw the miraculous birth of Jesus in Bethlehem, his crucifixion, and his resurrection.

The first disciples of Jesus didn't miss the connection. The Gospels are full of their comments about Jesus fulfilling one prophecy of Isaiah after another.

Jesus didn't miss the connection either. When he stood in his hometown synagogue, in Nazareth, he opened the scroll of Isaiah and read the first two verses of chapter 61.

Then he told his listeners, "What you have just heard me read has come true today" (Luke 4:21).

As fascinating as this is, however, the book of Isaiah is far more than a sneak preview into the life of Christ. It's a study of sin—of how it slowly destroyed two Jewish nations and of how God will one day wipe it from the face of creation. ❏

Famous Lines

- Unto us a Child is born, unto us a Son is given; and the government will be upon His shoulder. And His name will be called Wonderful, Counselor, Mighty God, Everlasting Father, Prince of Peace (9:6, New King James Version).

- They shall beat their swords into plowshares (2:4, New King James Version).

- "Here am I! Send me" (6:8, New King James Version).

- Though your sins are like scarlet, they shall be as white as snow (1:18, New King James Version).

- "Come now, and let us reason together" (1:18, New King James Version).

Behind the Scenes of Isaiah

⭐ Starring Roles

Isaiah, prophet whose ministry spans four kings (1:1)
Hezekiah, godly Judean king who usually follows Isaiah's advice (1:1)

📖 Plot

In an astonishing vision, God calls Isaiah to become a prophet during a critical time in Middle Eastern history. Assyria will destroy the northern Jewish nation of Israel, and the southern nation of Judah (Isaiah's country) will face the same threat. Isaiah's job is to deliver God's messages to his fellow Jews.

The prophet warns sinners of both Israel and Judah that God will punish them, using the Assyrians, then the Babylonians. But Isaiah also predicts that when the punishment has ended, God will send a Prince of Peace to restore the nation.

Woven into the plot are intriguing implications about the end of human history, when God punishes the entire world for sin, then makes a new world for the people who have been faithful.

🎥 What to Look For

Messages from God in the first person. Isaiah, like the other major prophets, doesn't deliver God's messages in the third person, as a reporter would. Isaiah won't say, for example, "God is sick of your offerings." Instead, he speaks the very words of God: "I am sick of your offerings." Isaiah,

Did You Know?

• The longest word in the Bible is the name of Isaiah's son: Maher-Shalal-Hash-Baz (8:1). It's a Hebrew phrase that means *invaders are coming soon.* Isaiah used this to emphasize that, before his newborn son could say "Mommy" or "Daddy," Assyria would crush Israel.

• Isaiah, the Old Testament book most quoted in the New Testament, is sometimes called the Fifth Gospel. That's because it's filled with prophecies about Jesus. Here are a few of the best known:

Birth—7:14; 9:6.
Character—11:1–5
Death—53:1–12

• The book of Isaiah breaks into two main sections: 39 chapters of judgment, followed by 27 chapters of comfort. Coincidentally, the Bible also breaks into two main sections: 39 books called the Old Testament, followed by 27 books called the New Testament.

• Isaiah walks barefoot and naked for three years, to forecast the fate of Egypt and to warn Judah not to join them in a rebellion against Assyria (20:1–6). Instead, Isaiah says, Judah should trust God for protection.

TIMELINE

BIBLE EVENTS

| God selects Isaiah to become a prophet 740 B.C. | Assyria destroys northern Jewish nation of Israel 722 B.C. | Hezekiah revolts against Assyria 705 B.C. | Assyria seizes Judah but can't capture Jerusalem 701 B.C. | Babylon destroys Jerusalem 586 B.C. | Jewish exiles return to Jerusalem 538 B.C. |

| 800 B.C. | 750 B.C. | 700 B.C. | 650 B.C. | 600 B.C. | 550 B.C. | 500 B.C. |

WORLD EVENTS

| First recorded Olympic games in Greece 776 B.C. | Chinese history confirms solar eclipse 775 B.C. | King Romulus founds Rome 753 B.C. | Assyrians choose Nineveh as capital and start rebuilding it 705 B.C. | Cyrus Cylinder confirms return of exiled Jews 539 B.C. Dates are approximate |

however, will introduce most prophecies with the phrase, "The Lord has said." This alerts the people that the words they are about to hear come directly from God.

Promises about a coming messiah. You'll find more references in Isaiah to the Messiah than in any other Old Testament book. New Testament writers often quote Isaiah to show that Jesus fulfilled prophecies about the promised Messiah.

Poetry and prose. In most Bible translations, it's easy to separate the prophecies from the stories. The prophecies are printed in poetic form and are usually indented. The stories and sermons are printed in paragraph form.

Vivid images. Isaiah is a genius of imagery. He's especially fond of treating inanimate objects as though they live and breath. "Mountains and hills will sing" and "trees will clap" (55:12). "The moon and sun will both be embarrassed and ashamed" (24:23). So don't take all the images literally.

Author and Date

According to tradition, the prophet Isaiah is the author. He is a prominent character throughout the book, and much of the material is written in the first person: "God said to me."

The first 39 chapters are from Isaiah's time. But because chapters 40—66 refer to Judah's exile in Babylon some 150 years later and the subsequent return home, many Bible experts think the book was written by two or three authors. Others think Isaiah wrote the later chapters by drawing on what God showed him about the future. (See "How many prophets does it take to write a book?" in Reviews.)

Isaiah's ministry spanned at least the last four decades of the 700s B.C., during the reigns of four kings: Uzziah, Jotham, Ahaz, and Hezekiah. Isaiah apparently lived at least another 20 years because he reports the murder of Assyrian King Sennacherib, who was killed by his own sons in 681 B.C.

Jewish legend says Isaiah was sawn in half at the order of Hezekiah's son and successor, Manasseh, who reigned from 696 to 642 B.C.

Other prophets during Isaiah's lifetime included Micah, Hosea, and Amos.

The book preserves Isaiah's attempt to convince the Jews to obey God or face the consequences. Tragically, by ignoring him, they chose the second option.

On Location

Isaiah prophesies in the southern Jewish nation of Judah and probably lives in the capital city of Jerusalem.

Later in the book the setting changes as Isaiah tells about the coming defeat of Judah, followed by the people's long exile in Babylon. ❏

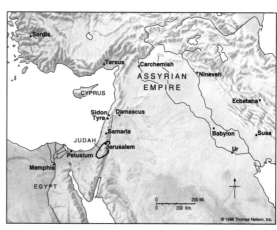

Big Scenes from Isaiah

Sometime during the year that King Uzziah died, in about 740 B.C., a young man described only as "Isaiah, the son of Amoz" has an incredible, bizarre vision. He sees God seated on a high throne in a temple. Surrounding the throne are glowing, heavenly beings.

God asks "Is there anyone I can send? Will someone go for us?"

Isaiah quickly replies, "Send me!"

God tells Isaiah to call the people of Judah back to obedience. But God warns that they won't listen. When Isaiah asks how long the people will disobey, God replies ominously, "Until their towns are destroyed and their houses are deserted, until their fields are empty, and I have sent them far way, leaving their land in ruins" (6:11–12).

With this promise of failure, Isaiah begins his ministry.

**God makes Isaiah into a prophet
(1:1; 6:1–13)** •

A few years later, the northern Jewish nation of Israel unites with Syria to fight for freedom from the Assyrian Empire. When Judah refuses to join the coalition, Israel and Syria try to force the issue.

Isaiah tells Judean King Ahaz to stand his ground because God says the kings of Israel and Syria are "nothing more than a dying fire" (7:4). Ahaz apparently doesn't trust God alone, so he calls on help from Assyria.

The Assyrians come and in 732 B.C. conquer Syria. Ten years later, they return and destroy Israel, burning the capital city and deporting tens of thousands of the leading citizens.

Judah pays dearly for trusting an alliance with Assyria instead of trusting God's promise: they lose their freedom and must pay taxes to Assyria each year.

Assyria destroys the northern Jewish nation of Israel
• **(8:1–10)**

In a prophecy possibly delivered at the coronation of one of Israel's most godly kings, Hezekiah, the prophet Isaiah appears to reflect back on the birth of the king and portray this birth as a sign of hope. New Testament writers also interpreted it as a signpost, pointing to the promised Messiah, Jesus.

"To us a child is born, . . . and the government will be on his shoulders. And he will be called Wonderful Counselor, Mighty God, Everlasting Father, Prince of Peace" (9:6, New International Version).

**"To us a child is born"
(9:2–7)** •

In yet another prophecy that may have been delivered at the coronation of one of Judah's kings, Isaiah speaks of the day when a ruler from the family of King David will lead the nation into an era of enduring peace.

Again, early Christians associated this with the coming kingdom of Jesus, in which God will defeat sin and restore the original beauty of creation. Isaiah describes natural enemies living in harmony, "and a little child will lead them" (11:6, New International Version).

When peace comes to stay
(11:1–16)

The fall of Babylon
(13:1–22)

Babylon is still just an emerging power in Isaiah's day, but the prophet foresees a time when it will become powerful and majestic. Yet Babylon will also become a brutal and godless empire—one that will level Jerusalem in 586 B.C.

Jewish survivors will lament the sins that caused their downfall, yet criticize God for punishing them with a nation that is even more sinful. Isaiah promises that Babylon will face its own Judgment Day. The devastation will be so thorough that "even nomads won't camp nearby." Babylon, 60 miles south of Baghdad, has been completely deserted since the A.D. 600s.

Before peace comes, however, God will purge the world of sin. This purging begins with the punishment of a long list of nations. Among the many that will suffer are Judah, Assyria, Babylon, Egypt, and Arabia. Then in chapters 24—27, which Bible scholars call the Apocalypse of Isaiah, the prophet says the entire planet will suffer.

"The Lord is going to twist the earth out of shape and turn it into a desert," Isaiah says (24:1).

The devastation is so extensive that it seems God is dismantling his physical creation. In fact, many experts think Isaiah is speaking about the end of human history. Yet, after the end comes a new beginning, a new creation—perhaps the kingdom that Jesus told his disciples he was preparing (John 14:2–3).

The Apocalypse
(24:1–23)

After 39 chapters, most of which are warnings about the fall of Judah and its neighbors, Isaiah does an about-face. Threats of doom turn to promises of comfort.

The setting moves in fast-forward, 200 years into the future. Jerusalem is destroyed, and the people of Judah are suffering through half a century of exile in Babylon.

Our God has said:

"Encourage my people! Give them comfort.
Speak kindly to Jerusalem and announce:
    Your slavery is past; your punishment is over"
(40:1–2).

**Comforting words for God's people
(40:1–31)** ••

One of the most captivating prophecies of Isaiah tells about a servant "despised and rejected by men, a man of sorrows, and familiar with suffering" (53:3, New International Version).

Jews reading this text in Babylonian exile may have thought Isaiah was talking about them, the outcast Jewish nation. Perhaps he was. But the New Testament writers also saw this as a portrait of Jesus (Matthew 8:17). Many phrases seem especially pertinent:

He was wounded and crushed because of our sins;
    by taking our punishment, he made us completely
    well.
He was painfully abused, but he did not complain.
He was silent like a lamb being led to the butcher
(53:5, 7).

**The Suffering Servant
(53:1–12)**
••

To a nation grieving over the lost glory of Jerusalem, a city the Babylonians had reduced to a massive pile of rocks, burned timber, and shattered pottery, Isaiah paints a glorious picture of the Holy City restored by God.

Isaiah uses the most lavish images available to describe what this new city will look like: "with stones of turquoise, . . . foundations with sapphires . . . battlements of rubies, . . . gates of sparkling jewels" (54:11–12, New International Version).

The first readers of these words may have considered the prophecy fulfilled when the Jews returned from Babylon and rebuilt their nation. But the meaning could reach well beyond this, to a time when God brings salvation to everyone, and once again God can look at his creation and declare, "It is good."

**The new city of Jerusalem
(54:1–17)** ••

Reviews

Goodbye, Babylon. "No one will live in Babylon," Isaiah prophesied. "Hyenas and wolves will howl from Babylon's fortresses and beautiful palaces. Its time is almost up!" (13:20, 22).

This once exquisite, sprawling city along the banks of the Euphrates River now lies in ruins in the rugged and hilly terrain outside of Baghdad. This, the home of Nebuchadnezzar and the capital of the Babylonian Empire, was abandoned by about A.D. 600.

How many prophets does it take to write a book? Many Bible experts think it took more than one prophet to write the book of Isaiah. Some scholars say the book reflects the work of two or three prophets, writing in different eras. Most of chapters 1–39 are set in Isaiah's lifetime and were probably written by him. But chapters 40–55 seem to be set in Babylon during the exile, 150 years after Isaiah. Chapters 56–66 seem to be set back in Israel, when the Jews are starting to rebuild their country. These last two sections, many scholars argue, were written by two other people, or perhaps by one person who lived during the exile and then returned to Israel.

Experts who say that Isaiah wrote the entire book argue that prophets do sometimes see into the future. They believe that consistency of writing style, choice of words (many of which are unique to the book), and recurring themes argue in favor of a single writer.

The oldest copy of the book, found among the Dead Sea Scrolls, was written about 100 B.C. It shows no break in the text, treating it all as a single work.

Prophecies don't name names. Isaiah actually names Cyrus—the Persian king who came along 200 years later—as the leader who would "set my people free" (45:13). This, say some experts, suggests the last half of the book was added long after Isaiah lived, because biblical prophecies aren't usually so specific. This material, they say, was written as history (that is after the fact), not as a prediction.

Some prophecies in Daniel, however, fit precisely the political jockeying that took place between Egypt and Syria in the time between the Old and New Testament. Of course some scholars argue that these, too, were written after the fact. Yet other scholars argue that God is God and so is fully capable of giving a specific prophecy. ❏

Encore

- For another Judean prophet's perspective on what life was like at the time, read the seven-chapter book of Micah.

- For a glimpse into how New Testament writers interpreted the words of Isaiah as prophecies about Jesus, read these texts: John 12:37-41; Acts 8:26-39; Romans 15:7-21. (There are many more.) ❏

JEREMIAH

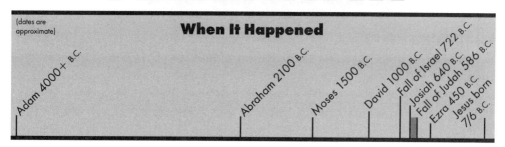

(dates are approximate)

When It Happened

Adam 4000+ B.C. — Abraham 2100 B.C. — Moses 1500 B.C. — David 1000 B.C. — Fall of Israel 722 B.C. — Josiah 640 B.C. — Fall of Judah 586 B.C. — Ezra 450 B.C. — Jesus born 7/6 B.C.

He Predicts Doom and Lives to See It

The prophet Jeremiah was an eyewitness to the most tragic event in his nation's history. He saw his people slaughtered, with survivors herded up and taken away. He saw Jerusalem burn. He saw his country die.

Actually, he had seen all this coming for 40 years. And he knew it didn't have to end like this. If only he could convince the people to turn back to God—to honor the agreement their ancestors had made with the Lord. If the nation would honor their obligations, which are summed up in the Ten Commandments, God would honor his by protecting and blessing the people. Since they chose to dishonor the covenant, however, God was bound by the agreement to punish them.

Sin had consequences; it was written into the covenant.

Sin still has consequences; it's written into the law of cause and effect, and expressed in wise sayings like "what goes around comes around." It's also repeated in God's Word, in memorable passages like "the wages of sin is death" (Romans 6:23).

Unfortunately, people today—as in Jeremiah's time—have the option of ignoring God's Word.

Jeremiah gives us a chance to learn from the mistakes of his era, for he opens a window that allows us to take a long, hard look at the wages of sin. ❑

Famous Lines

- Can a leopard remove its spots? (13:23).

- "I will write my laws on their hearts and minds.
  I will be their God, and they will be my people" (31:33).

- "Like clay in the hand of the potter, so are you in my hand, O house of Israel" (18:6, New International Version).

- The heart is deceitful above all things, and desperately wicked (17:9, New King James Version).

Behind the Scenes of Jeremiah

⭐ Starring Roles

Jeremiah, a prophet who witnesses Jerusalem's fall (1:1)
Baruch, the scribe who writes Jeremiah's dictated prophecies (32:12)
Jehoiakim, king who cuts up Jeremiah's first scroll of prophecies (1:3)
Zedekiah, last king of Judah; he takes his army and abandons besieged Jerusalem (1:3)

📖 Plot

The prophet Jeremiah, still a young man, begins his job of delivering God's word during a spiritually upbeat time in Judah's history. King Josiah, a godly ruler, is leading the nation in a revival. But it's too little, too late. The effects won't last, and the Jews will revert to their old ways of worshiping idols and treating each other like there's no such thing as compassion or the laws of God.

Judgment day is coming in the form of the merciless Babylonian army, and Jeremiah delivers this heartbreaking message. Unfortunately, his is one of the few hearts broken. Most people ignore him, as they do the other prophets. ❑

🎥 What to Look For

Poetry, stories, speeches. The prophecies of Jeremiah are easy to spot at a quick glance in most Bible versions; they're indented because they are poems. You'll also find in the book some stories and sermons or speeches, which are written in regular paragraph form.

Did You Know?

• Jeremiah has more words than any other book in the Bible.

• The prophet acts out many of his messages. For example, on one occasion he wears a yoke to symbolize that God expects the nations of the area to serve Babylon (27:2). Another time God tells him not to attend any funerals or show sympathy to the bereaved. This is to illustrate that God will have no pity on the Jews when it comes time to punish them (16:5).

• The new covenant, which New Testament writers said replaced the hundreds of laws that God gave Moses, is first mentioned here: "The time is coming," declares the Lord, "when I will make a new covenant with the house of Israel and with the house of Judah" (31:31, New International Version). That time arrived with the death and resurrection of Jesus, says the New Testament (Hebrews 8).

TIMELINE

BIBLE EVENTS	Jeremiah begins his 40-year ministry 626 B.C.	Babylon invades Judah and takes captives, including prophet Daniel 605 B.C.	Babylon suppresses Judean rebellion, taking more captives including Ezekiel 597 B.C.	Babylon destroys Jerusalem and other Judean cities, exiling many survivors 586 B.C. Dates are approximate
	650 B.C.		600 B.C.	550 B.C.
WORLD EVENTS	Babylon captures Assyrian capital of Nineveh 612 B.C.	Babylon crushes Egyptian forces 605 B.C.	Hinduism teaches that at death, the soul moves to another body or animal 600 B.C.	Founder of Buddhism is born 560 B.C.

Poetic repetition. The prophet Jeremiah understands the powerful impact of repeating a striking phrase or idea. This repetition is the most unique characteristic of Hebrew poetry, which does not rhyme or have rhythm.

Jeremiah's complaints. Scattered throughout the book are complaints and questions Jeremiah raises.

Once he complains, "I wish I had never been born! I'm always in trouble with everyone in Judah" (15:10).

Another time he wonders out loud about God's apparently distorted sense of justice: "Why is life easy for sinners? Why are they successful? You plant them like trees; you let them prosper and produce fruit. Yet even when they praise you, they don't mean it" (12:1–2). ❏

Author and Date

The book says Jeremiah dictated the poetic prophecies to his assistant, a scribe named Baruch (36:4). But the prose story sections, say many Bible experts, may have been added by Baruch and other writers.

Jeremiah prophesied in Judah for about 40 years, from 626–586 B.C. He dictated his prophecies, the heart of the book, during the reign of King Jehoiakim (609–598 B.C.).

The book confronts the Judeans with their sin, gives them a chance to repent, then records the horrifying consequences they suffer when they refuse. Yet throughout, it offers this promise: the nation of Israel will rise again.

On Location

Jeremiah delivers his prophecies in Jerusalem, capital of Judah. When Babylonian invaders conquer the land, they deport much of the population to Babylon, a city near what is now Baghdad. Jeremiah and a group of survivors who remain in Judah later escape to Egypt. ❏

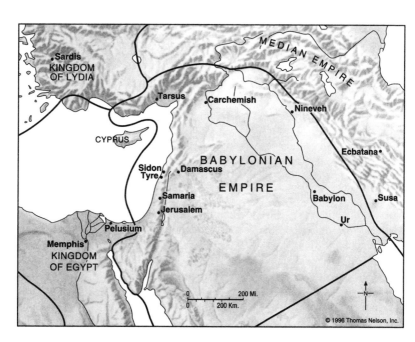

Big Scenes from Jeremiah

Jeremiah, the son of a priest raised just three miles from Jerusalem, has no desire to become a prophet. When God asks him to "speak for me to the nations," Jeremiah resists. "I'm not a good speaker," he replies, "and I'm too young."

"Don't say you're too young," the Lord answered. "If I tell you to go and speak to someone, then go! And when I tell you what to say, don't leave out a word! I promise to be with you and keep you safe, so don't be afraid" (1:5–8).

Later, God tells Jeremiah to go to the pottery shop. "When you get there," God says, "I will tell you what to say to the people."

As Jeremiah and others watch the craftsman at work, they see that when the pottery doesn't shape up well, the potter starts over. Jeremiah, acting on God's instruction, tells the spectators that God can do to the Jewish people what the potter has just done to the clay.

"I have decided to strike you with disaster," God says through Jeremiah, "and I won't change my mind unless you stop sinning and start living right. But I know you won't listen" (18:11–12).

This disaster would come in three waves of Babylonian invasions spread over nearly 20 years. In the first two invasions, the Babylonians would deport leading citizens. In the third invasion, they would destroy all the major cities, including Jerusalem, and deport much of the remaining population.

Jeremiah visits a potter's shop
(18:1–23) ••

Jeremiah, speaking God's words, harshly criticizes the unrighteous rulers of Judah. "You leaders of my people are like shepherds that kill and scatter the sheep. You were supposed to take care of my people, but instead you chased them away. . . . You will pay for your crimes!" (1–2).

Then, in a poetic prophecy, Jeremiah speaks of a coming ruler whom the Jews later associated with the promised Messiah.

> Someday I will appoint an honest king from the family
>   of David,
>   a king who will be wise and rule with justice.
> As long as he is king, Israel will have peace,
>   and Judah will be safe (5–6).

Early Christians would interpret this as a reference to Jesus, who could bring peace to the human heart and who would one day return to rule with wisdom and justice "forever and ever" (Revelation 11:15).

Someday a godly king will rule
•• **(23:1–8)**

For 23 years," Jeremiah says, "I have been telling you what the Lord has told me. But you have not listened" (25:3).

Now their time is up. God will invoke his rights according to the agreement that he and the Jewish people made with each other: "After I destroy your towns and ruin your land with war, I'll scatter you among the nations" (Leviticus 26:33).

"I will let you be attacked by nations from the north, and especially by my servant, King Nebuchadnezzar of Babylonia," God says through Jeremiah. "This country will be as empty as a desert, because I will make all of you the slaves of the king of Babylonia for seventy years" (25:9, 10–11).

The sentence: 70 years in exile
(25:1–14)

As Jeremiah had predicted, the Babylonians capture all the major cities of Judah except Jerusalem, which they have now surrounded. Inside is Jeremiah, under arrest in the palace courtyard for speaking out against King Zedekiah's policy of defending the city; Jeremiah had advised surrender.

While the siege is underway, Jeremiah buys a field in his boyhood home nearby. The sale is meant to serve as a symbol to Israel. God tells Jeremiah to put the bill of sale in a clay jar—the ancient version of a safety deposit box—so it will last a long time.

Jeremiah reports what God has told him: "I promise you that people will once again buy and sell houses, farms, and vineyards in this country" (32:15).

Jeremiah buys a field
(32:1–15)

The story flashes back about 20 years, to when God instructs Jeremiah to write down all the prophecies he has spoken. Jeremiah dictates the prophecies to a scribe, "Baruch, son of Neriah."

Later, Baruch takes the scroll to the temple and reads it to the people. When King Jehoiakim hears the words in a private reading he is not impressed. As the reader finishes a section, the king reaches over with a small knife, cuts it off, and tosses it in the fire. He does this to the entire scroll.

When Jeremiah hears of this, he vows that since the king threw away the words of God, the king will be killed and thrown out. Jeremiah dictates a second scroll, which becomes the core of the book bearing his name.

The king burns Jeremiah's prophecies
(36:1–32)

Fast-forward back to Babylon's siege of Jerusalem (the chronology of Jeremiah jumps around a bit). Four Jerusalem officials overhear Jeremiah telling some people that if they stay in the city they will die from disease, hunger, or battle. The officials report this to King Zedekiah.

"You should put Jeremiah to death," they argue, "because he is making the soldiers and everyone else lose hope."

"Do what you want with him," the king replies.

The officials take Jeremiah to an underground cistern, built to store rainwater. Using ropes, they lower him in, then leave him to die. There's no water in the cistern, but plenty of mud. And Jeremiah sinks deep.

Another official appeals to the king not to let Jeremiah starve down there, and the king relents. Jeremiah is returned to the palace courtyard, under arrest. There, the king calls Jeremiah aside and asks him for advice about the battle.

"If you surrender," Jeremiah says, "you and your family won't be killed, and Jerusalem won't be burned down."

"I can't surrender," Zedekiah says. He's afraid the enemy soldiers will turn him over to the Jews who have sided with Babylon, and that the Jews will torture him.

"If you will just obey the Lord," Jeremiah replies, "the Babylonians won't hand you over to those Jews. You will be allowed to live, and all will go well for you" (38:20).

Jeremiah imprisoned in a muddy cistern
(38:1–13) •

A year and a half into the siege, the Jews are starving to death. So the king and his army make a break for it under the cover of darkness. The unprotected citizens are left behind.

Babylonian soldiers, however, catch the fleeing king and capture the city. The last memorable scene King Zedekiah sees is the execution of his sons; then he is blinded, locked into chains, and taken to Babylon where he dies a prisoner.

Set afire are the temple, the palace, all the important buildings, and the homes. Then the protective walls of the city are broken down.

The Babylonian commander locates Jeremiah in a string of chained slaves bound for Babylon.

"I am taking the chains off your wrists and setting you free!" he tells Jeremiah. Jewish prisoners had apparently spoken of the prophet who tried to convince the king to surrender.

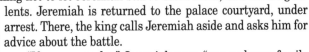

Jeremiah remains in Judea, under the care of the governor that Babylonian King Nebuchadnezzar appoints to rule the area. Sometime later, perhaps as long as four years, the Jews assassinate this governor. Fearing reprisal, they flee to Egypt and force Jeremiah to go with them. There, the Jews take up the worship of the goddess Astarte, "the Queen of Heaven." Jeremiah promises that this remnant of Judah will die in Egypt. Indeed, they disappear from the pages of history, as does Jeremiah.

Jeremiah survives the fall of Jerusalem
• **(39:1—40:16; 52:1–34)**

Reviews

The seal of Jeremiah's scribe. In 1975 a clay impression of an ancient seal used to validate official documents was discovered in Israel. The seal is inscribed with the words, "Belonging to Baruch son of Neriah the scribe." This is exactly how the Bible describes the associate who helped Jeremiah record his prophecies (32:12). Furthermore, the clay impression was scorched, indicating it had been burned, perhaps in the fire that destroyed Jerusalem in 586 B.C.

A second seal impression is also linked to the story of Jeremiah. This one belonged to Jerahmeel, King Jehoiakim's son, who was ordered to arrest Jeremiah and Baruch (36:26).

Letters from a doomed city. Just before the Babylonians conquered Jerusalem, they destroyed the nearby Judean cities of Azekah, then Lachish. Dramatic messages scribbled on broken pieces of pottery—ancient memo sheets—preserve some of the final, frantic military reports.

One message concludes, "We are watching for the fire signals according to the signs my lord has given, because we do not see Azekah."

No 70-year exile. Jeremiah said the exile would last "seventy years" (29:10). It lasted only about 50, because Persian King Cyrus released the Jews to return home in about 538 B.C., just after Persia defeated the Babylonians (2 Chronicles 36:22).

The 20-year difference remains a puzzle. But there are several possible solutions.

1. Jeremiah had in mind the first deportation of Judeans to Babylon. This happened in about 605 B.C., nearly 70 years before Cyrus' decree.

2. The exile extended from the destruction of the temple in 586 B.C. until its rededication in 516 B.C., 70 years.

3. Jeremiah didn't mean 70 literal years. He simply meant a long time. This number was used in this manner on other occasions in the Bible (2 Chronicles 36:21; Daniel 9:24). ❏

Encore

• For more on this era in Judah's history, read 2 Kings and 2 Chronicles 34–36.

• For the words of other Judean prophets who lived during Jeremiah's lifetime, read the books of Habakkuk, Zephaniah, and Nahum. ❏

LAMENTATIONS

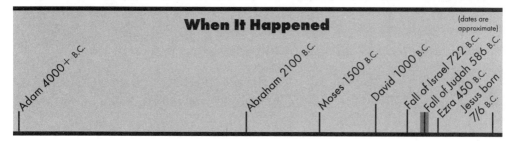

When It Happened
(dates are approximate)

Adam 4000+ B.C. | Abraham 2100 B.C. | Moses 1500 B.C. | David 1000 B.C. | Fall of Israel 722 B.C. | Fall of Judah 586 B.C. | Ezra 450 B.C. | Jesus born 7/6 B.C.

"My Eyes Are Red from Crying"

This may not be the book to read if you're depressed, unless misery loves miserable company. But it's the best place to go in the Bible if you want to understand how people feel when they've suffered an indescribable loss.

"My eyes are red from crying, my stomach is in knots, and I feel sick all over," the writer moans. "Just thinking of my troubles and my lonely wandering makes me miserable. That's all I ever think about, and I am depressed" (2:11; 3:19).

With good reason. He has lost nearly everything but his life—and he could lose that as quickly as a master could kill a slave.

His country is gone, the cities burned, and the leaders dead or arrested. The citizens are gone, slaughtered by Babylonian invaders or deported to faraway lands. Perhaps many of the writer's friends and close family members are among the dead. And perhaps he's all alone now.

Yet when he reaches deep within himself for a response to all this tragedy, he turns up a surprising, inexplicable revelation. It's obviously not an insight he worked out through his powers of reasoning, for it makes no sense.

Famous Line

- Great is thy faithfulness (3:23, King James Version).

"The Lord can always be trusted," he says. "Deep in my heart I say, 'The Lord is all I need'" (3:23–24).

Most people can't understand an attitude like this, bursting forth from deep despair. But gifts from God are sometimes hard to explain. ❏

Behind the Scenes of Lamentations

⭐ Starring Roles

Survivors of Judah, a nation defeated and dispersed (1:3)

📖 Plot

This is not a story with a plot, but a sad song about the death of the Jewish nation.

In a collection of five poems, the writer captures the intensity of his feelings about the unspeakable suffering he has witnessed. He knows his nation has sinned, but he can't understand why God has responded so viciously. "Think about it, Lord!" he complains, "Have you ever been this cruel to anyone before? Is it right for mothers to eat their children [while starving during Babylon's siege of Jerusalem], or for priests and prophets to be killed in your temple?" (2:20).

"Bring us back to you," is his plea. "Give us a fresh start" (5:21).

🎥 What to Look For

Twenty-two-verse chapters. There are five chapters in this book, and all but one have 22 verses. The only exception is chapter 3, which has 66 verses—3 times 22. There's a reason for this. In the 22-verse chapters, each verse begins with a letter of the Hebrew alphabet—starting with *aleph,* followed by *beth,* and continuing through the 22-letter alphabet. So each chapter forms an acrostic, using the Hebrew alphabet. Chapter three is a bit different; it begins every three verses with a new letter from the alphabet.

Chapter five is not an acrostic, but it follows the concept by limiting itself to 22 verses.

It took a lot of thought to create these acrostic songs.

Why the writer went to so much trouble is uncertain. Acrostics help people memorize poems and songs. Yet there may be another reason. For when the writer

> ### Did You Know?
>
> • This is the saddest book in the Bible, the only book made up entirely of mournful songs.
>
> • This collection of songs, along with some heart-wrenching songs in the book of Jeremiah, has earned Jeremiah the nickname, "the weeping prophet."
>
> • Many Jews today read this book at the Western (Wailing) Wall, where they still lament the destruction of the temple, and pray for the day it will be rebuilt.

TIMELINE	BIBLE EVENTS			
		Babylon destroys Jerusalem ⌐----- 586 B.C.	Jewish exiles return to Jerusalem 538 B.C. ---------┐	Temple rebuilt 516 B.C. -------┐ Dates are approximate
	600 B.C.		550 B.C.	500 B.C.
	WORLD EVENTS	Babylon crushes Egyptian forces ⌐-------- 605 B.C.		Cyrus Cylinder confirms return of Jews 539 B.C.

exhausts the entire alphabet, the song also symbolizes fullness. It's as though the writer is saying the Jews have suffered grief from A to Z, many times over.

Poetry with a beat. Lamentations is the one piece of Hebrew poetry in the Bible that breaks the rule that says Hebrew poetry has no rhythm. There's a beat that you can see not only in the original language, but in many English translations as well. The beat is usually 3–2, with three beats in the first line and two beats in the second line. Here's an example, with the beats marked:

*The leaders of Jerusalem / were purer than snow / and whiter than milk;
their bodies were healthy / and glowed like jewels* (4:7).

Author and Date

The writer is unnamed, but since ancient times has been identified as Jeremiah. This is because the poignant scenes suggest that the writer was an eyewitness to the fall of Jerusalem and the suffering that followed. For example, it seems likely that an eyewitness would report starvation becoming so intense in Jerusalem that "loving mothers have boiled and eaten their own children" (4:10).

There's also some similarity between Jeremiah and Lamentations in writing style and word choice.

Because the pain is so much on the surface of the writing, and without any clue that relief is in sight, most Bible experts say the songs were written shortly after the fall of Jerusalem in 586 B.C., and before the rebuilding of the temple 70 years later.

On Location

Some songs are set in Israel, as the Jews suffer near-annihilation. Others are set abroad, as survivors are forced to live in exile in Babylon (now Iraq). At least one group of survivors, Jeremiah included, escapes to Egypt. ❏

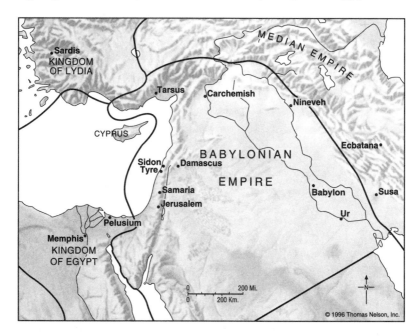

© 1996 Thomas Nelson, Inc.

Big Scenes from Lamentations

Somewhere in exile, far from Israel, a homesick poet writes songs about his once-proud Jewish nation, which now lies in ruins.

Jerusalem is a city of rubble, and its people an assembly of slaves "suffering in a foreign land, with no rest from sorrow."

The poet knows that his nation is being punished for its horrible sins, and that if God had not been merciful, "we would have been destroyed" (3:22). Yet he longs for an end to the torment.

**Jerusalem is gone
(1:1–22)** ••

We are like children whose mothers are widows," the poet writes. "Slaves are now our rulers and there is no one to set us free" (5:3, 8).

The poet finds it impossible to understand how God can allow such depth of suffering to go on for so long. He yearns for God to forgive Israel. "You will rule forever," he says to the Lord. "You are King for all time. Why have you forgotten us for so long? Bring us back to you! Give us a fresh start" (5:19–21).

The poet doesn't know how God will respond. But somehow, somewhere he finds a calming, healing assurance: "The Lord is all I need; I can depend on him" (3:24).

The Jews become like a nation of poor children
•• **(5:1–22)**

Reviews

Other songs sung blue. There are other ancient songs written in the despairing spirit of Lamentations. About 1,500 years before a Jew penned his lament about the fall of Jerusalem, another songwriter lamented the fall of Ur, a city in what is now Iraq. "The people lay in heaps," wrote the author of *A Lamentation Over the Destruction of Ur.* "Dead bodies, like fat placed in the sun . . . melted away." The author of Lamentations described similar conditions. "My people, both young and old, lie dead in the streets," he wrote. "My young men and women were brutally slaughtered" (2:21).

In search of an author. Some Bible experts say Jeremiah probably didn't write the book. They argue that ancient copies of the book don't even mention him, some of the language doesn't sound like him, and it's hard to imagine him complaining that Israel's prophets "don't have a message from the Lord" (2:9). Furthermore, Lamentations speaks of the people "hopelessly looking for help from a nation that could not save us" (4:17). Jeremiah preached the opposite—that the people should not look for help from Egypt (Jeremiah 37:7-10).

Other experts, however, say the language *does* sound like Jeremiah's, and that after Jerusalem was destroyed and Jeremiah left the region there *weren't* any prophets remaining to deliver God's message. Regarding the Jews expecting Egypt to save them, the writer may have been expressing not his hope, but the hope of the masses.

What does seem clear is that the author, whoever he was, witnessed the tragedy and shared the heartbreak. ❏

Encore

- For more songs of grief about the fall of Jerusalem, read Psalms 74, 79, and 137.

- Jesus' lament over the impending disaster of Jerusalem fits the pathos of Lamentations (Luke 13:34-35).

- For the history behind Lamentations, read Ezekiel and Zephaniah. ❏

EZEKIEL

When It Happened (dates are approximate)

Adam 4000+ B.C.   Abraham 2100 B.C.   Moses 1500 B.C.   David 1000 B.C.   Fall of Judah 586 B.C.   Ezra 450 B.C.   Jesus born 7/6 B.C.

Visions that Rattle the Bones

This is not a bedtime story. You'll not want to read it alone at night. And you'll certainly not want to read it to your children as you tuck them in.

The book is full of strange and unsettling images. In a vision of the throne room of God, the prophet Ezekiel reports seeing humanoid creatures, each with four faces, four wings, human hands, and calf-like hooves. This is part of Ezekiel's story about how God calls him to become a prophet.

Later, Ezekiel tells about his most famous vision: His spirit is transported to a valley filled with the scattered bones of human beings. Right before his eyes, these bones begin to rattle, snapping together to form skeletons. Muscles and skin then erupt onto the bones, quickly spreading and covering them to form lifeless corpses. Finally a wind begins to blow, breathing into the bodies the breath of life. This, God promises, is what he will do for Israel, destroyed by Babylon. As a nation, Jews will be resurrected.

Woven into the book's perplexing scenes are clear and important insights about God. For one, he'd rather forgive than punish. For another, he'll never give up trying to win back the loyalty and love of those who have turned their backs on him. ❏

Famous Lines

- Like mother, like daughter (16:44, New Revised Standard Version).

- Dry bones, hear the word of the Lord! (37:4, New International Version).

- There shall be showers of blessing (34:26, King James Version).

- The fathers have eaten sour grapes, and the children's teeth are set on edge (18:2, King James Version). *Ezekiel refutes this old adage, saying that God does not punish children for the sins of the parents. People are accountable only for their own sins.*

Behind the Scenes of Ezekiel

⭐ Starring Role

Ezekiel, Jewish prophet, priest, and prisoner in Babylon (1:1)

📖 Plot

Ezekiel is a 25-year-old priest in Jerusalem when Babylonian soldiers arrive to suppress a rebellion there. They take Ezekiel away as a hostage—one of 10,000 upper-class Judeans enslaved.

Five years later, in a bizarre vision filled with strange-looking creatures from heaven, God calls Ezekiel to become his prophet and to deliver his messages to the Jews in exile. For the next 20 years or more, Ezekiel does just that. First he warns the Jews that their beloved nation and capital city of Jerusalem will fall: "This is what the Sovereign Lord says to the land of Israel: The end!" (7:2, New International Version).

When the end arrives about eight years after he begins predicting it, Ezekiel radically changes his message, switching from doom to hope. The exiles will return to Jerusalem, the city and temple will be rebuilt, and the nations that hurt Israel will suffer terribly.

> ### Did You Know?
>
> • The song about the "foot bone connected to the leg bone" comes from one of Ezekiel's strange visions (37: 1–14).
>
> • "Son of man" is how God addresses the prophet—about 90 times in all. This title spotlights Ezekiel's humanity and his dependence on God. The prophet Daniel, however, uses the term to describe the future messiah (Daniel 7:13). Jesus used this title more than any other to describe himself.
>
> • The last word in the book of Ezekiel is the symbolic name of the new Jerusalem: "The-Lord-Is-Here."

🎥 What to Look For

Prophecies acted out. To help people see what he's talking about, Ezekiel sometimes acts out his prophecies.

Once, when his wife dies, he refuses to follow the Jewish mourning customs. He doesn't cry, put on torn and ragged clothing, or cover himself in dirt. When his neighbors ask why, he says the Jews are about to suffer something so horrible that it will leave them in a state of shock; they won't even be able to cry.

Another time, he shaves his head and beard. Some of the hair he burns, some he cuts with a sword, and the rest he scatters to the wind. This, he explains, is what will happen to the Jewish people.

TIMELINE

BIBLE EVENTS					
Babylon suppresses Judean rebellion and takes Judean hostages 605 B.C.	Babylon takes 10,000 more hostages, including Ezekiel 597 B.C.	Ezekiel begins his ministry as a prophet 593 B.C.	Babylon destroys Jerusalem and other Judean cities, exiling many survivors 586 B.C.	Persia defeats Babylon 539 B.C.	Exiles start returning to Jerusalem 538 B.C.	Temple rebuilt 516 B.C.

600 B.C.	550 B.C.	500 B.C.

WORLD EVENTS			
Babylon captures Assyrian capital of Nineveh 612 B.C.	Babylon crushes Egyptian forces 605 B.C.	Founder of Buddhism is born 560 B.C.	Cyrus Cylinder confirms release of exiled Jews 539 B.C.	Dates are approximate

Yet another time, he sleeps on his right side for 40 days, to symbolize that the Jews have 40 more years to suffer the consequences of their sins.

A lot of vivid symbolism. Don't always take Ezekiel literally. Sometimes it's easy to see he's speaking metaphorically. For example, he'll call Egypt a giant crocodile, and he'll call the seacoast city of Tyre a great ship. But other times it's not as obvious. For example, Ezekiel condemns the king of Tyre by saying he will be thrown out of a garden and cast into a fire (38:11–19). This is a poem in which Ezekiel apparently compares the coming fall of the king to the fall of Satan, who was thrown out of the Garden of Eden.

Don't let the symbolism hide the message. It's supposed to do the opposite. The message is often quite obvious; the colorful images and metaphors are to grab the attention of Ezekiel's listeners and to help them visualize what he's talking about.

Bad news first, good news last. The book divides into two parts. Chapters 1—24 contain Ezekiel's prophecies of warning made before the fall of Jerusalem. Using stern language, he condemns the Jews for arrogantly rebelling against God, and he warns them that judgment day is coming soon.

"I will tell the most wicked nations to come and take over your homes," Ezekiel says on behalf of God. "They will put an end to the pride you have in your strong army, and they will make your places of worship unfit to use" (7:24).

After the fall of Jerusalem, Ezekiel's message changes completely. He delivers good news for Judah. First, in chapters 25—32, he pronounces doom on the wicked countries that destroy the Jewish nation. Then in the final 16 chapters, 33—48, he promises the exiles that they will one day return to Jerusalem. ❏

Author and Date

The prophet Ezekiel wrote this book to Jewish exiles living in the Babylonian Empire. He was merely a priest, and not a prophet, until God came to him in a vision. Ezekiel was 30 years old at the time, and five years into his exile that probably began in 597 B.C. So the prophecies recorded in this book began in 593 B.C., about eight years before the fall of Jerusalem.

On Location

Ezekiel lives near the Chebar River, close to the Babylonian Empire's capital city of Babylon—about 50 miles south of the modern Iraqi capital, Baghdad. That's nearly a thousand miles from his home in Jerusalem by way of the ancient caravan routes. In chapters 47 and 48 he charts the division of the land after the exile. ❏

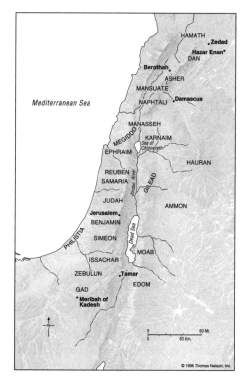

HAMATH
• Zedad
Hazar Enan•
DAN
Berothah •
ASHER
MANSUATE
Mediterranean Sea   NAPHTALI •Damascus
MANASSEH
MEGIDDO   KARNAIM
Sea of
Chinnereth
EPHRAIM
HAURAN
REUBEN
SAMARIA
GILEAD
JUDAH   AMMON
Jerusalem•
BENJAMIN
SIMEON   Dead Sea
PHILISTIA   MOAB
ISSACHAR
ZEBULUN   •Tamar
GAD   EDOM
• Meribah of
Kadesh

N
0   60 MI.
0   60 Km.

© 1996 Thomas Nelson, Inc.

Big Scenes from Ezekiel

While Ezekiel is living in the Babylon area, with other upper-class Jews deported from Judah, God selects him to become a prophet. Ezekiel will deliver God's message to the Jews in exile.

To graphically symbolize that Ezekiel's words will come from God, he is handed a scroll "filled with words of sadness, mourning, and grief."

"Eat this and fill up on it," God says. Afterward, Ezekiel is to go and speak to the people of Israel.

"I ate the scroll," Ezekiel reports, "and it tasted sweet as honey" (2:10—3:3).

**Ezekiel eats a scroll
(2:3—3:3)** •••

In a dramatic vision that begins in chapter 8, Ezekiel is transported to the Jerusalem temple. What he witnesses there becomes part of the tragic, unbelievable message he must deliver.

The temple represents the presence of God in Israel. The temple's back room, which contains the golden chest that holds the Ten Commandments, represents the earthly throne of God; it is the holiest site in Judaism. The Jews believe that God's presence has been there ever since King Solomon dedicated the temple.

Many Jews cannot conceive of God permitting the destruction of his 300-year-old temple and his holy city of Jerusalem. But what Ezekiel witnesses makes this not only believable, but probable. He sees the dazzling light of God's presence come out the door of the temple and ascend into the heavens.

God is gone.

The presence of God leaves the temple
•• **(10:1–22)**

Ezekiel," God says, "tell the people of Jerusalem: I have sharpened my sword to slaughter you; it is shiny and will flash like lightning!" (21:9).

Carrying God's sword of punishment will be an army of Babylonian soldiers. Ezekiel tells the Jews of his exiled community that Babylon will build dirt ramps to the top of Jerusalem's walls, invade the city, kill the people, and tear down the walls. The city—and the sacred temple—will smolder in ruins.

**Invaders from Babylon destroy Jerusalem and the temple
(21:1–32)** ••

After the messages of doom come messages of comfort. In a vision, Ezekiel is transported to a valley filled with dried-out human skeletons, broken and scattered about. The place looks like the site of a massacre long years ago.

God tells Ezekiel to speak to the bones. He's to say that God will "wrap you with muscles and skin and breathe life into you" (37:6).

Even before Ezekiel is finished speaking, he hears a rattling throughout the valley. Bones snap into joints. Muscles spontaneously grow. Skin envelops them. Then a wind sweeps into the valley, blowing across the corpses and bringing them to life. And in a shocking final scene, they all stand up.

"The people of Israel are like dead bones," God explains to Ezekiel. But God instructs the prophet to give this message to the people: "My Spirit will give you breath, and you will live again. I will bring you home" (37:14).

The valley of dry bones
•• **(37:1–14)**

In yet another vision, God takes Ezekiel to a mountain. The year is 573 B.C. (40:1), some 13 years after the temple was destroyed and 57 years before the Jews would finish and dedicate the replacement temple.

What Ezekiel sees is a new and glorious temple. More importantly, he sees the presence of God returning to this holy place.

"I saw the brightness of the glory of Israel's God coming from the east," Ezekiel says. "The sound I heard was as loud as ocean waves, and everything around was shining with the dazzling brightness of his glory" (43:2).

As Ezekiel bows, he sees the Lord's glory come through the east gate and into the temple, filling it with brilliance. God has returned to his people, and his people have returned to him.

This is a message of deep comfort for a nation living in exile, feeling estranged from God and spiritually dead.

A new temple in Jerusalem
(40:1–43:27) ••

Reviews

Ezekiel's the writer. Though Bible experts sometimes disagree about who wrote various books of the Bible, most agree Ezekiel wrote this one. No other prophet in Israel expressed himself in words and actions so distinctly. This unusual brand of writing is easy to recognize throughout the book.

Babylon unearthed. In 1899, archaeologists began digging up the city that Ezekiel and other prophets wrote about. What they found confirms the Bible's account of a massive, beautiful, pagan city. Even yet, the full extent of the city is uncertain. A writer in about 400 B.C. said the total length of the double walls, if arranged in one long line, would stretch out for 60 miles. Some of those walls were 100 yards high and nearly 30 yards thick. Inside the city were massive palaces and several temples to various Babylonian gods.

The eccentric. People reading this book for the first time may wonder if Ezekiel was an eccentric–or worse, crazy. His behavior at times was nothing short of bizarre: shaving his head, refusing to mourn his wife, cooking bread over manure, pretending to tremble as he ate–to name just a few. Yet what Ezekiel did, he did for a reason. And he explained the reasons.

The trembling hands during mealtime, for example, illustrated the fear that would soon overtake Judah; they, too, would eat with trembling hands.

Each of Ezekiel's dramatizations added power to his message. The people might forget the words, but they'd not likely forget the acted-out prophecy. And when the promises were fulfilled a few years later, the people would remember that Ezekiel said it would turn out this way. ❏

Encore

- The prophets Jeremiah and Daniel lived at the same time as Ezekiel–Jeremiah in Judah and Daniel in exile with Ezekiel. Read their books for more insight into the turbulent times.

- Some Bible experts believe that the writer of Revelation borrowed the strange and highly symbolic imagery from the books of Ezekiel and Daniel. Revelation also borrows some of the content. For example, like Ezekiel, Revelation talks about a new Jerusalem. ❏

DANIEL

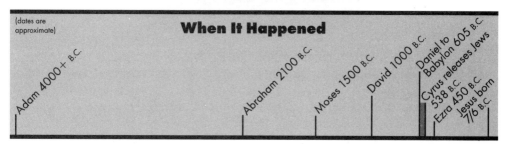

(dates are approximate) · **When It Happened**

Adam 4000+ B.C. Abraham 2100 B.C. Moses 1500 B.C. David 1000 B.C. Daniel to Babylon 605 B.C. Cyrus releases Jews 538 B.C. Ezra 450 B.C. Jesus born 7/6 B.C.

A Meal the Lions Skipped

Two of the Bible's most famous stories are reported in this book: Daniel in the lion's den, and the three young Hebrew men in the fiery furnace.

Part of what makes the book a classic is that all four men survived. It wasn't that the lions were stuffed, and the furnace was merely a sauna. The lions were hungry, and proved it the next morning by ravenously eating Daniel's accusers. The furnace was hotter than blue blazes, and instantly broiled the soldiers who pushed the Hebrews inside.

After these and other riveting stories come the lesser-known words of Daniel, in the second half of the book. The prophet tells about some of his incredibly strange visions concerning the future, and of angels explaining what the vision meant.

This short, 12-chapter book was apparently intended to comfort exiled Jews who wondered if God had forsaken them. But if allowed, the book could comfort all people. For through Daniel's stories and visions, God reminds us that he is Lord of creation. He has used his power to invade human history—making appearances in lion dens and kiln furnaces—and he will use that power to direct the future.

In the end, the goodness of his original creation will be fully restored. And when it is, "he will rule forever" (7:14). ❏

Famous Lines

- "My God knew that I was innocent, and he sent an angel to keep the lions from eating me" (6:22). *Daniel's explanation to the king of how he survived a night in the lion's den.*

- I saw what looked like a son of man coming with the clouds of heaven. . . . He will rule forever, and his kingdom is eternal (7:13-14). *One of Daniel's end-time visions, which New Testament writers say refers to the second coming of Jesus.*

Behind the Scenes of Daniel

⭐ Starring Roles

Daniel, Jewish prophet exiled in Babylon (1:6)
Shadrach, Meshach, Abednego, Daniel's friends who survive the fiery furnace (1:7)
Belshazzar, ruler who sees the handwriting on the wall (5:1)

📖 Plot

As a young nobleman in Jerusalem, Daniel is arrested by soldiers of the world's new superpower, Babylon. With many other Jewish leaders, Daniel is taken to Babylon and forced to live there. The Babylonians quickly realize how intelligent he is, and put him through a three-year training program to become a royal advisor.

With his colleagues, Shadrach, Meshach, and Abednego, he agrees to serve the king. But all four refuse to reject their faith in God. When they're ordered to worship an idol and to stop their daily prayers, they don't comply. This is a capital offense, but God protects them. Daniel's three friends survive a furnace. And Daniel survives a lion's den.

For 50 years or more Daniel serves various kings, first Babylonian, then Persian.

Did You Know?

• The old saying, "I could see the handwriting on the wall," comes from Daniel's story of a terrified king watching a disembodied hand write a message on the palace wall (5:5).

• Old Testament writers rarely speak about life after death. But Daniel does, offering the Old Testament's clearest insight into the resurrection: "Many of those who lie dead in the ground will rise from death. Some of them will be given eternal life, and others will receive nothing but eternal shame" (12:2).

🎥 What to Look For

God in control. The dramatic stories and astonishing visions of this book point to one main theme: God is in charge of human history.

At his command, Babylon rises and Babylon falls. When an emperor orders Daniel's friends executed, then another emperor condemns Daniel to death, God overrules. And when the Jews are discouraged, he gives them assurance through Daniel's visions of a glorious future.

TIMELINE	BIBLE EVENTS					
	Babylon invades Judea and takes captives, including Daniel 605 B.C.		Babylon destroys Jerusalem 586 B.C.	Daniel in the lion's den 539 B.C.	Jews return to Jerusalem 538 B.C.	Dates are approximate
	600 B.C.			550 B.C.		500 B.C.
	WORLD EVENTS	Temples to Zeus and other gods built in Olympia, Greece 600 B.C.			Pythagorus invents geometry theories 540 B.C.	

Part 1, Part 2. It's easy to spot the end of Part 1 and the beginning of Part 2. The first six chapters are stories about Daniel and his friends. The remaining six chapters are about the mysterious visions of Daniel.

Apocalypse, the genre. Daniel's visions are written in a style that became a genre: apocalyptic. Books of this genre—the most famous of which is the perplexing New Testament book of Revelation—are filled with stories about spirit-world creatures delivering messages to human beings concerning future events.

The symbolism is so thick that even Daniel, a respected sage and trusted interpreter of dreams and visions, needs an angel to tell him what his visions mean. Yet even the explanations of the angel leave questions unanswered. For example, Daniel has a troubling vision about four beasts—a lion, a bear, a leopard, and an unnamed beast with iron teeth. An angel later explains that the four creatures represent four kingdoms that will emerge, one after the other. Neither the angel nor Daniel identifies which kingdoms they are, but many Bible experts speculate they are Babylon, Medo-Persia, Greece, and Rome.

Some Christians look to the apocalyptic writings of Daniel and Revelation for clues about the end of human history and the second coming of Jesus. These people try to make connections between the ancient symbolism and today's headlines. For example, they may associate prophecies about Babylon with modern-day Iraq. But in doing this, these Bible students are trying to explain what wise men like Daniel found unexplainable.

The point of the visions is not to provide a coded road map to the future, but to assure the reader that God's doing the driving.

Author and Date

Many believe Daniel wrote the book sometime after Cyrus defeated Babylon in 539 B.C., because that's one of the last events described in the stories about Daniel.

Others says the book was written and compiled centuries later. (See "Looking for the Real Writer" in Reviews.)

On Location

The stories and visions take place in Babylon, capital city of the Babylonian Empire, to which Daniel and his friends are taken after the first Babylonian invasion of Judah in 605 B.C. ❏

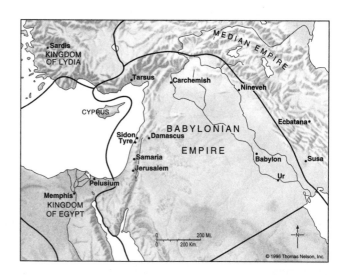

© 1996 Thomas Nelson, Inc.

Big Scenes from Daniel

When Babylon becomes the superpower, it steals some of the finest minds in the Middle East. Among many forced from Judah, with Daniel, are three men: Shadrach, Meshach, and Abednego. In recognition of their intelligence, they are trained to work in the palace.

Later, at a palace event, they refuse to bow in front of a new idol built for the king. As punishment, they are thrown into a furnace so hot that the flames leap out and kill the executioners. Yet inside the furnace, the three men walk around unharmed. With them is a fourth man who "looks like a god."

When the king calls the men back out, they aren't burnt, singed, or even smelling of smoke. The king vows to protect their right to worship God.

**Daniel's three friends in a fiery furnace
(3:1–30)** •

Years later, a new king throws a banquet for a thousand of his top-ranking officials. He gets drunk and orders drinks served in the sacred cups stolen from the Jerusalem temple. Suddenly a human hand appears and writes these words on the plastered palace wall: "Numbered. Numbered. Weighed. Divided." The king is terribly frightened.

He calls on Daniel, a respected advisor and interpreter of dreams, to explain what the words mean. "God has numbered the days of your kingdom," Daniel says. "He has weighed you on his balance scales, and you fall short of what it takes to be king. So God has divided your kingdom between the Medes and the Persians" (5:26–28).

That very night, Babylon falls to a coalition of Medes and Persians.

The handwriting on the wall

• **(5:1–30)**

When Daniel rises to become one of the top three officials in the Persian palace, jealous officials plot to kill him. They shrewdly convince King Darius to order the people to pray only to the king for the next 30 days, or face the lions. When the officials catch Daniel praying openly to God, they turn him in. The king is upset and tries to find a way to save Daniel. But his edict is irrevocable.

Daniel spends the night in a den of lions, but is protected by an angel.

After a sleepless night, the king rushes to the den to find Daniel alive. The king orders Daniel removed and his accusers thrown in. The death they wished upon Daniel is the death they receive.

**Daniel in the lion's den
(6:1–28)** •

Reviews

Looking for King Belshazzar. Many Bible experts once wondered if Belshazzar—who Daniel says was the last ruler of Babylon—was a fictional character. This is because ancient records show that Nabonidus was the Babylonian king overthrown by the Medes and Persians. More recent discoveries of Babylonian records reveal that Belshazzar was the son of Nabonidus, who during the last part of his reign shared power with his son.

This insight into Babylonian history answers another question that had vexed scholars: why Belshazzar asked Daniel to interpret the handwriting on the wall, then offered him not the number two position in the kingdom, but number three (5:7). Belshazzar himself held the second most influential position. The highest position he could offer was the number three spot.

Looking for the real writer. Daniel could not possibly be the writer of the book, some say. They cite many reasons. Here are two of the most frequently mentioned.

1. The book reads like it was compiled by someone else. The visions are in the first person, and might have been written by Daniel. But the stories are in the third person, as though written by someone else reporting Daniel's story. Also, the oldest copies of the book are written in two languages. The opening and closing chapters are written in Hebrew, and the other chapters are written in Aramaic, the language of the Babylonians and Persians.

2. Some of the visions so accurately reflect Middle Eastern history in the second and third centuries B.C. that they were likely written after those events—not as a prediction, but as history disguised as a prediction. For example, Daniel's description of what took place between the king of the north and the king of the south (chapter 11) matches history's account of what took place as the Ptolemies of Egypt and the Seleucids of Syria fought for control of the region after Alexander the Great died.

Bible experts who contend that Daniel *did* write the book say that God is fully capable of empowering his prophets to predict the future.

And though the writing styles and two languages used remain a puzzle, this doesn't mean that Daniel could not have done the writing at various times during his 50-year ministry. Jesus, in fact, commented about one of the visions "of the prophet Daniel" (Matthew 24:15). ❏

Encore

- The stories of heroic Daniel are in some ways similar to the stories about earlier Israelite heroes Joseph (Genesis 39–41) and Mordecai (Esther). There are dreams and interpretations, and there are Jews being saved from mortal danger brought on by foreign leaders.

- For more of the apocalyptic style of writing, read Ezekiel's visions as well as the visions in Revelation.

- To see how Jesus interprets Daniel's reference to someone committing sacrilege in the temple (9:27; 11:31; 12:11) read Matthew 24:15-28. Jesus tells people to run to the hills when they see this happening. About 40 years later, when Romans planted on the temple mount their flagpole-like standards decorated with idols, many Christians left. They escaped the destruction of Jerusalem, when in A.D. 70 Rome crushed the Jewish rebellion. ❏

HOSEA

(dates are approximate)

When It Happened

Adam 4000+ B.C.

Abraham 2100 B.C.

Moses 1500 B.C.

David 1000 B.C.

Fall of Israel 722 B.C.

Fall of Judah 586 B.C.

Ezra 450 B.C.

Jesus born 7/6 B.C.

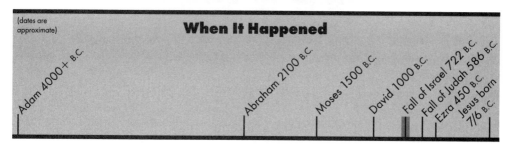

The Prophet and the Prostitute

"Hosea," God said, "Israel has betrayed me like an unfaithful wife. Marry such a woman" (1:2).

Hosea did. And the story that follows has gripped the attention of people ever since. It's a story of God's persistent love for the Jewish people. Centuries earlier he had entered into a covenant with them. He would be their God, they would be his people. He would take care of them, they would obey the laws he had given through Moses.

God fulfilled his part of the agreement, but Israel didn't. Throughout much of their history, they were not God's people and they did not obey God's laws.

Before invoking the punishment clause in the ancient agreement, God appointed prophets to deliver his messages to the Jews, urging them to come back and warning them about what would happen if they didn't.

But the people treated the prophets with the same disrespect they had shown God and his law. As Jesus put it 700 years later while standing in Jerusalem, "Your people have killed the prophets and have stoned the messengers who were sent to you" (Matthew 23:37).

Yet the story of Hosea isn't mainly about spiritual rebellion or divine punishment. It's about God's inexplicable, relentless love even for people who treat him like the enemy.

For those who think the Old Testament God is cruel, Hosea reveals a preview of God practicing the compassion that his Son would later preach: "Love your enemies" (Matthew 5:44). ❏

Famous Lines

- They sow the wind, and reap the whirlwind (8:7, New International Version). *Hosea's way of saying that if Israel doesn't repent, they'll pay for their evil. They'll sow idolatry, and reap annihilation.*

- You are not my people, and I am not your God (1:9, New International Version). *God's complaint about Israel, stated exactly opposite of the wording in the covenant agreement between Israel and God (Leviticus 26:12).*

Behind the Scenes of Hosea

⭐ Starring Roles

Hosea, prophet to the northern Jewish nation of Israel (1:1)
Gomer, Hosea's prostitute wife (1:3)

📖 Plot

God instructs Hosea to marry a prostitute as a living reminder that the people of Israel have spiritually prostituted themselves by worshiping the local gods. When Hosea's wife has three children, only the first of whom is clearly identified as her husband's, God instructs Hosea to give them names that symbolize Israel's potential fate: Jezreel, meaning "God Scatters," Lo-Ruhamah, meaning "No Mercy," and Lo-Ammi, meaning "Not My People."

Hosea's wife eventually leaves him and apparently moves in with another man who treats her as his legal property. Acting on God's order, Hosea buys her back. "Do this," God says, "to show that I love the people of Israel, even though they worship idols" (3:1).

Hosea then prophesies that the people will be punished if they don't quickly change their ways. Yet, in spite of their unfaithfulness, God pleads with them to come back by promising, "I will heal you and love you without limit" (14:4).

🎥 What to Look For

Gomer as an example of Israel. Notice the parallels between Gomer, Hosea's wife, and Israel. Both are unfaithful to their beloved. Both become enslaved, Gomer by an unnamed master (3:2), and Israel by Assyria (10:6). Both are sought back in spite of their unfaithfulness and their abandoning the one who loved them. ❏

Did You Know?

• Hosea's name, in Hebrew, is almost identical to the names of Jesus and Joshua. All three mean "God saves." Hosea saves his wife from slavery, Joshua saves Israel from defeat, and Jesus saves the world from sin.

• Hosea is the first of what are known as the 12 Minor Prophets. They're not "minor" because they have unimportant messages, but because their books are much shorter than those of the Major Prophets: Isaiah, Jeremiah, Ezekiel, and Daniel.

• Hosea was the only prophet from the northern Jewish nation of Israel who ministered to Israel. Amos, who also prophesied in Israel, came up from Judah to deliver God's message.

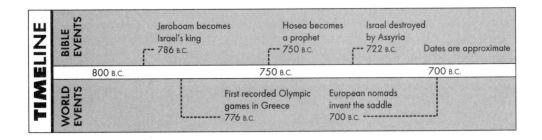

TIMELINE

BIBLE EVENTS

Jeroboam becomes Israel's king
786 B.C.

Hosea becomes a prophet
750 B.C.

Israel destroyed by Assyria
722 B.C.

Dates are approximate

800 B.C.   750 B.C.   700 B.C.

WORLD EVENTS

First recorded Olympic games in Greece
776 B.C.

European nomads invent the saddle
700 B.C.

Author and Date

The book starts by identifying the writer: "I am Hosea son of Beeri" (1:1). As is the case with most prophets, very little is revealed about him.

Hosea lived and prophesied during the last 20 years or more of Israel's existence, before Assyria conquered the nation in 722 B.C. Hosea said he was called to become God's prophet sometime during the 40-year reign of King Jeroboam II (786–746 B.C.).

On Location

Hosea's story takes place in the northern Jewish nation of Israel. The Israelites there seceded from the union about 200 years before Hosea's time, during the reign of King Solomon's son. ❏

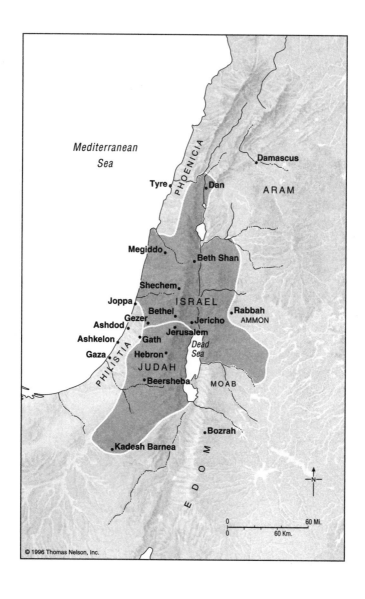

© 1996 Thomas Nelson, Inc.

Big Scenes from Hosea

In one of the most bizarre requests that God has ever made of a Bible character, he instructs the prophet Hosea to marry a prostitute. This marriage is to serve as a living, breathing symbol that Israel has broken its covenant with God, and has been unfaithful by worshiping idols.

"I married Gomer," Hosea reports. During the marriage, Gomer has three children: two sons and a daughter. They, too, become part of the living symbol, for Hosea gives them Hebrew names that point to Israel's potential fate: Jezreel, meaning "God Scatters;" Lo-Ruhamah, meaning "No Mercy;" and Lo-Ammi, meaning "Not My People." God's covenant with Israel has a punishment clause for breach of contract. If Israel fails to honor the agreement, God has the right to scatter them among the nations, show them no mercy, and disown them.

Hosea's marriage and family serve as a daily reminder to the people around him about the sins of the nation, and the consequences that the Jews will suffer if they don't change their ways.

Yet, even if Israel fails to repent, God promises that there is coming a day when the people of Israel will be called "Children of the Living God," "My People," and "Shown Mercy." They will return home and enjoy the rich blessings of God.

**Hosea's family portrait
(1:1–11)**

Gomer leaves her husband and family, apparently to return to her trade. For in a poetic lament, God's complaint of Israel seems to parallel Hosea's complaint of Gomer: "Accuse! Accuse your mother! She is no longer my wife, and now I, the Lord, am not her husband. Beg her to give up prostitution and stop being unfaithful" (2:2).

God then gives Hosea a second bizarre command. Hosea is to fall in love with Gomer all over again. He's to do this to show that God still loves Israel "even though they worship idols."

By this time, Gomer is living with another man. Perhaps she provides him with income from her prostitution, and he provides her with room, board, and protection. The Bible doesn't say. Whatever their relationship, Hosea needs to buy her back as one would buy a slave. The price is 15 silver coins and about 10 bushels of grain.

In the remainder of the book, Hosea warns that if Israel continues on its current course, God will use Assyria to destroy the nation and lead the people into captivity. But if they give up their idols, Hosea assures them, God will forgive.

**Hosea buys back his wife from another man
(3:1–5)**

Reviews

Prostitution an apt comparison. When God told Hosea to marry a prostitute as a living, breathing symbol of Israel's spiritual unfaithfulness, he chose an appropriate metaphor. The people of Israel not only prostituted themselves spiritually, they also did it literally—worship of Canaanite gods involved having sex with temple prostitutes.

Though many people continued to worship God, they also worshiped local gods as a kind of spiritual disaster insurance. The most popular god seemed to be Baal, thought to provide fertility in field, flock, and family. Worshipers believed, for example, that the rain was Baal's semen. And they apparently thought they could stimulate him or at least convince him to honor their request for rain by having sex with his priests and priestesses. Worshipers also entertained him with fertility rites in thanks for good crops, herds, and the birth of a child.

The Hebrew word describing Gomer, however, was a word that usually referred to a street prostitute, not a temple prostitute.

Hosea's marriage, fact or fable? God would not do such a distasteful thing as to order a prophet to marry a prostitute. That has been the conclusion of many respected Jewish and Christian Bible experts throughout the ages, including the famous Christian theologians Martin Luther (father of the Protestants), and John Calvin (theological forebear of Southern Baptists and Presbyterians).

The marriage never happened, some said. It was simply a make-believe story that symbolized Israel's religious adultery. Others suggest Hosea experienced the marriage in a dream or a vision. Still others argue that Hosea was probably married, but his wife was faithful—he portrayed her as a prostitute only to dramatize his point about the strained relationship between God and Israel.

Ancient Jewish commentators, however, had no trouble accepting the story at face value. They believed God told Hosea to marry a prostitute, and he obeyed. ❑

Encore

- For a second opinion into what life was like in Israel during Hosea's day, read the nine-chapter book of Amos. He prophesied just a few years before Hosea.

- Other prophets who lived and wrote in Hosea's time were Isaiah and Micah, though they ministered in the southern Jewish nation of Judah.

- To see how other prophets compare Israel to an unfaithful bride, turn to Jeremiah 2–3 and Ezekiel 16, 23.

- For a New Testament perspective on God's persistent love, read 1 John 4:7–21. ❑

JOEL

When It Happened

(dates are approximate)

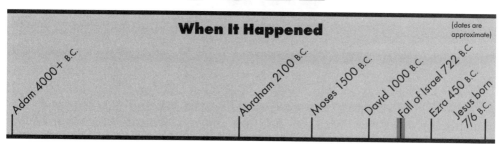

Adam 4000+ B.C.   Abraham 2100 B.C.   Moses 1500 B.C.   David 1000 B.C.   Fall of Israel 722 B.C.   Ezra 450 B.C.   Jesus born 7/6 B.C.

Year of the Locust

The poetry is masterful, the images stark and terrifying.

In the opening scene, locusts swarm in from the desert where predators are few and a single swarm can number into the billions. Starving and aggressive, they devour wheat, barley, figs, grapes, pomegranates—everything an insect can eat. Pastures are grazed to the ground, trees stripped to their naked branches.

As if this isn't bad enough, Joel warns the people that more trouble's ahead: to punish the nation for sin, God is allowing an invasion force to assemble somewhere up north. When it arrives, so does "the judgment day of the Lord" (2:1). But there's hope. "It isn't too late," the Lord says, "You can still return to me with all your heart" (2:12).

The choice confronting Israel is the choice confronting all of humanity. Joel says that one day, in "Judgment Valley," God will try the nations of the world and render his verdict. "I will punish the guilty," he promises, "and defend the innocent" (3:21). ❏

Famous Lines

- Beat your plowshares into swords, and your pruninghooks into spears (3:10, King James Version). *The exact opposite of what happens in the peaceful scene of Isaiah 2:4 and Micah 4:3. Joel warns the enemies of God to get ready for their last battle with him.*

- Multitudes, multitudes in the valley of decision (3:14, King James Version). *A poetic description of the nations assembled for judgment day.*

- The judgment day of the Lord is coming soon (2:1).

- Everyone who calls on the name of the Lord will be saved (2:32, New International Version).

Behind the Scenes of Joel

⭐ Starring Role

Joel, a prophet of God (1:1)

📖 Plot

Swarm after swarm of locusts invade Israel, devouring the crops and then planting eggs that will hatch and consume the next generation of plants. With harvest and pasture gone, people and livestock go hungry. Water holes lose their shade and dry up. Famine scars the land for years to come.

Joel uses this natural disaster to warn of an even worse catastrophe. Because the people have sinned—Joel doesn't mention how—a monstrously enormous army will invade the land and strip it bare. Joel may be talking about an ancient invasion, an end-time apocalypse, or both.

"It isn't too late," the Lord says through Joel. "You can still return to me" (2:12).

If the people do, they can escape a horrifying judgment that Joel simply calls "the day of the Lord."

"I am merciful, kind, and caring," God assures the people. "I don't like to punish" (2:13).

> **Did You Know?**
>
> • Swarms of 10 billion locusts, an aggressive kind of grasshopper, occasionally invade the Middle East. Eyewitnesses to a 1915 swarm in Israel said the locusts flew around for five days, darkening the sky. Afterward, they ate every plant they saw, then left their eggs behind. The eggs can be killed by plowing the ground.

🎥 What to Look For

The day of the Lord. This is an important phrase in Joel, repeated five times in the short, three-chapter book. Many prophets use this phrase to talk about any time God does something to a nation or a generation of people—whether to punish or protect.

Joel uses the phrase in both ways. It's a dark and dreadful day when God will punish his enemies, and it's a bright and glorious day when he will save the faithful. Joel also uses the phrase, in chapter 3, to hint of what other prophets and the New Testament describe as a final Judgment Day at the end of human history, when God destroys everything evil. (See "Day of the Lord" in Reviews.)

The coming of the Holy Spirit. God says through Joel that there is coming a day when "I will pour out my spirit. . . . Then everyone who calls on the name of the Lord shall be saved" (2:29, 32, New Revised Standard Version).

That day arrives about two months after the resurrection of Jesus, according to Peter, one of the original disciples. Before Jesus ascends to heaven he tells the disciples to wait in Jerusalem until the Holy Spirit comes upon them. On the day of Pentecost, a Jewish holiday 50 days after Passover, "the Holy Spirit took control of everyone" (Acts 2:4). Before a huge crowd of pilgrims from around the world, Peter declares that the prophecy of Joel has today been fulfilled.

Author and Date

The writer is the prophet "Joel the son of Pethuel" (1:1). He's not mentioned anywhere else in the Old Testament, though there are references to about a dozen other men with this popular name. The only other mention of the prophet Joel comes in a sermon by Peter on the day of Pentecost, when Peter declared that one of Joel's prophecies had just been fulfilled.

There are no solid clues about when Joel lived. His book is preserved among those of the prophets from the 700s B.C., just before Assyria destroyed the northern Jewish nation of Israel. Joel does talk about invaders coming from the north—as Assyria did in the 700s B.C., Babylon in the 500s B.C., and Alexander the Great of Greece in the 300s B.C. But Joel doesn't say who the invaders are, so Bible experts are left guessing.

On Location

It appears that Joel lived in the southern Jewish nation of Judah, which he mentions frequently. But he also speaks of Israel. The name "Israel" could refer either to the northern nation of Israel or to the entire Jewish race, in both Israel and Judah. He may have prophesied in the years before Assyria overran Israel. ❏

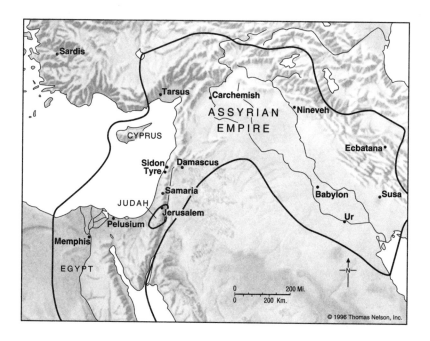

© 1996 Thomas Nelson, Inc.

Big Scenes from Joel

Swarm after swarm of locusts has attacked our crops, eating everything in sight," says the prophet Joel. "Mourn for our farms and our vineyards! There's no wheat or barley growing in our fields. Grapevines have dried up and so has every tree" (1:4, 11–12).

The food is gone. The rivers are dry. And the livestock wander aimlessly in search of pasture.

As terrible as this is, Joel warns, the worst is yet to come.

**Invasion of locusts
(1:1–20)** ••

The judgment day of the Lord is coming soon," Joel continues his ominous prophecy. "Troops will cover the mountains like thunderclouds. . . . They make the earth tremble and the heavens shake" (2:1, 2, 10).

But it's not too late. The people of Judah can escape the coming disaster if only they will return to God with all their heart. "I am merciful, kind, and caring," God says, "I don't like to punish" (2:13).

**Invasion of massive army
(2:1–27)**

•••

In the years to come, God says he will more than make up for the suffering that Israel has endured because of their sins. "Grain will cover your threshing places; jars will overflow with wine and olive oil" (2:24).

Later, God will give out his Spirit to everyone. "Your sons and daughters will prophesy. Your old men will have dreams, and your young men will see visions" (2:28). On the Jewish holiday of Pentecost, centuries later, Peter stood in the courtyard of Herod's temple and proclaimed that this prophecy had just been fulfilled—the followers of Jesus had been the first to receive the gift of the Holy Spirit (Acts 2:14–21). That day, 3,000 listeners believed him, were baptized, and received the Spirit.

**Young men and women prophesying
(2:28—3:21)** ••

Reviews

Northern army. Joel warns that unless the people stop sinning, God is going to punish them by letting a huge army invade from the north.

Throughout Israel's history, that's where most of the invaders came from. When God decided to punish the northern Jewish nation of Israel, Assyria invaded from the north and conquered the country in 722 B.C. When God decided to punish the southern nation of Judah, Babylon invaded from the north several times, eventually destroying Jerusalem in 586 B.C.

Later, Alexander the Great invaded from the north in the 300s B.C., followed by the Seleucids of Syria in the 200s B.C., then the Romans in the 100s B.C.

The day of the Lord. This is a waffling sort of a phrase. Over the millennium that it took to create the Old Testament, writers used this phrase inconsistently—sometimes presenting it as doomsday, and other times presenting it as deliverance day.

The single consistency is that it was always a time when God got involved in human history and changed the course of events. Writers described this divine action in many ways, including "that day," "then," "day of visitation."

Initially the phrase had a positive ring; it was a day the Israelites longed for—when God would deliver them from their enemies, as he had done by freeing the Israelites from Egypt. But later on, the prophets began charging that Israel *was* the enemy. And like other evil nations that refused to repent of sin, the Jews would die. So the anticipated day of the Lord became the feared day of doom.

Yet the prophets were unwilling to limit the phrase to doomsday, just as New Testament writers were unwilling to limit Judgment Day to the defeat of God's enemies. The prophets said that after punishment comes the restoration of God's people. And the New Testament says that after Judgment Day comes eternal life for the faithful.

The day of the Lord—any day God interrupts human history—is a bad day for the godless and a good day for the righteous. ❏

Encore

- To see what Peter said was the fulfillment of Joel's prophecy about the Holy Spirit, read Acts 1–2.

- For what other prophets say about the day of the Lord, read Amos 5:18-27; Zephaniah 1:14–2:3; Isaiah 13:6–14:2. For Jesus' insight, read Matthew 25:31-46.

- Revelation 19:11-21 and 20:11-15 are judgment scenes similar to that in Joel. ❏

AMOS

(dates are approximate)

When It Happened

Adam 4000+ B.C.   Abraham 2100 B.C.   Moses 1500 B.C.   David 1000 B.C.   Fall of Israel 722 B.C.   Ezra 450 B.C.   Jesus born 7/6 B.C.

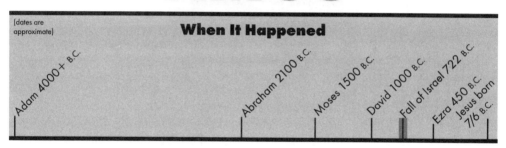

When Money Talks, Who Hears the Poor?

If you want to know what God thinks about a rich society that exploits the poor and lets money do the talking in the courts, read Amos.

Long before advocacy leaders and civil rights organizers, there was a sheepherder named Amos. With vicious honesty, he condemned the wealthy who "smear the poor in the dirt and push aside those who are helpless" (2:7).

Women who mistreat poor servants and beggars, Amos charged, are "fat cows" who will be dragged away by "sharp hooks," like those that butchers use to haul a carcass to the chopping block.

Amos also condemned leaders, nobles, and merchants who cheat honest people, tax them to death, and twist the face of justice until no one can recognize it anymore.

> ### Famous Lines
>
> • Prepare to meet your God (4:12, New King James Version).
>
> • Let justice roll on like a river (5:24, New International Version).

This criticism did not endear Amos to Israel's leaders. They had two words for him: "Get out!" (7:12).

But the judgment they imposed on him was the judgment they would face. God wouldn't stand for this kind of *status quo*. He stepped into human history and rearranged Israel's socioeconomic system. Suddenly, with the swooping of an Assyrian invasion force, the rich were on the same level as the poor.

God's concern about social issues didn't end in Old Testament times. Neither did his ability to step into history and change what greedy humans won't. ❏

Behind the Scenes of Amos

⭐ Starring Roles

Amos, prophet, shepherd, and fig farmer (1:1)
Amaziah, a priest who chases Amos off (7:10)

📖 Plot

God calls on Amos, a shepherd and fig grower, to leave his small village at the desert's edge in the southern Jewish nation of Judah. Amos' task is to deliver a prophetic message to the northern nation of Israel, which is wallowing in prosperity. Amos is to throw the spotlight on the nation's most blatant sins. Wealthy folks are getting richer at the expense of the exploited poor. In court, the verdict goes to the client with the most money. Father and son sleep with the same prostitute. People go through the motions of worship, thinking rituals are enough to appease God.

"I will crush you," God says through Amos (2:13). Soldiers will invade the land and carry the people away as captives.

A priest named Amaziah replies, "Amos, take your visions and get out!" (7:12).

Amos leaves, but not before promising that Amaziah's children will be killed in the war, and the priest will die in a foreign country. As for Israel, Amos leaves the people with a hopeful promise: God will one day restore the nation he has been forced to destroy.

Did You Know?

• Civil rights leader Martin Luther King, Jr., drew heavily from the ideas in Amos. In King's famous "I Have a Dream" speech, he said he dreamed that one day "the heat of injustice and oppression" would become "an oasis of freedom and justice."

• Amos was perhaps the first Bible prophet to write down his messages.

🎥 What to Look For

Crimes of injustice. Amos criticizes the people for doing nothing about social injustice running rampant. The poor don't have enough money for food and clothing, and are sold into slavery if they can't pay for a pair of sandals they buy on credit. Merchants regularly cheat people with rigged scales. Judges are bought and paid for. The poor and powerless don't have a chance, unless God steps in.

TIMELINE

	BIBLE EVENTS			
		Amos begins his ministry 760 B.C.	Northern nation of Israel destroyed 722 B.C.	Dates are approximate
	800 B.C.		750 B.C.	700 B.C.
	WORLD EVENTS	Ohio River people build earth burial mounds 800 B.C.	King Romulus founds Rome 753 B.C.	Ethiopia starts 50-year rule of Egypt 716 B.C.

The mere motions of worship. Many people do nothing more than go through the motions of worship. They think that bringing the appropriate sacrifice is all they need to do to please God. "Sin all you want! Offer sacrifices the next morning," Joel says sarcastically (4:4).

The day of the Lord. This is a phrase used by many Jews of the time. For them, it refers to a day when God will deliver Israel from harm and punish Israel's enemies. But like other prophets, Amos warns that the day of the Lord is nothing for Israel to look forward to: "You are in for trouble!" (5:18).

Author and Date

"I am Amos," the book begins. "And I raised sheep near the town of Tekoa" (1:1). Amos also tended a grove of fig trees. So he was both a herder and a farmer, living about 10 miles south of Jerusalem. He said he was not a prophet, until God gave him this message to deliver to Israel (7:14–15).

His eloquent prose and poetry suggest he was more than a hired shepherd and farmhand. He was apparently an educated man, and perhaps the owner of the flock and grove.

He says he lived when Jeroboam was king of Israel (786–746 B.C.). The national prosperity that Amos talks about fits the conditions during the later part of Jeroboam's reign, beginning about 760 B.C.

On Location

Amos leaves his hometown and country—Tekoa, 10 miles south of Jerusalem in the southern Jewish nation of Judah—and takes God's message to Bethel, a worship center in the northern nation of Israel. ❏

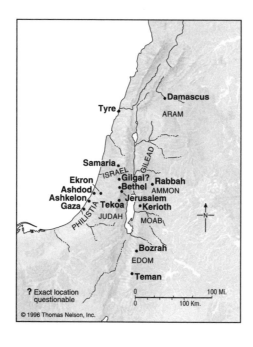

Big Scenes from Amos

Amos is not someone who earns his living as a prophet, advising national leaders.

"I'm not a prophet! And I wasn't trained to be a prophet," he tells his listeners. "I am a shepherd, and I take care of fig trees. But the Lord told me to leave my herds and preach to the people of Israel."

His herds are in a different country, the rival Jewish nation of Judah, in the southland. Acting on God's orders, Amos leaves his work. He also leaves his village of Tekoa, south of Jerusalem, and his country of Judah. He travels 20 miles north of his home to Israel's border town of Bethel, one of the worship centers in the northern Jewish nation.

**Amos leaves his flocks to deliver a message
(1:1; 7:12–15)** •••

The message Amos delivers is blunt. "The Lord said: 'I will punish Israel for countless crimes, and I won't change my mind. They sell honest people for money, and the needy are sold for the price of sandals. They smear the poor in the dirt and push aside those who are helpless'" (2:6–7)

For this, and more, God says he will "crush you, just as a wagon full of grain crushes to the ground. No matter how fast you run, you won't escape. No matter how strong you are, you will lose your strength and your life" (2:13–14).

In fact, the nation is strong and prosperous. Optimism is high. So the gloom and doom message of Amos is a bit hard for the citizens to swallow.

"I will punish Israel"

••• **(2:1–3:15)**

You women of Samaria are fat cows!" Amos says on behalf of the Lord. A more literal translation calls them "cows of Bashan." In Bible times, cattle from Bashan, in southern Syria, are famous as pampered, prime stock, well fed and well bred.

"You mistreat and abuse the poor and needy," Amos accuses these women. "Your time is coming. Not one of you will be left— you will be taken away by sharp hooks" (4:1–2). (Pictures chiseled into stone show Assyrian soldiers leading prisoners on ropes attached to hooks pierced through the noses or lips of captives.)

Amos says God has tried to get their attention, to convince them to return to righteous living. He has withheld rain. He has sent locusts to devour their orchards. He has even killed many people. "Even then," God says, "you rejected me. . . . Now, Israel, I myself will deal with you. Get ready to face your God" (4:8, 12).

**Rich people oppress the poor
(4:1–13)** •••

Even now, at this late date, God gives Israel a chance to mend its ways. "Turn back to the Lord," Amos pleads, "and you will live. If you don't, the Lord will attack like fire" (5:6).

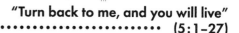

Until the Jews stop doing wrong and start doing right, God won't receive their worship. "I won't accept your offerings or animal sacrifices—not even your very best. No more of your noisy songs! I won't listen when you play your harps" (5:22–23).

What God wants is for his people to "let justice and fairness flow like a river that never runs dry" (5:24).

"Turn back to me, and you will live"
(5:1–27)

Israel is a crooked nation. God shows this to Amos in a vision.

"The Lord showed me a vision of himself standing beside a wall and holding a string with a weight tied to the end of it. The string and weight had been used to measure the straightness of the wall" (7:7).

What this plumb line shows is that the people of Israel "don't measure up." The wall is crooked. And like all crooked walls, it must come down.

Both literally and figuratively, the walls of Israel eventually collapse during a war instigated by God. "I will send war," Amos says, on behalf of God.

God measures Israel with a plumb line
(7:1–17)

Even if Israel refuses to repent—and refuse they do—all is not lost. Though God's contract with the Jews, spelled out in the law of Moses, gives him the right to annihilate Israel for breach of contract and to sever all relationship with any survivors, God refuses to do so.

Instead—even before the punishment arrives—God gives Israel a hopeful message. It's the final word he chooses to leave with them. "In the future," he says, "I will rebuild David's fallen kingdom. I will build it from its ruins" (9:11).

The rebuilding of Israel
(9:11–15)

Reviews

A prophecy fulfilled. "My eyes have seen what a sinful nation you are, and I'll wipe you out," God said through Amos. "Israelites who remain faithful will be scattered among the nations" (9:8 - 9).

Amos predicted this in the mid-700s B.C., when Israel's economy and national confidence were riding high. The superpowers of Assyria and Egypt weren't a threat because they were occupied elsewhere.

About a year after Israel's confidence-boosting king died, however, Tiglath-pileser rose to power in Assyria. About 40 years after Amos brought his message of doom to Israel, the Assyrians brought the horrifying reality. Israel's capital city of Samaria fell in the winter of 722 B.C.; many survivors were taken away in chains, never to return.

A prophecy not fulfilled. "I'll make Israel prosper again," God said. "I'll plant your roots deep in the land I have given you, and you won't ever be uprooted again" (9:14 - 15). That never happened in biblical times, nor does it seem likely that Israel—or any other nation in modern times—could bank on such a promise.

Some Bible experts say this will take place after the second coming of Jesus, either during a 1,000-year reign on earth or perhaps when all of God's people—Jews and non-Jews—are resettled in heaven.

Hope is an add-on. Some say that the book's hopeful conclusion, beginning at 9:11, was added later, perhaps by Amos after he returned home or perhaps centuries later by someone else. They argue that this conclusion reads like an afterthought and doesn't mesh with the prophet's message of doom.

But if the words aren't original to Amos, his prophetic book would have been the only one in the Bible to preach doom exclusively, without any reference to hope. ❏

Encore

- Besides Amos, two other prophets known for their concern about the poor and other social justice issues are Micah and Isaiah.

- You'll find social justice themes addressed in the New Testament by Jesus (Matthew 5–6; 25:31 - 46) and throughout the short book of James. ❏

OBADIAH

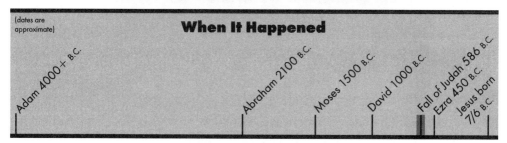

(dates are approximate)

When It Happened

Adam 4000+ B.C.   Abraham 2100 B.C.   Moses 1500 B.C.   David 1000 B.C.   Fall of Judah 586 B.C.   Ezra 450 B.C.   Jesus born 7/6 B.C.

Payback

We don't like to see the bad guys get away with something. Not in books, not in movies, and certainly not in life—especially our life. All human beings seem to share a concern for justice.

Obadiah saw injustice about as bad as it gets. He saw what happened after invaders swarmed on Judah. Jewish refugees ran for their lives to the neighboring country of Edom, racial cousins who, like Judah, had descended from Abraham and Isaac. But did Edom embrace their cousins? No, Edom ambushed them. Then Edom arrested them, turned them over to the invaders, and scavenged Judah for anything left behind.

The Jews would not live to see Edom get what it deserved. But the Jews had this promise from God: "Edom, you will pay in full for what you have done" (15).

If Obadiah and the other prophets said only one thing about God, they said this: God settles his accounts. And he does it justly. Sooner or later, sometimes later, sin is punished. Always. The story of Edom is just one of many examples in the Bible.

> ### Famous Line
>
> • As you have done, it will be done to you (15, New International Version). *Obadiah's warning to the country of Edom is the flip side of the Golden Rule: "Treat others as you want them to treat you"* (Matthew 7:12).

Justice may sometimes be outside our reach. But it's always within God's reach. And in due time, justice will win. The bad guys won't. ❏

Behind the Scenes of Obadiah

Starring Role

Obadiah, a prophet who warns the people of Edom that they'll get the punishment they deserve (1:1)

Plot

Invaders attack and destroy the southern Jewish nation of Judah. Edom, Judah's neighbor south of the Dead Sea, takes delight in this. Edom even arrests the Jewish refugees and turns them over to the invaders. Then Edom raids Judah to steal anything the attackers may have missed.

For this, Obadiah promises, Edom will be wiped out. Judah, on the other hand, will be restored.

What to Look For

Part 1 is doom, Part 2 is hope. Verses 1–14 talk about how God will punish the people of Edom for their cruelty. The rest of the short book (verses 15–21) promises that the Jews will one day return to their land, and will even capture the land of their enemies, including Edom.

Author and Date

Obadiah is the prophet who wrote this book. We know nothing about him except that he had a common name that means "worshiper of the Lord."

Because Obadiah talks about Edom's treachery against Judah, Bible scholars assume the book was written sometime after 586 B.C. That's when Babylon conquered Judah, with support from Edom.

> **Did You Know?**
>
> • The Jews and Edomites were related. Jews descended from Jacob. Edomites descended from his twin brother Esau.
>
> • Obadiah is the shortest book in the Old Testament, with only one chapter and 21 verses.
>
> • Edom was famous for its wise men. One of Job's well-educated friends came from there (Job 2:11).

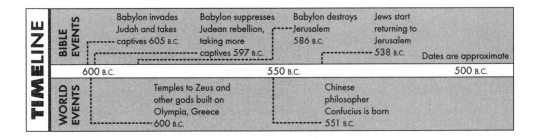

TIMELINE

BIBLE EVENTS
Babylon invades Judah and takes captives 605 B.C.
Babylon suppresses Judean rebellion, taking more captives 597 B.C.
Babylon destroys Jerusalem 586 B.C.
Jews start returning to Jerusalem 538 B.C.
Dates are approximate

600 B.C.   550 B.C.   500 B.C.

WORLD EVENTS
Temples to Zeus and other gods built on Olympia, Greece 600 B.C.
Chinese philosopher Confucius is born 551 B.C.

On Location

The events unfold in the southern Jewish country of Judah, and in Edom south of the Dead Sea. When Babylon conquered Judah, the Edomites collaborated with the invaders, working against their Hebrew cousins. ❏

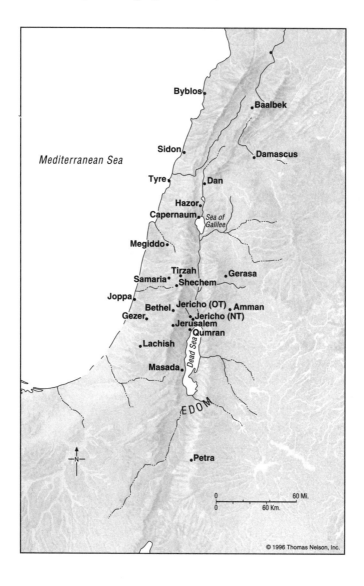

© 1996 Thomas Nelson, Inc.

Big Scene from Obadiah

The people of Edom live in mountaintop fortresses, secure in their defenses. "I will still bring you down," God promises, "even if you fly higher than an eagle or nest among the stars" (4).

What God vows to do is wipe them out and give their land to others. The reason? The Edomites, descendants of Esau, celebrate and even contribute to the destruction of Judah, descendants of Esau's twin brother, Jacob.

After invaders—probably the Babylonians—conquer Judah, the people of Edom tour the destroyed Jewish cities "sneering and stealing." Worse, they round up Jewish refugees and turn them over to the invaders.

It's true that God is punishing the Jews for their sins. But that doesn't give Edom the right to gloat or to profit from Judah's disaster. Yet Edom does both.

One day, when the Jews are done suffering the consequences of their sin, God promises to let them return home. When that happens, "Israel will be a fire, and Edom will be straw going up in flames" (18).

Obadiah's promise: Edom will fall (1–14) •

Reviews

Rock City abandoned. Obadiah says that though the people of Edom live in a rock fortress, they will be wiped out (3, 9). In Jordan, south of the Dead Sea and near the border with Israel, archaeologists have studied Petra—an Edomite city with homes and temples carved into the solid rock of a hillside.

What they found there and in other Edomite cities is that by the 400s B.C. Arabs had driven the people of Edom from their land. Ironically, the Edom refugees fled to Judah, where they lived. By the first century A.D., King Herod of the Jews was recognized as the ruler of Edom. But in A.D. 70, when Rome crushed a nationwide Jewish rebellion, the people of Edom disappeared from history.

The ruins of Petra are now a tourist attraction.

Obadiah the plagiarist? Compare verses 1–9 with Jeremiah 49:7–22. They're so much alike that either Obadiah was drawing from Jeremiah's work, or vice versa. Another possibility is that both men drew from the work of yet another prophet.

In our day, this would border on plagiarism. But in ancient times, there were no copyright laws. And, besides, both men credited the source of the words: God.

Throughout the Old and New Testaments, writers often referred to prophecies and teachings mentioned elsewhere in the Bible. Sometimes, the writers simply quoted the material. Other times, they condensed it or commented on it, in much the same way as preachers do today. Chronicles, for example, expands on some of the events described in Kings. ❏

Encore

• Read Jeremiah 49:7–22. The message is nearly identical to Obadiah 1–9.

• For other prophecies against Edom, read Amos 1:11–12; Isaiah 34; and Ezekiel 25:12–14. ❏

JONAH

(dates are approximate)

When It Happened

Adam 4000+ B.C.

Abraham 2100 B.C.

Moses 1500 B.C.

David 1000 B.C.

Divided Kingdom 931 B.C.

Fall of Israel 722 B.C.

Ezra 450 B.C.

Jesus born 7/6 B.C.

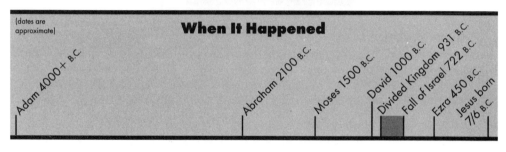

Prophet Overboard

This is not your standard book of prophecy.

It's the only book in which a prophet gets swallowed by a fish. And it's the only prophetic book that doesn't have a collection of prophecies. Instead, it serves up a minuscule one-sentence prophecy, which turns out wrong.

God tells the prophet Jonah to go east and deliver a message of doom to Assyria. Instead, Jonah goes west. He boards a ship on the Mediterranean. The Bible doesn't say why he ran. Maybe he was afraid the story would turn out like it did, and that he would be mortified when his prophecy didn't come true. Or perhaps he couldn't get enthusiastic about delivering death threats to an empire that thought fine art—suitable for framing on palace walls—was stone carvings that showed captured enemies getting impaled on stakes.

The Assyrians were ruthless. For entertainment, Assyrian soldiers cut open the stomach of live prisoners, inserted a live cat, and swiftly sewed the stomach back up. Then they watched the cat claw its way out.

In all of the Bible, Jonah is the only prophet of God whose ministry was not directed to the Jews. Despite his reservations, Jonah took his ministry to Assyria. In Jonah's time there was probably no better way to show that God's love is available to everyone. ❏

Famous Line

- The Lord sent a big fish to swallow Jonah (1:17).

Behind the Scenes of Jonah

⭐ Starring Role

Jonah, a Jewish prophet who reluctantly takes God's message to an Assyrian city (1:1)

📖 Plot

God tells Jonah to go to Nineveh, a huge city deep within the feared Assyrian Empire. Jonah's assignment is to warn the citizens that God will destroy their city in 40 days.

Jonah apparently fears the Assyrians more than he fears God, so he boards a ship headed in the opposite direction, some scholars think to Spain. A fierce storm erupts. To appease God, the sailors throw Jonah overboard. The prophet is swallowed by a large fish of some kind. Three days later the fish vomits Jonah onto a beach.

From there, Jonah walks to Nineveh and delivers the message. To his dismay, the people repent and God spares them. Angry that his prophecy hasn't come true, Jonah goes to the desert where he sits and pouts. The book ends abruptly with God explaining that he has a right to show mercy on the 120,000 citizens of Nineveh.

Did You Know?

• The Bible doesn't say a whale swallowed Jonah, only that a "big fish" did.

• In predicting his resurrection, Jesus compares his three days in the grave to the three days Jonah spends inside the fish (Matthew 12:40).

🎥 What to Look For

Only one sentence of prophecy. Books by other prophets contain a lot of prophecies. Not Jonah. It has one prophetic sentence: "Forty days from now, Nineveh will be destroyed!" (3:4). The rest of this short book tells the story of what leads up to this prophecy, and what happens afterward.

God's compassion extending beyond the Jews. Many Jews in Bible times consider themselves to be not just the chosen people of God, but the only people of God—the only ones who worship him, and the only ones he cares about. But as in the story of Ruth, a woman from Moab, the story of Jonah confirms that God cares deeply about non-Jewish people as well.

TIMELINE	BIBLE EVENTS	Jeroboam begins his 41-year reign ┌----- 786 B.C.		Jonah goes to Nineveh, perhaps before end of Jeroboam's reign ┌----- 746 B.C.	Dates are approximate
		800 B.C.	750 B.C.		700 B.C.
	WORLD EVENTS		Solar eclipse confirmed in Chinese history └----- 775 B.C.	Assyrians choose Nineveh as capital, and start rebuilding it 705 B.C. --------------	

🖥 Author and Date

We don't know if Jonah wrote the book, or if someone else did. But the story is about "Jonah, son of Amittai," a Galilean prophet from a village near Nazareth. This same "Jonah, son of Amittai" is identified as a prophet who supported King Jeroboam's successful efforts to expand the borders of Israel in the late 700s B.C. (2 Kings 14:25).

If Jonah wrote the book, he probably did it during the eighth century B.C., perhaps during the reign of Jeroboam (786–746 B.C.). It is possible, however, that someone else—perhaps centuries later—recorded this short, dramatic story that had been passed along by word of mouth for generations. The statement that Nineveh "was" a great city (3:3) could suggest the book was written after Babylon destroyed the city in 612 B.C.

🌍 On Location

The story begins in Israel, continues somewhere aboard a ship in the Mediterranean Sea, then inside a fish. It ends in Nineveh, an Assyrian city in what is now northern Iraq. ❏

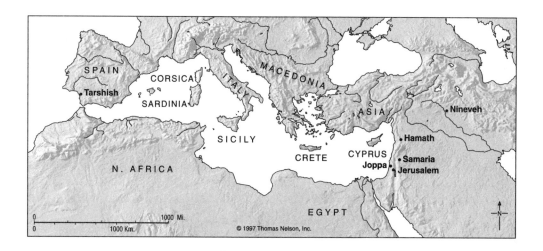

Big Scenes from Jonah

When God orders Jonah into the heart of the feared Assyrian Empire, to warn the people of Nineveh that their city is going to be destroyed, Jonah runs away. He books passage on a ship headed in the opposite direction.

God churns up a storm that nearly swamps the ship. Finally, in desperation, the sailors turn to prayer. Jonah confesses that he is the cause of their trouble, and he advises them to throw him overboard. Initially, they refuse and try rowing back to shore. But when they realize it's hopeless, they throw him overboard, and the sea calms down.

Jonah is swallowed by a huge fish of some type. He remains inside for three days, praying a mystifying prayer of thanks to God for rescuing him. Then the fish vomits him up onto a beach.

Jonah overboard
(1:1—2:10) •••

Jonah walks to Nineveh and delivers the assigned message: "Forty days from now, Nineveh will be destroyed!" (3:4).

For some unexplained reason, the Assyrians believe him—a stranger from another country. Yet back in Israel and Judah, the Jews are ignoring God's prophets.

The Assyrians—even the king—stop eating and drinking, dress in ragged clothes, and sit in the dust. They do this to show their sorrow. They won't even let their animals eat or drink.

When God sees this, he has pity and does not destroy them as he had planned.

Jonah preaches in Nineveh
(3:1–10)
•••

Jonah is incensed. "I knew from the very beginning that you wouldn't destroy Nineveh," he complains to God. "You are a kind and merciful God, and you are very patient. You always show love, and you don't like to punish anyone, not even foreigners. Now let me die! I'd be better off dead" (4:2–3).

Ironically, Jonah is one of the few prophets in the Bible who is successful. He convinces the people to repent. Yet he considers this anything but success. As far as he is concerned, success requires the annihilation of the 120,000 citizens of Nineveh. Fortunately for Nineveh, God disagrees.

The point of the entire story is that God deeply cares about everyone, and he is eager to show mercy to anyone genuinely sorry for the wrongs they have done. Anyone.

Jonah is furious that his prophecy doesn't come true
(4:1–10) ••

Reviews

God cares about non-Jews, too. The main point of the story—that God cares about everyone, not just the Jews—is a point repeated throughout the Bible.

When God selected Abraham to become the father of the Jewish nation, God said "Everyone on earth will be blessed because of you" (Genesis 12:3). Later, through the prophet Isaiah, God told the Jews, "I have placed you here as a light for other nations; you must take my saving power to everyone on earth" (49:6).

And Paul, writing to Christians in Rome, said that if a person has faith in God it doesn't matter if that person is a Jew or a Gentile. "There is only one Lord, and he is generous to everyone who asks for his help. All who call out to the Lord will be saved" (Romans 10: 12-13).

History or parable? Some Bible scholars say that the story of Jonah never really happened. The story, they argue, is a parable that uses the name of a real prophet, in much the same way that Jesus' parable about Lazarus and a rich man may refer to the Lazarus that Jesus raised from the dead.

The story shares a lot in common with short, dramatic parables that teach a message. For example, the 48 verses are packed with captivating miracles—the story's an attention grabber. And it ends abruptly, as soon as the moral is delivered. In addition, Jonah is like none of the other books of prophecy: it's nearly all story, with only one sentence of prophecy. Also, there is no record in Assyrian documents to confirm Jonah's story that Nineveh repented.

Other Bible experts say the story did take place. They argue that Jonah is mentioned in 2 Kings 14:25, and that Jesus compared his own burial with that of Jonah's three days in the belly of the fish (Matthew 12:40).

But whether Jonah is history or parable, the message remains unchanged: God cares about everyone, and he wants us to do the same. ❑

Encore

- For another story about God showing mercy to a non-Jew, read the short book of Ruth.

- For more about God's concern for non-Jews, read Genesis 12:1-3; Isaiah 42:6-7; 49:6; Romans 10—11.

- For background on what life was like in Israel during Jonah's day, read the book of Amos. The two prophets ministered about the same time. ❑

MICAH

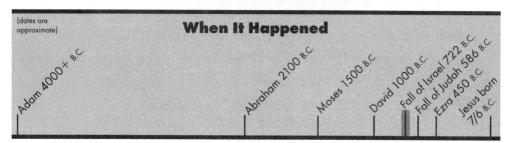

(dates are approximate)

When It Happened

Adam 4000+ B.C.

Abraham 2100 B.C.

Moses 1500 B.C.

David 1000 B.C.

Fall of Israel 722 B.C.

Fall of Judah 586 B.C.

Ezra 450 B.C.

Jesus born 7/6 B.C.

Painting a Portrait of God

Job one for the Bible is to show human beings what God is like. Micah shows there are two sides to God.

There's holiness, which means he's good and just. He takes a stand against us when we become evil and unjust.

And there's love, which means he's like a compassionate father. No matter what we do, good or bad, he loves us.

The book of Micah reads like the flip of a coin. Heads, you've sinned and God will punish you. Tails, he loves you and he'll forgive you. In an ongoing cycle, Micah identifies the sins of the Jews and the consequences they'll have to face. Then he consoles them with the promise that, no matter what, God loves them.

Three times Micah warns the Jews that because of their nation's long-standing sinfulness, the nation will die. Then he promises a saving miracle: one day the nation will be restored. Not because the Jews deserve it for good conduct, but because God loves them and forgives them.

This isn't just a history lesson. It's a glimpse into the character of God. What he did for the Jews, he continues to do for all people. He stands against people who do evil, but loves them nonetheless. ❏

Famous Lines

- They will beat their swords into plowshares and their spears into pruning hooks. Nation will not take up sword against nation, nor will they train for war anymore (4:3, New International Version).

- Bethlehem . . . you are one of the smallest towns in the nation of Judah. But the Lord will choose one of your people to rule the nation (5:2). *Because of this verse, some Jews in ancient times believed the Messiah would be born in Bethlehem, birthplace of Jesus.*

- What does the LORD require of you but to do justly, to love mercy, and to walk humbly with your God? (6:8, New King James Version).

Behind the Scenes of Micah

⭐ Starring Role

Micah, a rural Judean prophet who criticizes the leaders of Israel and Judah (1:1)

📖 Plot

This is not a story, but a collection of prophecies written as poetry. Micah denounces corrupt officials—religious and political—in both the northern Jewish nation of Israel and the southern nation of Judah. Judges take bribes, priests teach God's word only for money, and prophets tell fortunes for profit. Rulers mislead the people, nobles take advantage of the poor, and the masses take their pleas to idols.

For this, Micah says, God will destroy both nations. Assyria, in fact, destroys Israel during Micah's lifetime, in 722 B.C. Assyria also overruns Judah about 20 years later, stopping short of destroying it. But another nation, Babylon, decimates Judah in 586 B.C.

Micah promises, however, that a time will come when the Jewish nation will be restored and worship God.

> ### Did You Know?
>
> • Like Isaiah, Micah may have walked around naked for a time. This was to graphically show the fate of future prisoners who would be stripped and deported (compare 1:8 with Isaiah 20:1-4).
>
> • Micah may have personally known several famous prophets who lived when he did: Isaiah, Jonah, Hosea, Amos.

🎥 What to Look For

A pattern of doom and salvation. The prophecies are arranged in an obvious pattern: doom (1:1—2:11), salvation (2:12–13), doom (3:1–12), salvation (4:1—5:15), doom (6:1—7:7), salvation (7:8–20).

Old Testament prophets have an earned reputation as messengers of doom. But no book of prophecy in the Bible is without hope. Like the other prophets, Micah warns that sin has consequences and is punishable by God. But Micah also assures that punishment is not the last word. God still loves the people, and when the punishment is over he will prove it.

Charges of injustice. Micah, like the prophet Amos who lived at the same time he did, criticizes the leaders and nobles for misusing their power.

TIMELINE	BIBLE EVENTS		Micah begins several decades of ministry	Israel is destroyed by Assyria	
			- - - - - 742 B.C.	- - - - - 722 B.C.	Dates are approximate
	750 B.C.		725 B.C.		700 B.C.
	WORLD EVENTS		Ivory carvings popular in Samaria, Phoenicia, Egypt	Merchants in Greece prosper, farmers starve	
			- - - - - 750 B.C.	- - - - - 725 B.C.	

"Listen to me, you rulers of Israel!" God says through Micah. "You know right from wrong, but you prefer to do evil instead of what is right. You skin my people alive. You strip off their flesh, break their bones, cook it all in a pot, and gulp it down" (3:1–3). Using this kind of stark, symbolic imagery, Micah attacks the rich and powerful for wallowing in wealth and self-indulgence. Not only do they leave the helpless to fend for themselves, the leaders make dishonest decisions against the poor. They cheat families out of homes and land. They worship wealth, not God. They revere power, not justice. They admire achievement, not mercy.

Author and Date

The prophecies are from Micah, a rural prophet who lived in a small village about 25 miles southwest of Jerusalem.

Verse one says that his ministry took place during the reigns of three Judean kings: Jothan, Ahaz, and Hezekiah. These men reigned between 742 and 687 B.C. Decades later, the prophet Jeremiah quoted Micah, confirming that during the days of Hezekiah, Micah predicted "Jerusalem will be plowed under and left in ruins" (Jeremiah 26:18; compare to Micah 3:12). Micah lived to see the Assyrians destroy Israel.

On Location

Micah delivers his prophecies in the southern Jewish nation of Judah. But he criticizes both Judah and the northern Jewish nation of Israel, often addressing them by the names of their capital cities: Jerusalem (Judah) and Samaria (Israel). ❏

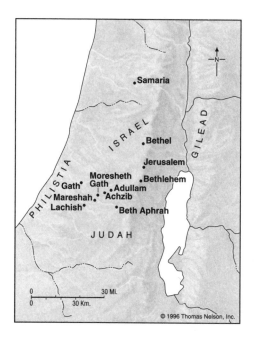

Big Scenes from Micah

For their many sins against God and each other, both Jewish nations will be destroyed.

"The LORD will leave Samaria in ruins—merely an empty field where vineyards are planted," Micah prophesies. "He will scatter its stones and destroy its foundations. Samaria's idols will be smashed" (1:6–7).

What happens to Samaria and the entire northern Jewish nation of Israel will also happen to Jerusalem and the southern nation of Judah. "Judah is doomed. Jerusalem will fall" (1:9).

Among the host of charges that God levels against the Jewish nations are these: "You hate justice and twist the truth. You make cruelty and murder a way of life in Jerusalem. You leaders accept bribes for dishonest decisions. You priests and prophets teach and preach, but only for money" (3:9–11).

Once Samaria, a capital city, now a vineyard (1:1–16) •

God refuses to abandon the Jewish people because of their sins. They *will* have to face the consequences of their sinful choices, but not forever. In the future, Micah prophesies, the Jewish people will repent of their sins, stop doing evil, and return to God. In return, God will bless them by sending a chosen leader—a messiah—who would lead into peace, like a shepherd leads sheep to quiet waters.

"Bethlehem," Micah says, "you are one of the smallest towns in the nation of Judah. But the LORD will choose one of your people to rule the nation—someone whose family goes back to ancient times" (5:2).

Seven hundred years later, wise men from an eastern nation followed a light to Israel because they believed that unusual astronomical events such as comets were signs that a future ruler had been born. When they arrived in Jerusalem and asked King Herod if they could see the child who had been born king of the Jews, Herod was upset. *He* was the king of the Jews, and he had no newborn son. Furthermore, he had already killed his brother to secure the throne. He would kill this newborn threat, too, if he could. Herod turned to the religious leaders and asked them where the messiah would be born. They turned to the book of Micah and found their answer: Bethlehem.

A ruler will be born in Bethlehem

• **(5:2–5)**

Reviews

Born in Bethlehem. About 700 years before Jesus was born in Bethlehem, Micah prophesied that the Messiah would come from this tiny village on the outskirts of Jerusalem.

Today, pilgrims go to Bethlehem to visit the oldest church in the world, built over a cave believed to be the birthplace of Jesus. The first known reference to the cave comes from Justin Martyr, a Christian who was born about the time the apostle John died, around A.D. 100. John took care of Mary after the Crucifixion. It seems reasonable that Mary told John where Jesus was born, and that the site was known and revered among Christians living in the Jerusalem area.

In A.D. 135, Roman Emperor Hadrian destroyed all sacred sites. He replaced them with shrines to Roman gods. Over a cave stable in Bethlehem, he built a temple to the god Adonis—ironically, known for his death and resurrection. Each winter, Adonis is said to go to the underworld. Each spring, he returns to earth.

Two centuries later another Roman emperor, Constantine, replaced the shrines with churches. The Church of the Nativity was built in about A.D. 325 to commemorate the birth of Jesus. It stands today.

Two themes, two writers. Some suspect the book was written by two writers—one who penned the words of doom, and another who wrote the words of hope. As the theory goes, one of the writers or perhaps a later editor compiled the prophecies into their current pattern, alternating the themes of doom and salvation.

The presumption here is that one writer couldn't write in two styles. But even today, writers can and do jump from style to style, genre to genre. ❏

Encore

- Amos was another prophet concerned about social problems.

- Read Matthew 2:1-16 to see how the Jews of Jesus' day interpreted Micah's prophecy about a Jewish leader coming from Bethlehem (5:2).

- To read more about the two sides of God—judgment and mercy—turn to Nahum.

- For more about the kind of social concern that Micah expressed in 6:8, read Isaiah 1 and the Sermon on the Mount (Matthew 5:1–7:29). ❏

NAHUM

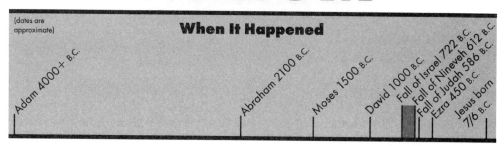

(dates are approximate)

When It Happened

Adam 4000+ B.C.

Abraham 2100 B.C.

Moses 1500 B.C.

David 1000 B.C.

Fall of Israel 722 B.C.

Fall of Nineveh 612 B.C.

Fall of Judah 586 B.C.

Ezra 450 B.C.

Jesus born 7/6 B.C.

Middle Eastern Reign of Terror to End

It seems an odd coincidence that Nahum, a prophet whose name means "comfort," delivers a message that sounds entirely vindictive.

At first glance it looks as though the Jews are supposed to take comfort in hearing the good news that God will soon annihilate Assyria, an empire that has too long terrorized the entire Middle East.

"Nineveh," Nahum says, addressing the Assyrian capital, "now it's your turn!" (3:11).

The language of Nahum is strong and staccato, like the rapid-fire jabs of an avenger. Yet the prophecy, written as a poem full of emotional symbolism, was not meant to condone revenge and violent retaliation. It was written to assure the Jewish people that Assyria's reign of terror was almost over.

Evil is real. The Jews knew that all too well. But so is the justice of God. Sooner or later, but always in God's timing, evil is stopped and the guilty are punished. It's in the deliverance from evil—not the punishment of the guilty—that the Jews found comfort.

In the meantime, throughout the suffering, the Jews could take heart in knowing that "the LORD is good, a refuge in times of trouble" (1:7, New International Version). We can take comfort in that, too. This doesn't necessarily mean we'll escape unharmed, or even with our physical life intact. But we will endure, and evil won't. ❏

Famous Lines

- The LORD is slow to anger (1:3, King James Version).

- Your people are sheep without a shepherd (3:18). *Nahum's description of Assyria, whose leaders have been killed by invaders.*

Behind the Scenes of Nahum

★ Starring Role

Nahum, Judean prophet who vows that God will punish Assyria for its cruelty (1:1)

Plot

For centuries the Assyrian Empire, headquartered in what is now northern Iraq, has been terrorizing the Middle East. At will, they crush nations. One of the victims is the northern Jewish nation of Israel, wiped out in 722 B.C. Many survivors are deported to central Assyria—especially craftsmen, teachers, and other skilled people who can make a valuable contribution to the empire.

Roughly 100 years later, while Assyria is still bullying the Mediterranean world, the Jewish prophet Nahum has a vision about the empire. He sees its savagery and its defiance of God. And he hears what God says he will do to Assyria: "I will send you to the grave. . . . You will never again make victims of others" (1:14; 2:13). Nahum delivers this message to the people of his nation, who are currently being forced to serve the empire by paying taxes to it.

> ### Did You Know?
>
> • English poet Lord Bryon (1788–1824) in his poem *The Destruction of Sennacherib* portrays the fierceness of the Assyrian army: The Assyrian came down like the wolf on the fold, and his cohorts were gleaming in purple and gold.
>
> • About 100 years before Nahum, the prophet Jonah told Nineveh it would be destroyed in 40 days. The people repented and were spared.

What to Look For

Assyrian terror. Nahum describes an empire so vicious and brutal that it epitomizes evil. When the Assyrians capture a city, they are merciless. Holding babies by the ankles, they swing them like clubs and dash them against stone walls. Members of enemy royal families are auctioned off to the highest bidder, or tortured and executed. (See "Vicious Assyria" in Reviews.)

Poetic justice. Nahum uses poetry and graphic symbolism to describe the coming destruction of Assyria. Don't read the descriptions literally. They are meant to express the seriousness of Assyria's crimes and the satisfaction that

TIMELINE	BIBLE EVENTS			
		Earliest possible date of Nahum's vision 663 B.C.		Dates are approximate
	700 B.C.		650 B.C.	600 B.C.
	WORLD EVENTS	Assyria sacks Thebes, Egypt 663 B.C.	Assyrian empire begins to crumble when King Ashurbanipal dies 630 B.C.	Nineveh—Assyrian capital—destroyed 612 B.C.

the Jews and the rest of the world will get when they find themselves freed from this international bully.

Author and Date

"I am Nahum from Elkosh," the book begins. We know nothing else about him. He is not mentioned in any other book of the Bible. Even the location of Elkosh remains a mystery.

Nahum probably had the vision described in this book sometime between 663 and 612 B.C. He said Thebes Egypt had already fallen (3:8–10); it fell to Assyria in 663 B.C. And he predicted the fall of Nineveh, which Babylon and coalition forces captured in 612 B.C. This time frame places Nahum alongside two other prophets: Zephaniah and a young Jeremiah.

On Location

The Assyrian Empire, centered in what is now Iraq, is the target of Nahum's prophecy. But the message seems intended for the people of Judah, to assure them that God will soon put an end to Assyria's tyranny. ❏

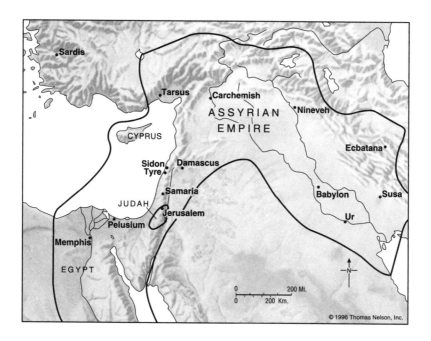

Big Scene from Nahum

To Assyria's complete surprise—but as Nahum had prophesied—the combined forces of Babylonians and Medes strike at the heart of the empire. Nineveh falls.

Assyria had been the evil superpower of the Middle East for centuries—taking whatever it wanted, whenever it wanted. It had taken the northern Jewish nation of Israel in 722 B.C., swallowing it whole and deporting the citizens. Afterward the empire had allowed the southern nation of Judah to survive, but only if Judah joined other countries in annually feeding money into the Assyrian treasury at Nineveh.

It must have been hard for the Jews to believe what Nahum predicted: "Nineveh is doomed! Destroyed!" (2:10).

For Assyria's long history of cruelty, God promised he would send an army to destroy them. The Babylonians and Medes arrived at Nineveh's doorstep in 612 B.C. Nahum had said that when this happens, "the river gates fly open" (2:6)—perhaps a reference to the Khoser River that ran

through the city to the nearby Tigris River. The writer of the ancient book *Babylonian Chronicles* says a flood washed away some of the walls. Perhaps the invaders broke a dam for this very purpose.

"The Lord All-Powerful is against you, Nineveh," Nahum said several years before the attack. "You will never again make victims of others or send messengers to threaten everyone on this earth" (2:13).

Nineveh is so utterly destroyed that its massive ruins do not resurface until 1845, when archaeologists finally uncover them.

**Nineveh falls
(2:1–13)** •

Reviews

Vicious Assyria. Nahum and other Bible prophets paint Assyria's portrait with dark and bloody colors. Assyria invaded nations as a source of income, slaughtered the young and old alike, then mutilated and tortured to death the leaders. Entire countries—such as the northern Jewish nation of Israel—were deported, and their homeland resettled with Assyrian pioneers.

The findings of archaeologists confirm that Assyria was as brutal as the Bible says. In laying siege to a city, Assyrian soldiers would impale captured enemies on wooden spikes as thick as a fencepost. Some Assyrian kings ordered the corpses stacked like cord wood beside the city wall. Assyrian king Shalmaneser III built a pyramid of decapitated heads in front of a besieged city.

Assyrian kings bragged about their battlefield ferociousness by hiring artists to recreate the grisly scenes in stone carvings mounted on the palace walls.

Vengeful book, vengeful God. Some say Nahum reads like a book solely about revenge, starring the god of vengeance. In fact, they say, it reads like the exact opposite of Jonah, a story about God showing mercy to the Assyrians.

"I will pull up your skirt," God tells the Assyrians through Nahum, "and let the nations and kingdoms stare at your nakedness. I will cover you with garbage, treat you like trash, and rub you in the dirt" (3:5-6).

This vicious-sounding poetry is not a portrait of the character of God; it's a mirror held up to the Assyrians. For treating others like trash, God was going to allow invaders to attack and defeat Assyria.

Pulling up Assyria's skirt is a metaphor that means this proud empire would suffer international humiliation. In ancient times, people publicly humiliated prostitutes and adulteresses by stripping them or by lifting their dress (Ezekiel 16:37-39). "Nakedness" was perhaps a Hebrew play on words, since it sounds much like "exile" which is what the Assyrians did to many captured enemies.

The message behind the evocative poetry is that though it looks like no one can stop Assyria from terrorizing the world, God can and will. ❏

Encore

- To see God showing compassion to Assyria, read Jonah.

- To read more about the two sides of God—judgment and mercy—turn to Micah.

- Just as Nahum portrays God as a divine warrior who will rescue his people from tyranny (1:2-10), so does the prophet Habakkuk (3:3-15). ❏

HABAKKUK

(dates are approximate)

When It Happened

Adam 4000+ B.C. Abraham 2100 B.C. Moses 1500 B.C. David 1000 B.C. Fall of Israel 722 B.C. Fall of Nineveh 612 B.C. Fall of Judah 586 B.C. Ezra 450 B.C. Jesus born 7/6 B.C.

Where Is God When People Suffer?

Why does God sit by and do nothing when good people suffer at the hands of the wicked? That's Habakkuk's question for God.

Judah had become a moral sewer. It bred extortion, violence, and swarms of criminals out for blood. Habakkuk wanted it to stop.

So what does God do? He decides that Judah should suffer at the hands of the Babylonians. Judah was a nation of saints compared to the Babylonians. Sure, the Judeans ignored the laws of God, sold debtors into slavery, and cheated the poor into starvation. But the Babylonians didn't even pretend to worship God, they stole entire countries, and raped the women and girls to death.

Habakkuk thought a follow-up question was in order: Why the Babylonians, of all people?

God didn't give a direct answer. He did assure Habakkuk that the Babylonians would eventually face their own judgment day. But essentially God left the prophet with this terse response: "Let all the world be silent—the LORD is present in his holy temple" (2:20).

When you can't understand what's going on, God was telling Habakkuk, understand this: the Lord is in control.

That was all this prophet needed to hear. Already—some 2,600 years ago—God had a reputation for knowing what he was doing. ❑

Famous Lines

• The just shall live by his faith (2:4, King James Version). God's expressed desire that people learn to trust him. Martin Luther zeroed in on this idea, as paraphrased in Romans 1:17, to launch the Protestant movement. Luther argued that people are saved by faith in God, not by performing church rituals.

• Fig trees may no longer bloom, or vineyards produce grapes . . . but I will still celebrate because the LORD God saves me (3:17-18).

Behind the Scenes of Habakkuk

⭐ Starring Role

Habakkuk, a prophet in Judah who asks God why he's not punishing the wicked (1:1)

📖 Plot

Habakkuk has a vision of engaging God in a two-way conversation. The prophet begins by asking God why he's allowing Judah to go unpunished for "terrible injustice. . . . violence, lawlessness, crime, and cruelty" (1:3). God answers that he will punish Judah by sending the Babylonians to destroy the nation and "gather captives like handfuls of sand" (1:9).

Habakkuk protests that God shouldn't use the Babylonians to punish the Jews. "Don't sit by in silence while they gobble down people who are better than they are," Habakkuk pleads (1:13).

God replies that he will punish the Babylonians later. But in the meantime he wants his people to learn to trust him. Habakkuk responds with a masterful and moving song of confidence in God.

🎥 What to Look For

A prophet talking with God. This is an unusual book of prophecy. Prophets usually deliver God's message to human beings. But here, the prophet is questioning God. So the book is not so much an oracle from God or a story about the life of a prophet as you'll find in other books of prophecy. It's a record of the dialogue between Habakkuk and God.

A song of trust in God. The third and final chapter in this short book is a song of confidence in God. Though Habakkuk is shaken by the news that Baby-

Did You Know?

• A legend recorded in *Bel and the Dragon*, a book of the Apocrypha, reports that Habakkuk took a bowl of stew to Daniel in the lion's den. An angel reportedly transported Habakkuk from Judah to Daniel's location in Babylon, then home again.

• Among the ancient library known as the Dead Sea Scrolls is a commentary on Habakkuk. The author, who lived when Rome occupied Israel, said Habakkuk's references to Babylon stood for Rome. In fact, as Babylon destroyed Jerusalem in 586 B.C., so did Rome in A.D. 70.

TIMELINE	BIBLE EVENTS			
	Habakkuk predicts the fall of Jerusalem (earliest likely date) 612 B.C. ----------------	Babylon invades Judah, takes captives 605 B.C. -----	Babylon suppresses Judean rebellion, taking more captives 597 B.C. ---	Babylon destroys Jerusalem and other Judean cities 586 B.C. Dates are approximate
	625 B.C.		600 B.C.	575 B.C.
	WORLD EVENTS			
	Athens gets a code of laws 621 B.C. --------	Babylon begins 70-year dominance of Middle East 612 B.C.		Babylon defeats Egypt at battle of Carchemish 605 B.C.

lon will conquer his homeland and destroy the holy city of Jerusalem, he praises the miracle-working God of creation and pledges unwavering allegiance to him. This song, like those of Psalms, is later set to music and sung or recited in worship services. As indicated in the closing note to the music director, the song was once accompanied by stringed instruments.

Author and Date

"I am Habakkuk the prophet," the book begins. Habakkuk is not mentioned by name outside this book. But several times the New Testament quotes the phrase from Habakkuk that would later launch the Protestant Reformation: "The just shall live by his faith" (2:4, King James Version; compare this with Romans 1:17; Galatians 3:11; Hebrews 10:38).

Habakkuk likely prophesied in the years just after Assyria had fallen (612 B.C.) but perhaps before the Babylonians had defeated Egypt (605 B.C.) to assume the role of top superpower in the Middle East. Babylon defeated Judah three times in the next 20 years, carrying off hostages each time: 605 B.C., 597 B.C., and 586 B.C. when Jerusalem was leveled.

Other prophets that Habakkuk may have known are Jeremiah, Zephaniah, and Nahum.

On Location

Habakkuk's conversation with God takes place "on the watchtower," probably somewhere along the walls of Jerusalem (2:1). It is here he gets word that the nation of Judah will fall to Babylonian invaders who "laugh at fortresses" (1:10). Judah becomes absorbed into the Babylonian Empire and many of its citizens are relocated. ❑

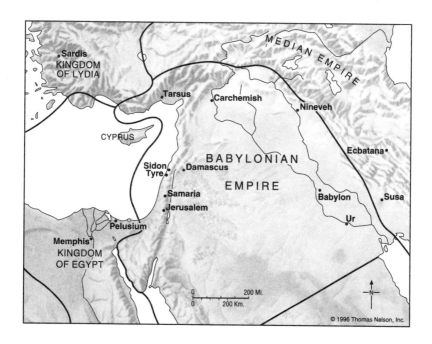

© 1996 Thomas Nelson, Inc.

Big Scene from Habakkuk

Our LORD, how long must I beg for your help?" Habakkuk pleads (1:2). His country of Judah is hopelessly bogged down in sin: "Laws cannot be enforced; justice is always the loser; criminals crowd out honest people and twist the laws around" (1:4).

"I am sending the Babylonians," God replies. "They are fierce and cruel—marching across the land, conquering cities and towns" (1:6).

This isn't the kind of help Habakkuk has in mind. "Don't sit by in silence while they gobble down people who are better than they are," the prophet implores (1:13).

God assures Habakkuk that after the Babylonians finish their job of punishing Judah, they will be punished for their own sins. In the meantime, the job of the righteous is to "live by faith" (2:4)—to trust God.

"I know your reputation," the prophet answers (3:2). On this basis, Habakkuk promises that no matter what happens he will trust in God. And if the Babylonians take everything—stripping vineyards, groves, and fields, and stealing all the livestock—Habakkuk will lean on God. "The LORD gives me strength. He makes my feet as sure as those of a deer, and he helps me stand on the mountains" (3:19).

Awaiting the invasion of Babylon (3:1-19) ••

Reviews

Arguing with God: a biblical tradition. When Habakkuk argued with God, he wasn't breaking new ground. He was joining a town hall meeting filled with inquisitive, respected biblical leaders.

Moses argued that he wasn't a good enough speaker to confront Pharaoh. Gideon couldn't believe God was calling him to lead an army, so he asked for—and got—miracles to prove that God would help him. Job insisted that he didn't deserve the horrors that had robbed him of his children, flocks, and health. Jeremiah resisted becoming a prophet, arguing that he was too young.

God dealt patiently with each of these men, as he did with Habakkuk.

Using evil to do good. Habakkuk fully expected God to punish Judah for becoming such a sinful country. But he was shocked when God told him that Babylon would do the punishing. Babylon was more godless than Judah. This was like assigning Hitler to execute a convicted war criminal, or Charles Manson to run a halfway house for celebrity stalkers.

But one of the Bible's many revelations about God is that he has the power to use evil to do good. For example, after Joseph's brothers sold him to slave traders, Joseph ended up in Egypt, second in power to the king. There, he was responsible for keeping the people from starving during a famine. When his brothers came to Egypt for grain, Joseph told them not to fear him: "You tried to harm me, but God made it turn out for the best, so that he could save all these people" (Genesis 50:20).

God uses people and nations—good and evil—to accomplish his goal of saving humanity from sin and restoring his creation to the paradise that was lost when sin contaminated it. ❑

Encore

- Habakkuk's description of God's power (chapter 3) is much like the description in Nahum 1:2-8.

- For insights from other prophets of the day, read the books of Jeremiah, Zephaniah, and Nahum.

- To see how the New Testament interprets Habakkuk's phrase, "The just shall live by his faith" (2:4, King James Version), read Romans 1:17; Galatians 3:11; Hebrews 10:38.

❑

ZEPHANIAH

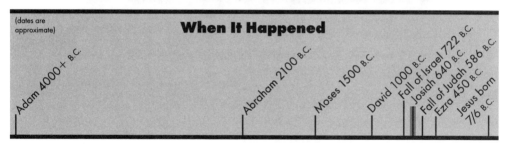

(dates are approximate)

When It Happened

Adam 4000+ B.C.

Abraham 2100 B.C.

Moses 1500 B.C.

David 1000 B.C.

Fall of Israel 722 B.C.

Josiah 640 B.C.

Fall of Judah 586 B.C.

Ezra 450 B.C.

Jesus born 7/6 B.C.

Good-bye, Human Race

This is probably not the book to turn to for comfort on the brink of a nuclear attack or as a monster asteroid speeds toward earth.

Hear the word of the Lord—the first words out of the mouth of the prophet: "I will sweep away everything from the face of the earth" (1:2, New International Version). That's a promise from God.

Zephaniah lived in a day when most Jews didn't worship God any longer. They worshiped gods of other nations, and even sacrificed their children to appease the idols. They cheated each other to accumulate wealth for themselves. They showed nothing but disdain for the people whom God repeatedly told them to take care of: the poor, the widows, the orphans.

God gave the Jews centuries to change their ways. He sent prophet after prophet to warn them about the consequences of their sins—consequences clearly written into the laws of Moses. Now, God had seen enough. Zephaniah said the Lord would punish the Jewish nation and ultimately bring an end to life on this planet.

Yet, the end is not the end.

The prophet also said that God will gather up the faithful to live in a mysterious time and place where sorrow is no more. Zephaniah's last words are that those who love the Lord can trust him, even when they can't trust anyone else. ❏

Famous Line

- I will wipe out the entire human race (1:3). God's promise of a coming judgment. Some scholars see this as extravagant exaggeration, common in ancient poetry, and say it refers to the imminent decimation of Judah. Others take it more literally, saying it refers to the end of humanity, when the faithful are gathered into heaven.

Behind the Scenes of Zephaniah

⭐ Starring Role

Zephaniah, a prophet who predicts the destruction of Judah and the surrounding nations (1:1)

📖 Plot

The three-chapter book of Zephaniah is not a story with a plot, but a prophecy written as a poem. Punishment for sin is the theme.

Judah will be defeated and plundered for a multitude of sins. But the wrath of God doesn't stop there. Zephaniah names countries to the north, south, east, and west of Judah—perhaps symbolizing the four points of the compass—and declares that the Lord will destroy them all. The graphic descriptions read like those of an end-time apocalypse.

Yet the prophet speaks of an assembly of righteous survivors living joyously in a restored Jerusalem. It's unclear if Zephaniah is referring to the city that the Jews rebuilt after their tragic defeat and exile, or to a heavenly city, or both.

🎥 What to Look For

Doom. Tagged by God for destruction are Judah and nations surrounding her on four sides: Philistia (to the west), Moab and Ammon (modern Jordan, east), Ethiopia (south), Assyria (Iraq, north). The "day of the Lord" devastation—brought on by sin—seems to engulf the entire planet. In fact, the prophecy reads like a reversal of the Creation story. For God had created fish, birds, land animals, and human beings, in that order. But now he is going to destroy "people and animals, birds and fish" (1:3).

To the ancient student of Jewish scriptures, the prophesied doom may have conjured up images of destruction as cataclysmic as the Flood. This next catastrophe, however, would apparently come by means of "a furious fire scorching the earth" and leaving the land "like Sodom and Gomorrah" (1:18; 2:9).

Did You Know?

• God sings. Zephaniah says God "celebrates and sings because of you" (3:17). This may be only a poet's way of describing God's joy. On the other hand, it doesn't seem too far-fetched to believe that the one who inspires so many songs could also sing them.

• Zephaniah was probably a prince. He's identified as the great-great-grandson of Hezekiah—likely *the* Hezekiah, former king of Judah (1:1).

TIMELINE				
	BIBLE EVENTS	King Josiah begins 31-year reign 640 B.C.	Zephaniah delivers his prophecy 630 B.C.	Jerusalem destroyed by Babylonians 586 B.C. Dates are approximate
		650 B.C.	600 B.C.	550 B.C.
	WORLD EVENTS	Japan founded, says a legend 660 B.C.	Assyrian Empire begins to crumble when King Ashurbanipal dies 630 B.C.	Horse racing becomes Olympic event 624 B.C.

Joyful survivors. Like all other prophets in the Bible, Zephaniah adds a message of hope. After the punishing destruction, God promises to gather up the scattered survivors who are his true worshipers. United, the people of God will celebrate the end of sorrow, violence, and injustice.

Poetic symbolism. Zephaniah writes in a poetic style that draws from vivid and, at times, exaggerated images. This makes it hard to interpret the words as precisely as we might like. It's clear that he's talking about God punishing the southern Jewish nation of Judah for turning its back on him and worshiping idols. It's also clear that Zephaniah foresees God punishing the surrounding nations. But whether or not the prophet is also foreshadowing the end of human history and the beginning of a new age in a celestial "Jerusalem" is less certain.

Author and Date

Zephaniah is the prophet behind this book. The unusual, four-generation genealogy in the first verse adds credibility to the theory that Zephaniah carried the royal blood of King Hezekiah.

The prophet says he received his message from God during the reign of King Josiah (640–609 B.C.). Josiah assumed the throne at age eight, and by age 20 began making religious reforms, such as tearing down pagan altars (2 Chronicles 34:3). Because Zephaniah describes the rampant idolatry in Judah, he probably prophesied before the reforms began in about 628 B.C. It's quite possible that Zephaniah's warning of a global disaster may have been a catalyst for the spiritual reform.

Zephaniah predicted the fall of Nineveh, so he apparently delivered his message before 612 B.C., when this prophecy was fulfilled.

On Location

Zephaniah delivers his prophecy in the southern Jewish nation of Judah, perhaps in the capital city of Jerusalem. ❏

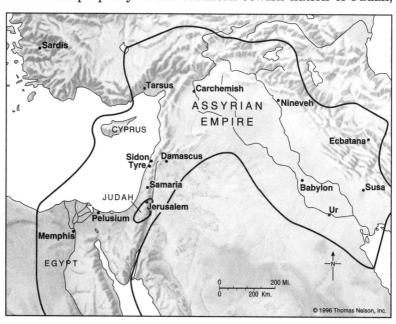

© 1996 Thomas Nelson, Inc.

Big Scene from Zephaniah

I, the LORD, now promise to destroy everything on this earth—people and animals, birds and fish. Everyone who is evil will crash to the ground, and I will wipe out the entire human race" (1:2–3).

This is the jaw-dropping lead of Zephaniah's prophecy. Zephaniah goes on to describe the doomed fate of his own country of Judah, along with the surrounding nations. All are destined for destruction. Judah will be demolished and plundered for abandoning God and worshiping the stars and idols. The other nations will be wiped out for worshiping their own pride, threatening the Jews, and mocking God.

Yet somehow, after God has destroyed the earth in his "fiery anger," he brings together "scattered people . . . true worshipers" who have apparently survived the holocaust (3:8, 10). And with this, a new age dawns. The people who survive "will live right and refuse to tell lies. They will eat and rest with nothing to fear" (3:13).

**The end of all life on this planet
(1:2–3)** ••

Reviews

Judah's tragic fall. Zephaniah's description of the fall of Judah, which took place about 40 years after the prophecy, accurately portrays what happened.

"National leaders and sons of the king" were punished (1:8). King Zedekiah was forced to watch his sons executed. Immediately afterward, his eyes were gouged out.

God's anger flared up "like a furious fire" (1:18). Babylon torched the cities after looting them.

The streets of Jerusalem and other Judean towns were "reduced to ruins and emptied of people" (3:6). The Babylonians knocked over the buildings and walls, then deported the surviving citizens.

The end is near. "The great day of the Lord is coming soon, very soon," Zephaniah said (1:14). Within a few decades, Judah was overrun and burned to the ground. But other aspects of "the great day" do not appear to have happened yet—2,600 years later.

All human and animal life on the planet has not been snuffed out (1:2). Nor has a mysterious group of survivors assembled to celebrate the end of sorrow (3:14, 18).

Old Testament prophecies, however, sometimes had two meanings: one referring to the immediate future, and another referring to the distant future. Jesus used the same technique when he gave signs about "the end of the world" (Matthew 24). Parts of the prophecy were fulfilled 40 years later, when the Romans destroyed Jerusalem. Other aspects are still unfulfilled, and many believe will unfold only at the second coming of Christ. ❏

Encore

• To learn about what Judah was like during Zephaniah's day, read 2 Kings 21–23 and 2 Chronicles 33–35.

• For more about the "the day of the Lord," a Judgment Day theme central to Zephaniah, read the book of Joel, which also emphasizes this idea.

• For more prophecies about what appears to be the end of human history, read Isaiah 24–27, a passage known by Bible experts as the Apocalypse of Isaiah. ❏

HAGGAI

(dates are approximate)

When It Happened

Adam 4000+ B.C.

Abraham 2100 B.C.

Moses 1500 B.C.

David 1000 B.C.

Fall of Judah 586 B.C.

Decree of Cyrus 538 B.C.

Ezra 450 B.C.

Jesus born 7/6 B.C.

Religion on Hold for Eighteen Years

If religion has taken a back seat to other things in your life, like making a living, the prophet Haggai has a word from the Lord for you.

Haggai lived about 2,500 years ago at a time when one of the most important ways that the Jews expressed their faith—especially Jews in the Jerusalem area—was to worship God at the temple. There they would sing praises, listen to the instruction of the priests, and offer sacrifices in thanks for God's goodness, or in sorrow for their sins.

But there was no temple anymore. The Babylonians had destroyed it, along with the rest of Jerusalem, before deporting the Jewish citizens. Some 50 years later the Persians defeated the Jews and freed them to go home. Once back in Jerusalem, one of the first things they did was to lay the foundation for a new temple. But opposition from outsiders forced them to stop. For the next 18 years the Jews went about their private business, abandoning the temple.

But along comes Haggai with a message from God for the Jews, and for us. Don't neglect the Lord. Don't exclude him from your life. Talk to him. Sing to him. Offer him expressions of your gratefulness and your sorrow. Worship him with an assembled community of believers. ❏

Famous Lines

- "Is it right for you to live in expensive houses, while my temple is a pile of ruins?" (1:4). *God's complaint to the Jews returned from exile.*

- "I am with you, says the Lord" (1:13, New King James Version).

Behind the Scenes of Haggai

⭐ Starring Roles

Haggai, prophet who urges Jews returned from exile to rebuild the temple (1:1)

Zerubbabel, Persian-appointed governor of Judah and descendant of King David (1:1)

Joshua, high priest, not *the* Joshua who led the Israelites into the Promised Land (1:1)

📖 Plot

After the Jews return from exile, they lay the foundation for a new temple. But neighboring communities convince Persian leaders to order the work stopped. Almost 20 years pass, and nothing more has been done to rebuild the temple, even though a new Persian king supportive of various religions has been on the throne for more than a year.

At the end of an apparently weak harvest season, Haggai tells the high priest and the governor of Judah that the reason the people have been suffering from crop shortages is because the temple has not been rebuilt. God will bless the people again, Haggai says, once they resume work on the temple.

About three weeks later, the rebuilding begins.

> **Did You Know?**
>
> • Haggai is the second shortest book in the Old Testament, after Obadiah.
>
> • If this book reports all the prophecies of Haggai, his ministry covered less than four months.

Though Haggai does not report the completion of the project, perhaps because he does not live to see it finished, Ezra says it takes about three and a half years (Ezra 6:15). The new temple is dedicated in the spring of 516 B.C., 70 years after Solomon's temple was destroyed.

🎥 What to Look For

⚠ **Connection between obedience and prosperity.** In no uncertain terms, Haggai bluntly tells the religious and civic leaders of Judah that the people are suffering from a bad harvest and a sour economy because the temple hasn't been rebuilt. Within about three weeks, construction begins. For such obedience, God tells the people through Haggai, "Although you have not yet harvested any

TIMELINE	BIBLE EVENTS	King of Persia decrees the exiled Jews can return home 538 B.C.	Jews complete the foundation of the temple 536 B.C.	Haggai urges the Jews to complete the temple 520 B.C.	The temple is completed 516 B.C. Dates are approximate
		550 B.C.		525 B.C.	500 B.C.
	WORLD EVENTS	Cyrus of Persia conquers Babylon 539 B.C.	Actor Thespis wins first prize in a tragedy competition in Athens 534 B.C.	Darius succeeds Cyrus as king of Persia 522 B.C.	Buddha, in India, preaches his first sermon 521 B.C.

grain, grapes, figs, pomegranates, or olives, I will richly bless you in the days ahead" (2:19).

The Bible as a whole doesn't teach that obedience guarantees prosperity. The story of Job dramatically proves that suffering can come to the most godly of people; for a time, Job was obedient *and* broke. But there are occasions—as Haggai reports—when God reserves the right to punish the disobedient with financial hardship and to reward the obedient with rich blessing.

Emphasizing a point. Haggai emphasizes key points by raising questions and by repeating important phrases.

One critical question he asks is this: "Is it right for you to live in expensive houses, while my temple is a pile of ruins?" (1:4).

Repeated phrases, as translated in the New International Version, include the following: "Give careful thought" (1:5, 7; 2:15, 18), "I will shake the heavens and the earth" (2:6, 21), and "I am with you" (1:13; 2:4).

Author and Date

The prophecies are from Haggai, a Jewish prophet whose name means "festival," suggesting he was born on one of the Jewish holidays. Another prophet, Ezra, said that Haggai and Zechariah both urged the Jews to rebuild the temple (Ezra 5:1; 6:14).

Haggai may have been an old man by the time he delivered this message, perhaps over 70. He implied that he remembered how glorious Solomon's temple once looked (2:3); it had been destroyed 66 years earlier, in 586 B.C.

Haggai delivered several prophecies from August through December in 520 B.C., "the second year that Darius was king of Persia" (1:1). Darius reigned from 522 to 486 B.C. The dating is unusually precise because Haggai reported the month and day of each prophecy, as well as the date that the Jews resumed work on the temple.

On Location

The story takes place in Jerusalem. ❏

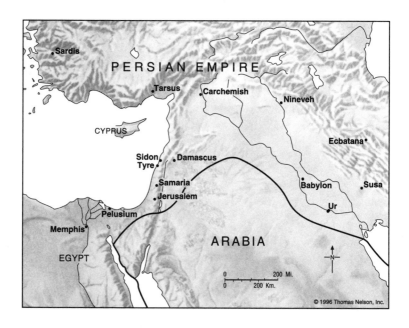

Big Scenes from Haggai

Nearly two decades after the first wave of Jews returned from exile, many are living in expensive homes. Yet, there is no temple for the Lord. For this spiritual negligence, Haggai reports, the people have been suffering from mildew, mold, and hail that have devastated the crops. This announcement comes in late August, near the end of a pitiful harvest.

Within about three weeks the Jews have organized a workforce and begin laying a new foundation. Cutting and transporting monster blocks, they finish the foundation before winter.

Pleased with their progress, Haggai assures the people that in the seasons ahead God will bless them with abundant harvests. Furthermore, Haggai adds, there is coming a day when nations will bring their treasures to Israel, the new temple will be more glorious than Solomon's, and peace will reign in Jerusalem.

**Laying the foundation of the new temple
(1:1–15; 2:18)** ••

Reviews

Darius's autobiography. Sources outside the Bible confirm that Darius was king of Persia, as Haggai reported. In fact, Darius had the story of his rise to power inscribed in three languages on a cliff wall in Iran. Archaeologists used this inscription to decipher cuneiform languages.

Darius was also open-minded about other religions, as the story of Haggai implies. Though Darius worshiped Persian gods, ancient records also say he rebuilt Egyptian temples.

Zerubbabel was no messiah. Haggai's closing prophecy suggests that Zerubbabel, who led the first wave of Jews back from exile, would also become the promised messiah who would destroy Israel's enemies and restore the nation to glory.

"Tell Governor Zerubbabel," God instructs Haggai, "that I am going to shake the heavens and the earth and wipe out kings and their kingdoms. . . . tell my servant Zerubbabel that I, the LORD All-Powerful, have chosen him, and he will rule in my name" (2:21-22, 23).

Furthermore, God told Haggai that the temple whose construction Zerubbabel supervised would be greater than Solomon's.

None of these prophecies was fulfilled in Zerubbabel's day. In fact, Zerubbabel disappeared from history even before his comparatively Plain Jane temple was finished. This has fueled speculation that he was executed for leading a movement to free Judah from Persian domination and to become king.

Was Haggai wrong?

Old Testament prophecies sometimes had both immediate and future meanings. This appears to be the case with Haggai's prophecy. Zerubbabel was God's chosen ruler, through whose leadership the temple was rebuilt. Five centuries later, King Herod renovated and expanded this temple to one much more spectacular than Solomon's. As for the kingdoms of earth falling, perhaps the fulfillment lies in the future. ❏

Encore

• For more about the rebuilding of the temple, read the books of Ezra and Zechariah. ❏

ZECHARIAH

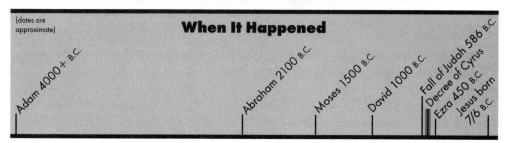

(dates are approximate)

When It Happened

Adam 4000+ B.C.

Abraham 2100 B.C.

Moses 1500 B.C.

David 1000 B.C.

Fall of Judah 586 B.C.

Decree of Cyrus

Ezra 450 B.C.

Jesus born 7/6 B.C.

Jews Rebuild Their Temple

The people of Jerusalem needed a shot in the arm, big time. They were back home from exile, but home to what? After nearly 20 years, they were still bankrupt spiritually, financially, and politically. Their temple lay in ruins. So did their harvests. So did their independence; Israel had been swallowed up by the latest and greatest superpower: Persia.

What could the Jews possibly do to turn all this around?

Nothing. That's the bad news.

The good news is that God is in control. That's the inspiring, motivating message of Zechariah, expressed in visions and prophecies. Furthermore, Zechariah said, God is going to see to it that the temple is rebuilt, prosperity returns to the land, and Israel is ruled by the king of peace.

Strangely enough, when the people started to believe this, they suddenly found themselves with the strength and determination to load a bundle of future history on their backs and carry it in the direction God intended it to go.

That's exactly what happened in Jerusalem. It's still happening among those who believe that God is the sovereign Lord over all creation. ❏

Famous Lines

• Strike the shepherd, and the sheep will be scattered (13:7, New International Version). *Jesus quoted this to describe what would happen to him and his disciples (Mark 14:27).*

• Everyone in Jerusalem, celebrate and shout! Your king . . . is coming to you. He is humble and rides on a donkey (9:9). *A verse the New Testament says is fulfilled on Palm Sunday, when the crowds cheer as Jesus rides into Jerusalem (Matthew 21:2–9; John 12:14–15).*

Behind the Scenes of Zechariah

★ Starring Role

Zechariah, a Jewish prophet and priest born in exile, in Babylon, but among the first Jews freed to return to Israel (1:1)

Plot

The book is not a story with a plot. It's a report of Zechariah's eight visions and his prophecies for the Jews who have returned to Israel, after enduring several decades of exile in Babylon.

The Jews have been back for almost 20 years, yet they have not rebuilt the temple. They had started the project right away, with the Persian king's blessing. But they abandoned it when local opposition convinced a new king that if the Jews rebuilt the city, they would rebel.

Now, however, yet another king is on the throne. And he's supportive of different religions. In this setting, Zechariah and the prophet Haggai both urge the people to finish what they started.

Zechariah's visions encourage the people to trust that God will help them rebuild not only the temple, but the nation. The prophecies in the second half of the book, chapters 9—14, are messages of punishment for the ungodly and salvation for the faithful. The closing prophecy looks forward to an end-time age when God defeats evil and reigns unopposed as the king of creation.

> ### Did You Know?
>
> • "Never again" is a phrase that many say in response to the Holocaust. God uses this phrase to describe a future age, perhaps after his people are assembled in heaven: "Never again will an oppressor overrun my people" (9:8, New International Version).
>
> • Though Zechariah has only 14 chapters, it's the longest of the 12 minor prophets.

What to Look For

The Messiah. This 14-chapter book talks more about the Messiah than any other Old Testament book, with the exception of the massive, 66-chapter book of Isaiah. New Testament writers, and Jesus himself, often quote Zechariah to show that Jesus fulfilled what was predicted.

Here's a partial review of the prophecies, and the New Testament fulfillment:
Ruler on the throne (2:10–13)—Revelation 22:1–5.
Holy priesthood (3:8)—1 Peter 2:5.

TIMELINE	BIBLE EVENTS			
	Zechariah and other Jewish exiles return to Jerusalem 538 B.C.	Zechariah's first reported message from God 520 B.C.	Jerusalem temple rebuilt 516 B.C.	Dates are approximate
	550 B.C.	525 B.C.		500 B.C.
	WORLD EVENTS	Temple of Artemis built in Ephesus 550 B.C.		Darius succeeds Cyrus as king of Persia 522 B.C.

Heavenly high priest (6:12–13)—Hebrews 8:1–2
Riding a donkey (9:9–10)—Matthew 21:4–5
Betrayal price: 30 pieces of silver (11:12–13)—Matthew 26:14–15
The money is used to buy potter's field (11:13)—Matthew 27:9
Body is pierced by spear (12:10)—John 19:34, 37
Good shepherd killed, sheep scattered (13:6–7)—Matthew 26:31

Angels. Angels appear to Zechariah in all eight of his visions, reported in chapters 1—6. These angels serve as God's messengers who help the prophet understand what each vision means. As elsewhere in the Bible, the angels aren't portrayed as figurative apparitions, but as living beings.

Part 1, Part 2. The book divides into two sections that are so different from each other that some say they are the work of two writers. Part 1, chapters 1–8, deals primarily with the visions of Zechariah concerning the rebuilding of the temple. Part 2, chapters 9–14, contains prophecies about God punishing Israel's enemies and rescuing Israel.

Author and Date

As stated in the first verse, the book was written by the prophet Zechariah, beginning in October or November of 520 B.C.

We arrive at this date because Zechariah said the word of God came to him in the second year and eighth month of Persian King Darius' reign. The eighth month on the Jewish calendar covers the end of October and the beginning of November. Zechariah's ministry spans at least two years, because his prophecy beginning in chapter 7 is from the fourth year of Darius' reign (518 B.C.).

Haggai was prophesying at the same time, in the same place (Jerusalem).

On Location

Zechariah ministers at Jerusalem in Judah. Though Judah was once a nation, now it's just a small province in the growing empire of Persia. ❏

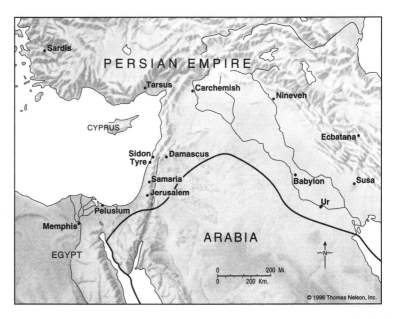

© 1996 Thomas Nelson, Inc.

Big Scenes from Zechariah

In a series of visions given to the prophet Zechariah, God motivates the Jews who have returned from exile in Babylon to finish rebuilding the temple. This is a job the Jews had started 18 years earlier, but one they halted because of local opposition.

"The city will be completely rebuilt," God reveals in the first of eight visions, "and my temple will stand again" (1:16).

Rebuilding the temple
(1:1–17) ••

Tied to God's assurance that the temple will be rebuilt is his promise that the cities of Judah will prosper again—especially the city of Jerusalem, his "chosen city."

Eventually, God says, the population will expand beyond the walls: "Jerusalem won't have any boundaries. It will be too full of people and animals even to have a wall. The Lord himself has promised to be a protective wall of fire surrounding Jerusalem, and he will be its shining glory in the heart of the city" (2:4–5).

Zechariah's message, with that of the prophet Haggai, must have struck a nerve. The people began rebuilding the temple, and saw it through to completion four years later.

Jerusalem becomes a thriving city again
•• **(1:17—2:5)**

In the most famous of his prophecies, Zechariah looks even deeper into the future—more than 500 years deep, to the time of Jesus.

"Everyone in Jerusalem, celebrate and shout! Your king has won a victory, and he is coming to you. He is humble and rides on a donkey. . . . I will bring peace to nations, and your king will rule from sea to sea."

Matthew and John both say this prophecy is at least partly fulfilled on the Palm Sunday when Jesus rides a donkey into Jerusalem, while crowds cheer his arrival as the promised Messiah (see Matthew 21:9; John 12:13–15).

Though God's kingdom of peace is not fully established then, it is started. And Zechariah promises that what God has started, he will finish.

The king of peace riding on a donkey
(9:9–10) •••

Reviews

Messiah arrives. Zechariah said that a Good Shepherd—a leader and deliverer sent from God—would replace the bad ones that had plagued Israel. The New Testament writers saw Jesus as the unmistakable fulfillment of Zechariah's many prophecies about this messiah. They saw it in the prophet's references to the leader riding into Jerusalem on a donkey, the 30 pieces of silver, suffering the pierce of a spear, and being killed. (See "The Messiah" in What to Look For.)

Author, author. Most Bible experts agree that Zechariah wrote chapters 1–8. But some suspect that a later writer, perhaps one or more of Zechariah's disciples, wrote the remaining six chapters. These scholars argue that the second half of the book—which they call Second Zechariah—is radically different in writing style, choice of words, and message.

In fact, the message at times seems opposite of First Zechariah. For example, chapters 1–8 paint a picture of national restoration, but chapters 9–14 reflect disillusionment with the restoration, and speak of warfare coming before peace. In addition, the later chapters say nothing of the Persians, but mention the Greeks—who defeated Persia in 332 B.C.

Scholars who contend that Zechariah wrote the whole book argue that the differences make sense: the first part of the book is prose—a reporting of visions, and the second part is poetry—prophetic messages from God about the future, both near and distant.

Whether or not Zechariah wrote the prophecy, New Testament writers as well as Jesus cited them as authentic messages from God. ❏

Encore

- For another perspective on what was happening in Jerusalem during Zechariah's day, read the two-chapter book of Haggai, a prophet who lived and ministered alongside Zechariah. The 10-chapter book of Ezra also reviews the history, though Ezra lived a generation or so later.

- Zechariah's sixth vision speaks about an evil woman. This concept is expanded in Revelation 17:1–19:4. ❏

MALACHI

When It Happened

(dates are approximate)

Adam 4000+ B.C.

Abraham 2100 B.C.

Moses 1500 B.C.

David 1000 B.C.

Ezra 450 B.C.

Jesus born 7/6 B.C.

Frauds and Freeloaders in God's House

Malachi is the final word in the Old Testament—the last message left stirring in the minds of people through the 400 years until Jesus was born.

For such an important location in the Bible—the finale of the First Testament—you'd think Malachi would have something important and enduring to say. You'd be right, though it might not look that way to you at first.

He tells the people to stop sacrificing sick, crippled animals. We don't sacrifice animals anymore, so this might not seem to apply to us. But if we go through the motions of worshiping God, without worshiping in a spirit of sincerity, the words do apply.

He tells the people to bring ten percent of their harvest and herds to the temple, as Jewish law required. Most of us aren't farmers, we don't worship in a temple, and we're not obliged to observe Jewish customs. But God's work goes on, and we can be a part of it.

Malachi also tells the people that the Lord is coming, bringing justice and healing. The message of the New Testament is that the Lord has come. He invites us to join his followers in seeking justice for the helpless and healing for the spiritually sick. ❏

Famous Line

• The sun of righteousness will rise with healing in its wings (4:2, New International Version). Malachi implies that in a future age, God will heal the sin-damaged creation by defeating evil and restoring justice.

Behind the Scenes of Malachi

⭐ Starring Role

Malachi, a prophet who condemns insincere worship (1:1)

📖 Plot

A century after the Jews have returned from exile in Babylon, they are again losing respect for God. They still go through the mechanics of offering sacrifices. But these sacrifices come from the bottom of the barrel—with a stamp of approval from the priests.

"I wish someone would lock the doors of my temple," God says through Malachi, "so you would stop wasting time building fires on my altar" (1:10).

Malachi urges the people to treat God with the respect due him. They're to treat each other with respect, too: not cheating in marriage, or lying in court, or taking advantage of employees, or ignoring the poor, or swindling foreigners.

In the end—and Malachi says the end is coming—God will settle all scores.

> **Did You Know?**
>
> • When Jews eat the *Seder* Passover meal, some leave the door cracked open, and set out an extra glass of wine called the "Elijah cup." They do this in anticipation that Elijah will someday return, as Malachi predicted, announcing the good news of salvation.
>
> • Jewish law required the people to give to the temple ten percent of their harvest and of the increase in their herd.

🎥 What to Look For

Insincere worship. Throughout this short book, Malachi complains that the people go through the motions of worship as though it's the motion that God wants.

They miss the point: God wants the motions to flow out of an inner sense of devotion and love. These people don't feel devoted. They feel obligated. Instead of bringing God the best they can, they bring the least they think they can get by with: crippled bulls, blind sheep, stolen goats.

Elijah. Malachi is the only prophet to announce that God will send the prophet Elijah as a messenger to prepare the way for the Lord's arrival, and the salvation to follow (3:1; 4:5). Jesus later explains that John the Baptist fills that role (Matthew 11:7–14; see also "Elijah's return" in Reviews).

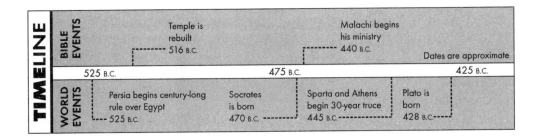

TIMELINE	BIBLE EVENTS			
		Temple is rebuilt ----- 516 B.C.		Malachi begins his ministry ----- 440 B.C.
				Dates are approximate
	525 B.C.		475 B.C.	425 B.C.
	WORLD EVENTS	Persia begins century-long rule over Egypt ---- 525 B.C.	Socrates is born 470 B.C. -------	Sparta and Athens begin 30-year truce 445 B.C. -----------	Plato is born 428 B.C.-----

Judgment day. Malachi vows "the day of judgment is certain to come" (4:1). When it does, justice comes with it. Evil is trampled and the righteous "will jump around like calves at play" (4:2).

Author and Date

"I am Malachi," the book begins. Nothing more is known about this prophet. Some Bible experts think "Malachi" is a title, not a name. The word means "my messenger." (See "Malachi who?" in Reviews.)

The book was written sometime after the temple was rebuilt (516 B.C.). Malachi's description of a decaying sacrificial system and his concern about Jews marrying non-Jews seems to fit the conditions around the time of Ezra and Nehemiah, roughly 450 B.C.

On Location

The prophet is one of several who addressed Jews in Jerusalem. ❏

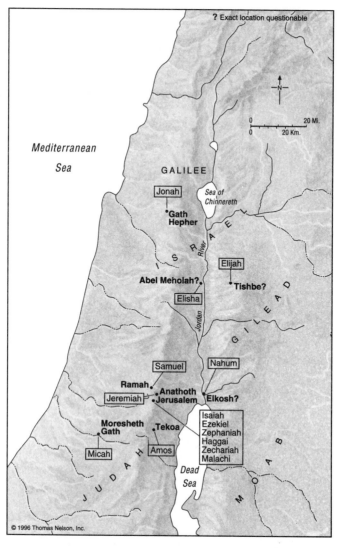

© 1996 Thomas Nelson, Inc.

Big Scenes from Malachi

God is insulted. He has allowed the Jewish people to return home from exile and to rebuild their temple and capital city. Yet, after some 100 years, they are becoming lax in their worship.

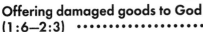

They're bringing damaged offerings even though Jewish law requires them to sacrifice animals without any kind of defect (Leviticus 22:18–23).

"Isn't it wrong," God asks rhetorically, "to offer animals that are blind, crippled, or sick? Just try giving those animals to your governor. That certainly wouldn't please him or make him want to help you" (1:8).

Priests are as guilty as the others, for they permit this to go on.

God, through the prophet Malachi, says, "You had better take seriously the need to honor my name" (2:2).

**Offering damaged goods to God
(1:6—2:3)** ••

You people are robbing me, your God," the Lord says. "You are robbing me of the offerings and of the ten percent that belongs to me" (3:8).

The Jews were supposed to bring a tenth of their harvest and herd to the temple. This was distributed as salary to the temple workers, as funds to maintain the temple facilities, and as charitable gifts to people in need.

"Bring the entire ten percent into the storehouse, so there will be food in my house," God says. "Then I will open the windows of heaven and flood you with blessing after blessing" (3:10).

The book—and the Old Testament—concludes with the promise that the Lord is coming, on the heels of a messenger who will prepare the way for him. Then the New Testament picks up the story of God's work among the human race. Jesus is born. And when he grows up, his ministry follows that of John the Baptist—the prophet who described himself as "someone shouting in the desert, 'Get the road ready for the Lord!'" (John 1:23).

**Bringing the tithe to the temple
(3:8–12)**

Reviews

Elijah's return. This concluding book of the Old Testament ends with the promise that the prophet Elijah will appear as a forerunner of the Lord's arrival—to prepare the Lord's way. The New Testament begins with the birth of Jesus, and tells of John the Baptist's ministry, which prepared the way for Christ's ministry.

John didn't realize he was the "Elijah" that Malachi was talking about. Even though John said he came to prepare the way for someone whose sandals he wasn't worthy to untie, when priests asked him if he was Elijah or perhaps the messiah, John replied, "No, I am not!" (John 1:21).

Jesus knew better. He said, "John is Elijah, the prophet you are waiting for" (Matthew 11:14).

Malachi who? Malachi might not have been the writer's name. Many scholars think the word was used as a descriptive title instead of a proper name.

Malachi means "my messenger," which was a common way of referring to God's prophets. In fact, the first Greek translation of the Old Testament—in about 250 B.C.—translated the term as a title, not a name.

The writers choice of the word *malachi* to describe himself may also have been a way of pointing toward the book's unique prophecy: "I, the Lord All-Powerful, will send my messenger" (3:1)—a reference to the prophet who would prepare the way for the Lord's arrival.

Whatever the author's name, New Testament writers quote the book with authority and respect—as does Jesus. ❏

Encore

- Malachi quotes God as saying "I hate divorce" (2:16, New International Version). For more on God's feeling about divorce, read the words of Jesus in Matthew 19:3-9.

- To see how the New Testament portrays John the Baptist as the promised Elijah, turn to Matthew 17:1-13.

- For more about the Jewish law of tithing, read Leviticus 27:30-32 and Numbers 18:21-24. ❏

MATTHEW

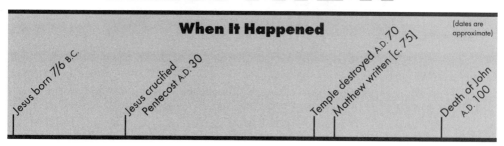

When It Happened

(dates are approximate)

Jesus born 7/6 B.C.

Jesus crucified
Pentecost A.D. 30

Temple destroyed A.D. 70
Matthew written [c. 75]

Death of John
A.D. 100

Jesus and His Teachings

Matthew is the first of four New Testament books about Jesus. Like any collection of stories about one person, each version is different. And there's something unique enough about Matthew's story to inspire Christian leaders long ago to put his ahead of all others in the New Testament.

Like the other three books about Jesus, Matthew is called a Gospel, meaning "good news." More than any other Gospel, Matthew zeroes in on exactly what that good news is, for he concentrates on the words Jesus spoke. He records accusing words (23:24), comforting words (28:20), and motivating words (5:9).

In Matthew, you'll not find as much dramatic action as you'll discover in Mark, or as many spotlights on compassion as you'll see in Luke, or as much proof of the deity of Jesus as you'll uncover in John. But in Matthew, you'll find the most complete record of what Jesus taught. And you'll learn how his teachings grow out of Old Testament scriptures.

Reading Matthew is as close as any of us can get to finding a soft clump of grass on a Galilean hillside, and sitting down to listen with thousands of others while Jesus teaches as though we, alone, are with him. ❏

Famous Lines

- Treat others as you want them to treat you (7:12). *The Golden Rule, from what has become known as Jesus' Sermon on the Mount.*

- Man shall not live by bread alone (4:4, King James Version). *Jesus' response when Satan asks him to prove he is the Son of God by turning stones into bread.*

- Blessed are the meek: for they shall inherit the earth (5:5, King James Version). *One of several "Beatitudes" from the Sermon on the Mount.*

- "He will be called Immanuel," which means "God is with us" (1:23). *Matthew's citation of Isaiah 7:14, given as one of many evidences that Jesus fulfills prophecies about the Messiah.*

Behind the Scenes of Matthew

⭐ Starring Roles

Jesus, God's son in a human body, and the Messiah that prophets said God would send to Israel (1:1)

12 apostles, working-class men whom Jesus recruits to become his disciples (4:18; 10:1–4)

📖 Plot

Jesus, a descendant of Abraham and King David, is born to a virgin. Astrologers arrive, saying they have followed a star they believe is a sign that the future king of the Jews has just been born. Herod, current king of the Jews, fears the child may be the Messiah, a king and deliverer promised by the prophets. Herod kills all the children ages two and under in the vicinity of Bethlehem. Jesus, however, escapes when his family flees to Egypt and stays there until Herod dies.

At about age 30, Jesus begins his ministry by being baptized, then by preaching and calling 12 men to join him as disciples. For perhaps three or four years he preaches and performs astonishing miracles in Galilee, his home region in what is now northern Israel. His most famous sermon, recorded only in Matthew, is called the Sermon on the Mount, a masterful summary on how to live as a citizen under God's government on earth.

Predicting his death, Jesus goes south to Jerusalem, healing people and teaching as he goes. In Jerusalem he faces the combative Jewish scholars entrenched in their traditions. When Jesus reveals that some of these traditions have no basis in Scripture, and—worse—that the leaders are hypocrites misleading the people, they become infuriated. They plot to kill him, but realize they have to do it secretly because he has a large following of people who believe he is either the Messiah or another great prophet.

During his prayer time one Thursday evening, Jesus is arrested, interrogated throughout the night, and tried the next morning by Pilate, the Roman governor. Reluctantly, Pilate gives in to the wishes of the assembled Jews and sentences Jesus to death. The execution is carried out immediately, and Jesus is dead before sundown.

On the following Sunday morning, he rises from the dead and appears to women who have come to his tomb. Later he meets with his remaining disciples and gives them what is now called the Great Commission: "Go to the people of all nations and make them my disciples" (28:19).

🎥 What to Look For

The Jewish angle. This is the most Jewish Gospel of all, written to convince Jews that Jesus is the Messiah that the prophets said was coming. That's one reason it comes first in the New Testament, right after Malachi, which ends with the promise of the Lord's coming.

More than the other Gospels, Matthew quotes Old Testament prophecies about the Messiah, to show that Jesus fulfilled them. Matthew cites the Old Testament no fewer than 57 times, compared with 30 in the runner-up, Mark.

A lot of comments on the death of Jesus. In all the Gospels, but especially in Matthew, look for a lot of material about the suffering and death of Jesus. The Gospel writers know they have a lot of explaining to do because the execution of Jesus, as a common criminal, is not what conventional wisdom says will happen to the Messiah. In reading the prophecies, most Jews expect the Messiah to restore the glory of Israel and the kingship of the nation. Jesus, however, is crowned with thorns and nailed to a cross, beneath a mocking sign that calls him king of the Jews.

The Gospel writers take the Jews back to the prophets to read other passages, which portray a humble Messiah, rejected by leaders, and sacrificed for the sins of others. Prophecies about a victorious, ruling Messiah, many believe, point to the second coming of Jesus.

> ### Did You Know?
>
> • In the family tree of Jesus are four women with tarnished backgrounds—not the kind of people Jews expect in the family tree of the great Messiah. There's Rahab, a pagan prostitute; Bathsheba, an adulteress; Ruth, a non-Jew who sneaks under the covers of a prospective husband; and Tamar, who becomes pregnant by her father-in-law. These memories of scandal would challenge the too-rosy memory of Jews conceited about their pedigree. And they would also counter attacks on the virgin Mary by reminding Jews that women with bad reputations are in the family tree of the great King David, forebear of the Messiah.

Five teaching sessions of Jesus. The book seems woven around five sets of teachings by Jesus. Some scholars believe these teachings were the original core of the book, provided by Matthew, and that the story line was added later.

These teachings are the Sermon on the Mount (chapters 5—7), commissioning the 12 disciples as ministers (10), parables revealing what the kingdom of heaven is like (13), guidelines on how to live as citizens in God's kingdom (18), and warnings about the end of the age and judgment day (24—25).

The kingdom of heaven. "The kingdom" refers to God's saving revolution on earth and to life set free by his government. Both the miracles and the teachings of Jesus show that God's reign applies not only to heaven and the future, but also to earth right now. God is revolutionizing "life as usual" through Jesus' ministry and wherever people embrace the policies of his government. Think of the Sermon on the Mount (5—7) as an Inaugural Address a U.S. President gives at the beginning of his term. In it Jesus, God's King for Jews and "all nations," outlines the policies of God's administration, showing people how to live as citizens of this kingdom.

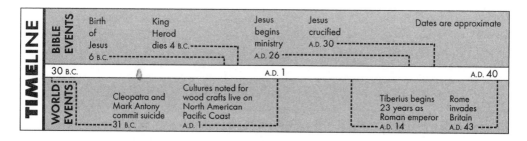

TIMELINE	BIBLE EVENTS	Birth of Jesus 6 B.C.	King Herod dies 4 B.C.		Jesus begins ministry A.D. 26	Jesus crucified A.D. 30	Dates are approximate
		30 B.C.			A.D. 1		A.D. 40
	WORLD EVENTS		Cleopatra and Mark Antony commit suicide 31 B.C.	Cultures noted for wood crafts live on North American Pacific Coast A.D. 1		Tiberius begins 23 years as Roman emperor A.D. 14	Rome invades Britain A.D. 43

Different responses to Jesus. Despite his astonishing miracles and compassionate teachings and manner, not everyone embraces his ideas. Many do, and crowds follow him. But his insights and unique interpretation of Old Testament Jewish laws make him seem like a threat to Jewish traditionalists who stubbornly cling to their understanding of what God expects from people.

Author and Date

Both the author and date are uncertain. The writer is not named in the book, but Christians writing in the second century said the book was written by Matthew, a tax collector who became one of the 12 original disciples of Jesus.

Clues within the book suggest it was written near the end of the first century, sometime after the Romans destroyed the Jerusalem temple in A.D. 70. Without the temple, there was no need for priests because there was no place to offer sacrifices. So the Jewish scholars, called Pharisees, rose to prominence. The book seems written especially to a Christian Jewish community trying to define and defend itself against traditional Judaism that—before the century was over—excommunicated Christian Jews from all synagogues. One clue that the Christian Jews faced such persecution appears in Matthew 23:34, which says the Jews "kill them or nail them to a cross or beat them in your meeting places or chase them from town to town."

On Location

The story of Jesus unfolds in what is now Israel, beginning in his hometown region of Galilee, and continuing southward through Samaria and into Judea, where he dies and is resurrected in the city of Jerusalem. ❏

Big Scenes from Matthew

Within about two years after Jesus is born, wise men from an unnamed country in the east arrive in Jerusalem. Ironically, these non-Jews become among the first in Matthew's Gospel to testify that Jesus is the long-awaited Messiah. "Where is the child born to be king of the Jews?" they ask. "We saw his star in the east and have come to worship him." Many in this day believe that a unique event in the sky, such as the arrival of a new star or a comet, is a sign that a great leader has been born.

King Herod, who has killed his own brother to protect the throne, is instantly worried. Consulting Jewish scholars, Herod learns that the Messiah will be born in Bethlehem. He reveals this to the sages, asking them to report back after they find the child, so he can "worship him too."

The wise men find Jesus, but in a dream are warned not to return to Herod. When Herod realizes the men aren't coming back, he orders all the boys executed who are two years old and under, living in the Bethlehem area. Jesus and his family escape to Egypt.

This story of the wise men probably troubles many orthodox Jews because they do not expect God to entrust such important news to pagan astrologers. But God does not allow human expectations to limit the good things he does for this world.

Wise men visit Jesus
(2:1 – 12)

John the Baptist, identified as the promised forerunner of the Messiah, reluctantly baptizes Jesus after expressing his hesitation: "I ought to be baptized by you."

John baptizes people as a symbol of their spiritual cleansing after repentance. Jesus is baptized to endorse John's ministry and, as a representative of all humanity, to be an example of humble obedience to God. Unlike all others, Jesus "did not sin" (Hebrews 4:15). Yet his baptism is clearly appropriate, for the sky opens and a voice from heaven says, "This is my own dear Son, and I am pleased with him."

Afterward, Jesus goes into the desert where he is tested by Satan.

Some Bible experts see in these scenes echoes from the Exodus, which helps Jews see Jesus as a living example of the child God wanted Israel to be. Like the Jews, Jesus is called out of Egypt (after Herod dies), he passes through the water, and he is tested in the desert. Only after passing the test does his ministry begin.

Baptism of Jesus
(3:13 – 17)

The Gospel of Matthew spends most of its time revealing what Jesus taught—not what he did or where he went. The most famous sermon of Jesus is called the Sermon on the Mount, delivered somewhere on a hillside possibly near the Sea of Galilee, where many of his disciples had worked as fishermen.

This sermon may actually be a collection of highlights from many sermons, for it succinctly captures the essence of what Jesus teaches. Here are the famous Beatitudes, which show that God's kingdom is not full of the high and mighty, but of people who are poor in spirit, humble, sorrowing, pure in heart, persecuted. Here, too, are Jesus' insights about criticizing others, adultery, divorce, revenge, loving our enemies, helping the needy, prayer, worry, judging others—to name a few.

Instead of giving detailed rules for people to follow, Jesus gives broad principles that make it incredibly difficult to find loopholes. When in doubt about what to do, Jesus says, "Act like your Father in heaven" (5:48). For those who don't know how God acts, Jesus shows them.

**Sermon on the Mount
(5:1—7:29)** •••

One day while Jesus is teaching, a government official rushes to him and, kneeling, says, "My daughter has just now died! Please come and place your hand on her. Then she will live again."

When Jesus arrives at the man's house, a crowd of mourners has already gathered. Jewish custom requires speedy burial, usually the same day. Jesus tells the people to leave. "The little girl isn't dead," he says. "She is just asleep."

Suddenly, cries of sorrow erupt into heckling laughter. The people eventually leave the house nonetheless. With that, Jesus takes the girl by the hand and helps her up.

News of this miracle worker quickly spreads throughout the region, producing mixed reviews. Many people are drawn to his message that points to the intent of the Jewish law: obedience to God. These supporters praise God for the miracles of healing they see Jesus perform. But others, including some Jewish scholars who don't agree with his interpretation of Scripture, charge that he gets his power from "the leader of the demons" (9:34).

**Jesus heals a "sleeping" girl
(9:18–26)**

•••

In the second of Jesus' five major teaching sections, he gives his 12 original disciples instructions for a mission they are to undertake. Jesus, like other ancient rabbis, has selected a small group of men to live and travel with him during his ministry, receive his teaching, watch his actions, follow his instructions, and continue his work when he is gone. The 12—apparently symbolizing the 12 tribes, or extended families, of Israel—are working-class men such as fishermen. Matthew is a tax collector, a profession hated among the Jews. Tax collectors in Israel at the time are usually Jews who collaborate with the Roman occupying force by assessing and collecting taxes, often overcharging and keeping the extra money.

The mission of the disciples, apparently short-term and perhaps a trial-run for the ministry they will perform when Jesus is gone, is to do what Jesus has been doing: teach about the kingdom of heaven, as well as heal the sick, exorcise demons, and even raise the dead. They are to take no pay. And when they aren't welcomed, they are to leave and "shake the dust from your feet at them" (10:14).

"Don't be afraid of people," Jesus says. "They can kill you, but they cannot harm your soul" (10:28).

Jesus sends out the Twelve
(10:1 – 42)

Jesus often teaches by using parables—short stories that are easy to picture and that communicate a spiritual meaning. Matthew says that Jesus' teaching method is yet another fulfillment of prophecy because the psalmist spoke of one who would teach with parables (compare Psalm 78:2 with Matthew 13:35). Matthew also says Jesus uses these stories to let his followers in on "the secrets about the kingdom of heaven."

The several parables in chapter 13 reveal mysteries about God's kingdom. The parable of the tall-growing mustard seed and of the yeast show that the kingdom will emerge suddenly in the world. The parables about the hidden treasure and the pearl show that people have to decide whether or not to become citizens of the kingdom. And the parable of the weeds in the wheat field reveal that people will be rewarded for choosing the kingdom and punished for rejecting it.

In this parable, Jesus compares himself to a farmer sowing good seeds that produce "people who belong to the kingdom. The weed seeds are those who belong to the evil one." At harvesttime—an expression of end-time judgment—the wheat is gathered in. But the weeds are separated and burned.

Parable of weeds among the wheat
(13:24 – 30, 36 – 43)

In a memorable scene told in all four Gospels, Jesus and his ministry-weary disciples sail away from the crowds for a rest. But the people on shore keep the boat in sight and follow it. When Jesus and his men arrive at a remote site, they are met by thousands—5,000 men, not counting the women and children.

As tired as he is, Jesus is still moved with compassion and heals everyone who is sick.

When the disciples suggest dispersing the crowd so they can get food, Jesus asks, "Why don't you give them something to eat?"

All that the disciples manage to round up is one boy's lunch: five pieces of barley bread and two small fish. Jesus takes it, looks to heaven and gives thanks for it, then hands it to the disciples to distribute. The people eat their fill, and the disciples collect 12 large baskets of leftovers.

Jesus feeds the 5,000
(14:13 – 21)

While in Caesarea Philippi, north of the Sea of Galilee and near Mount Hermon, Jesus asks the disciples who people say he is. They reply that some speculate he is the spirit of John the Baptist, who was recently beheaded. Others say he is the spirit of Elijah, Jeremiah, or some other Old Testament prophet.

When Jesus asks who the disciples think he is, one disciple boldly replies, "You are the Messiah, the Son of the living God."

Jesus gives this disciple, Simon, the new name of Peter, which means "rock." Then Jesus says, "On this rock I will build my church, and death itself will not have any power over it" (16:18). Later, on the day of Pentecost, when God sends the Holy Spirit to empower the disciples after the ascension of Jesus, it is Peter who preaches the first sermon (Acts 2).

Peter recognizes Jesus as the Son of God (16:13–20) •••

After Jesus begins preparing the disciples for his coming death and resurrection, he takes his three closest disciples—Peter, James, and John—to a hilltop. There they see Jesus changed into his glorified, heavenly form: "His face was shining like the sun, and his clothes became white as light" (17:2).

Suddenly, the prophets Moses and Elijah appear, also as beings of light, talking with Jesus. A glowing cloud rolls overhead, and from it a voice says, "This is my own dear son, and I am pleased with him. Listen to what he says!" (17:5).

When the disciples hear this, they drop to the ground, terrified. But Jesus tells them not to be afraid. When the men look up, Jesus is alone. He tells them to say nothing about this until after his resurrection.

Jesus transfigured into a being of light •• **(17:1–13)**

Jesus arrives in Jerusalem on what becomes the first Palm Sunday, just before his Friday crucifixion. Crowds who had heard of him cheer, welcoming him as the long-awaited Messiah who would save them from their enemies and restore righteousness to Israel.

Jesus is riding a donkey—just as the prophet Zechariah said the Messiah would arrive in Jerusalem (Zechariah 9:9). The people respond by paving the path with a carpet of palm branches and cloaks, befitting the arrival of a king.

"Hooray for the Son of David!" they shout. "God bless the one who comes in the name of the Lord." These words from Psalm 118:26, together with the actions of the crowd, reveal that many believe they are witnessing the arrival of the Messiah.

Jesus' triumphal entry into Jerusalem (21:1–11) 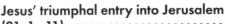 ••

When Jesus enters the temple courtyard—the worship area for non-Jewish believers—he sees the place filled with merchants selling sacrificial animals and exchanging foreign currencies for the Hebrew coins required in temple offerings.

Angrily, he flips their tables, quoting Isaiah: "The Scriptures say, 'My house should be called a place of worship.' But you have turned it into a place where robbers hide" (21:13).

Some ancient sources suggest that Jewish merchandising was later moved outside the temple area. But Jesus may be symbolizing what he later prophesies—the destruction of the temple. Romans level it in A.D. 70, while crushing a Jewish revolt. This ends the Jewish sacrificial system; they haven't had a temple since.

Jesus cleanses the temple
(21:12–17)

As Jesus and his disciples leave Jerusalem, to stay in nearby Bethany, they stop en route and rest on the Mount of Olives. There Jesus warns them about the coming fall of Jerusalem and the later end of the human age, saying he will return to take the citizens of God's kingdom to their eternal home.

No one knows when this will happen, Jesus says, so everyone needs to live in a state of readiness.

To illustrate the judgment that will follow his second coming, Jesus tells a story about sheep and goats, animals easily separated. The sheep, symbolizing godly and compassionate people who help the needy, are rewarded with "eternal life." The goats, representing the godless and selfish, "will be punished forever."

A parable about Judgment Day
(25:31–46)

The high priest and other members of the Sanhedrin, the top Jewish ruling body, plot strategies for arresting and executing Jesus because of his unorthodox interpretation of Scripture. The night of the arrest, Jesus arranges to eat a final meal with his disciples.

This meal is rich with symbolism that endures in the rite of Communion, or the Eucharist. He breaks bread and tells the men that it represents his body, which will soon be broken. Then he gives them wine and says it represents his blood, "poured out, so that many people will have their sins forgiven."

After singing a hymn, the group goes to a garden on the Mount of Olives to pray. There Jesus is arrested, betrayed for unknown reasons by Judas, who leads officers to him. The disciples scatter. Peter waits outside the home of the high priest, but vigorously and repeatedly denies knowing Jesus—as Jesus predicted he would do. Judas hangs himself.

The Last Supper
(26:17–30)

The Sanhedrin convenes an emergency session and spends the night interrogating Jesus. After lying witnesses fail to give enough evidence to warrant execution, the high priest, in frustration, asks Jesus, "Are you the Messiah, the Son of God?" (26:63). Jesus confirms he is. The court charges him with blasphemy and takes him to the governor, Pilate, who alone has authority to order an execution.

Pilate finds no cause to execute Jesus, but eventually gives in to the early-morning crowd of Jesus' opponents, viciously screaming, "Nail him to a cross!" Pilate publicly washes his hands, saying he is innocent of this man's blood. Then he orders Jesus crucified.

Pilate sentences Jesus (27:11–26)

Soldiers given custody of Jesus know that he claims to be the Messiah, king of the Jews. They dress him in a robe of scarlet, the color of royalty, then make him a crown from branches of a thornbush.

After beating him, they force him to make a humiliating march through the city, carrying the crossbeam on which his hands will be nailed. The vertical beam is fixed at the execution site outside the city walls.

Once crucified, Jesus hangs between two criminals. Above his head is a sign that reads, "This is Jesus, the King of the Jews."

With this execution, Jewish leaders hope to prove that Jesus is no messiah. Anyone "hung on a tree is under God's curse" (Deuteronomy 21:23, New International Version). And that, they believe, includes Jesus.

Yet when Jesus dies, his last words quote the beginning of a song about a servant of God who suffers and is later proven righteous (compare 27:46 with Psalm 22). Instantly, the earth shakes so violently that a soldier exclaims, "This man really was God's Son!"

Because Jesus had claimed he would rise on the third day, the Jewish leaders convince Pilate to seal the tomb and post a guard. This way, they argue, Jesus' disciples can't steal the body and claim he rose from the dead.

The execution of Jesus (27:33–66)

Early Sunday morning, when Sabbath is over, several women followers of Jesus go to the tomb to finish preparing his body for burial. There was no time for this Friday afternoon, as dusk and Sabbath approached.

But by this time, an angelic being of light had appeared and rolled back the stone, then sat on it. The guards were so terrified they passed out. When they came to, they reported to the Jewish priests, who bribed them to keep quiet.

When Mary Magdalene and at least two other women arrive, the angel is still there. "Don't be afraid!" the angel says, "I know you are looking for Jesus, who was nailed to a cross. He isn't here!

God has raised him to life, just as Jesus said he would"
(28:5–6).

As the women turn to leave, Jesus greets them. "Tell
my followers to go to Galilee," he says. "They will see
me there."

Jesus meets his disciples in Galilee. There, he gives
them what has become known as the Great Commission. "Go to the people of all nations and make them
my disciples," he says, "I will be with you always, even
until the end of the world."

Resurrected Jesus greets women at the tomb
(28:1 – 20)

Reviews

Jesus fulfills prophecies. More than any other Gospel, Matthew tries to prove to Jewish
readers that Jesus is the Messiah they've been anticipating—the Messiah that, for hundreds of
years, prophets have been saying God would send.

Many of the prophecies are especially convincing because they could not have been
artificially fulfilled. On the basis of what the prophet Micah said in 5:2, for example, the Jews
believed the Messiah would come from Bethlehem, hometown of their greatest king, David.
Jesus was born there.

Isaiah 53, known as the Suffering Servant passage, reads almost like an eyewitness account of the suffering and death of Jesus: "He suffered and endured great pain for us . . . He
was wounded and crushed because of our sins. . . . He was condemned to death without a
fair trial. . . . The Lord decided his servant would suffer as a sacrifice to take away the sin and
guilt of others" (4, 5, 8, 10).

Zechariah described the beginning of the messiah's kingdom: "Everyone in Jerusalem,
celebrate and shout! Your king has won a victory, and he is coming to you. He is humble and
rides on a donkey" (9:9). Matthew reveals that this prophecy is fulfilled in the Triumphal Entry, on the first Palm Sunday (21:1 – 9).

Jesus doesn't fulfill all prophecies. Though Jesus fulfills many prophecies about the
Messiah, other prophecies seem yet unfulfilled. For example, Isaiah says that when the Messiah comes, "the poor and the needy will be treated with fairness. . . . Leopards will lie down
with young goats, and wolves will rest with lambs" (11:4, 6). This utopian era of peace did
not follow the donkey-riding Jesus into Jerusalem. Nor did Jesus reestablish the great kingdom
of David, as many prophecies said he would.

But as Jesus told Pilate, "My kingdom doesn't belong to this world" (John 18:36). Many
believe that the prophecies about a glorious kingdom and everlasting peace will be fulfilled
when the Messiah returns in a Second Coming, to take the citizens of heaven home (1 Thessalonians 4:13 – 17).

Jesus doesn't speak kindly of non-Jews. "Stay away from the Gentiles," Jesus told
his disciples, when sending them on a tour of ministry throughout Galilee. "Go only to the
people of Israel" (10:5).

And later, when a non-Jewish woman asked Jesus to heal her demon-possessed daughter, Jesus replied, "I was sent only to the people of Israel!" When the woman pleaded, Jesus replied, "It isn't right to take food away from children and feed it to dogs" (15:24, 26).

It sounds like Jesus was calling non-Jews "dogs." Yet the woman apparently sensed something else in the tone of his voice, or perhaps glimpsed a twinkle in his eye. For she argued that even dogs deserve crumbs. "Dear woman," Jesus replied, "you really do have a lot of faith, and you will be given what you want" (15:28).

The ministry of Jesus did, in fact, seem to focus primarily on the Jews. And why not? He was a Jew and the Messiah that Jews, not Gentiles, had been waiting for. The Gospel of Matthew stresses Jesus' Jewishness and his mission first to his own people, to fulfill the promises God made to them, beginning with Abraham. Yet non-Jews are also included in the reach of the good news, as the beginning, middle, and ending of Matthew show: pagan astrologers are led by God to worship Jesus, the child-king (2:14); later, Jesus praises a Roman centurion who showed more faith than anyone else he had met (8:10); finally, he directs his followers to make disciples out of "the people of all nations" (28:19). ❏

Encore

- The Gospels of Mark and Luke are similar to Matthew's. John's Gospel is more theological, emphasizing the divinity of Jesus more than retelling the highlights of his life's story. But all three Gospels add depth to Matthew's portrait.

- Read some of the Old Testament prophecies that Matthew says Jesus fulfilled. For example: Jesus is Immanuel, God with us (1:23; Isaiah 7:14); born in Bethlehem (2:6; Micah 5:2); a healer of diseases (8:17; Isaiah 53:4). For more, see "Jesus fulfills prophecies" in the Reviews section.

- Read Acts to find out what happens after Jesus ascends into heaven, leaving the disciples behind. ❏

MARK

When It Happened

(dates are approximate)

Jesus born 7/6 B.C.

Jesus crucified / Pentecost A.D. 30

Mark written A.D. 62/63

Temple destroyed A.D. 70

Death of John A.D. 100

The Most Action-Packed Story of Jesus

It comes second in the New Testament, but it's probably the first Gospel worth reading—for many reasons.

It's short—the shortest of the four Gospels—and it's action-packed, jumping from one miracle of Jesus to another, and from one confrontation to another: silencing demons, feeding thousands, calming storms, walking on water, dying, rising to life.

When Matthew and Luke sat down to write their Gospels, they had probably already read Mark. Their works show signs of borrowing from the book.

One thing Mark helps us appreciate about Jesus, better perhaps than any other Gospel, is what Jesus suffered on our behalf. Some 40 percent of this short book lays out details of the final, traumatic week of Jesus' life. And the earlier part of the book throws the spotlight on the pain Jesus endured from the very beginning of his ministry: confrontation with hostile spiritual forces and with human beings intent on humiliating and then killing him. He even suffered the rejection of his family and his lifelong friends.

Words alone can't convey all that Jesus went through to help us understand how much God loves us. But the words of Mark are the place to begin. ❏

Famous Lines

• Many who are now first will be last, and many who are now last will be first (10:31). *Jesus tells his disciples that in the afterlife, some of this world's most respected people will be humbled, and the least respected will finally receive the honor due them.*

• I will make you fishers of men (1:17, New International Version). *What Jesus said to Peter and Andrew, fishermen he was inviting to become his disciples.*

• Give to Caesar what is Caesar's and to God what is God's (12:17, New International Version). *The answer Jesus gives to Jewish leaders trying to trick him into a traitorous quote by asking if Jews should pay taxes imposed by the Romans.*

Behind the Scenes of Mark

⭐ Starring Roles

Jesus, God's son, who has come to earth in human form (1:1)
12 apostles, men Jesus invites to join his ministry as disciples (1:16; 3:14–19)

📖 Plot

Surprisingly, Mark skips the childhood of Jesus altogether, beginning instead with John the Baptist preaching in the desert. This is a logical place to start, because John fulfills the Old Testament prophecy of the messenger who is to prepare people for the Lord's arrival.

Jesus arrives, is baptized by John, then retreats into the desert, where he overcomes several temptations offered up by Satan. Immediately afterward, Jesus begins his ministry in Galilee (northern Israel) by choosing four fishermen as the first of 12 disciples. Then comes a flurry of miracles—casting out demons, healing the sick—followed by calling the remaining disciples.

Jesus' ministry of teaching and healing continues, with dramatic results. Crowds, captivated by his new insights into ancient Scripture and astonished by his miracles, follow him by the thousands. But mingled in among the admirers are skeptics—Jewish scholars and religious leaders who don't agree with his non-traditional interpretation of Scripture. Repeatedly they try to humiliate him with trick questions, but each time they walk away humiliated themselves. By the third chapter, Mark reveals that these leaders intend to kill Jesus.

When Jesus turns south, taking his ministry to Jerusalem, he knows that the end is near—yet his disciples can't imagine a suffering Messiah. Everything they've heard about the promised Messiah is that he will reign in glory as a king with the stature of David.

Jesus enters Jerusalem on a Sunday, amid cheering crowds who give him a royal welcome. Five days later, by 9 A.M., he is nailed to a cross. By about 3 P.M., he is dead. But come Sunday morning, his tomb is empty, and an angel dressed in white is declaring that Jesus is alive and preparing to visit his devastated disciples.

🎥 What to Look For

Less talk, more action. Mark focuses more on what Jesus did than what he taught. In fact, this Gospel contains fewer teachings of Jesus than any of the four Gospels.

Like other action-packed stories, the pace is frantic. Mark jumps from one scene to the next, often saying that the subsequent scene happens "immediately." This conveys the image of a perpetually busy Jesus, and it leaves the reader empathizing with the weariness that he and his disciples must have experienced.

A suffering Jesus. There are only 16 chapters in this short book, and the last 6 are devoted to the final week of Jesus' life: his suffering and crucifixion.

There are perhaps two important reasons why Mark emphasizes this.

First, the Jews of Jesus' day cannot conceive of a suffering Messiah. They expect a king. That's why the disciples argue over who among them should be permitted to sit at the right and left of Jesus' throne, after he becomes king (10:37, 41). They argue this even after Jesus tells them—three times—that he is going to be executed. The Old Testament prophets have spoken of a suffering servant sent from God, but the Jews apparently don't associate these passages with the Messiah. Instead, they latch onto prophecies about the Messiah's glory days, which are yet to come.

> **Did You Know?**
>
> • More than 1,000 years after Jesus, knights of the Crusades search Israel for the Holy Grail—the cup of wine over which Jesus spoke the words, "This is my blood, which is poured out for many" (14:24). People in the Middle Ages collect sacred relics, which they believe have mystical power. Any trace of the blood of Jesus, they think, will be the most powerful relic of all.

Second, the suffering of Jesus has an important implication for the early Christians reading this Gospel. The book seems to have been written about 30 years after the time of Jesus, during the A.D. 60s. It is in A.D. 64 that Rome catches fire and Emperor Nero decides to lay the blame on Christians. This begins an empire-wide persecution of Christians. Many are martyred in ghoulish coliseum games. Others are executed. Peter and Paul are probably both killed during this holocaust of Christians. The followers of Jesus, during the days of Nero, have to be prepared to follow Jesus to the death.

Jesus keeping secrets. Apparently to keep his already imposing opposition to a minimum, to allow him time to complete his ministry, Jesus repeatedly tells people not to say anything about who he is or what miracles he has done.

When a demon addresses him as "God's Holy One," Jesus orders the spirit to "be quiet" (1:24–25). Jesus forces other demons to do the same (1:34). And when Jesus heals a man of leprosy, he urges the man to tell no one (1:44). Mark is full of other similar examples.

Jesus also uses parables as coded messages to followers—messages hidden from his opponents, who are perplexed by the symbolic stories (4:10–12).

So what's the big secret? Jesus himself. He is the Messiah, God's Son, and revealer of the kingdom of God. And this mystery of Jesus and the kingdom is revealed only to those who have the key that unlocks the door: faith.

Son of Man. This is Jesus' favorite way of describing himself. He uses it 14 times in Mark.

TIMELINE	BIBLE EVENTS	Birth of Jesus ---6 B.C.	Jesus begins ministry A.D. 26	Jesus crucified A.D. 30	Dates are approximate
		10 B.C.		A.D. 1	A.D. 40
	WORLD EVENTS		Trial by combat used among German tribes A.D. 1	Cremation preferred burial method by wealthy Romans A.D. 30	Nero is born A.D. 37

By applying this term to himself, Jesus suggests that he intends to fulfill the prophecy of Daniel 7:13–14: "I saw what looked like a son of man coming with the clouds of heaven, and he was presented to the Eternal God. He was crowned king and given power and glory, so that all people of every nation and race would serve him. He will rule forever, and his kingdom is eternal, never to be destroyed."

This image of a royal, victorious Messiah—which the disciples associated with Jesus—is one that many Christians believe will unfold only at the Second Coming, when Jesus returns to earth (Matthew 24:30).

Author and Date

The writer is unnamed, but Christian leaders in the early second century said it was written in Italy by John Mark, and was based on the memories of Peter. John (his Hebrew name) was also called Mark (his Latin name). It's unclear whether he ever met Jesus (see 14:51–52), but he was well-acquainted with the apostles. It was to the home of John Mark's widowed mother that Peter went, after an angel released him from prison one night (Acts 12:12). Her home was a meeting place for Christians, and a group was praying there when Peter arrived.

Most Bible experts say Mark was the first Gospel written, and that the writers of Matthew and Luke had access to Mark's manuscript, and borrowed from it. Matthew, for example, repeats 601 of the 678 verses in Mark. Most believe Mark was written in Rome by the early 60s. The story does contain Latin terms, and it explains Israel's geography and some Aramaic words, both of which would have been familiar to people living in Israel. The biblical evidence and early Christian writers indicate that both Peter and John Mark were in Rome during the Christian persecution of the 60s.

On Location

The story takes place primarily in what is now Israel, though some of the scenes show Jesus ministering east of the Jordan River, in what is now northern Jordan. The early part of Jesus' ministry takes place in his hometown region of Galilee, in northern Israel. His last week takes place in the Jerusalem area, in the region of Judea. (See map in Matthew, page 282.) ❏

Big Scenes from Mark

Before Jesus begins his ministry, he is baptized by John the Baptist, whom he recognizes as the Messiah's forerunner, prophesied in the Old Testament. Then Jesus goes into the desert for a time of prayer. The public opposition he will soon face is paralleled by the spiritual opposition he faces here. Satan tempts him, trying to get him to abandon his mission, but Jesus proves himself stronger than Satan. He eventually leaves the desert to begin his work.

To learn from him and carry on the work after he is gone, Jesus assembles a group of 12 men. The first four he calls are fishermen who work on the Sea of Galilee. As Jesus is walking along the shore, he sees the brothers Andrew and Simon (whom Jesus later renamed Peter), casting a net.

"Come with me!" Jesus says, "I will teach you how to bring in people instead of fish" (1:17). Both men join him immediately, perhaps because they've already heard his preaching and witnessed his power.

Further down the shore Jesus invites another team of brothers, James and John, bold men Jesus later nicknames "Thunderbolts." They, too, leave their nets and follow.

Later, Jesus selects his remaining apostles: Philip, Bartholomew, Matthew, Thomas, James son of Alphaeus, Thaddaeus, Simon, known as the Eager One, and Judas Iscariot, who would later betray him.

Jesus calls fishermen
•• **(1:14–20)**

Even before Jesus faces opposition from human beings, he faces it from cosmic, spiritual forces. While Jesus is teaching in a synagogue at Capernaum, a seaside fishing village in Galilee, a demon-possessed man storms into the service and interrupts.

"Jesus from Nazareth," the demon yells, "what do you want with us? Have you come to destroy us? I know who you are! You are God's Holy One."

"Be quiet," Jesus replies, "and come out of the man!"

The evil spirit shakes the man, screams, and departs. Jesus has overpowered the cosmic opposition, just as he will later overpower his human enemies.

All the people who witness this dramatic encounter are bewildered and wonder where Jesus gets his power. News of Jesus spreads quickly through the town and beyond, and people begin coming to him for healing. Lepers, lame, blind, demon-possessed—Jesus heals them all.

Jesus casts out an evil spirit
(1:21–28) ••

One Sabbath, the disciples of Jesus pick some heads of grain as they follow him through a field.

A group of Pharisees, a strict Jewish sect, sees this and confronts Jesus. The Pharisees believe that plucking even a few heads of grain is harvesting, which is work, which the Ten Commandments forbid on the Sabbath. Jesus disagrees and tells them the Sabbath was made to benefit people, not deprive them.

Later, Jesus does more "work" on the Sabbath by healing a man with a crippled hand. Rather than marveling at Jesus' obvious power, the Pharisees become so incensed that they start making plans to kill Jesus.

**Picking grain on the Sabbath
(2:23–3:6)** ••

Jesus knows that not everyone will accept his teachings. He reveals this in a clever story about a farmer sowing seeds.

Some seeds fall on the road and are taken by birds. These seeds symbolize people who hear Jesus' message but are snatched away by Satan. Some seeds land in shallow dirt resting on stones; the seeds spring up quickly but die. These are people who accept the message but don't develop spiritual roots. Some seeds land among thorns and get choked. These are people who accept the message but let it get squeezed out by preoccupation with other things, such as making money. Finally, some seeds land in good soil and produce a great harvest. These are people who accept Jesus' message and pass it on.

Through parables like this, Jesus is able to reveal mysteries about the kingdom of God to his followers, for they have the faith in him that it takes to understand the symbolism. But his opponents, who have nothing but contempt for him, often remain mystified by these stories.

Parable of the sower
••• **(4:1–20)**

While Jesus is walking in a crowd, a woman who has been suffering from menstrual bleeding for 12 years decides that even touching the robe of Jesus will bring her healing. When she touches him, Jesus feels a release of power.

"Who touched my clothes?" he asks. Ridiculous question, the disciples think, for they're all in a crowd. Jesus repeats himself, and the woman fearfully steps forward. "You are well now because of your faith," Jesus tells her.

Throughout his ministry, faith is the response Jesus looks for. Through faith, strangers and non-Jews are healed. But without faith, even Jesus' family and the Jewish leaders experience nothing. In Jesus' hometown, lack of faith limits his healings (6:5–6).

**Healed by touching Jesus' robe
(5:21–34)** ••

As Jesus had earlier fed 5,000 people, he again feeds a crowd of 4,000. Earlier, he had five patties of bread, probably pita-style, and two small fish. Here he has seven patties of bread and a few fish. But the result is the same: the people eat their fill, and the disciples collect many basketfuls of leftovers.

Showing an utterly amazing lack of insight about who Jesus is and what he can do, the disciples later suspect he is upset with them for bringing only one loaf of bread on a trip they're taking.

"Why are you talking about not having any bread?" Jesus asks. "Are your eyes blind? . . . Don't you remember how many baskets of leftovers you picked up?" (8:17–19).

Jesus feeds 4,000
(8:1 – 10)

The Son of Man will suffer terribly," Jesus says, speaking of himself. "He will be rejected and killed, but three days later he will rise to life" (8:31).

The disciples believe Jesus is the Messiah; Peter has already expressed this (8:29). But they

can't conceive of a suffering messiah—only a victorious one. When Peter advises Jesus to stop talking like this, Jesus responds, "Satan, get away from me! You are thinking like everyone else and not like God."

Jesus then tells the men that if they are to be his followers, they have to be willing to give up their lives. But he assures them that in so doing, they will preserve their souls. Six days later, Jesus gives Peter, James, and John a glimpse into the afterlife by allowing them to see him in his glowing, heavenly body as he talks with Moses and Elijah (9:2–8).

Jesus calls Peter "Satan"
(8:27 – 33)

While Jesus is teaching, some parents come forward, hoping to have Jesus bless their children. The people in Bible times believe that blessings, like prayers, can unleash a power that otherwise remains untapped.

When the disciples tell the parents to stop bothering Jesus, he quickly seizes the moment to teach his disciples two lessons. Blessing the children, he shows the kind of compassion he wants them to imitate. Then, calling attention to the trusting nature of children, he reveals how to become a citizen of God's kingdom.

But the disciples don't yet understand that God's kingdom is a spiritual one, not a physical one. They argue over which disciples deserve the honored seats beside the Messiah's throne (9:33–37; 10:35–45).

Little children with Jesus
(10:13 – 16)

At least three times Jesus has told the disciples he will die, yet it hasn't seemed to sink in. The jubilant scene as Jesus enters Jerusalem on Sunday gives the disciples all the more reason to anticipate a happy ending. Jesus rides in on a donkey, just like Zechariah 9:9 says the Messiah will arrive.

Crowds welcome Jesus with a carpet of palm branches and cloaks, while cheering him as the Messiah descended from King David: "Hooray! God bless the one who comes in the name of the Lord! God bless the coming kingdom of our ancestor David."

But this joyous scene begins the painful and predominant theme of Mark: the suffering and death of Jesus.

Immediately following this scene, Mark sets the stage for the final battle between Jesus and the Jewish leaders—and for God's rejection of the people who reject his Son. God's rejection of the unrighteous is symbolized first by a fig tree that Jesus kills with a curse, and second by Jesus' prediction that the temple will be destroyed—a prophecy fulfilled 40 years later. Neither the tree nor the temple provide what God intends they provide, so they are destroyed. Likewise, God will reject people who do not exhibit faith in Jesus.

The first Palm Sunday
(11:1–11)

Wednesday, the day before Jesus is arrested, he becomes the honored guest at a meal in Bethany, just outside of Jerusalem and across the ridge called the Mount of Olives. Back in Jerusalem, Jewish leaders are trying to figure out how to catch Jesus away from his admiring crowds, so they can arrest him without starting a riot, then quickly execute him.

But in Bethany, an unnamed woman opens a sealed, stone flask full of expensive perfume—worth a year's salary. This kind of perfume is used on special occasions, such as to anoint the body of a loved one who has just died. The woman pours this on the head of Jesus. Some of the guests quickly begin mumbling to each other about what a waste this is, since the woman could have sold the perfume and given the money to the poor.

Jesus silences the critics. "Leave her alone!" he says. "She has done all she could by pouring perfume on my body to prepare it for burial."

Afterward, Judas goes to the Jewish priests and offers to help them arrest Jesus. Why he does this, we don't know. Luke says only that Satan enters his heart (Luke 22:3). The following night, while Jesus is praying in a secluded place on the Mount of Olives, Judas leads temple officers to arrest him.

**Jesus is anointed at Bethany
(14:1–11)**

When the high priest learns that Jesus is in custody, he calls an emergency session of the Sanhedrin, a 70-member legislature-court of priests, scholars, and respected elders. They find Jesus guilty of blasphemy after he acknowledges that he is both Messiah and Son of God.

This is a capital offense, so at dawn they take him to Pilate, the Roman governor who alone has power to order an execution. Pilate sees no reason to kill Jesus, but the Jews are screaming their insistence. A politician with a knack for survival, Pilate yields to the will of the people and orders Jesus crucified.

At about 9 A.M., Roman soldiers nail Jesus to a cross.

Pleased with their success, Jewish leaders mock, "If he is the Messiah, the king of Israel, let him come down from the cross! Then we will see and believe" (15:32).

At noon the sky turns black and stays that way until 3 o'clock. About this time, Jesus dies. In that moment, an earthquake rips through the land, strong enough to tear the sacred curtain inside the temple. At the foot of the cross a soldier proclaims what the disciples of Jesus still do not seem to believe: "This man really was the Son of God!"

Jesus is executed
(15:21 – 47)

●●●

The body of Jesus is taken down before dusk, when Sabbath begins. There is no time to carefully prepare the body by anointing it with oil, as is the custom. But the corpse is wrapped in linen and placed in a tomb cut from solid rock. The entrance is sealed with a huge, disk-shaped stone that rolls along a stone-chiseled groove on the ground.

Sunday morning, three woman who have followed Jesus walk to the tomb to properly prepare his body for burial. They're worried how they're going to move the heavy stone by themselves. They needn't be. The stone is rolled away. Inside the tomb is a white-robed young man, instead of Jesus.

"Don't be alarmed," the man says. "You are looking for Jesus from Nazareth, who was nailed to a cross. God has raised him to life, and he isn't here" (16:6).

It's uncertain what the writer intends to say next, because there are several conclusions that show up in ancient manuscripts (see "The book's uncertain ending" in Reviews). But whatever happens next is enough to convince even the spiritually imperceptive disciples that Jesus is both the Messiah *and* the Son of God. Fifty days later, on the day of Pentecost, they boldly proclaim this at the temple.

That very day, some 3,000 people place their faith in these words—and the church is born.

Women at the tomb of Jesus
(16:1 – 8) ●●

●●●●●●●●●●●●●●●●●●●●●●●●●●●●●● **Reviews** ●●●●●●●●●●●●●●●●●●●●●●●●●●●●

Old Testament signs pointing to Jesus. Mark told the story of Jesus much like the disciples must have told it after the Resurrection. He builds on the foundation of Old Testament promises about the Messiah, beginning exactly where Malachi—the last book of the Old Testament—ends. He starts by introducing John the Baptist as the promised forerunner to the Messiah.

When the disciples ask Jesus why he speaks in perplexing parables, Jesus shows that he is fulfilling the prophecy of Isaiah 6:9 - 10 (Mark 4:10 - 12). And when Jesus warns the disciples that they will scatter when he is arrested, he confirms this by citing the prophet Zechariah (13:7; Mark 14:27).

The temple falls, as Jesus predicted. One day as Jesus was leaving the temple, one of his disciples expressed wonder at the beauty of the architecture. Jesus replied, "Do you see these huge buildings? They will certainly be torn down! Not one stone will be left in place" (13:2). Jesus then went on to talk more about the coming destruction of Jerusalem.

About 40 years later, in A.D. 70, Rome crushed a Jewish rebellion. They burned the city and leveled the last temple that the Jews have ever had.

The book's uncertain ending. It's a mystery how the writer intended to conclude his book, for there are several endings to choose from. The oldest Greek manuscripts end the book with three women running away from the empty tomb of Jesus, "too afraid to tell anyone what had happened" (16:8).

More recent manuscripts add endings that better match the other Gospels, with the women eventually reporting the news to the disciples, as the angel had told them to do (16:7).

It's possible that the writer died before he completed the book, since he apparently wrote in Rome when Nero was slaughtering Christians. Or perhaps the ending was torn off the original scroll, and other writers added what they knew to be the rest of the story.

Clashing facts. When you read the Gospels side by side, you'll notice some apparent discrepancies. For example, Mark reports that there were three women at the tomb of Jesus on resurrection Sunday, while Matthew speaks of only two. And Mark quotes Peter as declaring that Jesus is the Messiah, while Matthew quotes the apostle declaring Jesus is the Messiah *and* the Son of God.

If four members of a band wrote stories about life on the road with a famous musician, we would expect a lot of overlap, but also some variation. People see the same things differently. And they tend not to have tape recorders running, so their recollection of memorable quotes may not be word-for-word as spoken.

The core issue is whether or not the Gospels witness truthfully in answering the question: Who is this Jesus? The Gospels are early written witnesses to Jesus: They express the testimony of those who had been with Jesus during his ministry, after his resurrection, and (after his ascension to heaven) through the outpoured Holy Spirit. Through all their differences, the Gospels agree that Jesus rose from the dead and is now "both Lord and Christ" (Acts 2:36). And they agree that how people respond to this Jesus determines whether they live or die, eternally. ❏

Encore

• For more insights about Jesus, read the other three Gospels: Matthew, Luke, and John. For the Gospel least like Mark, begin with John.

• Read Acts to see how the disciples respond to their newfound faith that Jesus is the Son of God. ❏

LUKE

When It Happened

(dates are approximate)

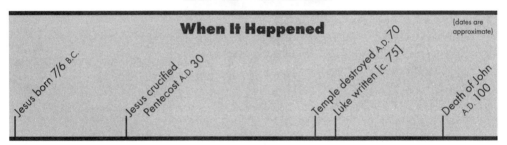

Jesus born 7/6 B.C.

Jesus crucified Pentecost A.D. 30

Temple destroyed A.D. 70

Luke written [c. 75]

Death of John A.D. 100

A Tender Physician's Story of Jesus

The Gospels seem so redundant—pretty much the same stories, same miracles. Why not drop one? Luke, for example?

If early Christians had cut Luke from the canon, we'd miss some of the best-loved stories in the Bible. Luke, a physician, is the only one who reports the birth of Jesus in such moving detail that listening to his version has become as much of a Christmas tradition as listening to carols: "And she brought forth her first-born son, and wrapped him in swaddling clothes, and laid him in a manger; because there was no room for them in the inn" (Luke 2:7, King James Version).

There's the story of the loving shepherd, leaving his 99 safe sheep to look for the lost one. And the story of the prodigal son, squandering his share of the family wealth, then returning home to the open arms of a loving father. And the story of the good Samaritan, a half-breed who shows compassion to an injured man after blue-blood Jews, supposed men of God, walk on by.

Fourteen such stories of Jesus are told only in Luke. There are six miracles, including the one of Jesus healing 10 lepers, and only one coming back to say thanks.

But perhaps what we would miss most is the word *Savior*. Though it shows up once in the Gospel of John (4:42), it's center stage in Luke, from beginning to end. From the choir of angels above a Bethlehem pasture to Jesus' resurrection and ascension, we are invited to witness God's salvation. ❏

Famous Lines

- Our Father which art in heaven, hallowed be thy name (Luke 11:2, King James Version). *The first sentence of the Lord's Prayer.*

- Glory to God in the highest, and on earth peace, good will toward men (2:14, King James Version). *The praise of angels in a shepherd's pasture on the night of Jesus' birth.*

- Physician, heal thyself (4:23, King James Version). *The words of Jesus, anticipating the command of his hometown critics, wanting to see him perform in Nazareth the miracles they hear he has done elsewhere.*

- I am sending you out like lambs among wolves (10:3, New International Version). *The warning of Jesus to 72 followers he is sending on a mission of preaching and healing.*

Behind the Scenes of Luke

⭐ Starring Roles

Jesus, God's son, who has come to earth in human form to offer salvation from sin, and eternal life to everyone who has faith in him (1:31)

12 apostles, men Jesus invites to join his ministry as disciples (5:10; 6:13–16)

📖 Plot

The angel Gabriel makes dramatic appearances to announce the coming birth of two men who will change the course of history: John the Baptist and Jesus. Gabriel tells Zechariah, John's future father, that his son will "go ahead of the Lord with the same power and spirit that Elijah had" (1:17). This foreshadows John's role in announcing the arrival of the Messiah. A month later, Gabriel tells Mary, a teenage virgin from a low-income family, that she will miraculously give birth to Jesus.

Both children are born. John begins his ministry, urging people to repent of their sins and then be baptized to show their devotion to God. Jesus is baptized and begins his ministry. A short time later, John's ministry ends when he is arrested and beheaded for criticizing the governor's marriage to a niece.

Jesus teaches and heals throughout his home region of Galilee for several years, establishing a following of people who believe he is the Messiah. But he draws the ire of Jewish leaders insulted that he doesn't share their interpretation of Scripture on many key points, such as how to show respect for the Sabbath. They keep close tabs on him, like religious police.

As he turns south, toward Jerusalem, his ministry is drawing to a close. But he continues preaching and healing, even among non-Jewish groups such as the Samaritans. When he finally arrives in Jerusalem, boisterous crowds welcome him as the promised Messiah-king. Yet Thursday evening, while praying, he is arrested and rushed to the Jewish leaders who try him all night, condemn him to death, then at daybreak on Friday they insist that the Roman governor issue the death sentence.

That same morning, Jesus is nailed to a cross. By early afternoon, he is dead. On Sunday, however, he is raised to life and later appears several times to the disciples. Some time afterward, on the Mount of Olives, the disciples watch him ascend into the sky.

🎥 What to Look For

The way of salvation. The one fact that drives this Gospel is that Jesus is the savior of the human race. What Luke chooses to report about Jesus—events, miracles, and teachings—all point to this single truth, which angels reveal to shepherds: "This very day in King David's hometown a Savior was born for you. He is Christ the Lord" (2:11).

The most comprehensive story of Jesus. Luke covers Jesus in more detail than any other Gospel, from the announcement of his birth to the report of his ascension into heaven. There's so much carefully reported detail that many Bible scholars refer to the author as the first Christian historian.

Good news for everyone. Luke uses many techniques to show that salvation through Jesus is available to everyone.

1. Throughout the book, Luke reveals that Jesus came not just for the Jews but also as "a light for revelation to the Gentiles," adding that "all mankind will see God's salvation" (2:32; 3:6, New International Version).

2. Unlike Matthew, Luke traces Jesus' genealogy back to Adam, father of all people, instead of stopping with Abraham, father of the Jews.

3. Luke reports Jesus' parable of the good Samaritan, which commends a race that many Jews hate.

4. Luke identifies a remarkable number of women, who in ancient times are usually treated as insignificant. The birth of Jesus, for example, is told from Mary's point of view—not from Joseph's, as is done in Matthew. And most of the male characters in Luke have female counterparts.

> **Did You Know?**
>
> • Luke is believed to be the only non-Jewish writer of Scripture. His literary contribution of the Gospel of Luke and its sequel, Acts, amounts to nearly one-fourth of the New Testament.
>
> • Legend says Luke was an artist, and that in A.D. 590 Pope Gregory the Great used one of Luke's paintings to lead a procession that stopped a plague. An angel is said to have appeared, sheathing its bloody sword, ending the plague. Luke, at least, was a painter of vivid word pictures that inspired many artists.
>
> • John the Baptist and Jesus were related, though the Bible doesn't say how (1:36).

A non-Jewish audience. The book seems written by a non-Jew, especially for non-Jews. The writer makes comparatively few references to the Old Testament, which would have been unfamiliar to Gentiles. Luke is also the only New Testament author who refuses to describe Jesus as a rabbi. Instead, Luke uses the Greek equivalent, a word meaning *master*.

Jesus' compassion for the needy. Luke's Gospel is full of stories showing how much Jesus cares about the poor and the social outcasts.

He announces that he has come "to tell the good news to the poor. . . . to free everyone who suffers" (4:18). "God will bless you people who are poor," Jesus says. "His kingdom belongs to you!" Then Jesus quickly adds, "But you rich people are in for trouble. You have already had an easy life!" (6:20, 24).

Jesus is drawn to the sinners, and even eats with tax collectors—people shunned as profiteering Jewish traitors who collaborate with the Roman enemy.

The prayer life of Jesus. Prayer is important to Jesus. He prays throughout this Gospel, including after his baptism, before selecting disciples, and be-

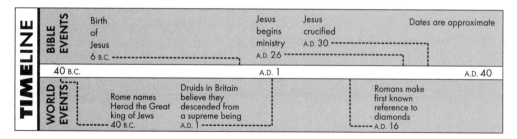

fore dying. He also teaches the disciples how to pray and tells the crowds several stories about the importance of taking requests to God (11:5–9; 18:1–8, 9–14).

Author and Date

Luke, a physician and an associate of the apostle Paul, is traditionally considered the writer of this Gospel, as well as its sequel, Acts. Though the book never names its writer, Christian leaders in the second century attributed the work to Luke. Certainly it makes sense that a physician would write the book that reports more healing miracles than any other Gospel. And leave it to a physician to give the most dramatic account of the birth of Jesus.

Both the Gospel and its sequel are addressed to "Honorable Theophilus," perhaps a Roman official who asked for information about Christianity. In response, the writer produces an eloquent composition, drawing from material gathered from a variety of sources, including eyewitnesses.

The book may have been written as early as the late 50s, before the execution of Luke's companion, Paul. But emphasis on Jesus' prophecy about the fall of Jerusalem, fulfilled in A.D. 70, suggests the book was written in the closing decades of the first century.

On Location

The story takes place primarily in what is now Israel, with some scenes east of the Jordan River, in what is now northern Jordan. Much of Jesus' ministry takes place in his hometown region of Galilee, in northern Israel. His last week takes place in the Jerusalem area, in the region of Judea. (See map in Matthew, page 282.) ❑

Big Scenes from Luke

After the angel Gabriel tells the virgin Mary that both she and her elderly relative Elizabeth will soon give birth to sons (Jesus and John the Baptist), Mary travels south to visit Elizabeth. There, Mary and Elizabeth's husband—the two who received Gabriel's messages—express their praise in what have become known as Mary's Song (also called the *Magnificat,* which means "glorifies") and Zechariah's Song.

Each hymn expresses themes that Luke will highlight throughout the book. "God gives the hungry good things to eat," Mary sings, "and sends the rich away with nothing" (1:53). "You, my son," Zechariah sings, "will tell [God's] people that they can be saved when their sins are forgiven" (1:76–77).

The moving story of Jesus' birth reveals that the first to visit the Savior were not wealthy rulers or prestigious Jewish leaders, but humble shepherds guarding their sheep near Bethlehem. They got an invitation they couldn't refuse: angels filled the night sky with the brightness of God's glory. "This very day in King David's hometown a Savior was born for you," an angel said. "He is Christ the Lord. You will know who he is, because you will find him dressed in baby clothes and lying on a bed of hay."

The shepherds rush to the place and tell Mary and Joseph what the angel said.

Shepherds visit newborn Jesus
•• **(2:1–20)**

Luke gives us the Bible's only glimpse of Jesus as an adolescent.

Each spring, Mary and Joseph take Jesus and their other children to Jerusalem, to celebrate the Passover festival that commemorates Israel's freedom from slavery in Egypt during the time of Moses. One year, when Jesus is 12, he accidentally gets left in Jerusalem after the festival. Mary and Joseph are traveling with a group of family and friends, and incorrectly assume Jesus is among the caravan.

Once they discover he is not, they frantically rush back to Jerusalem and begin searching throughout the city, which is crowded with holiday visitors. After three days they find their boy sitting in the temple courtyard, talking with sage teachers who are astonished at the lad's insight.

When Mary asks her son why he stayed behind and caused her such terrifying worry, Jesus replies, "Why did you have to look for me? Didn't you know that I would be in my Father's house?" (2:49).

Jesus grows wise and strong. "God was pleased with him and so were the people."

Young Jesus debating at the temple
(2:41–52) ••

At roughly 30 years of age, Jesus is baptized and begins his ministry of teaching and healing. Clearly and dramatically, he explains his mission by opening a scroll and reading a prophecy from Isaiah. On hand to hear this inaugural address, in his hometown of Nazareth, are family and friends who have shared a lifetime with him.

"The Lord's Spirit has come to me, because he has chosen me to tell the good news to the poor. The Lord has sent me to announce freedom for prisoners, to give sight to the blind, to free everyone who suffers" (4:18).

Jesus closes the scroll and reports, "What you have just heard me read has come true today."

The people can't believe their ears. As far as they are concerned, Jesus is Joseph's son—not the Messiah. Furious at his blatant blasphemy, they try to throw him from a cliff, but he slips through the crowd and leaves town.

**Jesus rejected in his hometown
(4:14–30)** •

The miracles of Jesus, and his unique insight into Scripture, quickly begins to draw huge crowds. One day as he is teaching in a house, some men can't get their paralyzed friend through the swarm of people. So they remove the roofing tile and lower their friend through the ceiling.

Jesus is so impressed by this show of faith that he says, "My friend, your sins are forgiven" (5:20).

When Jewish scholars instantly object, saying only God can forgive sins, Jesus asks which is easier—to heal the man or forgive his sins. Jesus says he has the power to do both.

"Pick up your mat and walk home," Jesus tells the now-healed paralytic. The man does just that, to the astonishment of everyone present.

Luke uses stories like this to allow Jesus himself to answer critics who, decades later, would raise the same objections that an earlier generation of Jewish scholars had expressed.

**Jesus heals a paralyzed man
(5:17–26)**

• •

A Roman soldier who is not a Jew but who worships God convinces some Jewish friends to do him a favor. They ask Jesus to heal a servant of his who is deathly sick. Jesus agrees and begins walking to the soldier's home, but he is intercepted by others bearing a second message from the officer.

The message is that Jesus need not trouble himself by coming, but can heal the servant from a distance.

"In all of Israel," Jesus says, "I've never found anyone with this much faith!" The servant is healed by the time the messengers get home.

**A soldier's faith
(7:1–10)** •

One evening Jesus decides to leave Galilee and sail across the lake, called the Sea of Galilee, to an area where mostly non-Jews live. In a remarkable story that emphasizes both his humanity and divinity, Jesus has become so weary that he falls into a deep sleep. He isn't even awakened by a sudden squall that terrifies the disciples—many of whom are seasoned fishermen.

"Master, Master!" they scream. "We are about to drown!"

Now awakened, Jesus asks, "Don't you have any faith?"

He tells the storm to be quiet, and the wind and waves fall placid.

Jesus calms the storm
(8:22–25)

After Jesus one day tells a Jewish scholar that the two most important laws are to love God and to love your neighbor, the scholar asks who is our neighbor. Jesus replies with this famous story, reported only in Luke.

A man walking the deserted, 15-mile path from Jerusalem to Jericho is attacked by robbers, stripped, beaten, and left for dead. Later in the day a priest approaches, but walks right on by.

Then comes another temple worker, but he walks by also. Finally a Samaritan arrives, helps the man, takes him to an inn, and pays the innkeeper to take care of the victim until he recovers. Samaritans are considered by Jews as hated half-breeds—descendants of Jews who intermarried with Assyrians and who mangled the Jewish faith by adding elements from pagan religions.

"Which one of these three people was a real neighbor?" Jesus asks.

"The one who showed pity," the scholar replies.

"Go and do the same," Jesus says.

Parable of the good Samaritan
(10:30–37)

Jesus frequently goes off by himself to pray. After one such session, one of his disciples asks that he teach them all how to pray. Jesus responds with an example that has become known as the Lord's Prayer, repeated in the Sermon on the Mount (Matthew 6:9–13).

"Father, help us to honor your name. Come and set up your kingdom. Give us each day the food we need. Forgive our sins, as we forgive everyone who has done wrong to us. And keep us from being tempted."

The Lord's Prayer
(11:1–4)

Jesus has what Jewish leaders believe is a terribly bad habit: he associates with known sinners. "He even eats with them," they grumble (15:2).

In response, Jesus tells three stories to show that the reason he came to earth is to find and save the lost. He tells a story about a lost sheep, a lost coin, and finally the beloved story of a lost son.

In this story, a son asks for and is given his share of the family property. He promptly leaves home and spends all the money in wild living. Broke, he finds himself eating pig fodder to survive. He decides to go home and ask his father for a job, since even the servants are better off than he.

On the son's last stretch home, his father spots him a long way off and takes off running, arms wide open.

This, Jesus is teaching, is how the Lord welcomes each sinner home to the kingdom of God.

**Parable of the prodigal son
(15:11–32)** ••

The story of Zacchaeus is a great example of what the Jewish leaders are talking about. Here Jesus associates with a tax collector—a Jew who collects Roman-imposed taxes from fellow Jews. Tax collectors routinely overtax and keep the extra money.

As Jesus is passing through Jericho on his way to Jerusalem—and to his inevitable crucifixion—a crowd meets him and begins walking with him.

Like others, Zacchaeus has heard of Jesus and wants to get a look at him. But Zacchaeus is too short. So he runs ahead and climbs a tree. When the crowd approaches the tree, Jesus stops, looks up, and says he'd like to stay the night at Zacchaeus' home.

By the time Jesus leaves Jericho, Zacchaeus is a changed man. He offers to give half his money to the poor and to repay everyone he has cheated—four times the amount.

**Zacchaeus the tax man
(19:1–26)**

•••

Jesus arrives in Jerusalem on what later becomes known as Palm Sunday, because cheering crowds welcome him with a carpet of palm branches. Sometime before his Thursday evening arrest, he stands with the disciples in one of the temple courtyards. There, they watch people dropping their offerings into temple collection boxes.

Some donors are rich, and make the size of their gift as conspicuous as possible. When Jesus sees a poor widow give what he knows is all she has, he turns to the disciples and says, "This poor woman has put in more than all the others."

**A widow's offering
(21:1–4)** ••

On Thursday evening, Jesus eats a final meal with his disciples. Then he leads them to the Mount of Olives, where he prays passionately for God to spare him from the crucifixion. Yet Jesus quickly adds, "Do what you want, and not what I want."

Led by Judas, a corps of temple guards arrive and arrest Jesus. They take him to the home of Caiaphas, the high priest, who convenes an emergency session of the Sanhedrin, a 70-member legislature-court of priests, scholars, and respected elders. After an all-night trial, they convict Jesus of blasphemy for claiming to be the Son of God.

At daybreak, the assembly leads Jesus to Pilate, the Roman governor, who alone has the authority to condemn a local prisoner to death. When Pilate refuses, not agreeing that blasphemy is a capital offense, the Jews charge that Jesus is an insurrectionist, stirring up the crowds for a possible revolt. Pilate remains unconvinced, as does Herod, governor of Galilee, who is also in town. But Pilate eventually gives in to the persistent assembly and orders Jesus executed immediately.

**Jesus prays in Gethsemane
(22:39 – 46)**

As Jesus is nailed to a cross he prays, "Father, forgive these people! They don't know what they're doing."

Some in the crowd hurl insults at him. One of the two criminals hanging beside him snaps, "Aren't you the Messiah? Save yourself and save us!" The other man, however, tells him to show some respect for God. Jesus replies by promising that the second man will join him this day in paradise.

Jesus dies about 3 P.M. and his body is entrusted to a Sanhedrin member who had objected to the council's sentence. Jesus is buried in this man's newly cut tomb, but by Sunday morning he is raised from the dead.

**Jesus is crucified
(23:26 – 56)**

On the day of his resurrection, Jesus joins two dejected travelers on their way to Emmaus, a village seven miles from Jerusalem. The two men don't recognize the Lord. They tell him about how the Crucifixion has dashed their hopes in Jesus, whom they had thought was the Messiah. But Jesus, without revealing his identity, replies, "Didn't you know that the Messiah would have to suffer before he was given his glory?" Then he teaches them a Bible lesson, proving his point by quoting the books of Moses and the words of the prophets.

Only later, as he breaks bread for them during a meal, do they recognize who he is. Then he disappears.

Luke and the other Gospels report that Jesus appears to his followers many times after the Resurrection. In his final appearance to the remaining 11 disciples—Judas has hanged himself—Jesus tells them to remain in Jerusalem "until you are given power from heaven" (24:49). After this, they are to tell others what they experienced in their few short years with Jesus.

The book of Acts reports the arrival of heaven's power some 50 days after the Crucifixion, followed by the birth of the church on that very day.

**Jesus on the road to Emmaus
(24:13 – 35)**

Reviews

The Galilee boat. During an Israel drought in 1986, the Sea of Galilee shoreline receded dramatically. Two men who lived nearby noticed in the mud below what looked like the outline of a boat. When they looked closer, it became clear that this was an ancient boat. Rains had recently returned, and the level of the lake was rising, so a team of archaeologists began working in 24-hour shifts to excavate the ancient treasure.

Within a few days they retrieved what they later discovered was a small fishing boat from Jesus' century—perhaps one much like Jesus and the disciples sailed on the evening they got caught in a sudden storm (8:23).

Buried in the mud, the boat was remarkably well preserved with the hull intact. Measuring nearly 27 feet long, 8 feet wide, and 5 feet high, it could carry at least 15 passengers. It would take at least four rowers and a helmsman to propel the craft.

The sudden storm. The squall that caught the disciples off guard one night is like many that still happen on the Sea of Galilee. Actually a freshwater lake, the sea rests in a deep basin 700 feet below sea level, almost completely surrounded by hills. Storms erupt when hot air trapped in this basin rises and collides with cool air blowing in from the Mediterranean Sea and pouring down the ravines.

The virgin birth. Many people, including some Christians, doubt what Matthew and Luke report as the virgin birth of Jesus.

In fact, Matthew's reference to Isaiah's prophecy, "A virgin will have a baby boy" (Matthew 1:23) translates into Greek a Hebrew word that means "young woman," not necessarily a "virgin." The translation that Matthew and Luke used is not unique to them. Jewish scholars translating Isaiah into Greek in the 200s B.C. also used "virgin," apparently wanting to stress what they believed would be God's supernatural involvement in the coming birth of a messiah.

Though Isaiah's prophecy may not point directly to a virgin birth, the reports of Matthew and Luke both say this is how Jesus was born.

Beyond criticizing the translation, some add that a virgin birth implies there is something dirty and sinful about human sexuality—sinful enough that God felt compelled to spare Jesus from any guilt by association. Yet Jesus spent his lifetime in close association with sinners, repeatedly taking flak from Jewish leaders for getting too cozy with the disreputable. And his first miracle in the Gospel of John is at a wedding. Jesus was no prude.

Many Christians view the virgin birth as one more piece of miraculous evidence pointing to what Jesus and the early Christians taught: Jesus is both fully human and fully divine— which, of course, takes us from one mystery to another: How could he be 100 percent both? This question leaves us standing on the foundation that Jesus taught was the most firm of all: faith in God. ❏

Encore

- Acts shows how the disciples boldly continued the work Jesus began, starting the Christian church.

- Matthew and Mark are two similar accounts of the life of Jesus. John also focuses on Jesus, but emphasizes primarily the teachings and miracles that show he is the Son of God. ❏

Behind the Scenes of John

⭐ Starring Roles

Jesus, God's son, who was present at the Creation of the world and who has come to earth in human form to offer eternal life to everyone who has faith in him (1:17)

12 apostles, men Jesus invites to join his ministry as disciples (1:40–45)

📖 Plot

Instead of starting with the birth of Jesus or the beginning of his ministry, John takes us all the way back to Creation. Jesus was there, John says. He was "with God and was truly God" (1:1). This launches the driving theme of the book: Jesus is not just a prophet or the Messiah—though he is certainly both—he is part of the Godhead. He is the Son of God, who has come from heaven and has taken the form of a human being to show people what God is like.

This stated, John introduces the promised predecessor of the Messiah—John the Baptist—who calls Jesus "the Lamb of God who takes away the sin of the world!" (1:29).

Jesus selects 12 disciples to learn from him, help him in ministry, and continue his work after he returns to heaven. Jesus then begins his work, engaging in detailed teaching sessions about who he is and why he has come, and performing miracles that convince many people he is both the Messiah and the Son of God. Most Jewish leaders, however, remain unconvinced that he is anything but a fraud who gets his power from the devil.

The second half of the book tells about the final week in the life of Jesus. He rides into Jerusalem amid cheering masses, washes the feet of the disciples at the Last Supper, then is arrested, tried all night long, and nailed to a cross the next morning. Two days later, Sunday morning, he is resurrected from the grave and is talking again with his disciples.

The book concludes by expressing the hope that readers will believe Jesus is the Son of God, and that through faith they will enter into the kingdom of God and live forever.

🎥 What to Look For

Jesus portrayed as God. John takes Jesus all the way back—to the beginning of Creation. This startling introduction presents Jesus as part of the Godhead. In words reminiscent of the Creation story, John begins his book: "In the beginning was the one who is called the Word. The Word was with God and was truly God" (1:1). *Word* is from the Greek term *logos,* which means different things to different people. The Jews think of it as the power of God, for all God has to do is speak the words, "Let there be light" (Genesis 1:3, New International Version) and there is light. The Greeks think of it as cosmic reason, the well-designed frame on which the universe is built.

Jesus is both of these—the power of God, and the one whose signature is stamped on the universe. But John takes the term still further. Just as a word reveals a thought, Jesus is the expression of God, physically revealing the invisible, spiritual presence of God.

JOHN

When It Happened

(dates ar
approxim

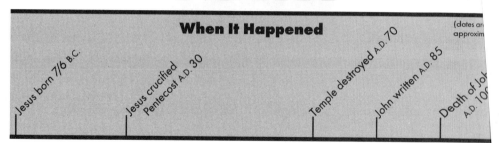

Jesus born 7/6 B.C.

Jesus crucified
Pentecost A.D. 30

Temple destroyed A.D. 70

John written A.D. 85

Death of Jo
A.D. 100

A Deep Thinker's Story of Jesus

John is the cerebral Gospel for thinking humans—perhaps too cerebral for some

If the action-packed Gospel of Mark was written for shorter attention spans, John has the opposite end of the spectrum in mind: people who enjoy peeling off layer upon layer of dramatic, insightful symbolism, and people who want nothing more than extensive, detailed teaching sessions led by the Master Teacher.

Ironically, the Gospel of John exists for one reason: to convince us to have faith in what he cannot possibly explain. The unexplainable is that Jesus and God are one, and that when Jesus lived on earth, he was both truly God and truly human.

John doesn't even try to explain how this could be. He simply reports that it is. He provides testimony from an intriguing array of witnesses, including Jesus himself. And he leaves us with a convincing string of miracles that bear the unmistakable signature of God.

Then John leaves us with a deep and sincere hope that we will have faith enough to believe. ❏

Famous Lines

- "I was blind but now I see" (9:25, New International Version). *A man's response to Jewish leaders who hope to prove that Jesus hasn't cured any blindness.*

- "For God so loved the world, that he gave his only begotten Son, that whosoever believeth in him should not perish, but have everlasting life" (John 3:16, King James Version). *Jesus' explanation of why he has come to earth.*

- "I am the bread of life" (6:35, New International Version). *Jesus' claim to be the source of spiritual nourishment that produces eternal life.*

Jesus is God who "became a human being and lived here with us" (1:14).

The book's purpose. The author himself explains why he wrote the book. "These [stories] are written so that you will put your faith in Jesus as the Messiah and the Son of God. If you have faith in him, you will have true life" (20:31).

What's missing. Notice what John leaves out. You'll not find a single parable. Nor will you find anything about the birth of Jesus, his baptism, temptation, the Last Supper, his agonizing prayer on the night of his arrest, or his ascension into the sky.

John, probably written last of the four Gospels, does not repeat most of stories that have been circulating for decades. Instead, it focuses on Jesus' deity, using carefully selected miracles and teachings that propel this theme.

Did You Know?

• "Doubting Thomas," the synonym for a skeptic, comes from the disciple Thomas, who didn't believe that the other disciples had seen Jesus alive after the Crucifixion (20:25).

• Early Christians gave animal symbols to each Gospel. John's symbol was the eagle. Like a bird of prey, the Gospel circles its target. That's what the writer does. He picks a theme—like his central theme of the deity of Jesus—and circles it many times by saying the same thing in many ways.

Seven miracles. John reports seven miracles of Jesus, which he calls "signs" that prove Jesus is God.

1. Jesus turns water into wine (2:1–12). This shows he is the source of physical life who can take one substance and make it into a new creation.

2. He heals a soldier's son by long-distance (4:46–54), showing he is not limited by geography.

3. He heals a lame man on the Sabbath (5:1–17), revealing he is not limited by time.

4. He feeds 5,000 people (6:1–14), then declares he is the bread of life—the source of both physical and spiritual nourishment.

5. He walks on water (6:16–21), as Lord of nature.

6. He heals a blind man (9:1–41), proclaiming himself the light of the world that can overpower any form of darkness.

7. He raises Lazarus from the dead (11:17–45), revealing his power over death.

Seven "I am" descriptions of Jesus. Jesus describes himself with seven revealing statements. All begin with "I am," the phrase God used to describe himself to Moses: "I am the eternal God. So tell them [the Israelites] that the LORD, whose name is 'I Am,' has sent you" (Exodus 3:14).

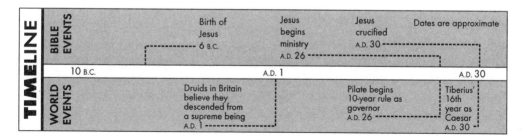

TIMELINE	BIBLE EVENTS				Dates are approximate
		Birth of Jesus	Jesus begins ministry	Jesus crucified	
		------------ 6 B.C.	A.D. 26 --------------	A.D. 30 -------------	
	10 B.C.		A.D. 1		A.D. 30
	WORLD EVENTS	Druids in Britain believe they descended from a supreme being A.D. 1 -------------		Pilate begins 10-year rule as governor A.D. 26 --------------	Tiberius' 16th year as Caesar A.D. 30

1. "I am the bread that gives life!" (6:35). Manna from heaven kept the Israelites from starving in the desert. Jesus says he is the source of spiritual nourishment: "No one who comes to me will ever be hungry."

2. "I am the light for the world! Follow me, and you won't be walking in the dark" (8:12).

3. "I am the gate for the sheep" (10:7), the only entrance into God's eternal kingdom.

4. "I am the good shepherd. . . . I give up my life for my sheep" (10:14–15).

5. "I am the one who raises the dead to life! Everyone who has faith in me will live, even if they die" (11:25). The body will die, but the soul that trusts in Jesus will live forever.

6. "I am the way, the truth, and the life! . . . Without me, no one can go to the Father" (14:6).

7. "I am the true vine" (15:1). Anyone cut off from him will wither and die, like pruned branches.

Several layers of meaning. John's language is rich in symbolism, often with more than a single meaning.

For example, when Jesus calls himself "the bread that gives life," early Christian readers probably envision many images. They think first of wheat or barley bread, one of their staple foods. They think also of the manna that God sent from heaven to keep the Israelites from starving, for Jesus comes from heaven. They think of the bread they eat each Passover to commemorate how God saved them from slavery, for Jesus offers freedom from slavery to sin. And they certainly think of the Last Supper, when Jesus breaks a loaf of bread and tells his disciples that this represents his body, which will be offered as a sacrifice for the sins of humanity. This Gospel invites readers to scan all of the Old Testament's library of images while pondering the meaning of Jesus.

Author and Date

The author is probably the apostle John, one of Jesus' three closest disciples. John is not mentioned in this Gospel, but he is named in the other three. His conspicuous absence here, along with the book's many references to a "favorite disciple" (13:23), suggest he was the writer. When the book was published, probably near the end of the first century, the church accepted it as the authentic testimony of the apostle John.

It's uncertain exactly when the Gospel was written. Some believe John wrote it around the middle of the century, perhaps the same time some of the other Gospels were written. Others suggest John wrote it late in the century, A.D. 85 or later, to supplement the other Gospels. Some Christian writers in the second century say this is exactly what happened, that an elderly John wrote it in Ephesus, a coastal city in western Turkey.

On Location

The story takes place primarily in what is now Israel, with some scenes east of the Jordan River, in what is now northern Jordan. Much of Jesus' ministry takes place in his hometown region of Galilee, in northern Israel. His last week takes place in the Jerusalem area, in the region of Judea. (See map in Matthew, page 282.) ❑

Big Scenes from John

Describing Jesus as the Word—the expression of God, in the way a word expresses a thought—John begins his Gospel by placing Jesus alongside God at the beginning of time.

"From the very beginning the Word was with God. And with this Word, God created all things" (2). Yet this Word "became a human being and lived here with us" (14). In this way, Jesus "has shown us what God is like" (18).

Since humanity first sinned, contaminating God's good creation, God has been working his plan to purge this contamination—to remove sin and its destructive effects. By associating Jesus with the first Creation, John also portrays Jesus as the one who will establish the New Creation, the kingdom of God.

Jesus at Creation
(1:1–18)

Jesus attends a wedding at the small village of Cana. When guests drink the last of the wine, Jesus' mother reports this to him, as though she expects him to remedy the problem.

He instructs the household servants to fill with water six stone jars—each jar holds 20–30 gallons. Then he tells them to dip some out and take it to the reception coordinator. The coordinator says this new wine is the best wine of the feast.

This miracle is the first of seven "signs" or proofs that John reports. These signs are intended to convince people that Jesus is God in the flesh. By turning the natural substance of water into the new creation of wine, Jesus shows he is the source of creation and the sustainer of life.

Jesus turns water into wine
(2:1–11)

While traveling home from southern Israel, Jesus arrives in a small town in Samaria. Tired and thirsty, he sits beside the village well, waiting for someone with a bucket. The disciples have gone to buy food.

When a woman arrives, Jesus asks for a drink of water. But she says she can't understand why he's talking to her, since Jews and Samaritans don't get along.

"You don't know who is asking you for a drink," Jesus replies. "If you did, you would ask me for the water that gives life" (10).

Before the visit is over, this woman has brought the entire village to Jesus, and the people have declared, "We are certain that he is the Savior of the world!" (42).

Jesus talks with a Samaritan woman
(4:1–42)

As Jesus continues his ministry of healing and teaching, huge crowds are drawn to him. One day, 5,000 people approach him in an isolated field along the shores of the Sea of Galilee. When they grow hungry, Jesus miraculously feeds them, using only five small loaves of barley and two fish. Everyone has plenty to eat, and the disciples gather up 12 large baskets of leftovers.

That evening, Jesus leaves the area. But by the next day, some of the people have tracked him down. Jesus accuses them of coming back not to learn, but to eat. They should be seeking spiritual bread from heaven.

"I am the bread that gives life!" he says. "Everyone who eats it will live forever" (48, 51).

Jesus feeds 5,000 people (6:1–59) •

The final and most dramatic of Jesus' seven miracles is the resurrection of Lazarus. As Lazarus lies dying, his sisters send word to their friend Jesus, expecting him to come quickly. But Jesus delays, telling his disciples that Lazarus' illness "will bring glory to God and his Son" (11:4).

By the time Jesus arrives, Lazarus has been dead four days. Jesus orders the tomb opened. And as the group of mourners watch, Jesus shouts, "Lazarus, come out!" Lazarus emerges, "wrapped with strips of burial cloth."

This graphically shows the power of Jesus over death. It also foreshadows his own Resurrection, perhaps a couple of weeks later.

Lazarus returns from the dead (11:1–44)
• •

Before eating the Last Supper, Jesus performs the humble chore of washing the feet of his disciples. It is something servants do for guests, or disciples for their rabbi.

This is not just an object lesson in humility, with deity teaching humanity how to behave. It's also a symbol of the spiritual cleaning that Jesus makes available to everyone. When Peter objects to the washing, Jesus gives a stern reply. "If I don't wash you," he says, "you don't really belong to me" (8).

Years later, when Paul converts, he too must be cleansed. "Wash away your sins," he is told, "by praying to the Lord" (Acts 22:16).

Jesus washes the feet of his disciples (13:1–17) •

At the Last Supper, shortly before his arrest, Jesus predicts that Peter will three times deny knowing him—this very night, before the rooster crows.

When officers arrest Jesus and take him to the high priest, Peter stands outside the priest's home with soldiers and servants, warming himself by a fire. One by one, throughout the night, people ask Peter if he is a disciple of the man inside. And one by one, Peter denies it. At the moment of the third denial, a rooster begins to crow.

By now, Jesus' trial is over and he is condemned of blasphemy. All that the Jews need is the Roman governor's order of immediate execution.

Peter denies knowing Jesus
•• **(18:15–27)**

Pilate, the governor, tries to talk the Jews out of the execution. "You want me to nail your king to a cross?" he asks.

"The Emperor is our king!" they reply (15).

This is a powerful, deeply symbolic moment. There was a time when God was Israel's king, but the Israelites demanded that Samuel choose them a human king. Though this made Samuel, God's prophet, feel like a failure, God consoled him: "I am really the one they have rejected as their king" (1 Samuel 8:7).

When the Jews reject Jesus, once again they reject the kingship of God.

Jesus is crucified
(19:28–42) ••

On Sunday morning, a resurrected Jesus appears to his disciples who are hiding behind locked doors. For some reason, Thomas is not there. Later, when the disciples tell him they've seen Jesus, Thomas says he'll believe it when he can touch the spear wound in Jesus' side and the nail scars on his hands.

A week later, Jesus returns. This time, Thomas is there.

"Look at my hands," Jesus says. "Put your hand into my side. Stop doubting and have faith!" (27).

Needing no more convincing, Thomas replies, "You are my Lord and my God!"

Jesus gently rebukes Thomas for needing proof—after all he has seen. And he commends those in years to come "who have faith in me without seeing me."

Doubting Thomas sees Jesus
•• **(20:24–31)**

Reviews

The anti-Semitic Gospel? John is more hostile to "the Jews" than any of the other three Gospels. When the other Gospels talk about the opponents of Jesus, they specify Jewish leaders, such as priests or scholars. But John simply calls them "the Jews" (5:16, New International Version).

John reports Jesus going so far as to say the Jews didn't descend from Abraham: "Your father is the devil" (8:44). Physically, they came from Abraham. But spiritually, there was no resemblance.

Not all Jews, however, opposed Jesus. In fact, Jesus was a Jew. So were all of his 12 disciples. So were the vast majority of his many other followers.

In the Gospel of John, "the Jews" is a technical term that means the opponents of Jesus, not all people who are racially Jews.

John probably wrote his Gospel in the last quarter of the first century, shortly after Jewish leaders had grown so weary of Jewish Christians worshiping with them that they expelled them from the synagogues. If so, this book was written during the height of an us–them, Christian–Jew antagonism. Many of the Christians were Jews, racially. And many continued to honor Jewish traditions, such as the Sabbath and Jewish holidays. But more and more they were also beginning to think of themselves as distinct. Religiously speaking, they were followers of Jesus. The Jews still worshiping in the synagogue, however, were not.

How many Gods are there? The Gospel asserts that the Word, Jesus, "was truly God" (1:1). Jesus also said he was the Son of God, and "one with the Father" (14:10). Yet when asked what the most important law was, he cited the creed of the Jewish people, first expressed in Deuteronomy 6:4: "Hear, O Israel, the Lord our God, the Lord is one. Love the Lord your God with all your heart" (Mark 12:29–30, New International Version).

The Lord is one. Not two. Not three.

So how can the Lord be one, as Jesus admitted, and yet seem to be more than one, with the Son on earth praying to the Father in heaven?

The Gospel of John doesn't explain how, but the Prologue clearly asserts that the Word-Son-Jesus is God, yet distinct from God the Father (1:1–18). And the end of the book includes another testimony to Jesus' unique identity. After he touches the wounds of the risen Jesus, Thomas exclaims "You are my Lord and my God!" (20:28). In telling us who Jesus is, John stresses both identity (Jesus is the Lord God) and distinction (the Son is closely related to but not identical with the Father or the Holy Spirit). The earliest Christians lived with this complex relationship but left it to theologians in later centuries to explain the complex oneness of God in the doctrine of the Trinity. ❏

Encore

- Other New Testament books traditionally attributed to John are the short letters of 1, 2, 3 John and the mysterious end-time prophecy of Revelation.

- Read Matthew, Mark, and Luke for additional details about the life and ministry of Jesus.

- Acts begins where the ascension of Jesus ends, with the disciples boldly reporting what Jesus taught them. ❏

ACTS

When It Happened

(dates are approximate)

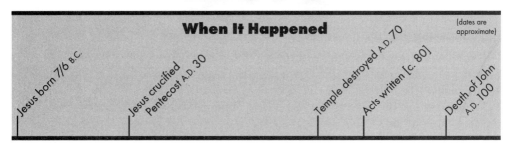

Jesus born 7/6 B.C.

Jesus crucified
Pentecost A.D. 30

Temple destroyed A.D. 70

Acts written [c. 80]

Death of John
A.D. 100

The Church Is Born

It's strange that the second book in a series should be so full of firsts.

Acts, a sequel to the Gospel of Luke, tells of Jesus' ascension into heaven, then proceeds to report on the first sermon by a disciple, the first miracle by a disciple, the first steps toward organizing the Christian movement, the first orchestrated persecution of believers, the first Christian martyr, the first non-Jewish convert, and the first missionary trip.

It's also strange how quickly the original disciples of Jesus become lost in the picture, like a dozen golden stems of wheat blurred amid a harvest field. The disciples are revered throughout their lifetime as leaders of the movement, because of their intimate association with Jesus and the eyewitness stories and divinely illumined insights they often speak about. But other leaders quickly rise, eclipsing the ministry of the disciples who are seldom mentioned in the rest of the Bible.

The book of Acts introduces these wonder-working, charismatic leaders, the most famous of whom is Paul. Acts also reminds us where this wonder-working power and spiritual vigor come from; at each bend in the road, early believers turn for guidance to the Holy Spirit. And like Jesus, the Holy Spirit never misleads.

God's Spirit making bold witnesses out of ordinary people is the reason behind the phenomenal success of the first-generation church. He'll also be the reason behind any successes of the 21st-century church. ❏

Famous Lines

• It is more blessed to give than to receive (20:35, King James Version). *Paul quoting a proverb of Jesus that does not appear in any of the Gospels.*

• Everyone who calls on the name of the Lord will be saved (2:21, New International Version). *Peter announcing that this prophecy of Joel's is now fulfilled.*

• "You will receive power when the Holy Spirit comes on you; and you will be my witnesses in Jerusalem, and in all Judea and Samaria, and to the ends of the earth" (1:8, New International Version). *The last words of Jesus to his disciples, spoken as he ascends to heaven.*

Behind the Scenes of Acts

⭐ Starring Roles

Paul, one-time Jewish persecutor of Christians, who converts to become missionary and advocate for non-Jewish Christians (13:9; in 7:58 by his Hebrew name, Saul)

Peter, leader of the 12 original disciples, who preaches the first sermon after Jesus' resurrection (1:13)

Stephen, the church's first martyr, killed by a Jewish mob (6:5)

Barnabas, Paul's missionary colleague (4:36)

📖 Plot

The story picks up where the Gospel of Luke leaves off, with the ascension of Jesus into heaven. As Jesus rises into the clouds he gives a final instruction to his disciples. He tells them to wait in Jerusalem for the Holy Spirit, who will fill them with power. Afterward, they are to tell everyone what they have witnessed during their few years with Jesus.

Ten days later, the Holy Spirit arrives with dramatic fury, filling the house with the sound of a powerful wind. Suddenly, the Holy Spirit enables the disciples to praise God in languages they have never learned. This amazes the throng of Jewish pilgrims in town from all over the Roman Empire for the holy day of Pentecost, a harvest festival of thanksgiving. Peter preaches the first sermon of the newborn church, and 3,000 people become followers of Jesus.

The believers begin to organize, selecting leaders to help the apostles. But the Jewish council that arranged for the execution of Jesus becomes alarmed at the growth of what they believe is just another heretical Jewish movement. They begin persecuting the believers, trying and imprisoning them. During the trial of Stephen, a newly elected church leader, the Jews become so furious that they drag him outside and stone him to death. Many Christians flee Jerusalem, taking the gospel with them.

One Jew named Saul tries to hunt them down. But on a search-and-arrest trip to Damascus, he meets Jesus and converts to Christianity. Sometime later Paul (Saul's Roman name) becomes a leader of a predominantly non-Jewish congregation in Syria. From there, at the prompting of the Holy Spirit, he and Barnabas are sent on a preaching tour to cities throughout Cyprus and western Turkey. Despite stiff resistance from orthodox Jews, enough people respond favorably that Paul decides to continue his traveling ministry. During about three decades of ministry, Paul starts congregations throughout the Roman Empire.

He is eventually arrested in Jerusalem and sent to Rome for an imperial trial that may have ended in his execution. As the book draws to a close, Paul remains under house arrest in Rome, bravely teaching others about Jesus.

🎥 What to Look For

The acts of Paul. Though the book is called Acts of the Apostles, the original disciples of Jesus quickly disappear from the scene. By chapter six, the book begins introducing other leaders of the rapidly expanding movement. And by chapter 13, Paul emerges as the book's main character and as leader in the ministry among the fastest growing segment of the church: non-Jews. Though the church starts among Jews, over the years the Jews increasingly reject the church and its message that Jesus is the Messiah and Son of God.

"We had to tell God's message to you before we told it to anyone else," Paul explains to a synagogue full of Jews. "But you rejected the message! This proves that you don't deserve eternal life. Now we are going to the Gentiles" (13:46).

God keeping his promises. One of the main points that Luke makes, in both the Gospel of Luke and in Acts, is that God keeps his promises. In the Gospel, Luke points out how Jesus fulfills Old Testament prophecies about the Messiah. And in Acts, Luke reports in meticulous detail of the apostles, Paul, and other godly men fulfilling Jesus' commission to the church: "Tell everyone about me in Jerusalem, in all Judea, in Samaria, and everywhere in the world" (1:8).

The story begins in a strictly Jewish setting, during the harvest festival of Pentecost in Jerusalem. There, the Holy Spirit-empowered church picks up where the ministry of Jesus ends. The apostles and others then take the news of Jesus outside the capital city, to the surrounding region of Judea. Next they start house churches in Samaria, the region to the north. And by the end of the book, the church has scattered across thousands of miles and is welcoming people of all cultures and nations.

The job of the Holy Spirit. Just as the Holy Spirit—the third person of the Godhead—fills Jesus at the beginning of his ministry (Luke 4:1), the Spirit also fills the apostles and other followers of Jesus, giving them supernatural power that helps convince many about the truth of their message (2:4, 43, 47).

Did You Know?

• The term "Christian" didn't surface until about a decade after Christ, perhaps as a demeaning term like "Moonie," used to describe a member of Sun Myung Moon's Unification Church. The earliest Christians called themselves followers of "the Way," short for "the way of God" (24:14).

• Though Acts is the first known history of the church, written as early as 30 years after the Resurrection, it is probably not the first Christian document. Most of Paul's letters were written even earlier, some as early as 20 years after the Resurrection.

• The two books of Luke—the Gospel of Luke followed by Acts—make up nearly one-fourth of the New Testament.

TIMELINE	BIBLE EVENTS	Jesus ascends to heaven A.D. 30	Stephen martyred A.D. 35 Paul converts A.D. 35	Paul's missionary journeys begin A.D. 46		Paul imprisoned at Rome A.D. 60	Dates are approximate
		A.D. 30	A.D. 40	A.D. 50	A.D. 60	A.D. 70	A.D. 80
	WORLD EVENTS	Gamaliel is leading rabbi of Pharisees A.D. 30	Emperor Claudius begins 13-year reign A.D. 41	Buddhism of India introduced to China A.D. 58	Rome burns; Christians blamed, persecuted A.D. 64	Jews in Israel revolt A.D. 66	Mount Vesuvius erupts, burying Pompeii A.D. 79

This Spirit continues filling believers from all walks of life, not only performing wonders through them but also helping them make important decisions (15:28; 16:6–7).

God's surprise attacks on barriers to the gospel. Notice how God continues to surprise church leaders—even the apostles—by knocking down one barrier after another that would restrict the expanding kingdom of God. Here are three examples.

Customs fall. Jewish Christians argue that all Christians need to observe Jewish dietary laws restricting what people can and cannot eat. To Peter's astonishment, God shows him a vision that repeats what Jesus had taught earlier: under God's new covenant with humanity—which replaces the old covenant with Israel—all food is kosher (Mark 7:19; Acts 10).

Racism falls. The gospel is extended to the Samaritans, a race of Jewish half-breeds that pure-blooded Jews hate (8:4–17).

Vengeance falls. Citizenship in the kingdom of God is extended to enemies of Israel, Roman soldiers occupying the land. Though independence-loving Jews will revolt in A.D. 66, Christians are to embrace Roman believers as brothers in Christ (chapter 10).

Author and Date

Luke, a physician and an associate of the apostle Paul, is traditionally considered the writer of this book, as well as its Gospel predecessor—Luke. Though neither book names its writer, Christian leaders in the second century attributed both to Luke.

The two books share a unique writing style and are both addressed to "Theophilus," perhaps a Roman official who asked for information about Christianity. In response, the writer produces an eloquent composition, drawing from material gathered from a variety of sources, including eyewitnesses and perhaps his own travel diary (sometimes when reporting about Paul's ministry the writer refers to "we," as in Acts 16:10).

The book may have been written in the early 60s, before the execution of Luke's companion, Paul, perhaps during Nero's persecution of Christians beginning in A.D. 64. But emphasis in the Gospel of Luke on Jesus' prophecy about the fall of Jerusalem, fulfilled in A.D. 70, suggests to many experts that both books were written later.

On Location

The story covers the first 30 years of Christian history, beginning in Jerusalem. There, the apostles witness the ascension of Jesus into heaven. Ten days later, when the promised Holy Spirit arrives and fills them with power and boldness, the men immediately start preaching the good news about Jesus. Thousands convert. The church quickly expands beyond Jerusalem into most of the Roman Empire. Within three decades Christians are worshiping in house churches throughout what is now Israel, Syria, Turkey, Greece, and even Rome, some 2,000 miles away. ❏

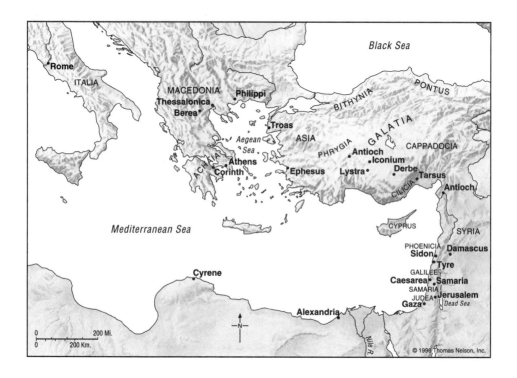

Big Scenes from Acts

Jesus remains with his disciples 40 days after the Resurrection. Then he leads them to the Mount of Olives, across the valley from Jerusalem. "Don't leave Jerusalem yet," he says. "Wait here for the Father to give you the Holy Spirit."

"Then," Jesus says, "you will tell everyone about me in Jerusalem, in all Judea, in Samaria, and everywhere in the world." With this, Jesus rises into the sky and out of sight.

The disciples stare into the clouds, perhaps feeling abandoned. But two angels suddenly appear with this comforting message: "Jesus has been taken to heaven. But he will come back in the same way that you have seen him go."

**Jesus ascends to heaven
(1:1–11)** •••

The disciples return to Jerusalem and select Matthias to replace Judas, who had betrayed Jesus and then hanged himself. After about 10 days the Spirit arrives, flooding the room with the sound of a mighty wind. Above each person's head hovers a flame, perhaps symbolizing the presence of God.

The Spirit's arrival marks a turning point in the way God communicates with human beings. Until now, God has sent the Holy Spirit to only select individuals, such as prophets who conveyed God's instructions to the people. But today, the promise God had made to Joel comes true: "I will give my Spirit to everyone" (Joel 2:28). All who call on the Lord personally receive the presence of God. With this, the mission of Jesus is transferred to the apostles, then to the converts.

The Holy Spirit fills the disciples
•• **(2:1–13)**

When the Holy Spirit arrives, the disciples are mysteriously enabled to speak in different languages. This is a timely miracle, since foreign-speaking Jews from all over the world are in town to celebrate the harvest festival of Pentecost.

At 9 A.M. Peter boldly addresses the crowd, which includes Jewish leaders who 50 days earlier had executed Jesus. Instead of denying that he knows Jesus—as he did the night of Jesus' trial—Peter proclaims that Jesus is Messiah and Lord, and that "God has raised Jesus to life!"

Some 3,000 believe what they hear, perhaps because Peter's words are backed up by miracles. The converts repent of their sin, are baptized, then spend time with the apostles learning more about Jesus.

The church is born.

**Three thousand converts in one day
(2:14–47)** ••

Compassion for the needy becomes a trademark of the fledgling Christian movement. When someone has a need, others sell property and possessions and bring the money to the apostles, who oversee the compassionate ministries.

A man named Ananias and his wife Sapphira decide to sell some property, give part of the money to the apostles, and keep the rest. Appearing before Peter individually they each lie and say they have donated all the money from the sale. When Peter replies that they have lied to God, the accusation strikes them like a blow, and they drop dead. The Bible doesn't state the cause of death. But believers realize the power of the Holy Spirit is not to be trifled with.

A husband and wife die
(5:1 – 10)

Among several Spirit-filled men that the apostles choose to help them is Stephen. He is such a compelling speaker that some Jews have him brought up on charges of "saying terrible things about this holy temple and the Law of Moses" (6:13).

Standing before the same Jewish council that tried Jesus, Stephen doesn't defend himself. He reminds the tradition-minded Jews that God is not confined to any temple built by humans and that their ancestors killed the prophets who spoke of the coming Messiah. Then Stephen has a vision: "I see heaven open and the Son of Man standing at the right side of God!"

Enraged, a mob drags Stephen from the courtroom and stones him to death. Standing nearby, holding the cloaks of the executioners is Saul, better known by his Roman name, Paul.

Stephen becomes the first Christian martyr
(7:1 – 60)

That very day, Jews begin hunting down and imprisoning people who believe as Stephen did. Many believers leave town, taking their teachings about Jesus with them throughout the territories of Judea and Samaria. Philip, who like Stephen is one of seven chosen to help the apostles, travels north to Samaria, a region Jews tend to avoid. Many Jews believe Samaritans are physical and spiritual half-breeds—former Jews whose blood and religion have been contaminated by foreigners.

Despite this prejudice, Philip invites them to become citizens in the kingdom of God. Many accept, prompted by healing miracles that Philip performs.

Philip takes the gospel to Samaria
(8:4 – 8)

Among Jews committed to chasing down these heretics is Saul, whose Roman name is Paul. As he nears Damascus, a brilliant light from the sky strikes him, driving him to the ground. As he trembles in the dirt a voice asks, "Saul! Why are you so cruel to me?"

"Who are you?" Saul replies.

"I am Jesus."

The Lord tells Saul to go on to Damascus and wait for instructions. When the light disappears, Saul is blind. His traveling companions escort him into the city, where he refuses to eat or drink.

God directs a believer living in the city to go to Saul and to pray for his healing. Before Saul leaves town, he is telling others about Jesus, perhaps even quoting the sermon of Stephen.

**Paul's conversion
(9:1 – 19)** ••

At noontime one day, Peter goes to his rooftop to pray. There he sees a vision. Animals prohibited from the Jewish diet since the days of Moses are lowered from heaven.

"Peter, get up!" says a voice. "Kill these and eat them."

The apostle refuses to break the Law of Moses. But the voice replies, "When God says that something can be used for food, don't say it isn't fit to eat."

Peter is baffled by this vision. While he's still thinking about it, messengers from a Roman soldier arrive and ask him to come with them. Peter goes, and the soldier's entire household is converted. When these non-Jews (often called Gentiles) receive the Holy Spirit and praise God in other languages, Peter realizes what the vision means: God's new covenant with Jesus' followers now embraces the entire world.

**Peter's strange vision of animals
(10:9 – 23)**

••

Saul is invited to help lead a growing congregation in Antioch, Syria, about 100 miles from his hometown of Tarsus. Most of the believers are non-Jews, drawn to this new religion teaching that you don't have to be a Jew or observe Jewish customs about diet and circumcision before God will accept you.

While Paul is there, the congregation and leaders alike feel impressed by the Holy Spirit to send him and Barnabas on a ministry tour to other cultures.

The men board a ship and set sail for the island of Cyprus, where Barnabas was raised. There,

Saul converts a high Roman official, Sergius Paulus. From then on the Bible identifies Saul by his Roman name: Paul. Perhaps Paul employs this name to honor the Roman, or perhaps it shows that he has stepped out of the Hebrew culture to minister almost exclusively to the Greek-speaking world.

The journey continues into western Turkey, where the men start tiny congregations in one city after another. Before Paul dies, he will make several such missionary trips, covering about 10,000 miles, planting churches from Turkey to Italy, and earning a reputation as God's apostle to the non-Jews.

**Saul begins his missionary trips
(13:1 – 3)** ••

The church's first big controversy is over whether or not to make non-Jews observe the laws of Moses, especially laws about circumcision and diet, which have kept many people from converting to Judaism.

Peter stands and tells the group about his earlier vision and about the Spirit filling the household of a Roman soldier. Peter argues that this shows God has invited non-Jews to join his people. Paul and Barnabas reinforce this argument by reporting miracles they saw among non-Jews during their recent missionary trip.

In what is apparently a split decision, the council decides against ordering non-Jews to obey Jewish laws. This ruling confirms what many Jewish Christians like Paul have long been teaching: you don't have to be a Jew to be a Christian.

Paul argues against making non-Jews follow Jewish laws (15:1–21)

On a second missionary trip, Paul and his colleague Silas arrive in Philippi, a city in northern Greece. There, Paul exorcises a demon from a slave girl. This infuriates her owners, who have been making money from her demon-powered ability to tell the future. The businessmen convince city leaders to beat and imprison the two strangers for disturbing the peace.

About midnight, as Paul and Silas are singing and praying, a powerful earthquake breaks open the prison doors. The jailer prepares to kill himself because jailers are usually executed when prisoners escape. Paul stops him, calling out that no one has left.

The jailer apparently recognizes the authenticity of their faith, for he takes the two home, treats their wounds, and is baptized as a new believer. The next morning, Paul and Silas are released and escorted out of town.

Paul and Silas in prison (16:16–40)

During his third and final missionary trip, Paul arrives in Ephesus, a bustling city in western Turkey. Ephesus is famous as the worship headquarters for Artemis (the Romans called her Diana), goddess of the hunt, harvest, and childbirth. Her huge temple here is one of the seven wonders of the ancient world.

Paul's preaching winds up cramping the business of craftsmen who make silver statues of Artemis. The craftsmen call a town meeting in the theater, then work the city into a riot by claiming that Paul's preaching is not only hurting the economy, but also undermining the worship of Artemis.

When Paul hears about this, he wants to defend himself before the crowd. But believers convince him not to go near the theater. When the uproar is over, he slips out of town, leaving behind a committed core of Christians.

Riot at Ephesus (19:23–41)

When Paul leaves Ephesus, he returns to Jerusalem where he anticipates arrest. With him he carries an offering he has collected among non-Jewish congregations for poverty-stricken Jewish Christians. Paul hopes this will help ease tensions between Jews and non-Jews. It does not. His presence at the temple sparks a riot that results in Roman soldiers taking him into protective custody and whisking him off to the regional government headquarters in Caesarea, 50 miles away.

In a trial before the Roman governor, Felix, Jewish priests charge Paul with instigating riots and desecrating the temple by bringing in a non-Jew. Apparently unconvinced that Paul has done anything wrong, Felix placates the Jews by holding Paul in prison for two years, until Festus is appointed governor. After two more indecisive trials, one before Festus and another before Agrippa, Roman-controlled ruler of the Jews, Paul appeals his case to the emperor's court in Rome.

**Paul on trial before the governor
(24:1–27)** •••

Late in the year, when sailing can be treacherous, Paul is put aboard ship in the care of a sympathetic Roman officer transporting several prisoners to Rome. After approaching the island of Crete in the hopes of finding a safe winter harbor, they get caught in a two-week storm that blows them 600 miles west. The ship eventually breaks apart in shallow water near Malta, an island south of Italy and Sicily. Miraculously, everyone survives.

Three months later they set sail on a ship that wintered in Malta. By spring, Paul arrives in Rome.

**Paul is shipwrecked
(27:1–44)**

•••

For two years Paul waits for his case to come to trial. Although under arrest and constantly accompanied by a guard, he is free to teach any who come to him. Paul also writes letters to encourage congregations he helped start, such as those in Ephesus and Colossae.

Oddly, the book ends without reporting what happens at the trial. This may be because the case hadn't been tried yet, or because the tragic fate of Paul is so well known that Luke decides to leave the reader with a scene that he believes Paul would like to be remembered by.

Early Christian writers say Paul was beheaded in Rome. The execution may have taken place after this trial. But Clement of Rome, a Christian leader writing in the late A.D. 90s, says Paul was martyred on his second trip to Rome after going to the "extreme limit of the west" (probably Spain, the western extent of the empire).

**Paul preaching, under house arrest at Rome
(28:16–31)** •••

Reviews

Bold disciples confirm the resurrection. Once you've read the early chapters of Acts, and compared them to the closing chapters of any of the Gospels, you can't help but notice the radical change in the disciples. On Passover weekend, in early spring, they run for their lives when Jesus is arrested. They are afraid to stand with him when he faces death. Peter, the lead disciple, won't even admit to household servants that he is a disciple.

Fifty days later, each disciple is willing to face death alone on behalf of Jesus. In the temple courtyard, within the viewing of Jewish leaders who plotted the execution of Jesus, they speak the same words that got Jesus killed: they proclaim him Messiah and Son of God.

Something happened during those 50 days to change the disciples—something that wiped away their fear of death.

They had seen the afterlife. They talked with the resurrected Jesus and ate fish with him along the seashore. Months before they had heard his words, "Do not be afraid of those who kill the body but cannot kill the soul" (Matthew 10:28, New International Version). But now they believed him. And then the Holy Spirit fell upon them, making them bold to witness to the risen Jesus, who is Lord over all.

Fearless of death, they witness to Jesus by continuing His teachings and actions. Eventually, early Christian writers report, this costs them their life. But, Jesus would quickly add, not their soul.

Why did God change his mind about dietary laws? God himself told Moses what kind of animals the Jews could and could not eat. The list is in Leviticus 11. Cattle, sheep, and even grasshoppers are kosher. Pigs, rabbits, and shellfish are not.

Suddenly Jesus comes along and declares all meat edible (Mark 7:19). And God confirms this in a vision to Peter (Acts 10:9 - 16).

The dietary laws were part of God's agreement, or covenant, with Israel. If the Jews obeyed the laws given through Moses—some of which seem to have served no purpose other than to function as a badge of distinction, marking the Jews as a unique race set aside to serve God—Israel would be protected and blessed by God. Repeatedly, the people broke even the most basic laws, expressed in the Ten Commandments (Exodus 20).

"The time will surely come when I will make a new agreement," God said through the prophet Jeremiah (31:31). In this new covenant, New Testament writers explain, God writes his most fundamental laws onto the human heart, so we know right from wrong. This new agreement is for Jews, but also for "everyone who has faith in him . . . God's Son" (John 3:16, 18).

God's plan was to entrust the Jews with a mission: "I selected and sent you to bring light and my promise of hope to the nations" (Isaiah 42:6). Through Jesus, a Jew, God accomplishes just that. ❏

Encore

- Read the Gospel of Luke. This is Part One in the two-part work of the writer, and the volume referred to in Acts 1:1: "Theophilus, I first wrote to you about all that Jesus did and taught from the very first until he was taken up to heaven."

- The 21 New Testament letters that follow, especially letters by Paul, fill in details about events described in the last half of Acts. ❏

ROMANS

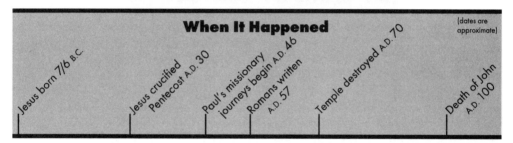

Jesus born 7/6 B.C.

Jesus crucified Pentecost A.D. 30

Paul's missionary journeys begin A.D. 46

Romans written A.D. 57

Temple destroyed A.D. 70

Death of John A.D. 100

Paul Explains What Christians Believe

Second to Jesus, Paul is the most influential Christian of all time. That's primarily because of the legacy he left in the letters he wrote. Romans, his letter to a congregation in Rome, is Paul's masterpiece—a skillfully crafted summary of many important Christian beliefs.

Paul writes the letter as a seasoned minister, 20 years deep in the faith. Out of all he has experienced and witnessed, he shares what he believes are some of the most important lessons of life.

Lesson one: Everyone has sinned and stands in the need of God's forgiveness (3:23).

Lesson two: God not only wants to forgive us, he sent his Son to make forgiveness available to everyone. If we simply have faith in Jesus, Paul explains, God "sets us free from our sins" (3:24).

Lesson three: We should live like we're taking our cue from God, not from the devil. "Dear friends, God is good," Paul says. "Do everything that is good and pleasing to him" (12:1–2).

Romans is not a light read. Though the letter ends with a few chapters of easy-reading, practical advice about everyday living, the earlier chapters are thick with theology, a word that means "God talk." But this theology is important because it explains why Christians believe and behave the way they do. Christians who understand the reasons behind their faith are better motivated, more effective servants of God. History is full of examples (see Did You Know?). The future will be, as well. ❏

Famous Lines

- The wages of sin is death; but the gift of God is eternal life (6:23, King James Version).

- All have sinned, and come short of the glory of God (3:23, King James Version).

- All things work together for good to them that love God (8:28, King James Version).

Behind the Scenes of Romans

★ Starring Role

Paul, a formerly ultraconservative Jew who becomes the early church's leading minister to non-Jewish Christians (1:1)

📖 Plot

This is a letter with a theme—salvation—not a story with a plot. But the letter has a background that helps us understand what is on Paul's mind as he writes.

Two decades into his ministry, Paul is near the end of his third and final missionary trip. He feels like he has done about all he can in the eastern Mediterranean. So he's going to deliver an offering he has collected for poverty-stricken Jewish Christians in Jerusalem. Then he hopes to take his teachings about Jesus to Spain, at the western perimeter of the Roman Empire. On the way, he'll stop in Rome to meet believers there.

So before returning to Jerusalem—where he will be arrested—he writes the Romans to tell them of his plans and to solicit their help. Because Paul wants them to know who they will be helping, he tells them about his beliefs.

Paul says that everyone—Jew and non-Jew alike—has sinned and needs the forgiveness and salvation of God. Without these, people remain covered in guilt, unfit to stand in the presence of a holy God. So God is forced to condemn them to an eternity of separation from him. But Paul says it doesn't have to be this way. God has provided forgiveness and salvation through the sacrificial death of Jesus. All that human beings need to do to receive both of these is to have faith—an attribute with a long Jewish tradition dating to the time when elderly Abraham, father of the Jews, trusted that God would give him a son and make their descendants into a nation.

When people are saved, Paul says, the Holy Spirit makes himself at home inside them. The Spirit empowers people to live a godly life—to say no to evil desires that once controlled them like domineering bosses, and to pursue sacred opportunities they would not otherwise have seen.

🎥 What to Look For

The reason Paul writes the letter. Paul has never been to Rome and was apparently not involved in starting the congregation there. But he writes "there is nothing left for me to do in this part of the world, and for years I have wanted to visit you. So I plan to stop off on my way to Spain. Then . . . I hope you will quickly send me on" (15:23–24). In this last sentence Paul appears to hint that he would appreciate it if believers in Rome would help back his trip, with prayer and funds.

Romans is like an ambassador's letter of introduction, identifying who Paul is ("a servant of Jesus Christ," 1:1) and what message he intends to preach in Spain, in order to prepare the way for a good reception when he arrives.

An introduction to basic Christian beliefs. In short order, Paul's words stop sounding like a letter and start sounding like a textbook for Christianity 101. Paul's thesis is this: "I am proud of the good news! It is God's powerful way of saving all people who have faith, whether they are Jews or Gentiles" (1:16).

Paul then explains what this good news is: "You will be saved, if you honestly say, 'Jesus is Lord,' and if you believe with all your heart that God raised him from death" (10:9). Paul goes on to talk about the radically new life of such a person, carefully explaining religious ideas that are sometimes hard to understand: sin, grace, faith, justification, redemption, salvation, sanctification, death, and resurrection.

Of sanctification, for example, a word that means holiness, Paul says that the Holy Spirit makes "Gentiles into a holy offering" (15:16). This doesn't mean they become morally perfect. It means that God has seen their faith and he has separated them from the faithless. "Holy" means reserved for God's purpose. And it's God who makes the reservation, not on the basis of our behavior but on the basis of our faith, which inevitably changes our behavior.

> **Did You Know?**
>
> • Romans has been a life-changing read for many. After Martin Luther read in it that salvation is through faith and not church rituals, the Protestant Reformation was born. Woman-chasing, pleasure-loving Augustine was converted after reading Romans 13:13 – 14, a passage about turning from reckless living and embracing Jesus. Methodist founder John Wesley felt "strangely warmed" after studying the book. A revival in England followed.
>
> • Romans is the first letter in the New Testament because it's the longest of the letters. The letters were originally arranged from longest to shortest, but that order changed a bit over time.

Four big ideas. Paul has created, in Romans, a study filled with deep theological insight. So Bible experts have broken the work down into many possible outlines—the raw frame on which they believe Paul built the letter. Here's one of many outlines.

After introducing himself, Paul shows that everyone has sinned and needs salvation (1:18—3:20). He explains how God has made salvation available through Jesus (3:21—8:39). Next Paul assures everyone that there's ample room in the kingdom of God for Jews (9—11). Paul closes with lessons about how to behave (12—15), followed by a chapter of personal notes concerning many individuals.

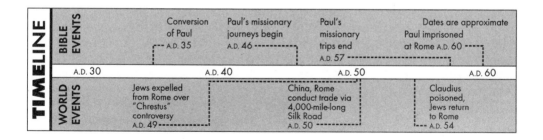

TIMELINE	BIBLE EVENTS		Conversion of Paul A.D. 35	Paul's missionary journeys begin A.D. 46	Paul's missionary trips end A.D. 57	Dates are approximate Paul imprisoned at Rome A.D. 60
		A.D. 30	A.D. 40		A.D. 50	A.D. 60
	WORLD EVENTS		Jews expelled from Rome over "Chrestus" controversy A.D. 49		China, Rome conduct trade via 4,000-mile-long Silk Road A.D. 50	Claudius poisoned, Jews return to Rome A.D. 54

Author and Date

Paul wrote the letter in about A.D. 57, possibly in Corinth, Greece, near the end of his third and final missionary journey.

"I am now on my way to Jerusalem," he writes, "to deliver the money that the Lord's followers in Macedonia and Achaia collected for God's needy people. . . . After I have safely delivered this money, I will visit you and then go on to Spain" (15:25–28).

Unfortunately, Paul was arrested when he got to Jerusalem and imprisoned for two years. When he finally does arrive in Rome, in about A.D. 60, he is a prisoner waiting for trial in the emperor's court. It's unclear if Paul is executed after this trial, or if he is released, only to be executed following a later trial in the city after returning from Spain.

On Location

Paul addresses a Christian congregation in Rome, capital of the Roman Empire. Paul has ministered throughout the eastern Mediterranean, in what is now Israel, Syria, Turkey, and Greece. (See map in Acts, page 323.) Now he hopes to visit Rome on his way to taking the gospel to Spain, at the western edge of the empire. ❏

Big Scenes from Romans

After 20 years of ministry in the eastern Mediterranean, Paul feels he has done all he can there and that it's time to move on.

"I want you to know that I have often planned to come for a visit," Paul writes to the congregation in Rome. "But something has always kept me from doing it. I want to win followers to Christ in Rome, as I have done in many other places. It doesn't matter if people are civilized and educated, or if they are uncivilized and uneducated. I must tell the good news to everyone" (1:13–15).

After spending time in Rome, Paul says he hopes the believers there will help send him on to Spain. But because most people in the congregation know Paul only by reputation, he writes a letter introducing himself and his beliefs. Most likely, the letter is read aloud during one of the meetings, which are often held in the larger homes of the more wealthy church members. Because Paul's letter is such a masterfully crafted summary of important Christian beliefs, it is probably copied and circulated among churches throughout the empire.

Christians worshiping in Rome
•• **(1:1–17)**

A hallmark of Paul's beliefs is that people become acceptable to God through faith—not through making sacrifices or observing Jewish customs, such as circumcision, dietary restrictions, and annual religious holidays.

This is great news to people from non-Jewish backgrounds. Many of them have worshiped God, but have stopped short of converting to Judaism because of the seemingly harsh requirements. On the other hand, most Jews—even Jewish Christians—believe that their traditions come from God and are sacred. They don't believe that mere faith can save anyone.

To prove that faith is enough, Paul reminds his readers that God singled out Abraham to become father of the Jews because of Abraham's faith—not because he followed the rules. Most of the rules, in fact, didn't arrive until several centuries later, in the time of Moses.

"You cannot make God accept you because of something you do," Paul writes. "God accepts sinners only because they have faith in him" (4:5).

As convincing as Paul could be, age-old traditions die hard. And throughout Paul's lifetime and beyond, this remained a touchy topic for Jewish and non-Jewish Christians worshiping together, as they likely did in Rome.

Abraham, an example of faith
(4:1–25) ••

All of us have sinned and fallen short of God's glory," Paul writes. "But God treats us much better than we deserve, and because of Christ Jesus, he freely accepts us and sets us free from our sins" (3:23–24).

Paul explains what the story of Genesis reveals, that sin and death entered the world when Adam and Eve disobeyed God and ate forbidden fruit. God's good creation became contaminated. "Adam sinned, and that sin brought death into the world," Paul explains. "Now everyone has sinned, and so everyone must die."

The problem is that a holy God cannot coexist with sin. The sin must be cleansed, or the sinner removed from the presence of God. In Old Testament times, God set up the sacrificial system as a way to allow people to find cleansing and forgiveness. The death of the animal graphically

reminded everyone of the deadly seriousness of sin. Later, God sent Jesus as the ultimate and final sacrifice, launching a new means of spiritual cleansing. In a way that we can't fully understand, Christ's sacrifice and resurrection provided a way for individual human beings to correct the damage done by Adam. We correct the damage when we have faith that Jesus is the remedy for sin and death.

"Adam disobeyed God and caused many others to be sinners," Paul says. "But because of the good thing that Christ has done, God accepts us and gives us the gift of life" (5:19, 18).

**Adam brings death,
Jesus brings life
(5:12—6:14)** ••

The church gets its start among Jews who believe Jesus came to earth as the Messiah and Son of God. But as time passes and the church realizes that this means the prophesied age of the new covenant has arrived, and the age of the old covenant had ended—with all of its laws about circumcision, diet, and rituals—Jews become increasingly hostile toward Christianity. By the end of the century Jews will prohibit Jewish Christians from worshiping in synagogues.

Paul realizes that non-Jewish believers might begin looking down on Jews, including Jewish Christians. But Paul reminds his mostly non-Jewish readers that God has carefully cultivated the Jewish people, just as a farmer cultivates and purposefully prunes an olive tree.

"You Gentiles are like branches of a wild olive tree," Paul says, which has been grafted to the "cultivated olive tree" (11:17).

Paul's point is clear. The roots of Christian faith are Jewish. For it is the Jews who have long been drawing spiritual nourishment from God. And it is through Jews—such as Jesus, the disciples, and Paul—that God extends salvation to the rest of the world.

Even though most Jews reject God, Paul says, "they are still the chosen ones, and God loves them" (11:28). In the end, Paul adds, Israel will return to God and be saved.

**Jews and non-Jews
become children of God
(9—11)**

•••

Paul explains that when Jesus sacrificed himself for the sins of the human race, this rendered the Jewish sacrificial system obsolete. In practice, Romans ended it 40 years later when they destroyed the temple. Since A.D. 70 the Jews have not had a temple for making sacrifices. A 1,300-year-old mosque now sits on the temple hilltop.

Instead of offering animal sacrifices, Paul urges the people to offer their bodies "as a living sacrifice, pure and pleasing. That's the most sensible way to serve God. Don't be like the people of this world, but let God change the way you think. Then you will know how to do everything that is good and pleasing to him" (12:1–2).

This letter makes such an impression on the Romans that when Paul finally arrives in Italy, as a prisoner on his way to court, many of the congregation travel 40 miles to meet and accompany him on the last leg of his journey (Acts 28:15).

**Behaving like children
of a loving God
(12:1–21)**

·················· **Reviews** ··················

Tension between Christians and Jews. Paul talks a lot about Jews having the right to membership in the church, as though he's addressing a predominantly non-Jewish congregation that wonders if Christianity is big enough for both.

First-century Roman historian Suetonius says that in A.D. 49 there was such an uproar among Jews over "Chrestus," probably Christ, that Emperor Claudius expelled the Jews from Rome. They weren't allowed to return until Claudius died in A.D. 54, just a few years before Paul reminded the mostly non-Jewish church of Rome that in God's eyes there's no difference between Jew and non-Jew: "No one who has faith will be disappointed, no matter if that person is a Jew or a Gentile," Paul writes. "There is only one Lord, and he is generous to everyone who asks for his help. All who call out to the Lord will be saved" (10:11 – 13).

Politically incorrect about homosexuality. Some describe Paul as homophobic. He says homosexuality is "not natural," even "shameful." He stops only a hair shy of name-calling when he implies that practicing homosexuals are perverts: receiving "due penalty for their perversion" (1:27, New International Version).

Creative Bible interpreters say that when Paul spoke of "unnatural" sexual behavior he was condemning homosexual acts by heterosexuals. But this interpretation doesn't come from Paul. It comes from the prevailing belief today that homosexuality is natural for some people.

As politically incorrect as it may be, when Paul says homosexual acts are unnatural, he means they're sinful, they're contrary to God's plan. Paul is repeating what God revealed to Moses more than a thousand years earlier. For along with prohibiting adultery, incest, and having sex with animals, God said: "It is disgusting for a man to have sex with another man" (Leviticus 18:22).

Even if homosexual tendencies are determined by genetics or by events in life, and therefore we are not responsible for our sexual desires, we are responsible for our actions. And though it would seem unfair for God to place such a burden on human beings, people in this sin-damaged world carry a wide variety of burdens.

"If you are tired from carrying heavy burdens," Jesus once said, "come to me and I will give you rest. Take the yoke I give you. Put it on your shoulders and learn from me" (Matthew 11:28 – 29).

Whatever the burden, Jesus promises to help us carry it and learn from it. ❏

·················· **Encore** ··················

- Read Galatians for another in-depth, but more freewheeling, emotion-packed glimpse into Paul's beliefs.

- For more about how Christianity grows out of the Jewish faith, and fulfills it, read Hebrews. ❏

1 CORINTHIANS

When It Happened

(dates are approximate)

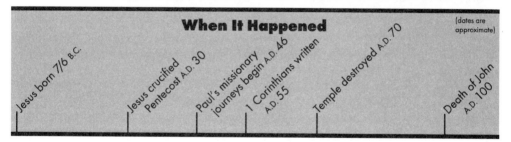

Jesus born 7/6 B.C.

Jesus crucified Pentecost A.D. 30

Paul's missionary journeys begin A.D. 46

1 Corinthians written A.D. 55

Temple destroyed A.D. 70

Death of John A.D. 100

Paul's Letter to a Fractured Church

There's no such thing as a perfect church when human beings are on the roll. Never has been, never will be, until the roll is called up yonder.

Consider the church founded by the most notable, influential, successful Christian minister of first-generation believers. Paul didn't stay in Corinth only a few days or weeks, as he did in most cities. He stayed for two years, training and nurturing the spiritual infants. Several years later, however, the Corinthians were still behaving like disobedient, rebellious kids.

They were arguing over who in the church was most important, suing each other in court, turning a blind eye to incest among the congregation, and showing that they were thoroughly confused about key Christian beliefs such as the Resurrection.

In a blunt though loving letter, Paul replies to an array of practical questions the Corinthians raised in a letter to him. But he also confronts issues they were apparently too embarrassed to mention.

This is not a boring letter.

First Corinthians is gripping because of the deeply emotional issues Paul tackles. And it's timely because, unfortunately, there's a little bit of Corinth in every church—a lot of Corinth in some. ❑

Famous Lines

• Let's eat and drink. Tomorrow we die (15:32). *Paul quotes a Greek proverb to suggest what our attitude should be if Christ was not raised from the dead.*

• O death, where is thy sting? O grave, where is thy victory? (15:55, King James Version). *A praise of believers who realize that, like Jesus, they too will be resurrected.*

• God is faithful; he will not let you be tempted beyond what you can bear (10:13, New International Version).

• Your body is a temple where the Holy Spirit lives (6:19). *Paul's reminder to the Corinthians to take good care of their bodies.*

Behind the Scenes of 1 Corinthians

★ Starring Role

Paul, leading minister to the non-Jewish world, and founder of the church at Corinth, Greece (1:1)

Plot

A couple of years after leaving the church he started in Corinth, Paul receives troubling news. Messengers arrive with a letter from the congregation asking for his help in solving a number of divisive problems. Not all the bad news is in the letter. The messengers and other sources report additional problems: power struggles among the leadership, cliques in the congregation, an I-don't-want-to-get-involved attitude about church members engaged in illicit sex, Christians suing Christians.

Paul begins his letter by dealing with these problems first, since they reflect a deep-seated misunderstanding about what it means to be a Christian. Only then, beginning with chapter 7, does he address the questions that the Corinthians asked—questions about more practical issues of everyday living and worship services. Questions such as, "Is it best for people not to marry?" (7:1). And is it okay to eat "food offered to idols" (8:1), which priests sell wholesale to meat vendors who resell it at a profit in the meat markets?

In all of Paul's advice, he urges the believers to act in unity and love. If they can do this, he teaches, their other problems will wither and die.

What to Look For

A power struggle in the church. The congregation is breaking into factions that prefer one of at least three leaders: Paul, Peter, or Apollos (1:12). Apollos, mentioned in Acts 18:24–28, is an Old Testament scholar and a charismatic speaker. Peter, one of the original disciples of Jesus, may have appealed to Jewish Christians at Corinth. Paul, founder of the church and advocate for non-Jewish believers, maintained a loyal core of supporters.

"Don't take sides," Paul advises. "Has Christ been divided up? Was I nailed to a cross for you?" (1:10, 13).

Christians behaving badly. Besides the power struggle, there are other problems in the church—many stemming from Christians behaving as if they have a license to sin. There is a man who has married his stepmother, in defiance of both Roman and Jewish law that considers this incest (Deuteronomy 27:20). Paul is shocked that the congregation lets this man remain in the church, as though he is doing nothing wrong.

Though God judges people outside the church, Paul says, Christians have an obligation to judge and discipline their members. Paul advises the Corinthians to stay away from professing believers who are blatantly "immoral or greedy or worship idols or curse others or get drunk or cheat" (5:11). In even sterner advice Paul adds, "Chase away any of your own people who are evil" (5:13).

Another example of bad behavior is Christians suing each other in "a court of sinners" (6:1).

"Can't you settle small problems?" Paul asks. "Why do you take everyday complaints to judges who are not respected by the church?" (6:2, 4).

Practical advice about life and worship. In chapter 7 Paul starts answering a variety of questions the church has asked him.

Here's a sampling of the topics.

Marriage. Paul apparently expects Jesus to return soon, so he advises people not to get married, but he concedes "it is better to marry than to burn with desire" (7:9).

Eating food offered to idols. Paul says this issue is not particularly important, since all food comes from God. Paul does say, however, that Christians should be sensitive to other believers who have scruples against eating such food (8:1–13).

Dressing for worship services. People should dress appropriately, Paul says, not as trend-setters calling attention to themselves or as lures for the opposite sex (11:1–16).

The Lord's Supper. This is a shared celebration of the death and resurrection of Jesus, Paul explains. But Corinth has turned it into a segregated potluck, where rich members cluster in cliques to eat rich folks' food, while the poor eat comparative crumbs (11:20–33).

Spiritual gifts. God gives different abilities to different people, Paul says. Each gift is important and useful in God's work (12:1–31).

A beautiful hymn about love. One of the most famous chapters in the Bible is Paul's lyrical message about love. The poem comes immediately after Paul has talked about other gifts from God, to emphasize that all talent is useless if it doesn't flow from a heart of love. "What if I could speak all languages of humans and of angels?" Paul asks. "If I did not love others, I would be nothing more than a noisy gong or a clanging cymbal" (13:1).

The ability to love others, Paul argues, is the greatest gift of all—greater than hope, and even greater than faith (13:13). This is a powerful message especially in Corinth, a city famed for its great temple of Aphrodite, goddess of love.

Author and Date

"I am signing this letter myself: PAUL" (16:21). This conclusion, along with the introduction, "From Paul," (1:1), clearly identifies who the writer is.

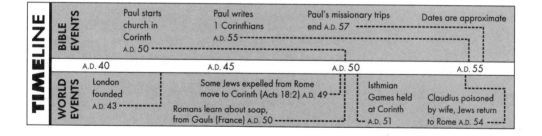

		Paul starts church in Corinth A.D. 50	Paul writes 1 Corinthians A.D. 55	Paul's missionary trips end A.D. 57	Dates are approximate
TIMELINE	**BIBLE EVENTS**	A.D. 40	A.D. 45	A.D. 50	A.D. 55
	WORLD EVENTS	London founded A.D. 43	Some Jews expelled from Rome move to Corinth (Acts 18:2) A.D. 49 / Romans learn about soap, from Gauls (France) A.D. 50	Isthmian Games held at Corinth A.D. 51	Claudius poisoned by wife, Jews return to Rome A.D. 54

Early church leaders included this letter in the New Testament because they believed it came from the pen of Paul, the most influential minister among first-generation Christians.

Paul wrote the letter from Ephesus in about A.D. 55, two or three years after leaving Corinth. Some five years earlier Paul first arrived in the city and started the church during the second of his three missionary trips throughout the eastern Mediterranean. Paul didn't usually stay in a town longer than a few weeks, but he made an exception for Corinth, a busy port city full of international travelers who might hear his message and take it home with them. Paul stayed in Corinth for two years, then returned after writing 1 Corinthians, during his third missionary trip.

On Location

Paul's letter is addressed to Christians in a young church he started a few years earlier, during his second missionary journey (shown on the map), at Corinth, perhaps the busiest city in ancient Greece. Located south of Athens, Corinth is near a four-mile-wide land bridge separating the Aegean Sea in the east and the Adriatic Sea in the west.

Eastern trade ships carrying products destined for Rome and other western cities would often stop in Corinth. If the ship were small enough, it could be hauled up onto a huge wagon, wheeled across the isthmus, then launched into the Adriatic. This saved merchants a 200-mile trip around the tip of Greece, sparing them from storms and pirates. Larger ships unloaded their cargo and had it hauled to other ships waiting at the Adriatic port. Nero started a canal in A.D. 66, but the project was stopped after engineers doubted it could be done and Corinthians complained that a canal would keep travelers from stopping in the city. The project was completed in 1893 and is still used. ❏

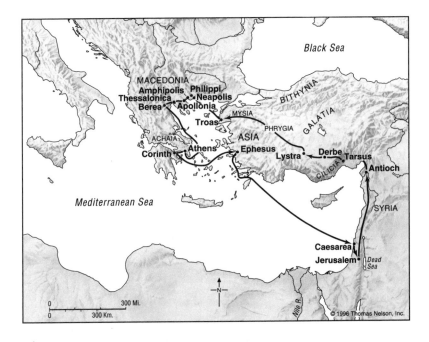

Big Scenes from 1 Corinthians

A few years after Paul leaves the church he founded in Corinth, continuing his preaching trips throughout the eastern Mediterranean, the congregation splits into squabbling factions. Some prefer the guidance of their founding minister. Others prefer the interpretations of Peter, who is still observing many Jewish customs and probably living in Jerusalem. Others gravitate to Apollos, a brilliant scholar and dynamic speaker living in Corinth.

Paul begs the Corinthians to stop arguing, since only Christ is the leader of the church. "Was I nailed to a cross for you?" Paul asks. "Were you baptized in my name?" (1:13).

All three leaders are merely servants of God, Paul says. "Paul and Apollos and Peter all belong to you" (3:22). Comparing God's spiritual kingdom to a garden, Paul says "I planted the seeds, Apollos watered them, but God made them sprout and grow" (3:6).

Christians quarrel over who's in charge (1:10–31)

Paul is shocked to find out that a member of the church has married his stepmother, and the church has taken no action to discipline him. By both Roman and Jewish standards, the man has committed incest.

"In my other letter [before 1 Corinthians] I told you not to have anything to do with immoral people," Paul says. "But I wasn't talking about people of this world. You would have to leave this world to get away from everyone who is immoral or greedy or who cheats or worships idols. I was talking about your own people" (5:9–11). Paul explains that God judges those outside the church, but believers have a responsibility to protect the name of Jesus by disciplining those who call themselves Christians.

Paul's advice: "Expel the wicked man from among you" (5:13, New International Version). This harsh judgment is not to condemn the man to everlasting banishment, but to bring him to his senses so he will repent and return to Christ and the church.

Immorality in the church (5:1–13)

Bickering among the church gets so bad that Christians start taking each other to court.

"Why should one of you take another to be tried by unbelievers?" Paul asks. "Aren't any of you wise enough to act as a judge between one follower and another?"

Roman courts operated without the notions we cherish today: fairness and justice being blind. Roman judges were expected to decide in favor of the wealthier, more influential party. The poor and other persons of low social standing feared being hauled into court, because—guilty or innocent—their misery would surely be multiplied if their accuser were higher class or wealthier. In prohibiting lawsuits between believers, Paul protects the socially weaker members and calls the whole church to its responsibility to apply God's wisdom to disagreements among themselves.

Christians suing Christians (6:1–11)

In many churches, Corinth included, when believers observe the ritual of the Lord's Supper by eating bread and drinking wine that represents the body and blood of the crucified Jesus, they also eat a full meal called a "love feast."

A problem develops.

"You don't really celebrate the Lord's Supper," Paul writes. "You even start eating before everyone gets to the meeting, and some of you go hungry, while others get drunk" (11:20–21).

The love feast is apparently like a potluck, held at a large meeting place, often the home

of wealthy members. Church members cluster in socio-economic cliques—rich folks eating fancy food together and poorer families and slaves eating the meager morsels they can bring.

This dishonors Christ, Paul says, and it divides people who should be united in gratitude for what Jesus did for them on the Cross.

Paul advises the people who are hungry to eat before they come to worship, so they can concentrate on the ritual meal and thank Jesus for the gift of salvation and the promise of a resurrection.

More of a segregated feast than a Lord's Supper (11:17–34) ••

Paul writes that God has entrusted to the people at Corinth a wide variety of talents, or gifts: prophecy, healing, teaching, speaking in other languages. All of these are important because they allow Christians to help others. But Paul says the greatest gift of all—the gift that channels our talents in the right direction—is the gift of love.

"What if I could prophesy and understand all secrets and all knowledge?" Paul asks. "I would gain nothing, unless I loved others."

Compassionate love—inspired by Christ's death for humanity—produces a selfless people who are kind and patient, not boastful or easily angered, always supportive and hopeful, never keeping a record of the wrongs that others do.

Christians don't start out this way, Paul says. "When we were children, we thought and reasoned as children do. But when we grew up, we quit our childish ways" (13:11).

Growing Christians cultivate an attitude of love above all others. Among the three most noble traits—faith, hope, and love—Paul says "the greatest is love."

God's greatest gift: the ability to love
•• **(13:1–13)**

Some Corinthians are confused about the resurrection of Jesus and what it has to do with them. Some apparently don't believe that bodies will be resurrected. Instead, these people have adopted the Greek understanding that only the soul is immortal. Paul teaches that Jesus—soul and glorified body—were both resurrected and witnessed by hundreds.

"Unless Christ was raised to life, your faith is useless," Paul explains. "But Christ has been raised to life! And he makes us certain that others will also be raised to life. Just as we will die because of Adam, we will be raised to life because of Christ" (15:20–21).

Paul reveals that some day, in an instant, "our dead and decaying bodies will be changed into bodies that won't die." Our former bodies made from dust will become like that of "the one who came from heaven."

When this happens, Paul says, the prophecies of Isaiah and Hosea will be fulfilled, and people will praise God saying, "Death has lost the battle! Where is its victory? Where is its sting?" (Isaiah 25:8; Hosea 13:14).

The resurrected Jesus meets with his disciples
(15:1–58)

Reviews

Erastus was here. Erastus is identified in the New Testament as a colleague of Paul (Acts 19:22; 2 Timothy 4:20) and as the Corinth city treasurer (Romans 16:23). These references may have been about two people. Even if that's so, both were Christians, and the Erastus of Corinth was a member of the church there.

Archaeologists working in the ruins of ancient Corinth found a block of pavement stone with this inscription, written in the Roman language of Latin: "Erastus, commissioner of public works, bore the expense of this pavement."

The inscription may be identifying the same Corinthian Christian and city treasurer that Paul wrote about.

Isthmian Games. The Isthmian Games, an athletic competition second in popularity only to the Olympics, were held in Corinth every four years—including A.D. 51, when Paul was in town. The Isthmian Games featured a wide variety of races by runners, horsemen, and charioteers.

Probably not coincidentally, Paul's first use of athletic imagery appears in his letter to the Corinthians. Comparing Christians to runners in a race, Paul says, "You know that many runners enter a race, and only one of them wins the prize. So run to win!" (9:24).

"Athletes work hard to win a crown that cannot last," Paul adds, "but we do it for a crown that will last forever" (9:25). In fact, winners' crowns at the Isthmian Games were woven from withered stalks of celery.

Women, keep quiet in church. Sometimes Paul comes across as the first liberationist. After all, he's the one who said, "Faith in Christ Jesus is what makes each of you equal with each other, whether you are a Jew or a Greek, a slave or a free person, a man or a woman" (Galatians 3:28). Unfortunately, to many readers Paul looks more like a chauvinist in 1 Corinthians: "When God's people meet in church, the women must not be allowed to speak. They must keep quiet and listen. . . . If there is something they want to know, they can ask their husbands when they get home" (14:33 – 34).

On the topic of women, Paul can be puzzling. On the one hand, he commends Phoebe as a church deacon (Romans 16:1) and even describes a woman named Junias by using the rare and highest church leadership title of "apostle" (Romans 16:7). Yet in other letters he insists that men should be in charge (1 Corinthians 11:2 – 16) and that women should be subject to men in everything (Ephesians 5:24).

How could Paul say all these things? Some scholars suggest that Paul struggled between male-female equality in Christ and the traditional female subordination of his day. Some think that Paul affirmed that men and women are equal in worth before God but are given different roles within that equality. God made men responsible for leading, but he requires them to lead like Christ leads the church. Other scholars say that Paul restricted women's activities only in the churches where women were abusing leadership. ❏

Encore

- Read Paul's follow-up letter: 2 Corinthians. ❏

2 CORINTHIANS

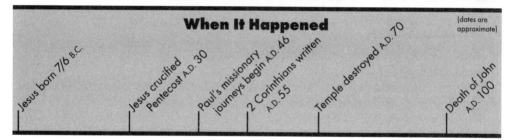

When It Happened

(dates are approximate)

Jesus born 7/6 B.C.

Jesus crucified Pentecost A.D. 30

Paul's missionary journeys begin A.D. 46

2 Corinthians written A.D. 55

Temple destroyed A.D. 70

Death of John A.D. 100

Paul Fights a Hostile Takeover

Ministers and congregations have a long history of not getting along. The first case on record is of Paul and the church he started in Corinth. Paul plants the church like a seedling, then stays for two years and nurtures it. Eventually, he moves on to start other churches. That's when trouble starts.

Arguments break out in Corinth about who's in charge, how Christians should behave, and how they should worship. By long-distance courier and by a personal visit, Paul addresses these problems. Then, within the year, another crisis strikes. Others who claim to be apostles arrive in Corinth and begin wooing church leaders away from Paul's leadership. Second Corinthians doesn't say exactly what these fraudulent apostles teach, but Paul accuses the intruders of repackaging the gospel with "another Jesus," "another spirit," and "a different message" (11:4).

Paul refuses to back off. He fights for the hearts and minds of the Corinthians. It's a battle he knows he might lose. If he were concerned about his personal pride and reputation, he'd walk away and turn his energy to the many other churches that appreciate him more. But Paul cares about the Corinthian people. He's willing to endure whatever heartache and humiliation it takes to win them back to the true Jesus, the true spirit, and the genuine message. ❏

Famous Lines

- God loves a cheerful giver (9:7).

- A thorn in the flesh (12:7). Paul's mystifying description of an unnamed problem that tormented him.

Behind the Scenes of 2 Corinthians

Starring Roles

Paul, leading minister to the non-Jewish world, and founder of the church at Corinth, Greece (1:1)

Titus, Paul's associate who carries a letter to Corinth that tries repairing the damaged relationship between Paul and the congregation (2:13)

Plot

Shortly after the Corinthian Christians receive Paul's letter known to us as 1 Corinthians, some outsiders arrive. Paul doesn't say who these people are, but clearly their take on Christianity differs from his. Paul calls the intruders "false apostles" who "only pretend to be apostles of Christ" (11:13). They apparently represented Jewish Christianity, yet 2 Corinthians says nothing about observing such Jewish matters as circumcision, food restrictions, and religious holidays.

The relationship between Paul and the Corinthians already was badly strained. The church itself had started fracturing into cliques and arguing over lifestyles and worship practices. After writing 1 Corinthians, Paul makes a visit to the church. But this only aggravates the tension.

Intruder alert.

Gifted in the art of persuasion, the newly arrived intruders lob charge upon charge at Paul. All we know of the charges is what we can infer from Paul's defense, preserved in 2 Corinthians. But the outsiders seem to attack his authority and motives. In response, Paul presents himself as an honest and sincere minister of Christ who cares deeply about the Corinthians.

What to Look For

Verbal attacks against Paul. Religious teachers arrive in town, saying they are Christians. They quickly show they are opponents of Paul, because they begin turning the church against their founding minister.

Here are what seem to be several main points of attack, along with excerpts of Paul's defense.

1. Paul is a self-appointed apostle, not one personally commissioned by Jesus, as were the original disciples. "When I was with you, I was patient and worked all the powerful miracles and signs and wonders of a true apostle" (12:12).

2. Paul is self-promoting. "We are not preaching about ourselves. Our message is that Jesus Christ is Lord" (4:5).

3. Paul can't be trusted, since he didn't come to Corinth when he said he would. Paul replies by saying that his last visit was so painful that he decided a cooling off period was in order. "I have decided not to make my next visit with you so painful. . . . I didn't want to make you feel bad. I only wanted to let you know how much I cared for you" (2:1, 4).

4. Paul is pocketing money collected for the poverty-stricken believers in Jerusalem. "Unlike so many, we do not peddle the word of God for profit" (2:17, New International Version). Paul implies that the intruders are seeking donations for themselves from the Corinthians. Paul had refused to do this (12:13).

Instead, he earned his keep by working as a tentmaker (Acts 18:3).

5. Paul barks boldly in his letters, but in person he's a coward who has nothing worth saying (10:10). "When I am with you, I will do exactly what I say in my letters" (10:11).

Paul's reluctant bragging about his sufferings. Bible experts call 11:16—12:13 the "Fool's Speech" because Paul says "let me be a fool and brag a little" (11:16). Paul feels uncomfortable bragging about anything except the Lord. But he feels that his back is to the wall and his ministry in Corinth will be over if he doesn't speak up.

The Fool's Speech might look like self-defensive bragging, but it's not. It's a parody on ancient speeches and letters that commend a person. This is an appropriate defensive technique because the intruder-critics in Corinth have come with letters of commendation.

In a sarcastic reversal of typical commendations, Paul begins bragging about experiences that show him as a victim—a loser by the world's standards. Paul reports suffering one tragedy after another—all because he is doing God's will and on behalf of the Corinthians.

The readers can't help but be reminded of how Jesus suffered for the same reason.

For many Corinthians, this speech likely generates a renewed sense of gratitude for what Paul and Jesus have endured on their behalf.

Paul's "thorn in the flesh." In describing what he has suffered throughout his ministry, Paul speaks of a "thorn in the flesh" that torments him and keeps him from getting conceited (12:7, New International Version).

Paul shows himself to be weak in that, though he asks God three times to remove the "thorn," God refuses. Jesus, too, asked to be spared the suffering of the cross. Because Jesus suffered, Paul is willing to do the same—even if it makes him look weak in the eyes of the world.

Paul never says what the "thorn" is. Bible experts have many theories, including some kind of physical problem such as malaria or poor eyesight (he

---

Did You Know?

• The Corinthian congregation apparently got over their bickering, eventually. In the final decades of the first Christian century, Roman church leader Clement complimented them in a letter. He wrote that they "bore no malice to one another. All sedition and all schism was abominable to you."

• Paul wrote at least four letters to the Corinthians: (1) a letter mentioned in 1 Corinthians 5:9, warning believers to stay away from sexually immoral people; (2) 1 Corinthians; (3) the stern letter of reprimand mentioned in 2 Corinthians 2:4; and (4) 2 Corinthians.

TIMELINE

BIBLE EVENTS	Paul begins missionary trips	Paul starts church in Corinth	Paul writes 1, 2 Corinthians		Paul's missionary trips end	Dates are approximate
	A.D. 46	A.D. 50	A.D. 55		A.D. 57	
	A.D. 45		A.D. 50		A.D. 55	A.D. 60
WORLD EVENTS	Famine strikes Jerusalem sometime within next 7 years A.D. 46		Some Jews expelled from Rome move to Corinth (Acts 18:2) A.D. 49		Claudius poisoned by wife, Jews return to Rome A.D. 54	

writes in big letters, Galatians 6:11), or his never-ending persecutions, or his rejection by the Corinthians.

Personal information about Paul. This letter reveals more autobiographical information about Paul than any of his other letters. Much of this comes in chapters 11—12, where he talks about how he suffered as a minister: beatings, jailings, shipwrecks, stoning, public humiliation. The list goes on. He also describes what sounds like a vision or an out-of-body experience in which he caught a glimpse of the afterlife (12:1–6).

An impassioned fundraising letter. Surprisingly, in this letter that includes a defense against charges that he's preaching for profit, Paul asks for money.

But the money is not for him. In fact he makes it a point to remind the Corinthians that during the two years he lived among them he did not accept their money. The donation he is now requesting is for poverty-stricken Christians in Jerusalem. This is a special offering Paul has been collecting from churches throughout the eastern Mediterranean.

Paul applies some gentle pressure by telling the Corinthians that he has bragged about their generosity. "I know how eager you are to give. I have proudly told the Lord's followers in Macedonia [a comparatively poor province to the north] that you people in Achaia [Greece] have been ready for a whole year. Now your desire to give has made them want to give. . . . This [donation of yours] will prove that we were not wrong to brag about you" (9:2–3).

Author and Date

The letter is "From Paul, chosen by God to be an apostle of Jesus Christ" (1:1), along with his associate, Timothy.

Paul wrote the letter a few months after writing 1 Corinthians, during his third and final missionary trip. Drawing on clues from the text, some Bible experts speculate that he wrote 1 Corinthians in the spring while staying at Ephesus, then 2 Corinthians in the winter while in Macedonia.

On Location

Like 1 Corinthians, Paul's letter is addressed to Christians in a young church he started a few years earlier at Corinth, Greece. Located south of Athens, Corinth is near a four-mile-wide land bridge separating the Aegean Sea in the east and the Adriatic Sea in the west. (See map in 1 Corinthians, page 342.) Paul apparently assumes that other churches in the region will read circulated copies of the letter, since he also addresses "all of God's people in Achaia," the Roman province that is now Greece. ❏

Big Scenes from 2 Corinthians

Paul begins his emotional letter by saying how glad he is that God always comforts us when we suffer. This is an apt introduction since Paul is going to spend much of the rest of his letter talking about the torment he has endured from the Corinthian church and from others.

Paul says that followers of Christ in this generation—and especially ministers—should expect hardship, opposition, and rejection because these are what Christ got. To illustrate two extremes in the way people react to the gospel, Paul draws on an image familiar to citizens of large cities in the Roman Empire. It's the scene of a Roman procession: soldiers marching in a victory parade after a battle. On display are the prisoners of war who will be executed for the emperor's pleasure or sold as slaves. Along the roadway, citizens cheer and fill the air with the sweet smell of burning incense. To the conquerors, this perfumed scent is fragrant and welcome. To the captives, the smell means death.

Paul then paints a picture of himself and other Christian ministers marching in a victory parade led by Jesus. "For people who are being saved," he says, "this perfume has a sweet smell and leads them to a better life. But for people who are lost, it has a bad smell and leads them to a horrible death."

Some people welcome the gospel and its messengers. But many reject both and resist them with a vengeance.

Roman conquerors in a victory march
•• **(2:14 – 17)**

Paul is amazed that God would entrust a message as important as the gospel to frail human beings.

"We are like clay jars in which this treasure is stored," Paul says. "We often suffer, but we are never crushed. Even when we don't know what to do, we never give up. In times of trouble, God is with us, and when we are knocked down, we get up again. We face death every day because of Jesus" (4:7–11).

Paul doesn't have an inordinate fear of death because he believes the only thing to die will be the body, which God will replace with an eternal body.

"Our bodies are like tents that we live in here on earth," Paul writes. "But when these tents are destroyed, we know that God will give each of us a place to live. These homes will not be buildings that someone has made, but they are in heaven and will last forever."

Human bodies are like tents: temporary
(5:1 – 10) ••

Torment stalks Paul like a predator everywhere he goes. Many Jewish Christians, for example, vehemently disagree with the Jerusalem council's decision, years earlier, to allow non-Jewish believers to join the church without having to observe long-standing Jewish laws such as those about circumcision, kosher food, and religious holidays (Acts 15). So they follow Paul, who is famous as a minister to non-Jews, and try to undo the damage they believe his preaching has done.

To help diffuse this tension, Paul tries to unify Jewish and non-Jewish factions of the church with a tangible expression of concern: he collects an offering from his predominantly non-Jewish churches for poverty-stricken Jewish Christians in Jerusalem. Actually, Paul says this isn't his idea, but that it comes out of the Jerusalem council meeting (Galatians 2:10). Yet Paul gets 100 percent behind the suggestion and promotes the offering throughout his travels, as shown by references in Acts, 1 and 2 Corinthians, and Romans.

The Bible doesn't say how the Jerusalem believers got poor. One theory is that the spirit of generosity that started at Pentecost spurred many believers to give away nearly everything they owned (Acts 4:32–37). Another suggestion growing out of Scripture is that a famine hit the region sometime after Paul began his first missionary trip in about A.D. 46 and before Emperor Claudius died in A.D. 54 (Acts 12:27–30). Yet another reason may be because older Jews often move to Jerusalem to spend their final days in the Holy City and be buried there. The church may have had to bear the brunt of caring for women whose husbands preceded them in death.

Whatever the reason for the poverty, the offering for Jerusalem is important to Paul. He pleads with the Corinthians to be generous.

"But don't feel sorry that you must give and don't feel that you are forced to give," he adds. "God loves people who love to give" (9:7).

Paul later delivers the offering in person, fully aware that he may be arrested and tried for heresy by the same Jewish legislative body that tried Jesus. In fact, Paul is arrested and eventually transported to Rome for trial in the emperor's court. That's the last the Bible says of Paul. Christian writers at the end of the century report that Paul was executed.

A collection for the poor of Jerusalem (8:1—9:15)

In the closing chapters of his letter, Paul grapples with the biggest problem now threatening the Corinthian church: "false apostles" who have arrived with letters of commendation and who are winning control of the church (11:13).

Paul takes an incredibly creative approach to winning back his congregation. Instead of bragging about his spiritual power and influence—as the intruders have done about themselves—Paul writes a sarcastic parody on self-promotion; he brags about his weaknesses and the humiliations he has suffered.

Once, he admits, he had to sneak out of Damascus like a criminal, lowered over the city wall in a basket. This took place shortly after his conversion. Jews had posted guards at the city entrance and had planned to kill him as a religious traitor when he came out (Acts 9:20–25).

In this humiliating litany, Paul shows what great dangers and hardships he has endured out of love for God and for the Corinthians.

"Five times my own people gave me thirty-nine lashes with a whip. Three times the Romans beat me with a big stick, and once my enemies stoned me. I have been shipwrecked three times, and I even had to spend a night and a day in the sea. . . . My life has been in danger in cities, in deserts, at sea, and with people who only pretended to be the Lord's followers" (11:24–26).

The climax of this parody comes when Paul reveals that Jesus, too, suffered terribly because of the gospel message. "He was weak when he was nailed to the cross," Paul says, but now Jesus "lives by the power of God."

The Corinthians should see how only Paul—not the crowd-pleasing latecomers—fits the pattern established by Jesus and is therefore their genuine apostle.

Paul escapes Damascus in a basket (11:16–33)

Reviews

Paul wasn't much to look at. The Bible gives only scant hints of what Paul looked like, but those hints mesh with the earliest surviving description of him, preserved in a second-century book.

Writing in the *Acts of Paul,* the Christian author describes Paul as "a man of middling size, and his hair was scanty, and his legs were a little crooked, and his knees were far apart; he had large eyes, and his eyebrows met, and his nose was somewhat long."

Paul quoted his critics as saying, "Paul's letters are harsh and powerful. But in person, he is a weakling" (10:10). The New International Version translates "weakling" as "unimpressive," while the New Revised Standard Version puts it this way: "his bodily presence is weak." Whatever the description meant, it was no compliment.

Paul didn't deny that he appeared weak to people who evaluated him by worldly values. On the contrary, he admitted it, then built on it by reminding the Corinthians that Jesus was crucified in weakness.

"Although he [Jesus] was weak when he was nailed to the cross, he now lives by the power of God. We are weak, just as Christ was. But you will see that we will live by the power of God, just as Christ does" (13:4).

In other words, the Lord has a remarkable capacity for turning weakness into power. "If Christ keeps giving me his power," Paul adds, "I will gladly brag about how weak I am" (12:9).

More than one letter. Second Corinthians is a cut-and-paste job drawing from two or more of Paul's letters, some scholars say.

The letter is anything but smooth-flowing literature, seamlessly blending one topic into the next. Reading it is like taking a ride in a four-wheel-drive vehicle. One moment your chauffeur is cruising you down the expressway, chatting about how fulfilling his job is. The next moment he has ripped into a cornfield and is suddenly talking politics.

Abrupt sidetracks, radical changes from pleasant tones to harsh tones, and the variety of topics—rebukes, fundraising, sarcasm (to name just a few)—lead some Bible experts to conclude that 2 Corinthians is a composite of two or more letters. One theory is that the intense, heartbreaking letter Paul mentions in 2:4 is at least partly preserved in chapters 10–13 and has been tacked onto the letter that came after it: 2 Corinthians 1–9.

Other scholars, however, see 2 Corinthians as a single letter that addresses the many-faceted problems in Corinth. These scholars suggest that Paul's gentle tone at the beginning, followed by the stern tone at the end, shows that Paul was trying to mend bridges before crossing over to confront the big problem: fake apostles trying to take control of the church.

Early church leaders treated 2 Corinthians as a single letter. And none of the earliest Greek manuscripts show evidence that the letter was pieced together. ❑

Encore

- Read Paul's earlier letter to the church: 1 Corinthians.

- For another emotional defense of Paul's ministry, read his letter to the church in Galatia.

- Philippians is another letter in which Paul's gentle tone changes abruptly. In strong language he condemns people who argue that non-Jews must observe the rite of circumcision. ❑

GALATIANS

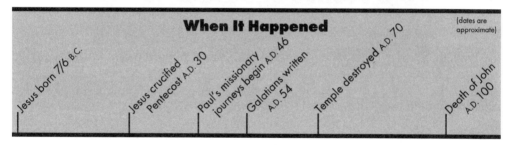

When It Happened

(dates are approximate)

Jesus born 7/6 B.C.

Jesus crucified Pentecost A.D. 30

Paul's missionary journeys begin A.D. 46

Galatians written A.D. 54

Temple destroyed A.D. 70

Death of John A.D. 100

The Church that Enrages Paul

This is the most emotionally charged book of the Bible. As you read it, you can almost see the thick purple veins popping out on Paul's neck as he unloads on the misguided Christians of Galatia.

"I am shocked," Paul begins.

He has taught them God saves them by trusting in Christ alone, not in doing religious things. And now he gets word that they don't believe this anymore. Instead they believe some newly arrived missionaries who teach that Christians have to obey the Jewish laws.

Paul is adamant that the Law has nothing to do with salvation now that Jesus has come. And with fervent emotion he reminds the Galatians of the miracles and the gift of the Holy Spirit they experienced when Paul was still in the area. "How were you given God's Spirit?" Paul asks. "Was it by obeying the Law of Moses or by hearing about Christ and having faith in him? How can you be so stupid?" (3:2).

Frankly, it's hard to understand the rage and intensity that drives Paul to say what he does, the way he does. This holy apostle uses some of the most vehement language in Scripture. Yet in an oddly familiar way, when he detonates his anger all over the Galatians and the people leading them in the wrong direction, he sounds like a furious but loving parent reading the riot act to a child who just did something incredibly stupid and nearly got killed.

Sometimes love is silent. But sometimes love is a vein-popping scream, calling one back from the brink of disaster. ❏

Behind the Scenes of Galatians

⭐ Starring Roles

Paul, an apostle famous for his ministry among non-Jews; founding minister of churches throughout Galatia (1:1)

Peter, leader of the 12 original disciples, who draws a sharp rebuke from Paul for avoiding non-Jewish Christians (1:18)

📖 Plot

While traveling throughout Galatia, in western Turkey, Paul had told the Jews and non-Jews living there that they needed only faith in Jesus to become Christians. Many had accepted his teachings, which were backed up by miracles.

Now, several years later, Paul gets word that other Christian teachers have arrived in the area and are contradicting him. These teachers, Jews who accept Jesus as the Messiah, insist that all non-Jews (Gentiles) must trust Jesus *and* obey the laws given by Moses. This is a controversial issue previously argued and supposedly settled in Paul's favor at a Jerusalem summit meeting of Christian leaders in about A.D. 49 (Acts 15).

Paul writes an eloquent, sometimes bitterly harsh, defense of his teaching and his authority as an apostle commissioned by God to "announce his message to the Gentiles" (1:16). He tells of his miraculous conversion while en route to arrest Christians, of seeing Jesus, and of the struggles he faced defending the gospel. He appeals to the example of Abraham, a man who lived before the time of the Jewish laws, to show that God accepts people because of their faith, not because of their obedience to rules.

The Jewish law, Paul argues, was intended to serve only until the Messiah arrived (3:19). With the sacrificial death of Jesus, God established a new covenant that liberated humanity from the law. Instead of needing to follow rules, Paul writes, "you are guided by the Spirit. . . . If you obey the Spirit, the Law of Moses has no control over you" (5:16, 18).

🎥 What to Look For

Anger. "You stupid Galatians!" (3:1). That's Paul talking. He's more upset in this letter than in any other letter he writes.

He's so angry that he skips the note of appreciation and praise that usually begins each ancient letter, much like modern letters begin with "Dear." Instead, Paul quickly jumps on the Galatians' case: "I am shocked that you have so quickly turned from God. . . . You have believed another message, when there is only one true message" (1:6–7).

Paul's anger reflects the seriousness of the problem more than the frailty of his ego. If the Galatians cling to the revised gospel message they have accepted, Paul knows that as far as they are concerned, Jesus will have died for nothing (2:21).

Makings of the first major split in the church. The first split in the Christian church came over the very issue that erupted in Galatia. The divisive question was this: Do people have to become Jews before they can become Christians?

Paul said no. Many other Jewish Christians said yes, everyone must obey the laws of Moses.

If the Jewish Christians had won the debate, Christianity might not have become a major world religion. It could have become just another branch or denomination in Judaism. Added to the Jewish branches of Reform (the least traditional), Conservative, and Orthodox (the more traditional), all of Christianity would be a branch of Jews who accept Jesus as Messiah, but who feel obligated to observe Jewish laws about circumcision, kosher food, and religious holidays.

Did You Know?

• Whirling dervishes, Muslim monks who dance into a spinning trance while trying to seek God, got their start in the 1200s in a 4,000-year-old city near Lystra, Galatia, where Paul started a church.

• The Roman province of Galatia got its name from the Gauls of western Europe who began settling there about 200 years before Christ.

Paul defending his apostle status. Paul reminds the Galatians of how God chose him to preach especially to the Gentiles, and of how the original disciples of Jesus accepted him as a minister of equal authority. The disciples agreed that Paul and Barnabas "would work with Gentiles and that they would work with Jews" (2:9).

Paul arguing with Peter. Paul is on such an equal par with the original disciples that he feels free to argue with Peter, leader of the Twelve, when Peter makes a big mistake. This happens when Peter visits the church that Paul and Barnabas are pastoring in Antioch, Syria. Peter, feeling pressured by Jewish Christians who still observe the laws of Moses, stops eating and socializing with Gentile members of the church. According to Jewish law, Gentiles are considered ritually unclean. Jews who come into contact with them have to perform cleansing rituals before they can worship God at the temple.

What Peter's behavior amounts to is religious segregation within the church. At best, both groups would have considered themselves separate but equal. More likely, each group would have considered itself superior.

Other Jews follow Peter's lead, until Paul publicly confronts him, saying: "If we can be acceptable to God by obeying the Law, it was useless for Christ to die" (2:21).

Principles of living, instead of rigid laws. Though Christians are free of Old Testament rules, Paul says believers must live godly lives nonetheless.

TIMELINE

BIBLE EVENTS	Paul starts churches in Galatia on first missionary trip A.D. 46	Jerusalem council grants Gentiles waiver from Jewish laws A.D. 49	Paul visits northern Galatia during second missionary trip A.D. 50	Paul's third missionary trip ends A.D. 57	Paul imprisoned at Rome A.D. 60
	A.D. 45	A.D. 50	A.D. 55	A.D. 60	
WORLD EVENTS	Jews expelled from Rome over controversy about "Chrestus" (probably "Christ") A.D. 49	Romans learn about soap, from Gauls (France) A.D. 50	Buddhism of India introduced to China A.D. 58	Dates are approximate	

Paul explains that the Holy Spirit leads people away from evil. "God's Spirit makes us loving, happy, peaceful, patient, kind, good, faithful, gentle, and self-controlled" (5:22).

Author and Date

The letter is "from the apostle Paul" (1:1) to all the churches in Galatia, a Roman province in western Turkey.

It's unclear exactly when Paul wrote. The letter provides no solid clues about the date, where Paul was when he wrote it, or which churches in Galatia he had in mind. Because the theology in the letter resembles Paul's early letter of 1 Thessalonians more closely than his later letter of Romans, Bible scholars speculate that Paul wrote Galatians sometime around A.D. 55 or a few years earlier.

On Location

Paul writes to unnamed churches he started in Galatia, a strip of territory roughly 300 miles long and 100 miles wide, located in western Turkey. It's unknown if Paul intended the letter for churches he founded in southern Galatia on his first missionary trip (churches named in Scripture) or churches he started in northern Galatia on his second trip (churches not named in Scripture). Perhaps he had both in mind. ❏

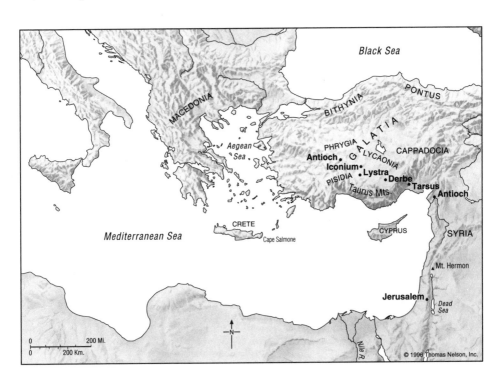

Big Scenes from Galatians

After Paul leaves Galatia, Jewish-Christian missionaries arrive and contradict his teaching that people are saved only by faith in Jesus. Faith in Christ is not enough, they argue. Anyone who wants to be a Christian must also obey the laws of Moses.

This is an old heresy, Paul explains in his letter of defense to the churches in Galatia. He tells the Galatians that years ago he had to publicly correct Peter for this same mistaken belief. When Paul was pastoring in Antioch, Syria, Peter came for a visit. At first Peter ate with the non-Jewish members and treated them as spiritual brothers and sisters. But later, when other church leaders from Jerusalem arrived, Peter suddenly became afraid of associating with non-Jewish Christians. Apparently these visiting dignitaries believed like other Jews that Gentiles were ritually unclean.

"We know that God accepts only those who have faith in Jesus Christ," Paul tells Peter. "If we can be acceptable to God by obeying the Law, it was useless for Christ to die" (2:15, 21).

Peter would later side with Paul on this matter in a Jerusalem summit meeting of Christian leaders (Acts 15). And though Jerusalem leaders concur, finding in favor of Peter and Paul, many Jewish-Christian dissenters take their case on the road—to Galatia and beyond.

Paul argues with Peter
(2:11–21)

If the teaching of Paul had been eclipsed by that of his opponents who got a foothold in Galatia, Christianity could have turned out much differently. All Christians might have become Jews, bound by the restrictions of Jewish law. Christianity might not have become a major world religion, but only one of several branches or denominations in Judaism. And non-Jews who converted to the Christian branch of Judaism might have been treated as lower-status members, just as Gentile converts to Judaism are in many synagogues today.

Paul wants nothing to do with a status-conscious Christianity that puts some people ahead of others. "Faith in Christ Jesus is what makes each of you equal with each other, whether you are a Jew or a Greek, a slave or a free person, a man or a woman. So if you belong to Christ, you are now part of Abraham's family" (3:28–29).

Freedom from the restrictive Jewish laws, however, does not mean freedom from accountability. "You cannot fool God," Paul warns, "so don't make a fool of yourself! You will harvest what you plant. If you follow your selfish desires, you will harvest destruction, but if you follow the Spirit, you will harvest eternal life" (6:7–8).

Equals in the eyes of God
(3:26—4:7)

•••••••••••••••••••••••••• **Reviews** ••••••••••••••••••••••••

The traits of a Christian. The traits of a Christian, which Paul identifies in Galatians 5: 22 - 23, are incredibly consistent with traits that Paul mentions in several other letters: 1 Corinthians 13:3 - 8; Philippians 4:8; and Colossians 3:12 - 16.

Compare, for example, Galatians and Philippians:

"God's Spirit makes us loving, happy, peaceful, patient, kind, good, faithful, gentle, and self-controlled" (Galatians 5:22 - 23).

"Keep your minds on whatever is true, pure, right, holy, friendly, and proper" (Philippians 4:8).

Paul, the bitter hypocrite? How could Paul write that God's Spirit makes people "gentle, and self-controlled" (5:23) just a few paragraphs after wishing that Jewish missionary intruders in Galatia "would not only get circumcised, but would cut off much more!" (5:12)?

And why would a gentle, self-controlled apostle ask Galatians who accepted the Jewish version of the gospel this rhetorical question: "How could you be so stupid?" (3:3).

This is one blistering letter.

Whether Paul let his human emotion get the better of him, only Jesus who flipped tables of businessmen at the temple can judge (Matthew 21:12). But like Jesus, perhaps Paul knew when a vital issue demanded a stern response. ❏

•••••••••••••••••••••••• **Encore** ••••••••••••••••••••••••

• For a report of the Jerusalem summit meeting that debated the same issue the Galatians confronted, read Acts 15.

• To better understand Paul's teaching about salvation through faith, read Romans 3:21 – 4:25. ❏

EPHESIANS

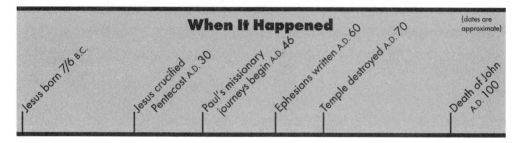

When It Happened

(dates are approximate)

Jesus born 7/6 B.C.

Jesus crucified Pentecost A.D. 30

Paul's missionary journeys begin A.D. 46

Ephesians written A.D. 60

Temple destroyed A.D. 70

Death of John A.D. 100

Job #1 for the Church

The church has a job. Paul's vision of what that job is may surprise you, for it's one that doesn't show up on agendas of church leadership meetings.

The job is not as material as fund-raising, not as mundane as counting warm bodies, not as simple as telling stories of people who lived 2,000 years ago or longer.

Christ's church has a job that's harder, playing a key role in a plan as old as Adam and Eve. God's plan is to save humanity from the destructive effects of sin, and to restore his creation to the holiness and peace it once exhibited. This sounds impossible, but God has been known to do the impossible.

God made human beings to be like him (4:24) and to live with him as his people (1:4). But God's holiness and human sinfulness are as incompatible as matter and anti-matter. So God provided a way for humanity to be cleansed of sin: we humans are to do exactly the opposite of Adam and Eve by obeying God in something we don't fully understand. We are to simply trust that the sacrificial death of Jesus makes us worthy to stand before God: "We can come to God by faith" (3:12).

The church's job is to be the people of faith—God's people.

How do we measure our success? The measuring is God's job. But the goals before us, Paul says, are unity among believers, following the Spirit within us, maturing in our faith, defeating spiritual forces allied against us, and—perhaps hardest of all—getting along with the people we live with every day.

Can the church ever hope to accomplish all of this? Paul replies confidently, "God will do all that he has planned" (1:10). ❏

Famous Lines

- Don't go to bed angry (4:26).

- Husbands, love your wives (5:25, King James Version).

- Our struggle is not against flesh and blood, but against the rulers, against the authorities, against the powers of this dark world and against the spiritual forces of evil in the heavenly realms (6:12, New International Version). *Paul explains there are evil spiritual forces that are every bit as real as the physical world. These forces oppose both God and God's people.*

- Put on the whole armor of God, that you may be able to stand against the wiles of the devil (6:11, New King James Version). *To defend against evil spiritual forces, Paul urges Christians to protect themselves with godly attributes such as truth, justice, and faith.*

Behind the Scenes of Ephesians

⭐ Starring Role

Paul, a traveling minister who starts churches throughout the Roman Empire, and who is most successful in non-Jewish cultures (1:1)

📖 Plot

Ephesians reads like a beautiful, poetic sermon written for just about any congregation. It's not a story with a plot, or a letter with a problem-solving agenda. It is, however, a compelling meditation with a deep and lasting message: God has a plan to return unity and peace to his creation, and the church will play a leading role in that plan.

"When the time is right," Paul says, "God will do all that he has planned, and Christ will bring together everything in heaven and on earth" (1:10).

🎥 What to Look For

No problems. After reading 1, 2 Corinthians and Galatians, this letter comes as a pleasant surprise. Paul isn't scolding anyone, correcting warped theology, or defending his authority as an apostle sent by God.

Instead, he's stretching and exercising the faith and mind of his readers, helping Christians improve their understanding of what God is doing in the world and how he is doing it. The short answer to the "what" question is that God is restoring his relationship to human beings, and human relationships to one another. The "how" is through Christ, and the church he started from a motley crew of a dozen common folk, the likes of fishermen and tax men.

The flow of the letter. Paul begins by pulling out a cosmic canvas and painting a picture of God's plan for all of creation—heaven and earth—to be holy and blessed (1:3–23). Next, Paul explains how Christ has made all believers—Jew and non-Jew alike—key players in this plan (2:1–22). Then, Paul explains the role that believers play through the church (3:1—5:20) and through their personal relationships at home and work (5:21—6:9). Finally, with powerful imagery from the battlefield, Paul tells Christians how to tap into God's unlimited power to defeat evil spiritual forces allied against them (6:10–20).

Practical advice for everyday living. The last half of the book throws the spotlight on practical ways for the church to fulfill its role in God's plan.

TIMELINE	BIBLE EVENTS					
		Paul converts A.D. 35	Paul's missionary journeys begin A.D. 46		Paul writes Ephesians, during Rome imprisonment A.D. 60	Dates are approximate
		A.D. 35	A.D. 45		A.D. 55	A.D. 65
	WORLD EVENTS		Buddhism of India introduced to China A.D. 58		Mayans are building a great civilization in Central America A.D. 60	

1. Live in unity. "Patiently put up with each other and love each other. Try your best to let God's Spirit keep your hearts united" (4:2–3).

2. Grow spiritually mature and serve others through the church (4:11–13).

3. Seek spiritual renewal. "Let the Spirit change your way of thinking and make you into a new person" (4:23–24); "let the Spirit fill your life" (5:18).

4. Put others first. "Submit to one another out of reverence for Christ" (5:21, New International Version). This involves all personal relationships, especially husbands and wives, children and parents, workers and bosses.

5. Resist evil spiritual forces. "We are not fighting against humans. We are fighting against . . . rulers of darkness and powers in the spiritual world. So put on all the armor that God gives. . . . And when the battle is over, you will still be standing firm" (6:12–13).

Author and Date

The letter claims Paul as its writer (1:1), and speaks in the voice of a prisoner "in jail" (6:20). For about 1,700 years no one questioned that Paul wrote Ephesians. But in recent centuries, scholars comparing this letter to others that Paul wrote have noticed some substantial differences. For more, see "Who wrote the letter?" in Reviews.

If Paul wrote the letter, he may have done so during his two-year imprisonment at Rome, which began about A.D. 60. If someone else wrote it in Paul's name, applying his theology to later circumstances in the church, the writing may have occurred in the closing decades of the first century.

On Location

Though the letter claims to be written "to God's people who live in Ephesus" (1:1), this introduction is excluded from the oldest manuscripts. Nor does the letter contain any of Paul's characteristic personal greetings to individuals, or references to circumstances in this major port city in western Turkey. Paul may have intended Ephesians as a general letter, for circulation among as many churches as possible. Or perhaps he did address it to Ephesus, fully expecting that believers there would make copies for distribution to other congregations. (See map in Acts, page 323.) ❏

Big Scenes from Ephesians

From the beginning of time, Paul says, God has wanted human beings "to live with him and to be his holy and innocent and loving people" (1:4). Yet from Adam's time onward, humanity has chosen sin over obedience. God in his mercy, however, has made provision for people to find forgiveness for sin: first through sacrificial rituals, then through the sacrifice of Jesus, who gave "his life's blood to set us free, which means that our sins are now forgiven" (1:7–8).

By the time Paul writes this letter, Jews are increasingly rejecting the Christian gospel, and the church is becoming more and more Gentile. So much so, that many non-Jews are developing an us-them attitude, with "them" being the Jews—outsiders to the church.

But the church, Paul reminds his mostly non-Jewish readers, is made up of the forgiven—Jew and Gentile alike. "Christ has made peace between Jews and Gentiles, and he has united us" (2:14).

Unity, Paul says, should be one of the hallmarks of every congregation. For by getting along with each other, the apostle explains, we fulfill one of the main reasons the church exists. "Let God's Spirit keep your hearts united," Paul says. "All of you are part of the same body" (4:3–4). That body is the church.

Jew and Gentile, united in Christ (2:11–3:13) •••

Paul says that when people become followers of the Lord, they slowly but certainly begin to resemble their creator. "You were created to be like God," Paul says, "and so you must please him and be truly holy" (4:23).

This doesn't mean Christians never make mistakes and always do the right thing. But it does mean they have accepted their role as human beings devoted to God, their holy father. And it means they live in such a way that others can see the resemblance. "Holy," in reference to anything in the physical world, means "set apart" or "dedicated" to God. It doesn't mean "perfect" in behavior.

On the other hand, Paul quickly adds that Christians who are growing spiritually are learning to replace bitterness, anger, and criticism with kindness, mercy, and forgiveness.

"Do as God does," Paul urges. "After all, you are his dear children. Let love be your guide. . . . Don't let it be said that any of you are immoral or indecent or greedy" (5:1–3).

Get rid of malice (4:17–5:20)

•••

Honor Christ and put others first," Paul says. Christians who listen to the Spirit of God within them will increasingly learn to do this in all their relationships—especially in relationships closest to home.

Husbands and wives will love and care for one another, each doing as much as possible to meet the needs of the other.

Children, young and old, will treat their parents with respect. This isn't a one-way street.

"Parents, don't be hard on your children," Paul instructs. "Raise them properly. Teach them and instruct them about the Lord" (6:4).

In ancient times, it was as acceptable for people to have slaves as it is today for corporate managers to have employees. (And many overworked, underpaid employees today can easily see a parallel.) Paul isn't interested in starting a slave-liberating revolution, at least not from the outside, in. What he calls for, however, would eventually accomplish this, by working from the inside, out.

"Slaves, you must obey your earthly masters. Show them great respect and be as loyal to them as you are to Christ. Try to please them at all times, and not just when you think they are watching" (6:5–6).

For slave owners, Paul offers these instructions: "Treat your slaves with this same respect. Don't threaten them. They have the same Master in heaven that you do, and he doesn't have any favorites" (6:9).

Does this sound like a recipe for Utopia? This is God working his plan through the church. It may sound unrealistic, but Paul assures his readers that "when the time is right, God will do all that he has planned" (1:10).

**Put others first
(5:21—6:9)**

• •

For the moment, we live in a physical world made up of elements we can see and touch and smell and taste. But Paul says there's an overlapping spiritual world that we can't see, yet it's as real as clouds and rocks and flowers and honey.

Mysteriously, in this spiritual world there are two forces at work. There are the forces of God and the forces of Satan. Both can influence us—God for the better and Satan for the worse.

In fact, Paul says, the biggest battles we face in this life are not confrontations with other human beings. "We are fighting against forces and authorities and against rulers of darkness and powers in the spiritual world. So put on all the armor that God gives" (6:12–13).

Comparing God's arsenal to the uniform of a Roman soldier, Paul tells believers to strap on truth like a belt, God's justice like armor, the good news of peace like shoes, faith like a shield, and God's saving power like a helmet.

Then when evil attacks, through temptation or whatever other means are at its disposal, "you will be able to defend yourself. And when the battle is over, you will still be standing firm."

**Dressing for spiritual success
(6:10 – 18)**   •

·················· **Reviews** ························

Husbands and wives: Submit to each other. Lots of sermons have touted the verse, "Wives, submit to your husbands as to the Lord" (5:22, New International Version). Fortunately for the ladies, Paul's thought begins one verse earlier: "Submit to one another out of reverence for Christ" (New International Version).

In this letter's original language, Greek, there is just one verb for the entire section that discusses husband and wife relationships. That verb is "submit," in 5:21. Everything that follows is built on this verb, to illustrate how each is to submit to the other.

"Wives should always put their husbands first, as the church puts Christ first" (5:24).

"A husband should love his wife as much as Christ loved the church and gave his life for it, . . . as much as he loves himself" (5:25, 28).

Who wrote the letter? Most scholars agree that Paul wrote Romans, 1 and 2 Corinthians, Galatians, Philippians, 1 Thessalonians, and Philemon. These books clearly sound like Paul in choice of words, style of writing, and theology. Ephesians, however, uses important words that don't appear in Paul's undisputed letters. And some of the familiar words have been tagged with different meanings entirely. Also, the prose is more flowery and wordy than Paul's other cut-to-the-chase-scene letters.

Some Bible experts suggest that one or more of Paul's associates, such as Timothy, wrote the letter after Paul died. This associate applied Paul's theology to current issues, such as the growing division between Jews and Gentiles, and honored his master teacher by writing in Paul's voice and by signing Paul's name. This was a common practice among Greek and Jewish writers of the time. It was exactly the opposite of plagiarism; it was giving credit instead of taking it, and it was an expression of humility instead of pride.

Other experts argue that Paul was quite capable of growing and adapting, using new terms and vesting old terms with new and rich meaning. The wordy writing, they suggest, may have come from Paul's use of well-known hymns and prayers, which he wove into the letter. And he may have used a writer or secretary, who expressed Paul's ideas in the writer's words, with the apostle's approval. ❏

·················· **Encore** ························

• Colossians, in both writing style and teachings, is strikingly similar to Ephesians. ❏

PHILIPPIANS

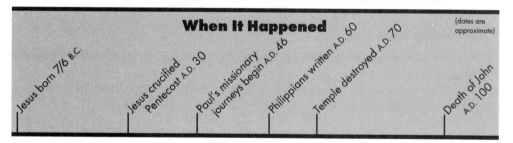

When It Happened

(dates are approximate)

Jesus born 7/6 B.C.

Jesus crucified Pentecost A.D. 30

Paul's missionary journeys begin A.D. 46

Philippians written A.D. 60

Temple destroyed A.D. 70

Death of John A.D. 100

A Joyful Letter from Paul in Jail

Paul does strange things in jail. When he sat in a Philippian jail, the year he founded the church in that city, he sang hymns (Acts 16:25). Now, as he sits in some other jail and writes to his beloved Philippians, he speaks of happiness.

He says he's happy that he has such caring friends. He's even happy that he's suffering for Christ because his suffering is inspiring other Christians to preach more boldly. And he says if need be, he will be happy to die because he will go to be with Christ, which is a much better place than where he is now.

As Paul faces death and ponders his mortality, his thoughts are drawn to the Source of immortality. "If I live, it will be for Christ, and if I die, I will gain even more" (1:21).

Paul wants the Philippians to experience this same peaceful joy when they reflect on their lives. So in the spirit of a gentle father, he advises them "to discover what it really means to be saved. God is working in you to make you willing and able to obey him. . . . Try to shine as lights among the people of this world, as you hold firmly to the message that gives life" (2:12–13, 15–16).

Paul's words are captivating, coming from the brink of death. ❏

Famous Lines

• At the name of Jesus everyone will bow (2:10).

• My God shall supply all your need according to His riches in glory by Christ Jesus (4:19, New King James Version).

• For to me to live is Christ, and to die is gain (1:21, King James Version). *Paul plans to live for Jesus, then enjoy an afterlife of eternity in heaven.*

Behind the Scenes of Philippians

⭐ Starring Roles

Paul, apostle, traveling preacher, frequent prisoner, and founder of the church at Philippi (1:1)
Epaphroditus, a member of the Philippian church who brings gifts from the congregation to jailed Paul (2:25)

📖 Plot

While Paul is in jail, perhaps in Rome during the early A.D. 60s, a messenger arrives from the church at Philippi, in northern Greece. Some 10 years earlier, during Paul's second missionary trip, Paul had arrived in Philippi and established what became the first church in Europe. Throughout his traveling ministry, the Philippians continue to support Paul with money and gifts. As soon as they learn of Paul's imprisonment, they dispatch one of their trusted members—Epaphroditus—who brings the apostle some gifts. These may have included funds to help defray his expenses while enduring two years of house arrest.

Epaphroditus becomes deathly ill, but manages to recover. Paul then sends him home, with a joyful letter of thanks we now know as Philippians. In this letter, the apostle expresses joy for the longstanding support that the Philippians have given him, and for the recent gifts, as well as for the recovery of Epaphroditus. But Paul also warns the believers that one day they may have to suffer as he is suffering now. "Be brave," Paul says (1:28), for God can use suffering to accomplish good. "What has happened to me," Paul explains, "has helped to spread the good news. . . . The Lord's followers have become brave and are fearlessly telling the message" (1:12–13).

🎥 What to Look For

No quotes from the Old Testament. Paul is a converted Pharisee, a scholar in the Jewish scripture. So it's unusual for him to write about religious matters without quoting the Old Testament. Yet there's no mention of the Old Testament in this letter. This may be because nearly all the believers in Philippi are non-Jews, unfamiliar with sacred Jewish scripture. When Paul first arrived in the town, there apparently was no formal synagogue—just a riverside gathering place outside the city, where a few Jews met for prayer on the Sabbath (Acts 16:13).

Why Paul writes the letter. Paul makes several key points in Philippians, one of his most affectionate letters.

1. Paul thanks the Philippians for their ongoing support, and for their recent gifts (1:3–11; 4:10–20).

2. He warns them that they may have to suffer, as Christ did and as Paul is doing now. But he urges them to stand firm in their faith. And drawing from his own experience, he shows how God can use difficult situations to help spread the good news about Jesus (1:12–29).

3. He urges them to remain united, and to imitate the humility of Jesus, who "gave up everything and became a slave" and to whom God awarded "the highest place and honored his name above all others" (2:7, 9).

4. Paul also warns the Philippians to "watch out for those people who behave like dogs!" (3:2). These are apparently Jews who profess Jesus as Lord, but who insist—against Paul's teaching—that all Christians must observe the Jewish laws recorded in the Old Testament.

> **Did You Know?**
>
> • Philippi was named after the father of Alexander the Great, King Philip.
>
> • Paul went to Philippi and the surrounding province of Macedonia only after seeing a vision of a man begging him, "Come over to Macedonia and help us!" (Acts 16:9).

Joy. For someone writing from prison and facing the threat of death, Paul speaks a lot about happiness. He uses the word "joy" in some form or another sixteen times in this short letter.

He remembers the Philippians with joy (1:4). He will be "completely happy" if the believers there will live in harmony with each other (2:2). The Philippians are his "pride and joy" (4:1).

A moving song about Jesus. Paul quotes part of what many Bible experts believe is an early song about Jesus (2:6–11). Paul uses the song merely as an illustration, to urge the Philippians to imitate Christ's humility and his willingness to suffer for others. But the song also shows what the earliest Christians believed about who Jesus is: "truly God," "he became like one of us," he is now "honored . . . above all others," and one day "at the name of Jesus everyone will bow."

Author and Date

Paul, writing from jail in an unnamed city, writes this letter to the Philippians to express thanks for gifts they sent him.

If Paul wrote from Rome, as many scholars believe, then Philippians is a product of his two years of house arrest, beginning about A.D. 60. This would have been during the final years of his ministry, which began with his conversion some 25 years earlier.

TIMELINE	BIBLE EVENTS	Paul starts church in Philippi, during second missionary trip A.D. 50		Paul writes Philippians, during Rome imprisonment A.D. 60	Dates are approximate
		A.D. 50	A.D. 55	A.D. 60	A.D. 65
	WORLD EVENTS		China, Rome conduct trade via 4,000-mile-long Silk Road A.D. 50	Rome burns; Christians blamed, persecuted A.D. 64	

On Location

Paul writes from prison to a church in Philippi, a large city on one of the main roads connecting Rome with territories to the east. He visited it twice on his third missionary journey (see map).

Where Paul is during the writing remains a mystery. He speaks of "Roman guards" (1:13) and employees "in the service of the Emperor" (4:22). This leads some to conclude Paul is writing from Rome. But Roman guards and imperial employees are scattered throughout the Roman world. So Paul could be writing from one of many other jails in which he spent time. Paul admits he was imprisoned many times (2 Corinthians 11:23). Acts names three: Philippi, when he started the church (16:23–40); Caesarea (23:23—26:32), and Rome (28: 16–31). Other possible jailings took place in Corinth and Ephesus. ❏

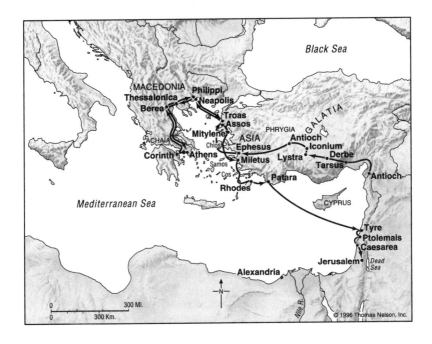

Big Scenes from Philippians

When the church at Philippi hears that Paul their founding minister is in jail, they send a courier with gifts. In response, Paul writes a joyous letter of appreciation.

"Every time I think of you, I thank my God," Paul writes. "This is because you have taken part with me in spreading the good news from the first day you heard about it. . . . You have a special place in my heart" (1:3, 5, 7).

Paul encourages the people not to feel badly about his imprisonment. He says "what has happened to me has helped to spread the good news. The Roman guards and all the others know that I am here in jail because I serve Christ. Now most of the Lord's followers have become brave and are fearlessly telling the message" (1:12–14).

Paul warns that one day the Philippians may also have to suffer for Christ. If they do, he says, they should be brave and remember that the love of Christ will comfort them.

Paul writes from prison
(1:1–29)

Not only will the Philippians be comforted, Paul adds, they will be rewarded. To illustrate this he draws from a beautiful poem about Jesus, perhaps the lyrics of a hymn: "Christ was humble. He obeyed God and even died on a cross. Then God gave Christ the highest place and honored his name above all others" (2:8–9).

Paul asks the Philippians to continue being his "pride and joy" (4:1) by living in harmony with each other and by following his example if they have to face suffering. "I run toward the goal, so that I can win the prize of being called to heaven," Paul writes (3:14).

"Finally," the apostle adds, "keep your minds on whatever is true, pure, right, holy, friendly, and proper. . . . God, who gives peace, will be with you" (4:8–9).

Jesus, the suffering servant now glorified
(2:1–18)

Reviews

Citizens of heaven. "We are citizens of heaven and are eagerly waiting for our Savior to come from there" (3:20). When Paul says this, he uses a technical term that appears only here in all of the New Testament. The word is "citizen," but it refers to a colony of settlers or retired soldiers who secure a conquered land. This is a term especially pertinent to the residents of Philippi, for this city began as such a frontier town. Residents in cities like this were awarded a legal status equal to that of people born in the imperial capital of Rome.

The Philippians took great pride in their citizenship, because their city enjoyed the highest legal privilege attainable in the empire. Paul wanted Philippian believers to take just as much pride in their church, which he described as a colony of heaven ruled by Jesus.

Three letters in one? Some Bible scholars say Philippians is a collection of three letters. They suggest this because of some abrupt changes in topic and tone, and because Polycarp, a second-century Christian writer, spoke of Paul's "letters" to the Philippians.

Especially obvious, though buried in the middle of the letter, is Paul's sudden and sarcastic attack on Jewish Christians who are trying to convince non-Jewish believers in Philippi to observe Jewish laws. Paul describes these people as evil, as enemies of the cross of Christ, and as behaving like dogs (3:2, 18). This digression seems far astray from a letter otherwise filled with words of happiness. Also, it seems odd to some that Paul waits until the end of the letter to thank the Philippians for the gifts they sent him.

For these reasons, some scholars propose that Paul wrote three letters, later combined into one: 1:1-31 with 4:4-9, 21-32; 3:2-4:3; and 4:10-20.

Other scholars argue that the writing style, choice of words, and themes all blend together to form a single letter. They add that when Paul urges the Philippians to "face your enemies" (1:28), he is anticipating the harsh comments ahead, with which he condemns Jewish-Christian intruders trying to impose Jewish laws onto Gentiles (3:2-4:3). ❑

Encore

- To read about how Paul started the church of Philippi, turn to Acts 16:11-40.

- Second Timothy is one of Paul's final letters. It includes a moving passage about his approaching death (4:6-8). ❑

COLOSSIANS

When It Happened

(dates are approximate)

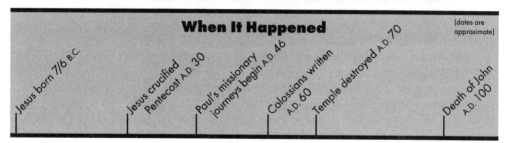

Jesus born 7/6 B.C.

Jesus crucified Pentecost A.D. 30

Paul's missionary journeys begin A.D. 46

Colossians written A.D. 60

Temple destroyed A.D. 70

Death of John A.D. 100

Fake Religions Ahead

Just enough truth to be dangerous—that's what Paul sees in a new religious movement catching fire in Colossae. For years Paul has defended Christianity against major religions of the day: Judaism, worship of Roman and Greek gods, along with mysterious cults that promise eternal life.

Now Paul faces a movement led by religious philosophers gifted in the art of accessorizing. These teachers take a little from Christianity, a little from Judaism, a little from the mysterious cults, and suddenly they have a new religion that looks deceptively familiar. This religion teaches that angels exist, it honors religious holidays, and it urges people to seek God. All this looks so familiar, in fact, that it makes the Christians of Colossae begin to wonder if this new teaching is simply a more insightful way of interpreting old truths.

It's not, Paul insists. It's just another set of human teachings that "come from the powers of this world and not from Christ" (2:8).

For the people of Colossae—and for Christians of all ages who become perplexed by new takes on old-time religion— Paul offers sage advice: "You have accepted Christ Jesus as your Lord. Now keep on following him. Plant your roots in Christ and let him be the foundation for your life" (2:6–7).

What people need is not "fancy talk" (2:3), not "senseless arguments" (2:8), not "human teachings" (2:8)—just Jesus Christ. ❏

Famous Lines

• Whatsoever ye do in word or deed, do all in the name of the Lord Jesus (3:17, King James Version).

• Christ is all, and in all (3:11, King James Version). *Paul's declaration that Jesus is what matters most in life, and that his Spirit lives in everyone who invites him in.*

Behind the Scenes of Colossians

⭐ Starring Roles

Paul, traveling minister who starts churches throughout the Roman Empire, and who advises even churches he has not started—such as the one in Colossae (1:1)

Epaphras, founding minister of the church in Colossae, and an associate of Paul (1:7)

📖 Plot

While sitting in prison awaiting trial, Paul gets word that Christians in Colossae are confronting a new teaching that could destroy the church. The threatening movement seems to blend elements of many religions into a convincing belief system.

"Don't let anyone fool you," Paul warns. "These arguments may sound wise, but they are only human teachings. They come from the powers of this world and not from Christ" (2:8).

Paul reminds the Colossians that they accepted Jesus Christ, and they should now follow him "just as you were taught" (2:7).

The apostle closes his letter with a list of everyday traits that true Christians exhibit, as well as traits they shun (chapter 3).

🎥 What to Look For

The problem. When Paul hears that a religious teaching that combines Jewish beliefs and other religions is making inroads into the church at Colossae, he writes a letter to urge the people to trust only in the power of Jesus to save them.

It's unclear what the heresy is, or even if it has a name. Paul's rebuttal, however, gives clues about what the heresy emphasizes.

1. Follow rules about food, religious holidays (2:16–17), and circumcision (3:11). These teachings may have come from Judaism.

2. Deprive your body, to show you have control over it (2:21–23). This resembles the ascetic practices of isolationist religious groups such as the Jewish Essenes who produced the Dead Sea Scrolls, and of Christian monks in later centuries.

TIMELINE	BIBLE EVENTS	Paul converts ---- A.D. 35	Paul's missionary journeys begin A.D. 46 ---------		Paul writes Colossians, during Rome imprisonment A.D. 60 -----------	Dates are approximate
		A.D. 35	A.D. 45		A.D. 55	A.D. 65
	WORLD EVENTS		Buddhism of India introduced to China A.D. 58 -----------------			Mayans are building a great civilization in Central America ---- A.D. 60

3. Worship angels, who provide visions, more knowledge about God, and more access to him (2:18). This emphasis on having secret knowledge about God and salvation may represent the seed of a heresy that develops into a major movement in the second century: Gnosticism, from a word for "knowledge."

The supreme power of Jesus. Paul refutes this speculative religion by reminding the Colossians that their salvation doesn't depend on such a wide variety of spiritual power sources. Christ is the supreme power on which people depend.

Christ's sacrifice eliminates the need to observe ancient Jewish rules, which were built around the sacrificial system (1:20). Christ is Lord of the "body," a word that symbolizes both the church and the individuals in it (2:19–23). And Christ had a role in creating all life, including angels (1:16).

A song about Jesus. To refute the heresy, Paul draws from what may have been a well-known song about Jesus. At least part of the hymn appears in 1:15–20. These lyrics, with Paul's additional comments, produce the New Testament's strongest statement about the authority of Jesus.

Instructions for daily living. After teaching about the power of Jesus to save, Paul shows how Christians should respond: adopt attitudes and a lifestyle that reflects a close relationship with Jesus. "You have been raised to life with Christ. Now set your heart on what is in heaven. . . . Be gentle, kind, humble, meek, and patient. Put up with each other, and forgive anyone who does you wrong, just as Christ has forgiven you" (3:1, 12–13).

Author and Date

The writer is identified as "Paul, chosen by God to be an apostle of Christ Jesus" (1:1). For background on why some scholars doubt this, read "Who wrote the letter?" in Reviews.

Because of similarities between this letter and the letter written to the Ephesians, both were likely penned about the same time. If Paul wrote the letter, he may have done so during his two-year imprisonment at Rome, beginning about A.D. 60. If someone else wrote it as a tribute to Paul, applying the apostle's theology to the heresy confronting Colossae, the writing may have occurred in the closing decades of the first century.

On Location

Paul writes from jail (4:3), perhaps in Rome, to a church he has never visited. Colossae is 100 miles west of Ephesus, where Paul once lived for two years. The church was apparently started by a student minister Paul sent: Epaphras (1:7). (See map in Acts, page 323.) ❏

Big Scenes from Colossians

A new teaching that urges people to pray to angels arrives in Colossae, a busy city on an important east-west trade route in Turkey. Paul feels compelled to write to the believers there and remind them to hold fast to their traditional faith, which they received from one of his associates.

There's no need to pray to angels, Paul says. "Christ is exactly like God. . . . Everything was created by him, everything in heaven and on earth" (1:15, 16). Paul explains that faith in Christ is all that anyone needs for salvation.

**Jesus at creation
(1:15–20)** ••

The heretical teaching, which Paul calls "senseless arguments," apparently has a long to-do list for people who want God's forgiveness that leads to salvation. In addition to praying to angels, people are expected to observe rules and religious holy days dictated by the teachers.

This is all wrong, Paul argues. God took away our sins when he "nailed them to the cross" (2:14). We become God's people not by obeying rules, praying to angels, or discovering spiritual secrets in visions. We become his people by trusting him.

Paul illustrates this with the familiar ritual of baptism. "When you were baptized, it was the same as being buried with Christ. Then you were raised to life because you had faith in the power of God, who raised Christ from death. You were dead, because you were sinful and were not God's people. But God let Christ make you alive, when he forgave all your sins" (2:12–13).

Other than believing this, Christians have no required to-do list for salvation.

**Jesus, taking our sins to the cross
(2:6–23)** ••

In words resembling Ephesians 4 and 5, and probably written about the same time, Paul says that genuine Christianity shows itself in the way people live.

"Each of you is now a new person. You are becoming more and more like your Creator" (3:10). Paul says this means, for one thing, that we learn to control our body—not as ascetics do by depriving themselves of nourishment—but by doing away with harmful thoughts.

In addition, we try to become more kind, patient, and forgiving, all of which are motivated by nothing less than love.

When we're in doubt about what to say or do, Paul offers this suggestion: "Whatever you say or do should be done in the name of the Lord Jesus" (3:17).

**Live like people of God
(3:1–25)** •••

Reviews

Paul's touch. Though some scholars question whether Paul or a later associate such as Timothy wrote this letter, the message reflects what Paul said in many other letters.

For example, one repeated theme is that as far as Christ is concerned, all believers are equal: "It doesn't matter if you are a Greek or a Jew, or if you are circumcised or not. You may even be a barbarian or a Scythian [people from southern Russia, known for their savagery], and you may be a slave or a free person" (3:11). Paul says much the same in other letters: Romans 10:12; 1 Corinthians 12:13; Galatians 3:28; and Ephesians 6:8.

Who wrote the letter? For many of the reasons that some scholars think Ephesians was written after the death of Paul, they think the same of Colossians. The writer's use of words and ideas don't mesh well with those of Paul in other letters.

For example, Paul often confronts opposition by using the style of a well-reasoned argument or debate. In Colossians he uses a more poetic style that joyously celebrates Jesus. Also, Paul writes with uncharacteristically long and complex sentences, which most English translations simplify.

In addition, part of the heresy addressed in the book seems remarkably close to Gnosticism, a movement that became popular only in the second century. And other teachings, such as the portrayal of Christ at the beginning of creation (1:16), appear only in Christian writings believed to have been written near the end of the first century—some thirty years or more after Paul died.

Bible experts who argue that Paul wrote Colossians say the variations show he was able to change with the times, using new terms and giving old terms new meaning. The wordy writing, they suggest, may have come from Paul's use of well-known hymns and prayers, which he wove into the letter. Also, the heresy in Colossae may have been the seed from which Gnosticism grew. ❏

Encore

- The letter of Colossians resembles Ephesians in both tone and teachings. Both, for example, have advice for everyday living, and both emphasize the church, which the writer symbolically calls the body of Christ. ❏

1 THESSALONIANS

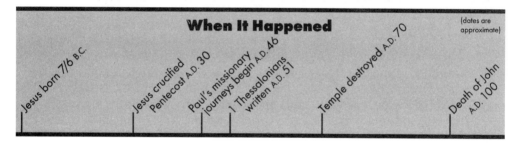

When It Happened

(dates are approximate)

Jesus born 7/6 B.C.

Jesus crucified Pentecost A.D. 30

Paul's missionary journeys begin A.D. 46

1 Thessalonians written A.D. 51

Temple destroyed A.D. 70

Death of John A.D. 100

When Will Jesus Come Back?

The infant church of Thessalonica, in ancient Greece, wants Jesus to come back soon and whisk them off to the eternal delights of heaven. This seemingly is their greatest desire—the one subject they think about most.

It's not hard to understand why. Paul is able to spend only a few weeks with them, before he is run out of town by Jews who believe he is preaching heresy. Left behind, and alone, is this unorganized core of converts, united only by their experience of salvation and the belief that one day the Lord will return to take the faithful to their everlasting reward in heaven.

Though the Thessalonian believers stand united, they stand alone—or so it must have seemed—for they begin cultivating a lifestyle of holiness while living in a sprawling port city that teems with immorality, greed, and deception. In addition, they worship Jesus as God's Son and as ruler of the heavenly kingdom, while Jews insist God has no son and Romans in the city worship the emperor, ruler of the largest earthly kingdom.

For Thessalonians, and all Christians who feel out of sync in their world, Paul encourages them not to focus their energy on the return of Jesus. Instead, we are to work hard, live honorable lives, and earn the respect of others. By doing this, we draw people to Jesus just as a lighthouse draws to safety one lost ship after another. ❏

Famous Line

• The Lord will come like a thief in the night (5:2, New International Version). *When asked about the timing of Christ's return, Paul replies with this phrase, meaning that no one can predict the Second Coming.*

Behind the Scenes of 1 Thessalonians

⭐ Starring Roles

Paul, leading minister to the Gentile world, and founder of the congregation at Thessalonica and other major cities throughout the Roman Empire (1:1)
Timothy, Paul's associate who visits Thessalonica then reports back to Paul about the progress of the new converts and the questions they have (1:1)

📖 Plot

About 1,000 miles into his second missionary trip, Paul has a captivating vision one night: he sees a man pleading with him to leave Turkey and come to Macedonia, a Roman province in northern Greece. Paul complies, taking the gospel to Europe. He arrives in Philippi, but stays only a short time before he is charged with disturbing the peace and is forced to leave town. He proceeds on to Thessalonica, capital and largest city of Macedonia. Some 200,000 people live in this busy port town on the main east-west trade route to Asia.

Paul preaches in the synagogue for about three weeks before the Jews realize that what he's teaching requires an end to traditional Judaism. They riot, forcing Paul to escape to Athens, 200 miles south. But not before some Jews and many non-Jews convert to Christianity.

Within perhaps a month or two, while Paul is staying in Corinth, he sends his young associate, Timothy, to check on the Thessalonian believers. Timothy returns with a good report. But he also brings word that the people are facing persecution, and that they have questions about the Second Coming. By this time Paul is deeply involved in starting the Corinthian ministry; he can't leave. So he comes up with an innovative solution that's not unlike a correspondence school. He decides to encourage and teach the believers of Thessalonica by letter.

Paul praises their faith, answers their questions about the Second Coming, then urges them to live in a way that would please the Lord.

🎥 What to Look For

The Second Coming. The questions most on the mind of new converts in Thessalonica have to do with the return of Jesus. Questions like these: When is he coming? How can we know he will accept us? What will happen to Christians who die before Jesus arrives?

Paul says no one knows when Jesus will return, but he assures the Thessalonians that as long as they trust in Jesus for their salvation, they won't be disappointed. As for dead Christians, Paul says they will not miss out on eternal life. After they die, they will be "raised to life" (4:16).

Paul covers several topics in this short letter, but the Second Coming is the main idea. Every chapter ends with a reference to it. And 4:13—5:11 describes what it will be like, beginning with the call of an angel and a trumpet blast, and concluding with Christians rising into the heavens to meet the Lord in the air.

Guidelines for holy living. Thessalonica is anything but a city of saints. It's a thriving port town on a major trade route. So it has all the sinfulness of any large city, along with the emphasis on sex that could be expected in a town that draws traveling merchants and sailors just passing by.

Paul knows that it's hard to live in a town like this without getting swept into the powerful current of passion and greed. So he gently warns the new believers, "Don't be a slave of your desires or live like people who don't know God" (4:4). Instead, Paul says, "Try your best to live quietly, to mind your own business, and to work hard. . . . Then you will be respected by people who are not followers of the Lord" (4:11–12).

> **Did You Know?**
>
> • First Thessalonians is probably the oldest piece of literature in the New Testament, written about twenty years after the death and resurrection of Jesus. The Gospels, describing the life of Jesus, were written a decade or more later, to preserve the stories the disciples had told.

No quotes from the Old Testament. Paul was raised a Pharisee, a Jewish scholar. When he talks about religious matters, it's common for him to draw from his expertise and quote the Jewish Scriptures. The fact that he doesn't do this in his letter to the Thessalonians suggests that most of the believers there are non-Jews, unfamiliar with Scripture.

The story of Paul's visit to Thessalonica, reported in Acts, suggests that only a few Jews accepted his message, compared to "a large number of God-fearing Greeks" (Acts 17:4, New International Version). God-fearing Greeks are non-Jews who worship in the synagogue, but who stop short of converting to Judaism. Major roadblocks to conversion are the painful rite of circumcision and the restrictive dietary regulations of the Jews.

By the time Paul writes this letter, there may be even fewer Jewish Christians—perhaps none. He describes congregation members as having "turned away from idols to serve the true and living God" (1:9).

Author and Date

The letter is written by Paul, who is accompanied by his traveling associates Timothy and Silas (1:1). Bible experts agree that this letter reads like other authenticated letters of Paul. Early Christian writers, beginning with Marcion in A.D. 140, confirm that Paul was the author.

Paul wrote this letter in about A.D. 51, during his second missionary trip, while he was starting a church in Corinth. For archaeological evidence supporting this date, read "Gallio was here" in Reviews.

TIMELINE	BIBLE EVENTS	Paul's missionary journeys begin A.D. 46	Paul starts second missionary trip A.D. 50	Paul writes Thessalonians while in Corinth A.D. 51	Dates are approximate
		A.D. 40	A.D. 45		A.D. 50
	WORLD EVENTS	China, Rome conduct trade via 4,000-mile-long Silk Road A.D. 50	Jews expelled from Rome over controversy about "Chrestus" (probably "Christ") A.D. 49	Isthmian Games held at Corinth A.D. 51	

On Location

Thessalonica is a bustling trade town in northern Greece. The city profits from a port in the Thermatic Gulf of the Aegean Sea, and from its location on the Via Egnatia, an east-west Roman road that stretches across northern Greece and into Turkey. Paul writes the letter from Corinth, some 250 miles south. (See map in 1 Corinthians, page 342.) ❑

Big Scene from 1 Thessalonians

During Paul's second missionary journey, which takes him into what is now Greece, the apostle spends only a few weeks in Thessalonica. But this is long enough to convince many people that the Messiah has come, been executed, and raised from the dead. It's also long enough to instill in the new converts an urgent sense of expectation; they believe Jesus will return at any moment.

Some apparently quit their jobs, feeling that they shouldn't waste their time on trivial matters. As the waiting goes on for weeks and perhaps months, the people begin to have doubts about what Paul told them. They want to know when Jesus is coming, and what is going to happen to Christians who die before he arrives.

Paul writes that no one knows exactly when Jesus will return: the event will be as unexpected "as a thief coming at night" (5:2). This Thief, however, will be welcome because he will come to take his followers to heaven.

Paul outlines the course of events: "With a loud command and with the shout of the chief angel and a blast of God's trumpet, the Lord will return from heaven. Then those who had faith in Christ before they died will be raised to life. Next, all of us who are still alive will be taken up into the clouds together with them to meet the Lord in the sky. From that time on we will all be with the Lord forever" (4:16–17).

In the meantime, Paul says, believers should not be idle, but should work hard, live godly lives, and patiently endure the religious persecution they will most certainly encounter.

**The Second Coming
(4:13–5:11)**

Reviews

Gallio was here. An ancient Greek inscription adds evidence that Paul was, in fact, at Corinth in about A.D. 51, when he wrote to the Thessalonians.

Acts 18 says the Corinthian Jews brought Paul up on charges before Gallio, governor of the southern Greece province of Achaia, and that Gallio threw the case out of court.

An inscription found at Delphi, a worship center in the region, confirms that Gallio was governor of Achaia from about A.D. 51 - 53. Gallio was also the brother of Seneca, a philosopher and a tutor of Nero. Seneca describes his brother as fair and likeable. "No other human being is so charming to just one person as he is to all people," Seneca writes.

Paul misjudged the Second Coming. Paul not only preached that Jesus had come to save human beings from sin, Paul also taught that Jesus was coming back. And from what Paul told the Thessalonians, he seemed certain the Second Coming would happen in his lifetime.

This is implied in the answer he gave to people wondering what would happen to Christians who died before Jesus returns: "We [the living] won't go up to meet him [Jesus] ahead of his followers who have already died" (4:15).

Not only did Paul believe in the imminent return of Jesus, he managed to pass this sense of the approaching Second Coming on to his converts. Some believers apparently had gone so far as to quit working to wait for the Great Return (4:11 - 12; 2 Thessalonians 3:6 - 15).

Paul, however, tells the Thessalonians to get back to work and to remember that no one can predict when Jesus will return.

Later in Paul's ministry he realizes he will not live to see the Second Coming. "Now the time has come for me to die," he writes to Timothy, his close friend (2 Timothy 4:6). When that moment arrives, Paul believes he will be raised to life and ushered into the presence of God. As he once explained to the Corinthians, to be absent from the body is to be present with the Lord (2 Corinthians 5:8). ❏

Encore

- To learn how the church at Thessalonica began, read Acts 17:1 - 10.

- For Paul's follow-up letter, read 2 Thessalonians.

- For Paul's most extensive statement about the return of Jesus, read 1 Corinthians 15. ❏

2 THESSALONIANS

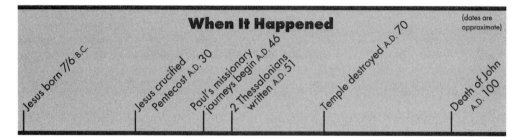

When It Happened

(dates are approximate)

Jesus born 7/6 B.C.

Jesus crucified Pentecost A.D. 30

Paul's missionary journeys begin A.D. 46

2 Thessalonians written A.D. 51

Temple destroyed A.D. 70

Death of John A.D. 100

Obsessed with the Second Coming

Once people start thinking about Jesus coming back to earth at any moment and whisking them to heaven, it's hard to think about much else—especially if life is as tough as it was for the persecuted Thessalonians.

Preoccupation with the Second Coming can sidetrack Christians, however, as it did in Thessalonica. Instead of going out to spread good news that Jesus came, Christians hang out and wait for better news that he has come back. Some actually quit their jobs.

This sabotages the mission Jesus gave the church: "Tell everyone about me" (Acts 1:8). Paul knows this, and in the first letter tells the believers to keep busy. In this second letter, he puts it more bluntly: "Now we learn that some of you just loaf around and won't do any work, except the work of a busybody. So, for the sake of our Lord Jesus Christ, we ask and beg these people to settle down and start working for a living" (3:11–12).

To get their minds off the Second Coming, Paul reminds them of other end-time events that must come first. We don't know how the Thessalonians reacted to this, but in later centuries Christians became preoccupied with "signs of the times." They tried to figure out where they were on God's end-time timetable.

For those of us who know believers doing this Paul says, "Don't consider them your enemies, but speak kindly to them" (3:15). And what exactly did Paul say kindly? "Settle down" (3:12). Perhaps he also reminded them of what the angels told the disciples after Jesus ascended into heaven: "Why are you men from Galilee standing here and looking up into the sky?" (Acts 1:11). ❏

Famous Lines

- If you don't work, you don't eat (3:10). *Paul's attitude toward people who quit work so they can wait for the Second Coming of Jesus.*

- Do not grow weary in doing good (3:13, New King James Version).

Behind the Scenes of 2 Thessalonians

⭐ Starring Role

Paul, leading minister to the Gentile world, and founder of the congregation at Thessalonica and other major cities throughout the Roman Empire (1:1)

📖 Plot

Sometime after Paul writes 1 Thessalonians, primarily to answer the church's questions about the Second Coming, Paul writes a second letter that arrives perhaps a few months later.

Excitement about the Lord's return has nearly consumed the believers. Part of the reason, perhaps, is because of Paul's teaching while he was in town, and his follow-up letter urging the Christians to remain alert and ready for Jesus' return. In addition, the believers are facing a lot of persecution—the violent kind that earlier had driven Paul out of town. These believers would have welcomed a quick escape to eternal bliss.

Paul, however, reminds them of events that must happen before the Lord returns. And he tells the believers to get on with their lives, sternly rebuking those who have quit work to await the Great Return.

🎥 What to Look For

Second Coming. Like 1 Thessalonians, the main reason Paul writes this letter is to clear up confusion about the Second Coming.

The return of Jesus is apparently all the Christians want to talk about. This excitement is likely fueled by Paul's earlier preaching on the subject, by his letter urging them to stay alert, and by a wave of anti-Christian persecution.

"The wicked one." To calm the believers down and get their minds focused on working in this world instead of anticipating the next, Paul reminds them of his earlier teaching about events that will precede the Lord's coming.

"Before the Lord returns, the wicked one who is doomed to be destroyed will appear. He will brag and oppose everything that is holy or sacred. . . . When the wicked one appears, Satan will pretend to work all kinds of miracles, wonders, and signs. Lost people will be fooled by his evil deeds" (2:3–4, 9–10).

The people of Thessalonica know exactly what Paul is talking about: "Don't you remember that I told you this while I was still with you?" (2:5). But we don't know what he's referring to. Bible experts have suggested several possibilities:

1. "The wicked one" may be an evil religious leader who is an antichrist, opposed to everything Jesus stands for. John refers to many antichrists (1 John 2:18).

2. He could be a wicked spiritual entity.

3. Or perhaps "the wicked one" refers to the Roman Empire, or to an emperor. If so, Paul would have had good reason not to be more specific in this public letter. One of the characteristics of end-time literature, a genre called apocalyptic, is that the writers often use code words that the recipients understand, but that no one else does. This allows writers to criticize powerful leaders without getting caught.

Persecution. The Christians of Thessalonica are suffering because they are Christians. Paul writes that he knows they are "going through a lot of trouble and suffering" (1:4). It's probably the same kind of violence mixed with legal wrangling that had earlier forced Paul out of town (Acts 17:5–10).

These harsh conditions would have added fuel to the bonfire of hope for a speedy return of the Lord.

Christians not working. Since Christians were sure that Jesus was coming right away, some apparently saw no reason to plant crops, work in their shops, or repair their houses. In time, these people began to live off the generosity of others. Paul has stern words for these folks, and how to treat them. "I beg you not to have anything to do with any of your people who loaf around," he says. "Follow our example. We didn't waste our time loafing, and we didn't accept food from anyone without paying for it. . . . We also gave you the rule that if you don't work, you don't eat" (3:6–10).

> **Did You Know?**
>
> • Some of the best-selling Christian books in the past century speculate on when Jesus will return, and under what conditions. Perhaps most famous is the 1976 book *The Late Great Planet Earth*, which has sold over 11 million copies. Four million copies of the booklet *88 Reasons Why the Rapture Will Be in 1988* were published.

Author and Date

The letter begins by announcing that it comes from Paul and his associates, Timothy and Silas. It ends with Paul's signature: "I always sign my letters as I am now doing: PAUL" (3:17).

Some Bible scholars, however, suggest that one of Paul's associates may have written the letter on his behalf, perhaps after his death. They base this on the observation that the teaching about the Second Coming is different from that in the first letter. Also, the second letter is written in a more formal style, and it uses some terms that don't appear in any of Paul's other letters—such as the words translated "the wicked one" (2:3). Other scholars argue that the changes in the second letter reflect the changing situation in Thessalonica. For more on this, see "Second Coming, revised" in Review.

Because the two letters address the same topics, they were probably written about the same time, perhaps a few months apart. Paul likely wrote them during his two-year stay in Corinth, which began in about A.D. 50.

TIMELINE	BIBLE EVENTS				
		Paul's missionary journeys begin A.D. 46	Paul starts second missionary trip A.D. 50	Paul writes 2 Thessalonians while in Corinth A.D. 51	Dates are approximate
		A.D. 40	A.D. 45		A.D. 50
	WORLD EVENTS	Jews expelled from Rome over controversy about "Chrestus" (probably "Christ") A.D. 49	China, Rome conduct trade via 4,000-mile-long Silk Road A.D. 50	Isthmian Games held at Corinth A.D. 51	

On Location

Thessalonica is a bustling trade town in northern Greece. The city profits from a port in the Thermatic Gulf of the Aegean Sea, and from its location on the Via Egnatia, an east-west Roman road that stretches across northern Greece and into Turkey. Paul writes the letter from Corinth, some 250 miles south. (See map in 1 Corinthians, page 342.) ❏

Reviews

Siding with the prophets. When Paul says a wicked and God-insulting leader will come before Jesus returns, the apostle is confirming end-time prophecy from the Old Testament. Daniel speaks of an evil leader who will "insult the only true God" (11:36) and of a "Horrible Thing" (9:27) that will desecrate God's holy temple.

Jesus also spoke of this "Horrible Thing" (Matthew 24:15), which may have been a prediction about the Roman destruction of the temple in A.D. 70 as well as a horror yet to come. John, writing in Revelation perhaps in the A.D. 90s, tells of a coming "beast" (13:5-8) who will claim to be God and who will rule the earth for a time. In the end, John says, the beast will be destroyed. Paul describes the death this way: "Jesus will kill him simply by breathing on him" (2:8).

This is a powerful description that connects Jesus to Creation. God "breathed life into the man" (Genesis 2:7), and at sometime in the future Jesus will breathe the life out of "the wicked one."

Second Coming, revised. Paul's teaching about the Second Coming of Jesus is so different here than it is in 1 Thessalonians that some scholars doubt Paul wrote the second letter.

In 1 Thessalonians, Paul tries to prepare the church for the soon-approaching return of Jesus. He calms their anticipation by urging them to go about their lives, yet he cautions them to stay alert and be ready when Jesus comes (1 Thessalonians 5:4-8).

In 2 Thessalonians, however, Paul backpedals so much that he looks like he's in full retreat. It's unclear if Paul was refuting that "the Lord has already come" (2:2) or that the coming was near. The original Greek could be translated either way. But whichever the case, Paul threw cold water on the anxious crowd by reminding them of his earlier teaching about the events that must precede the Second Coming.

We know very little about what these events are, but they involve the arrival of a mysterious entity or organization that Paul describes as "the wicked one" through whom "Satan will pretend to work all kinds of miracles" (2:9).

Paul probably didn't backpedal because he had changed his mind about the Second Coming. He probably saw that Second Coming fervor was getting out of hand in Thessalonica. And he realized he needed to calm the people down so they could get on with the business of living and serving God. ❑

Encore

- Read 1 Thessalonians, the letter Paul wrote the congregation first.

- To learn how the church at Thessalonica began, read Acts 17:1-10.

- For Paul's most extensive statement about the return of Jesus, read 1 Corinthians 15. ❑

1 TIMOTHY

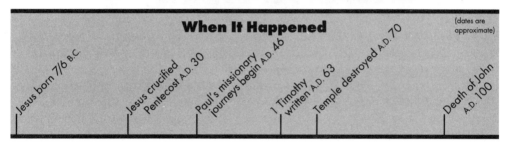

When It Happened

(dates are approximate)

Jesus born 7/6 B.C.

Jesus crucified Pentecost A.D. 30

Paul's missionary journeys begin A.D. 46

1 Timothy written A.D. 63

Temple destroyed A.D. 70

Death of John A.D. 100

Tips on How to Be a Pastor

Four years in Bible college, three years in seminary. That's the prescribed course of study for many ministers today. But for those interested in Paul's priorities for church leaders, there's a thirty-minute correspondence course: his two letters to Timothy, who is pastoring in Ephesus, and his one letter to Titus, on the island of Crete.

Timothy and Titus had each served several years of rigorous apprenticeship. They had accompanied Paul on some of his missionary trips, and they served as trusted emissaries who delivered his messages to churches and helped answer questions and defuse explosive situations. Timothy, for example, draws the unenviable assignment of delivering 1 Corinthians, Paul's letter to the troublesome congregation that hadn't bothered to discipline a member who was committing incest with his stepmother (1 Corinthians 4:17; 5:1).

Even after years of experience, both men receive continuing education on the basics of ministry, courtesy of their protective mentor. Because of these letters, we discover not only some of Paul's ministry fundamentals—such as resisting the temptation to get rich—we also learn that Paul believes older, seasoned ministers should gently share their wisdom with younger ones.

Paul supported the ministers in his care. Congregations can do the same. ❏

Famous Line

- The love of money is the root of all evil (6:10, King James Version).

Behind the Scenes of 1 Timothy

Starring Roles

Paul, traveling minister who covers some 10,000 miles and starts churches throughout the Roman Empire (1:1)

Timothy, one of Paul's most devoted traveling companions, whom Paul appoints to lead the church in Ephesus (1:2)

Plot

When Paul leaves Ephesus to travel on to Macedonia in northern Greece, he assigns his associate, Timothy, to stay behind and lead the congregation. The Christians there are being confronted and confused by several religious teachings. Paul believes that Timothy can help the Ephesians sort out the truth and the lies.

Sometime later, perhaps while Paul is in Greece, he writes Timothy this letter giving guidance on a wide array of issues that surface in local congregations. These topics include conducting worship services, choosing church leaders, ministering to the poor, and even ministering to the rich.

What to Look For

Lots of advice for ministers. The three letters of 1 and 2 Timothy along with Titus are known as the Pastoral Letters because they contain Paul's advice to these two men who are pastoring churches.

False teachings. Based on what Paul writes, it seems that the Ephesians are grappling with at least three kinds of religious teaching, all of which are at odds with Christianity.

1. References to "senseless stories and endless lists of ancestors" (1:4) and to "teachers of the Law of Moses" (1:7) point to the Jews, who take great pride in their family tree. The "stories" may refer to Jewish legends, which are popular in Paul's day.

2. "These liars will forbid people to marry or to eat certain foods" (4:2–3). This clue points to monk-like ascetics who try to make themselves holy by controlling their body. But in the process, they treat important elements of God's good creation—such as sex and food—as though they are sinful. Some later Christian leaders fast so much that they do permanent damage to their digestive system—among them, Protestant reformer Martin Luther.

3. "Stupid talk that sounds smart" (6:20) implies that the second-century heresy of Gnosticism (from a word meaning "knowledge") is already getting

TIMELINE	BIBLE EVENTS	Paul arrives at Ephesus, staying more than 2 years A.D. 53 ---┐	Paul imprisoned at Rome A.D. 60 --------┐	Paul writes 1 Timothy, possibly after release from ┌--- Rome A.D. 63	Paul executed, possibly after second imprisonment in ┌--- Rome A.D. 67
		A.D. 50	A.D. 60		A.D. 70
	WORLD EVENTS	Rome burns; Nero blames Christians, launches persecution A.D. 64 --------------------┘		Nero commits suicide A.D. 68 --------┘	Dates are approximate

started. Paul's Greek word for "smart" is *gnosis*. The Gnostics believe they have received from God unique knowledge about their true nature, and that this knowledge guarantees them eternal life. Some Gnostics teach that nothing their body can do will affect the fate of their soul—so they do as they please. Others go to the opposite extreme, trying to strengthen their true spiritual nature by depriving the body of physical necessities.

> **Did You Know?**
>
> • Though Paul argues that Jewish laws have become obsolete, including the law of circumcision, he arranges the rite of circumcision for Timothy, whose mother is a Jew. Evidently, this is to help Timothy get along with the Jews. Paul adamantly refuses, however, to have another associate circumcised: Titus, a full-blooded Greek (Galatians 2:3 - 5).

Qualifications for church leaders. Among the ranks of church leadership, the highest standards are required of the officiating minister. Ministers must have a solid reputation, strong social skills, and be able to teach (3:2). Paul has nothing but harsh words for profiteering preachers who love money and "think religion is supposed to make you rich" (6:5).

Church officers who help the minister should be honest, generous, and firm believers in the teachings about Jesus. Before they are appointed to their position, "they must first prove themselves" (3:10). This is not a job for new and struggling Christians.

Author and Date

The letter begins: "From Paul" (1:1). When Christian leaders in the early centuries referred to 1 Timothy, they identified it as the work of Paul. In fact the reason the letter survives in the New Testament is because early Christians accepted it as Paul's. For arguments suggesting that someone else wrote it, see "Who wrote Timothy and Titus?" in Reviews.

Scholars aren't sure when Paul wrote the letter. Paul says that after the two visited Ephesus, he left Timothy behind and continued on to Greece without him (1:3). But this doesn't fit with the travels described in Acts; Timothy accompanied Paul to Greece (Acts 20:4).

Some suggest Paul wrote this letter after the events described in Acts. If so, Paul was released from imprisonment in Rome in about A.D. 62, then made a fourth missionary trip. During that trip, as the theory goes, Paul assigned Timothy to Ephesus, then was later arrested and sent to Rome again. This time he was executed in about A.D. 67, during Nero's persecution of Christians.

On Location

Paul addresses his letter to Timothy in Ephesus, apparently writing from the northern Greece province of Macedonia. (See map in 1 Corinthians, page 342.) Ephesus, a harbor town in western Turkey, is one of the largest cities in the Roman Empire. The town boasts a population of somewhere between 200,000 and 500,000. Ephesus is also a Roman seat of government, home to Rome's governor of Asia. In addition, the city is a famous center of worship to Artemis, a fertility goddess whose temple there is four times larger than the Parthenon in Athens. ❑

Big Scenes from 1 Timothy

Timothy has learned a lot from Paul during the many years they traveled together, starting churches throughout the eastern Mediterranean, and dealing with questions and problems that arise later. But now Timothy is on his own, pastoring the church in Ephesus. Paul loves this young man like a son; he continues to train and encourage him by offering advice about how to run the church.

"When I was leaving for Macedonia, I asked you to stay on in Ephesus and warn certain people there to stop spreading their false teachings," Paul reminds Timothy. "You must teach people to have genuine love, as well as a good conscience and true faith" (1:3, 5).

**Paul writes to Timothy
(1:1–20)** •

Paul gives his coworker, whom he addresses as "my son" (1:18), advice on more than how to cope with false teachings. Paul tutors him on the wide range of topics that any local church leader would confront: how to conduct worship services, how to choose church leaders, and how to minister to the different kinds of people in the church.

In church services, for example, Paul says, "I want everyone everywhere to lift innocent hands toward heaven and pray, without being angry or arguing with each other" (2:8). Paul also wants the people to dress modestly, remembering that they come together to focus on God, not to show off their wardrobe, jewelry, and make-over hairstyle.

Church leaders, Paul says, "must have a good reputation and be faithful in marriage. They must be self-controlled, sensible, well-behaved, friendly to strangers, and able to teach." In addition, the apostle says, they should "be kind and gentle and not love money" (3:2, 3).

In advising young Timothy about ministering to various groups, Paul says, "Don't correct an older man. Encourage him, as you would your own father" (5:1). In addition, Timothy is to treat older women "as you would your own mother," and younger women as "your sister" (5:2).

After packing a wealth of practical counsel into this short letter, Paul closes with a final request and a promise.

"Timothy, guard what God has placed in your care!" he says. "I will pray that the Lord will be kind to all of you!" (6:20–21).

Early church worship service in a private home
• **(2:1–3:16)**

Reviews

Timothy, Paul's best friend. Though some scholars question that Paul wrote 1 and 2 Timothy, Paul's young associate was a prime candidate for the assignment in Ephesus and for the fatherly letters that came afterward.

Timothy was Paul's closest friend and a devoted associate who worked by his side among congregations in Turkey, Greece, and Italy. When believers of Thessalonica had questions about the second coming of Jesus, it was Timothy that Paul trusted to deliver his two letters and help resolve the confusion. And when Paul spent two years starting the church in Corinth, Timothy was at his side assisting in the preaching duties.

There's yet another reason Timothy was a logical choice to pastor the Ephesians. He was from the same Greek culture they were. Timothy grew up in Lystra, about 300 miles east of Ephesus. Yet Timothy also understood the Jewish community as well, because his mother and grandmother were Jews (Acts 16:1; 2 Timothy 1:5).

Who wrote Timothy and Titus? Some scholars doubt that Paul wrote the two letters to Timothy and the single letter to Titus. These scholars suggest that someone else penned the words after Paul died, perhaps drawing from his letters and sermons and applying them to later circumstances. This was a common and accepted practice among Jews and non-Jews of the time. (For more on this, see "Who wrote the letter?" in the Reviews section for Ephesians, page 366.)

One reason many Bible experts believe this is because some of Paul's pivotal ideas—such as those about faith, Jewish law, and righteousness—are treated differently in this letter. Here, for example, "faith" means Christianity. But in Paul's other letters, it describes a person's trusting relationship with Jesus.

Other scholars argue that Paul wrote the letters, as second-century church leaders testify. These Bible experts say that the differences in word use and the absence of themes important in Paul's other letters (such as the ministry of the Spirit, and freedom from Jewish law) confirm that Paul wrote these near the end of his ministry, perhaps ten to fifteen years after his first letters.

Women in the church. Paul told Timothy that women in church "should be silent and not be allowed to teach or to tell men what to do" (2:12). This is much the same message that Paul gave to the church in Corinth. Yet in congregations where there were no problems among the women, Paul puts no restriction on them. (See "Women, keep quiet in church," in the Reviews section of 1 Corinthians, page 346.) ❏

Encore

- To read about the founding of the church in Ephesus, turn to Acts 18:18–19:41.

- For insights into the Ephesus congregation by the turn of the first century, read Revelation 2:1–7.

- Paul gives further ministerial advice in the letters of 2 Timothy and Titus. ❏

2 TIMOTHY

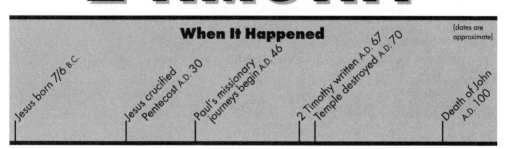

When It Happened

(dates are approximate)

Jesus born 7/6 B.C.

Jesus crucified Pentecost A.D. 30

Paul's missionary journeys begin A.D. 46

2 Timothy written A.D. 67

Temple destroyed A.D. 70

Death of John A.D. 100

The Last Words of Paul

When we know we're about to die, the last words we speak and the last actions we perform show what is most important to us.

The last we hear of Paul he's chained inside a Roman dungeon, awaiting execution. The imperial trial may still be underway, and if so, it's not going well.

Paul unrolls a strip of parchment, perhaps given to him by Luke, the only colleague in the area who hasn't abandoned him. Then Paul writes a letter to the man who is likely his best friend on earth, Timothy.

A preacher to the end, Paul repeats some of what he has said before: Don't be ashamed of the gospel. Don't be fooled by false teachings. Live like children of a holy and loving God. Timothy, who had traveled with Paul for many years, must have heard this a hundred times. But the words are important enough to Paul that he says them again.

Paul's final action—his last known request—is one that any hospice nurse would understand: "Come to see me as soon as you can" (4:9). Paul wants to die in the company of those he loves.

In words and actions, Paul shows what is most important to him: the gospel he has preached, and the people he has loved. ❑

Famous Line

- I have fought the good fight, I have finished the race, I have kept the faith (4:7, New King James Version). *Paul's reflection on his life as he sits in prison, expecting to be executed soon.*

Behind the Scenes of 2 Timothy

⭐ Starring Roles

Paul, traveling minister who starts churches throughout the Roman Empire, but who is now in jail awaiting execution (1:1)

Timothy, one of Paul's most devoted traveling companions, whom Paul appoints to lead the church in Ephesus (1:2)

📖 Plot

The end is near for Paul, and he knows it. So he writes this, his last and most moving letter. He addresses it to Timothy, a young friend he thinks of as a son. Paul is not writing from the comfort of the house arrest described at the end of Acts. Though he's in Rome—as he was before—he now languishes in a cold dungeon, chained like a dangerous criminal.

Paul is lonely, having been abandoned by colleagues who apparently realize the hopelessness of his situation. He asks Timothy to come and be with him before his execution. He also warns his devoted friend that sufferings are bound to come his way, too. Perhaps Paul is writing in the mid-60s, when Emperor Nero is having Christians killed throughout the empire—many in arenas, as blood-spectacle entertainment. But Paul urges Timothy to be brave and to cling to the hope of spending eternity with Jesus.

🎥 What to Look For

The intimate tone of the letter. Notice how personal the letter is—at times even private. Though Paul intends for the entire church of Ephesus to read it, and he refers briefly to false teachings, end times, and the traits of godly people, the aging apostle—perhaps now in his late 50s—is talking especially to Timothy. "You are like a dear child to me," Paul writes (1:2).

The approaching death of Paul. This letter may be the last surviving words of Paul, for he is convinced he is about to die. Paul has already endured at least part of a trial—perhaps all of it (4:16). And he's not expecting to be released.

"I am locked up in jail and treated like a criminal," Paul writes (2:9). He is further restricted, and humiliated, by having to wear a chain (1:16, New King James Version).

But in a poignant and inspired moment, Paul expresses his incredible faith: "Now the time has come for me to die. My life is like a drink offering being

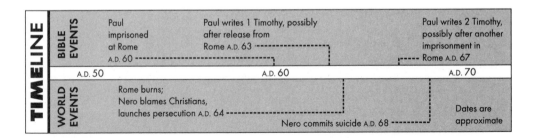

		Paul imprisoned at Rome A.D. 60	Paul writes 1 Timothy, possibly after release from Rome A.D. 63	Paul writes 2 Timothy, possibly after another imprisonment in Rome A.D. 67
TIMELINE	**BIBLE EVENTS**			
		A.D. 50	A.D. 60	A.D. 70
	WORLD EVENTS	Rome burns; Nero blames Christians, launches persecution A.D. 64	Nero commits suicide A.D. 68	Dates are approximate

poured out on the altar. I have fought well. I have finished the race, and I have been faithful. So a crown will be given to me for pleasing the Lord" (4:6–8).

Paul's request for Timothy to come. Like the last request of a dying man, Paul asks for his dearest friend to make a 1,000-mile journey across land and sea.

"I want to see you," Paul writes (1:4). "Come to see me as soon as you can" (4:9). Most of Paul's other associates have deserted him, and he is obviously lonely. He is also cold, and apparently hungry for God's Word, for he kindly asks Timothy to "bring the coat I left at Troas. . . . Don't forget to bring the scrolls, especially the ones made of leather" (4:13).

> **Did You Know?**
> • One of the oldest structures in Rome is Mamertine Prison, a dungeon carved out of solid rock 600 years before Christ. Early Christian writers say Paul was kept there before his execution.

A call to courage. Timothy is going to face persecution, Paul says he is certain of that. "But you must stay calm and be willing to suffer. You must work hard to tell the good news" (4:5). This certainly would have frightened Timothy. But Paul adds a comforting note of assurance: "Timothy, my child, Christ Jesus is kind, and you must let him make you strong" (2:1). Everyone who remains faithful to Jesus, Paul says, will rule for an eternity with the Lord (2:11).

Author and Date

The letter is from Paul, in a jail at Rome (1:1, 16–17). He is writing to his young friend, Timothy, whom he appointed to lead the church in Ephesus. Some scholars say that this letter, like 1 Timothy and Titus, was written a generation after Paul, perhaps to address Christian persecution going on at that time. (See "Who wrote Timothy and Titus?" in the Reviews section of 1 Timothy, page 395.) Others argue that the deeply personal nature of this letter confirms what early church leaders believed—that Paul wrote it.

It's unclear exactly when Paul wrote the letter. One popular theory is that Paul was released from the Roman imprisonment described at the end of Acts. But after continuing his missionary work he was again arrested, taken to Rome, tried during Nero's crackdown on Christians, and executed in about A.D. 67.

On Location

Paul writes from a jail in Rome. (See map in Acts, page 323.) He addresses the letter to Timothy, pastor of the church in Ephesus, a major Roman city about 1,000 miles east, along the Mediterranean coast of Turkey. ❏

Big Scene from 2 Timothy

As death approaches, the elderly and imprisoned Paul sits alone with his memories.

"Timothy," he writes, "you are like a dear child to me" (1:2). Paul says he remembers a time when Timothy cried, and Paul remembers laying hands on this young friend, blessing him for ministry. "I want to see you," Paul pleads, "because that will make me truly happy" (1:4).

A wave of anti-Christian sentiment and persecution is apparently sweeping across the empire, forcing the more timid believers to keep their faith a secret. But Paul pushes Timothy toward courage and boldness: "Don't be ashamed to speak for our Lord. And don't be ashamed of me, just because I am in jail for serving him" (1:8).

"Anyone who belongs to Christ Jesus and wants to live right will have trouble from others," Paul explains (3:12). But how people respond to this suffering, Paul says, will determine our destiny: "If we deny that we know him [Jesus], he will deny that he knows us." On the other hand, "If we don't give up, we will rule with him" (2:11–12).

"Come to me as soon as you can," Paul asks.

Then, drawing the letter to a close, Paul expresses confidence in the Lord even in the face of death. "When I was first put on trial, no one helped me. . . . But the Lord stood beside me. He gave me the strength to tell his full message, so that all Gentiles would hear it. . . . He will bring me safely into his heavenly kingdom. Praise him forever and ever! Amen" (4:16–18).

**Paul writes his last known letter
(3:10—4:18)** •

Reviews

Roman persecution was real. The violent persecution that Paul describes in this letter matches what Roman historians said about how the government treated Christians.

Paul speaks of once being spared from "hungry lions" (4:17) and of "fighting wild animals in Ephesus" (1 Corinthians 15:32). In both cases, Paul may have been speaking figuratively. But for many Christians during Nero's wave of terror in the mid-60s, there was nothing metaphorical about the wild beasts and executioners they faced in Roman arenas.

Historian Tacitus, writing about the fire that consumed two-thirds of Rome in A.D. 64, expressed his sentiments toward the "detestable superstition" of Christians—whom Nero blamed for starting the fire. Yet even Tacitus felt that Nero's tortures were excessive. The historian reports that some Christians were covered with fresh animal skins, then torn apart by starving dogs. Other believers were nailed to crosses, or were burned alive.

Even Nero's suicide in A.D. 68 didn't end the persecution. In the decades that followed, the oppression came and went, like a tide rolling in and out. Pliny the Younger, Roman governor of a territory near Timothy's church in Ephesus, revealed as much in a report he sent to Emperor Trajan in A.D. 112. Pliny said he had tried many people accused of being Christian: "I asked them whether they were Christians, and if they confessed, I ordered them executed."

The last days, 2,000 years ago. Paul wrote about "the last days" as though they were just around the corner. He said that in those final days of human history, before Jesus returns, "people will love only themselves and money. They will be proud, stuck-up, rude, and disobedient to their parents. They will also be ungrateful, godless, heartless, and hateful" (3:1-3).

The list goes on.

Then Paul told Timothy, "Don't have anything to do with such people" (3:5), as though Timothy would witness the last days.

Was Paul wrong?

If Paul expected Jesus to return within a few years, then he was wrong about that. But throughout the Old and New Testaments, "the last days" was a phrase that meant more than the months or years just before the Second Coming. It also meant "the age of the Messiah." The birth of Jesus became not only the event around which the human race built its calendar; that birthday also marked the beginning of the end of God's plan to save the world from sin.

When will God finish what he started?

"Only the Father knows," Jesus said (Matthew 24:36). ❏

Encore

• Paul gives more advice to ministers in the letters of 1 Timothy and Titus. ❏

TITUS

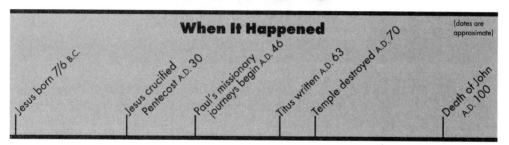

When It Happened

(dates are approximate)

Jesus born 7/6 B.C.

Jesus crucified Pentecost A.D. 30

Paul's missionary journeys begin A.D. 46

Titus written A.D. 63

Temple destroyed A.D. 70

Death of John A.D. 100

Ministering to Liars and Lazy Gluttons

Some pastors *feel* like they're ministering to a congregation of two-faced folk. In the case of Titus's church, however, this was widely assumed to be true.

Paul quotes one of Crete's own highly respected writers and teachers as saying, "The people of Crete always tell lies. They are greedy and lazy like wild animals" (1:12). Ancient Greek writings confirm this snake's-eye view of Cretans, for in Greek "cretanize" is a verb that means "to lie."

Paul assigns Titus to organize churches among these people, ironically giving him an order that must have sounded like an oxymoron: appoint as church leaders Cretans who "have a good reputation" (1:6).

The apostle and his associate know the reputation of the Cretans, and that it's deserved (see "Paul slanders the Cretans" in Reviews). But the ministers also apparently remember what Jesus said when religious folks scolded him for hobnobbing with liars, crooks, other shady characters: "The Son of Man came to look for and to save people who are lost" (Luke 19:10).

Paul reminds Titus that Jesus can make a difference for people everywhere, even on Crete, because Jesus made a difference in them: "We used to be stupid, disobedient, and foolish. . . . Everyone hated us, and we hated everyone. . . . Jesus treated us much better than we deserved. He made us acceptable to God and gave us the hope of eternal life" (3:3, 7). ❑

Famous Line

- Cretans are always liars, evil beasts, lazy gluttons (1:12, New King James Version). *The words of a Cretan writer and prophet, whom Paul quotes apparently to warn Titus that ministry in Crete will be a challenge.*

Behind the Scenes of Titus

⭐ Starring Roles

Paul, traveling minister who covers some 10,000 miles and starts churches throughout the Roman Empire (1:1)

Titus, one of Paul's non-Jewish traveling companions, whom Paul appoints to organize the churches on the island of Crete (1:4)

📖 Plot

During one of his missionary trips, Paul visits the island of Crete, south of Greece. Paul feels the need to continue his journey, but he leaves behind one of his traveling associates, Titus, "to do what has been left undone and to appoint leaders for the churches in each town" (1:5).

Sometime later, Paul writes this short letter to Titus. Paul may have written about the same time he wrote 1 Timothy, after assigning Timothy to the church in Ephesus. Both letters cover much the same material. Paul instructs Titus in the qualities that he should look for when selecting church leaders. Paul also tells Titus how to advise different groups of people in the church. Older women, for example, "must not gossip about others or be slaves of wine" (2:3).

Paul closes the three-chapter letter by urging Titus to insist that the people get along with each other and get away from false teachers.

🎥 What to Look For

Advice for a minister. This letter is a seasoned minister's advice to a younger minister. Bible experts call the three letters of 1 and 2 Timothy and Titus the Pastoral Letters, because they contain Paul's counsel to these two men who were once his traveling associates but who are now pastoring churches.

Qualifications for church leaders. Part of Titus's assignment in Crete is to choose leaders for each church on the island. Because Paul knows that a bad leader could kill a congregation, he gives Titus a list of qualifications. Church leaders "must have a good reputation and be faithful in marriage. Their children must be followers of the Lord and not have a reputation for being wild and disobedient" (1:16). In addition, Paul says, church officials "must not be bossy, quick-tempered, heavy drinkers, bullies, or dishonest in business. Instead, they must be friendly to strangers and enjoy doing good things. They must also be sensible, fair, pure, and self-controlled" (1:7–8).

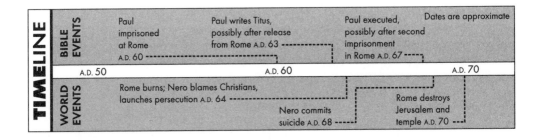

TIMELINE

		BIBLE EVENTS				
	Paul imprisoned at Rome A.D. 60		Paul writes Titus, possibly after release from Rome A.D. 63		Paul executed, possibly after second imprisonment in Rome A.D. 67	Dates are approximate

| A.D. 50 | A.D. 60 | A.D. 70 |

WORLD EVENTS

Rome burns; Nero blames Christians, launches persecution A.D. 64

Nero commits suicide A.D. 68

Rome destroys Jerusalem and temple A.D. 70

False teachings. Titus faced some of the same kinds of religious competition as Timothy does in Ephesus. "Don't have anything to do with stupid arguments about ancestors," Paul says. "And stay away from disagreements and quarrels about the Law of Moses. Such arguments are useless and senseless" (3:9; this advice is similar to 1 Timothy 1:4, 7). Paul is apparently talking about Jewish Christians, many of whom take great pride in their family tree and

believe that all Christians—even non-Jews—should obey the Jewish laws that God gave to Moses. Paul teaches that the age of the Law came to an end when Jesus was sacrificed for the sins of humanity (Colossians 2:14).

Author and Date

The letter is written "From Paul" (1:1) to Titus, who is directing the work of several churches in Crete. Some scholars, however, suggest that one of Paul's associates wrote the letter after Paul died, drawing from the apostle's letters and sermons, then applying the messages to problems that developed later in Crete. (For arguments about who wrote the letter, turn to "Who wrote Timothy and Titus?" in the Reviews section of 1 Timothy, page 395.)

It's uncertain when the letter was written. There's no mention of Paul visiting Crete, either in the stories of Acts or in any of his letters outside this one. For this reason some suggest Paul wrote the letter after the events described in Acts. If so, Paul was released from imprisonment in Rome in about A.D. 62, then made a fourth missionary trip. During that trip Paul likely assigned Titus to Crete, then was later arrested and sent to Rome again. This time Paul was executed in about A.D. 67, during Nero's persecution of Christians.

On Location

Paul addresses his letter to Titus, who is organizing churches on the island of Crete, some 100 miles south of Greece. (See map in Galatians, page 358.) The island is about 150 miles east to west, and 35 miles north to south—in square miles it's about the size of Rhode Island. This is a short-term assignment for Titus. Paul says he will send a replacement soon, and that he wants Titus to join him in Nicopolis, a city on the western coast of Greece. ❏

Big Scene from Titus

After Paul arrives on the island of Crete and starts churches in several cities, he decides to move on. But he assigns Titus, one of his associates, to stay behind long enough to appoint church leaders and to clear up confusion about some false teachings that quickly begin to threaten the churches.

Paul keeps in contact with Titus by letter, advising him how to choose good leaders and how to fight teachings that undermine Christianity.

Church leaders, Paul said, should have a solid reputation and a friendly disposition. And these leaders should be in full agreement with the core teachings of Paul, which emphasize that salvation comes through faith in Jesus—not through obeying Jewish laws.

Paul suggests a two-prong attack against false teachings.

First, he urges Titus to fight false teachings with true teachings: "Titus, you must teach only what is correct" (2:1). Paul then explains how Titus can measure his effectiveness: faith in Jesus should begin expressing itself in the lives of the people. Elderly men will become more patient, elderly women will give up gossiping, young women will become more kind, and young men will learn self-control.

Second, Paul tells Titus to stay away from false teachers who stir up trouble in the church. "Warn troublemakers once or twice. Then don't have anything else to do with them. You know that their minds are twisted, and their own sins show how guilty they are" (3:10–11).

Paul concludes with the same prayer that ends many of his letters: "I pray that the Lord will be kind to all of you!"

**Titus teaches a congregation in Crete
(2:1—3:11)** ••

Reviews

Paul's teaching: Obey rulers. The writer's choice of words and teachings suggest to some scholars that Paul didn't write this letter. And the implied well-developed organizational structure of the church suggests that the writing took place decades after Paul, when the church began growing more institutionalized. Yet some of the core material in Titus repeats what Paul said in other letters.

For example, Paul told Titus, "Remind your people to obey the rulers and authorities and not to be rebellious" (3:1). Paul said the same thing to Christians in Rome, in a letter that most scholars agree is genuinely his (Romans 13:1-2).

Paul slanders the Cretans. "Stupid, vulgar, or insensitive person." These are modern definitions of a *cretin*. Paul offered his own similar definition of Cretans by quoting a limerick from the sixth century B.C. Cretan poet and prophet Epimenides: "The people of Crete always tell lies. They are greedy and lazy like wild animals" (1:12). To this poetic verse, Paul adds a nod: "That surely is a true saying" (1:13).

Why would Paul slander the very people he says he's trying to help?

Perhaps Paul said what he did because the islanders had earned their bad reputation, and Paul didn't want Titus to think that ministry problems in Crete were the fault of the minister.

A thousand years earlier, Crete had been famous for its skilled architects and engineers; Greeks traveled there to study the architecture. But later, business moved elsewhere and Crete became infamous for harboring pirates and mercenaries. ❏

Encore

• For more of Paul's advice to a minister, read 1 and 2 Timothy. The letter to Titus is so much like 1 Timothy that both may have been written about the same time. ❏

PHILEMON

When It Happened

(dates are approximate)

Jesus born 7/6 B.C.

Jesus crucified Pentecost A.D. 30

Paul's missionary journeys begin A.D. 46

Philemon written A.D. 60

Temple destroyed A.D. 70

Death of John A.D. 100

A Runaway Slave Turns Himself In

Paul has a gift for being politically incorrect on social issues.

Take slavery, the subject of his letter to a Christian slave owner named Philemon. Paul is as out of sync with our day as he is with his own.

We want him to take a stand against slavery. We want to hear him tell Philemon to free the runaway slave Onesimus—and any other slaves he has.

On the other hand, the people of Paul's day would have been shocked at how freely he associates with slaves. And they would have taken him to task for insisting that everyone deserves equal treatment, slave or free. After all, they would argue, how could any slave owner treat a slave like he's free? Would a man work your fields all day, every day, for nothing but room and board? And could you snatch a citizen out of his home and sell him for a profit?

The answer seems obvious. You can't treat slaves like they're free until you free them—which is exactly what Paul wants Christians to discover, and what he wants Philemon to do to Onesimus.

Two thousand years later humanity has made progress. Most of our cultures have gotten rid of slavery. Yet that's just a mile marker along the road that Paul mapped out for us. He's pointing us farther up the hill, to equality. ❏

Famous Line

- [Welcome him] no longer as a slave but more than a slave, a beloved brother (16, New Revised Standard Version). *Paul's advice to a slave owner on how to treat the runaway slave who has come back.*

Behind the Scenes of Philemon

⭐ Starring Roles

Paul, traveling minister who starts churches throughout the Roman Empire, and who advises even churches he has not started—such as the one in Colossae (1:1)

Philemon, a Christian slave owner, master of Onesimus, and one in whose home the Colossians meet for church services (1:1)

Onesimus, runaway slave converted by Paul and sent back to his master (1:10)

📖 Plot

Onesimus, a runaway slave, meets Paul and converts to Christianity. Paul, consistent with his teaching in several letters, convinces Onesimus to return to his slave owner, Philemon.

Paul wields influence over Philemon, a church leader, and he uses it on behalf of Onesimus. From jail in an unnamed city—perhaps Rome—Paul writes a short but gripping letter for Onesimus to take to Philemon. In this letter Paul asks Philemon to receive the slave in kindness. Paul also hints—from the letter's beginning to its end—that Philemon should free Onesimus so he can help Paul.

🎥 What to Look For

A masterpiece of tactful persuasion. Paul doesn't come right out and ask Philemon to free Onesimus. But Philemon would likely have realized that this is what Paul wanted. The pressure Paul applies, though subtle, is certainly not gentle. It's powerful and compelling. Consider these seven pressure points:

1. Paul compliments Philemon on his growing faith in Jesus and his "love for all of God's people" (5)—slaves included.

2. "I would like to keep him [Onesimus] here with me, where he could take your place in helping me," Paul writes. "But I won't do anything unless you agree to it first. I want your act of kindness to come from your heart, and not be something you feel forced to do" (13–14). The implication is that Paul, as an apostle, has the authority to order Philemon, a church leader, to free Onesimus and return him to Paul's side.

3. "Onesimus is much more than a slave. To me he is a dear friend," Paul adds. "Welcome Onesimus as you would welcome me" (16–17). Certainly Philemon would not punish a visiting Paul as he would a runaway slave.

TIMELINE	BIBLE EVENTS		Paul converts		Paul's missionary journeys begin	Paul writes Philemon, during Rome imprisonment	Dates are approximate
			⌐------------ A.D. 35	⌐------------ A.D. 46		⌐-------- A.D. 60	
		A.D. 30	A.D. 40	A.D. 50	A.D. 60	A.D. 70	A.D. 80
	WORLD EVENTS		100-year anniversary of Spartacus's doomed slave revolt A.D. 28		Buddhism of India introduced to China A.D. 58 ----	6,000 captured Jewish rebels become Nero's slave labor force A.D. 67	

4. Paul says he will pay back anything Onesimus may have taken to finance his escape. "Charge it to my account," Paul says, adding, "But don't forget that you owe me your life" (18–19). Paul apparently converted Philemon. The implication is that Philemon owes Paul, and in gratitude should write off any debt.

5. This is not a private letter. It's to Philemon and "the church that meets in your home" (2). Others will read it and realize what Paul is asking Philemon to do—peer pressure at its finest.

6. When Paul gets out of jail, he plans to visit Philemon (22). This will be one awkward meeting if Onesimus is not free by then.

7. Paul is not alone in asking for kindness on behalf of the slave. Paul sends greetings from four associates, including Mark and Luke, implying that they support his request.

A lighthearted play on words. To lighten up the deadly serious topic of runaway slaves, Paul makes a play on words. The slave's name, Onesimus, means "useful." Paul acknowledges that Onesimus caused trouble for Philemon, the slave owner. But Paul argues that things are different now: "He was useless to you, but now he is useful both to you and to me" (11).

Author and Date

"From Paul, who is in jail for serving Christ Jesus. . . . to you [Philemon] and to the church that meets in your home" (1–2). Philemon lived in Colossae, in western Turkey.

It's uncertain when and where Paul wrote, though some ancient manuscripts add a postscript saying he wrote from Rome during his two-year imprisonment, which started in about A.D. 60. Some scholars doubt this. They argue that Rome, 1,000 miles from Colossae, is a long way off for a runaway slave with limited resources. They suggest Paul wrote from a closer jail, perhaps in nearby Ephesus.

On Location

Philemon and Onesimus live in Colossae, about a week-long trip east of Ephesus, Turkey (Colossians 4:9). (See map in Acts, page 323.) ❏

Big Scene from Philemon

Onesimus, a slave living in western Turkey, gets a chance to run away—and he takes it. During his flight to freedom, however, who does he run into but Paul, the apostle who teaches, "Slaves, you must obey your earthly masters" (Ephesians 6:5). Paul converts Onesimus to Christianity, then convinces him to return to his master, Philemon, a church leader in Colossae.

Fortunately for Onesimus, Paul also teaches that slave owners should reciprocate, treating slaves with respect, and keeping in mind that slaves "have the same Master in heaven that you do,

and he doesn't have any favorites" (Ephesians 6:9).

Paul, writing from prison somewhere, sends Onesimus home with a letter to Philemon. "Sending Onesimus back to you makes me very sad," Paul writes. "I would like to keep him here with me" (12–13). That's a strong hint for Philemon to free Onesimus.

The apostle promises to pay back anything Onesimus may have taken before leaving. Then Paul asks Philemon to welcome Onesimus not as a slave, but "as you would welcome me" (17).

Without actually using the words, Paul pleads for Philemon to send Onesimus back to him as a free man.

A runaway slave returns to his master
(1 – 25) ••

Reviews

Bishop Onesimus. About fifty years after Paul, a church leader named Ignatius wrote a letter to Bishop Onesimus, leader of the church in Ephesus.

It's uncertain if this bishop is the same slave who once lived in nearby Colossae. But it is possible. If Paul wrote the letters of Ephesians, Colossians, and Philemon all during his imprisonment in Rome—as many believe—the Ephesian people may have met Onesimus while he was on his way back to his master. This is quite possible because Onesimus traveled with Tychicus, who delivered the letters of Ephesians and Colossians (Ephesians 6:21; Colossians 4:7-9).

Many scholars who doubt that Paul wrote Philemon from Rome suspect he wrote from jail in Ephesus. If so, the Ephesians would have become acquainted with Onesimus during his conversion and perhaps after his return to Paul, if Philemon took the hints and freed him.

Paul's stand on slavery. Though Paul never outright said slavery is acceptable, he never condemned it, either. And when a runaway slave showed up, Paul converted him to Christianity and then returned him to his slave owner. Runaway slaves who returned were not usually welcomed with a hug. They were punished, sometimes executed, as an example to others.

The apostle's decision to send Onesimus back not only put the slave at risk, it seemed to condone slavery, and it certainly set back any movement that would have outlawed this flesh-peddling institution. It took nearly 1,000 years for the church to discover that there's nothing Christian about slavery. In the meantime, slaves served church members, ministers, and congregations.

Paul wasn't interested in starting a slave-liberating revolution, at least not from the outside, in. What he called for, however, would eventually accomplish this by working from the inside, out.

As he told the Ephesians, "Slaves, you must obey your earthly masters. Show them great respect and be as loyal to them as you are to Christ. Try to please them at all times, and not just when you think they are watching" (Ephesians 6:5-6). And for slave owners Paul offered these instructions: "Treat your slaves with this same respect. Don't threaten them. They have the same Master in heaven that you do, and he doesn't have any favorites" (Ephesians 6:9).

Instead of changing the system that would influence people, Paul changed people who would influence the system. ❏

Encore

- For more on Paul's view of slavery, read 1 Corinthians 12:12-31; Galatians 3:23–4:7; Ephesians 6:5-9; Colossians 3:11–4:1; Titus 2:9-10. ❏

HEBREWS

When It Happened

(dates are approximate)

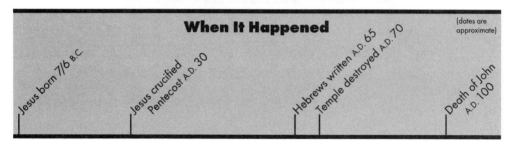

Jesus born 7/6 B.C.

Jesus crucified
Pentecost A.D. 30

Hebrews written A.D. 65
Temple destroyed A.D. 70

Death of John
A.D. 100

Advice for Christians About to Give Up

Hebrews is a book for potential Christian dropouts.

In a first-pass read, it looks like the unidentified writer has targeted only Jewish Christians on the verge of returning to their spiritual roots: Judaism. The writer certainly has targeted these people, because in this, the longest sustained argument in the Bible, he presents a staggering array of evidence to convince them that Jesus Christ—and faith in him—fulfills God's promises to Israel. He says that the old covenant, or agreement between God and Israel, has given way to the new agreement that Jeremiah predicted. God's law written on scrolls has been replaced by God's law written on the human heart. And animal sacrifices for sin have become obsolete because of the sacrificial death of God's Son.

This is a book for Jewish Christians, all right. But it's also a book for any other Christians facing obstacles to their faith: temptations, frustrations, disenchantment. The second thoughts that first-century Jewish Christians experienced were likely generated by Romans and orthodox Jews who were persecuting them.

Whatever the obstacle, the writer to Hebrews encourages Christians to keep their eyes on the finish line. "We must get rid of everything that slows us down," he says. "We must be determined to run the race that is ahead of us. We must keep our eyes on Jesus, . . . seated at the right side of God's throne!" (12:1–2). ❏

Famous Lines

• Jesus Christ is the same yesterday and today and forever (13:8, New Revised Standard Version).

• Faith is being sure of what we hope for and certain of what we do not see (11:1, New International Version).

Behind the Scenes of Hebrews

⭐ Starring Role

Jesus, God's Son, who establishes a new agreement between God and humanity—a covenant better than the one instituted by Moses and practiced in the temple (2:9)

📖 Plot

About a generation after Jesus' resurrection, some Jewish Christians are beginning to abandon the early Christian movement and return to the Jewish faith, perhaps because of persecution. To win back their loyalty, an unidentified church leader writes the book of Hebrews, an essay arguing that faith in Christ is better than Judaism.

The writer makes three main points: (1) Jesus is superior to Old Testament heroes, including the prophets, Moses, and even the angels. (2) Jesus is superior to the high priest, who serves as an intermediary between God and humanity. (3) Jesus is a better sacrifice than any animal offered on an altar.

Further, the writer adds, Jesus has rendered obsolete the old agreement, which was based on rules preserved on the pages of the first five books in the Bible. In its place is a new agreement, based on laws God has written onto the human heart. For Jewish Christians, the writer explains, there is no turning back—for there is nothing to turn back to.

🎥 What to Look For

Old Testament quotes. To convince Jewish Christians that the Christian faith is both God's idea and an outgrowth of Judaism, the writer quotes about forty passages of the Old Testament to support his arguments.

For example, he says animal sacrifice isn't what pleased God. Animal sacrifice was simply a means to an end—a way to remind people that sin is wrong. To prove his point, he quotes Psalm 40:6, "Sacrifices and offerings are not what please you." That passage goes on to reveal that what God really wants is for people to trust and obey him.

Jesus, the better way. Notice that the writer compares Jesus to many people and practices revered in Judaism. Notice, too, that Jesus always comes out the winner.

TIMELINE

BIBLE EVENTS				
		Unidentified author writes Hebrews		Dates are approximate
		.... A.D. 65		
A.D. 60	A.D. 70	A.D. 80		A.D. 90

WORLD EVENTS				
		Jews in Israel revolt A.D. 66	Rome destroys Jerusalem and temple A.D. 70	Roman bishop, Clement, quotes Hebrews A.D. 95 ---------
	Rome burns; Christians blamed, persecuted A.D. 64			

Better than angels, prophets, Moses. Angels worship him (1:6). Prophets are only spokespersons for God; Jesus is God's Son (1:1–2). Moses told God's people what the future would be like; Jesus is in charge of the future (3:5–6).

Better than a high priest. High priests intercede for the people in a temple; Jesus intercedes in heaven (7:23—8:1). High priests have sinned; Jesus has not (4:15).

Better than animal sacrifices. An animal is usually sacrificed for one sin, one person; Jesus was sacrificed for all the sins of all people (9:26).

Author and Date

The writer doesn't identify himself. In the mid-second century, some Christian leaders attributed the book to Paul. But it is unlikely that Paul wrote it. He identified himself in his other letters, and he wrote in a simpler style. Hebrews was likely written by someone who, unlike Paul, had never seen Jesus but who had heard about the Lord from eyewitnesses (2:3).

Two strong candidates for authorship are Barnabas and Apollos, associates of Paul. As early as A.D. 200, a theologian named Tertullian quoted from Hebrews, which he identified as "an epistle to the Hebrews under the name of Barnabas." Barnabas was co-pastor with Paul at a church in Antioch, Syria. Later, Barnabas served as a missionary who preached throughout the Eastern Mediterranean. Apollos was "a learned man, with a thorough knowledge of the Scriptures" (Acts 18:24, New International Version). It would take a well-educated Jew to write Hebrews, which is among the most sophisticated writing in the New Testament and which is so intimately connected to the Jewish Scripture.

The date of the writing is also uncertain. It was likely written sometime in the A.D. 60s, as the second generation of Christians began to emerge as church leaders. The book's many references to the Jewish temple and sacrificial system suggest the writer completed it before A.D. 70—when Rome destroyed the temple, bringing the sacrificial era to an abrupt halt. Clement, a church leader in Rome, quoted several sections of the book in a letter he wrote in A.D. 95.

On Location

The message seems addressed to Christians all over the Roman Empire, but especially to those of Jewish heritage. The writer sends greetings from believers in Italy, suggesting he lived there, perhaps in Rome (13:24). This possibility is strengthened by the fact that in A.D. 95, Clement, bishop of Rome, quoted from the book. (See map in Acts, page 323.) ❑

Did You Know?

• "Some people have welcomed angels as guests, without even knowing it" (13:2). Examples from the Bible include Abraham (Genesis 18), Gideon (Judges 6), and Manoah (Judges 13).

• The sacrifice of Jesus ended the need for people to offer sacrifices to God. Forty years later, Rome forcibly terminated the Jewish sacrificial system by destroying the temple, which has never been rebuilt. A 1,300-year-old mosque now sits on the Jerusalem hilltop where Jews once worshiped.

Big Scenes from Hebrews

To Jewish Christians on the verge of quitting Christianity and returning to Judaism, the writer of Hebrews reminds them of what they will be leaving.

Jesus, the writer explains, is superior to prophets, Moses, and even angels. "After the Son had washed away our sins, he sat down at the right side of the glorious God in heaven. . . . God never said to any of the angels, 'Sit at my right side'" (1:3, 13).

Hebrews also presents Jesus as superior to any high priest who ever interceded to God for the people. Jesus doesn't need to address God through rituals at a temple; Jesus has direct access to God in heaven.

**Jesus at the right side of the Father
(1:1 – 14)** •••

Jews who want forgiveness offer an animal sacrifice. This is not to placate an angry God, but to give the people a means of forgiveness and a graphic reminder of the seriousness of sin. When Jews lay their hands on the head of an innocent sheep—symbolizing the atonement that the animal will make for their sin—and when the people see the blood drain out of the animal, the life-and-death seriousness of sin becomes dramatically real.

"Life is in the blood," God told Moses, "and I have given you the blood of animals to sacrifice in place of your own" (Leviticus 17:11).

But as promised through the prophets, God establishes a new means of forgiveness. Jesus died as the final sacrifice, replacing the sacrificial system. "By this one sacrifice," Hebrews explains, "he [Jesus] has forever set free from sin the people he brings to God" (10:14).

**The sacrifice for sins
(10:1 – 18)**

•••

Faith makes us sure of what we hope for and gives us proof of what we cannot see," Hebrews says. "It was their faith that made our ancestors pleasing to God" (1:1–2).

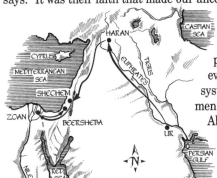

Drawing from a huge cast of Old Testament heroes, the writer proves his point that God is pleased by the trust that people have in him. Faith is more important to God than the Jewish rituals ever were—even before they became obsolete. Before Israel had a system of laws and religious rituals, the faith of godly men and women gave God immense pleasure—people like Abel, Noah, Abraham, Sarah, Isaac, Jacob, and Moses.

The writer urges his readers to hold firmly to their faith in God's Son: "The people God accepts will live because of their faith" (10:38).

**Abraham comes to Canaan, proving his faith
(11:1 – 40)** •••

Reviews

The promised new covenant. Jews were understandably reluctant to abandon the laws and rituals prescribed in their holy scriptures—rules that God himself had given through Moses, their most revered prophet. The Law, as the rules are called, represented Israel's part of an agreement God made with them. If the Jews obeyed these laws, then God would protect and bless their nation.

That's a big "if." Throughout Israel's long history, the people repeatedly broke the Law—sometimes abandoning it entirely, when godless kings reigned.

"The time will surely come when I will make a new agreement with the people of Israel and Judah," God said through the prophet Jeremiah. "It will be different from the agreement I made with their ancestors when I led them out of Egypt. Although I was their God, they broke that agreement. Here is the new agreement that I, the LORD, will make with the people of Israel: 'I will write my laws on their hearts and minds. I will be their God, and they will be my people'" (Jeremiah 31:31-33).

The writer of Hebrews explains that "when the Lord talks about a new agreement, he means that the first one is out of date. And anything that is old and useless will soon disappear" (8:13). As Moses delivered the first agreement to Israel, Jesus delivered the new one: "Christ died to rescue those who had sinned and broken the old agreement. Now he brings his chosen ones a new agreement with its guarantee of God's eternal blessings!" (9:15).

No second chance? To Jewish Christians thinking about returning to Judaism, the writer of Hebrews offers an ominous warning. He says that if Christians turn their back on Jesus, "there is no way to bring them back." To do so, he explains, "is the same as nailing the Son of God to a cross and insulting him in public!" (6:6).

This is a passage that has mystified Bible scholars.

To the casual reader, the words can sound like a minister's last, desperate, exaggerated attempt to keep a group of members from leaving the church: "Walk through that door and you've forever walked out of God's kingdom!"

Some scholars take the passage literally, insisting that Christians who recant faith in Jesus are hopelessly lost. Other scholars suggest that backsliders are people who have merely sampled Christianity but have never experienced a genuine faith in Jesus.

Still others argue that the believer's faith is authentic, yet so is that person's right to accept or reject Jesus—even after conversion. Fallen believers such as this remove themselves from the foot of the cross, and relocate themselves among the jeering crowd of sinners that crucified Jesus. And because God refuses to drag people into his kingdom against their will, there is nothing he can do to save them. If they want back inside, these scholars contend, repentant backsliders have only to follow this advice of Jesus: "Ask, and you will receive. Search, and you will find. Knock, and the door will be opened for you" (Matthew 7:7). ❏

Encore

- The writer of Hebrews compares Jesus to the priesthood and sacrificial system of the Old Testament. To review some of the source material with which the writer worked, turn to Leviticus, especially chapters 1–9. ❏

JAMES

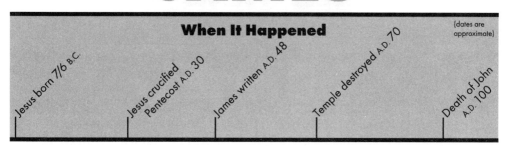

When It Happened
(dates are approximate)

Jesus born 7/6 B.C.

Jesus crucified
Pentecost A.D. 30

James written A.D. 48

Temple destroyed A.D. 70

Death of John
A.D. 100

Real Christians Do More than Talk

James has little patience with do-nothing Christians. When confronting them, sometimes he's diplomatic, and often he's not.

"Does some stupid person want proof that faith without deeds is useless? Well, our ancestor Abraham pleased God by putting his son Isaac on the altar to sacrifice him. Now you see how Abraham's faith and deeds worked together. He proved that his faith was real by what he did" (2:20–22).

Clearly James is quite tired of hearing Christians talk the talk. He wants to see some proof that the faith they're talking about is real. So James writes a short letter of instructions for Christian living. In it, he tells believers exactly what he expects of them.

For starters, they'll remain faithful even when others attack their beliefs. And when they see someone in need, they'll lend a hand. And when they have an opportunity to slander someone, they'll keep their mouth shut.

The entire book is a series of examples showing how James expects Christian faith to express itself in wise and compassionate ways.

The language is often vivid and picturesque—sometimes even forceful. But James knows that it can take a lot of energy to propel dead weight into motion. ❏

Famous Lines

- Resist the devil and he will flee from you. Draw near to God and He will draw near to you (4:7-8, New King James Version).

- Be quick to listen and slow to speak or to get angry (1:19).

- Faith without deeds is useless (2:20). *James teaches that true faith isn't kept inside, it's expressed through acts of kindness.*

Behind the Scenes of James

★ Starring Role

James, possibly the brother of Jesus and leader of the church in Jerusalem (1:1)

📖 Plot

The letter of James is not a story with a plot. It doesn't even seem to address a particular problem. Instead, it's a collection of practical lessons about Christian living.

Among the lessons are these: If you are poor, don't worry about it. If you are rich, worry like crazy—and give some money to the poor. Don't give in to temptation. Be slow to get angry. Don't treat rich people better than poor people. Do kind things for others. Watch your mouth. Run away from the devil and into the arms of God. Pray for people who need God's help.

🎥 What to Look For

Practical advice for everyday living. James is brimming with practical advice on how Christians should live. Some scholars call it Wisdom Literature of the New Testament, because it sounds so much like the wise sayings of Proverbs. In fact, much of what James says has been said before in Old Testament writings.

Here are a few excerpts of his advice:

"If you think you are being religious, but can't control your tongue, you are fooling yourself, and everything you do is useless" (1:26).

"You must not give the best seat to the one in fancy clothes and tell the one who is poor to stand at the side or sit on the floor" (2:3).

"Don't say cruel things about others" (4:11).

"You rich people should cry and weep! Terrible things are going to happen to you. . . . You refused to pay the people who worked in your fields, and now their unpaid wages are shouting out against you" (5:1, 4).

Jewish perspective. If you read carefully, you'll notice that the letter sounds like it's written by a Jew, for Jews.

James addresses his letter to the twelve tribes, a common way of referring to Israel. He uses the Greek word for synagogue to describe the meeting place

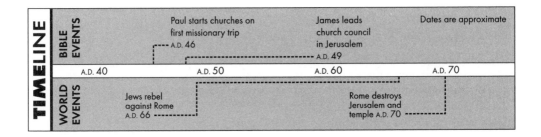

mentioned in 2:2. He uses the Hebrew title for God, *sabaoth*, in "Lord All-Powerful" (5:4). And he often speaks of the Jewish law, always with reverence (2:8–13).

Paul, on the other hand, does not always show such enduring respect for the Jewish law. When writing to his predominately non-Jewish constituency, Paul says, "Once a person has learned to have faith, there is no more need to have the Law as a teacher" (Galatians 3:25). For more on the apparent clash between James and Paul, see "James vs. Paul" in the Reviews section.

Did You Know?

• Martin Luther, father of Protestant religions, said this book doesn't belong in the Bible. He said it emphasizes good works too much and faith too little. Luther lived in a day when most Christians believed they were saved through church rituals, not through faith in Jesus.

Author and Date

The writer identifies himself only as "James, a servant of God and of our Lord Jesus Christ" (1:1). At least four men in the New Testament share this name, including an apostle. But since early Christian times the writer has been identified as the oldest of Jesus' four younger brothers (Mark 6:3). James rose to become leader of the Jerusalem church. He also headed the first church council meeting, which ruled that Gentiles did not have to follow Jewish rules about circumcision and food (Acts 15).

It's uncertain when James wrote the letter. A Jewish historian named Josephus, who lived in the first century, said Jewish leaders stoned James to death before Rome destroyed Jerusalem in A.D. 70. So if the brother of Jesus wrote it, he must have done so before then. Some scholars say that the Jewishness of the letter suggests it was written when most of the church was still Jewish—before Paul began to enjoy sweeping success among the Gentiles. If so, the letter could have been written in the A.D. 40s and might be the oldest literature in the New Testament.

On Location

James writes to "the twelve tribes scattered all over the world" (1:1). This may mean Jews who have become Christians. Or it can mean the entire Christian church, which James may be portraying as the New Israel. (See map in Acts, page 323.) ❑

Big Scenes from James

My friends," James says in an open letter to Christians throughout the Roman Empire, "what good is it to say you have faith, when you don't do anything to show that you really do have faith? If you know someone who doesn't have any clothes or food, you shouldn't just say, 'I hope all goes well for you. I hope you will be warm and have plenty to eat.' What good is it to say this, unless you do something to help? Faith that doesn't lead us to do good deeds is all alone and dead!" (2:14–17).

James anticipates that some Christians will disagree with him. Some, he says, may argue that belief in God is enough. But James replies that even demons believe in God.

"Anyone who doesn't breathe is dead," James declares, "and faith that doesn't do anything is just as dead!" (2:26).

**Christians are people helping people
(2:14–26)** ••

Probably the most memorable piece of advice James gives is that people should watch what they say: "If you can control your tongue, you are mature and able to control your whole body" (3:2).

The tongue is small, James adds, but so is a ship's rudder, and so is the spark that starts a forest fire.

"All kinds of animals, birds, reptiles, and sea creatures can be tamed and have been tamed," James observes. "But our tongues get out of control" (3:7–8).

For people with a tongue that flaps viciously in the heated breath of anger, James says simply, "Be quick to listen and slow to speak. . . . If you are angry, you cannot do any of the good things that God wants done" (1:19–20).

Harnessing the power of the mouth
•• **(3:1–12)**

Reviews

Rich vs. poor. One way to tell that James is an authentically Christian book is to study what he says about the rich and the poor.

The prevailing belief among Jews in Bible times is that the wealthy are rich because God has rewarded them for their goodness. Jesus and his followers, however, side with Old Testament prophets like Amos who say that too often the wealthy get rich by trampling poor people into the ground and then robbing them.

"It's easier for a camel to go through the eye of a needle than for a rich person to get into God's kingdom," Jesus said (Matthew 19:24).

James, like his big brother, has strong words for the rich: "While here on earth, you have thought only of filling your own stomachs and having a good time. But now you are like fat cattle on their way to be butchered. You have condemned and murdered innocent people, who couldn't even fight back" (5:5–6).

James vs. Paul. Paul says we're saved by faith alone, not by anything we do (Ephesians 2:8–9). But James argues that faith without deeds is worthless: "Can that kind of faith save you?" he asks (2:14). That's a rhetorical question; he expects us to answer no.

Critics of the Bible, and even famous Christians like Martin Luther, see a stark clash between James and Paul.

But James doesn't argue that we're saved by doing kind works—that we earn our salvation. Instead, he says that genuine faith in Jesus will naturally express itself in kindness. In a way, James is saying that if sin were a disease, and salvation were the cure, compassion would be a side-effect we'd have to live with.

Paul agrees. "Do as God does," he tells believers of Ephesus. "After all, you are his dear children. Let love be your guide. . . . Don't let it be said that any of you are immoral or indecent or greedy" (Ephesians 5:1, 2, 3).

The two men apparently came at the topic of faith from different perspectives. James seems to have ministered among do-nothing believers. And Paul has seen his share of I-can't-do-enough Gentiles who thought they needed to obey all Jewish laws and customs to earn salvation. Both extremes are wrong.

We're saved by faith. And when we're saved, it shows, because authentic faith works. ❏

Encore

• For more wise sayings, read the Old Testament books of Proverbs and Ecclesiastes. ❏

1 PETER

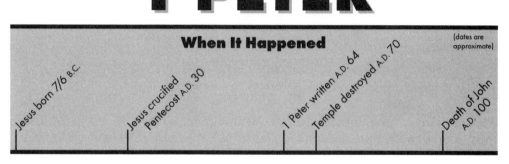

When It Happened
(dates are approximate)

Jesus born 7/6 B.C.

Jesus crucified
Pentecost A.D. 30

1 Peter written A.D. 64

Temple destroyed A.D. 70

Death of John A.D. 100

When We Suffer Because We're Christian

It's unnatural for humans to suffer in silence. Somebody has to tell us to do it—especially when we know we're right, and that we're suffering unfairly.

For Christians scattered throughout western Turkey, suffering simply for being Christians, Peter is that somebody.

Not only do we have to be told to suffer in silence, we need an explanation—a really good explanation. Peter gives several. For example, Christians who show respect to political authorities and who live a godly life have the power to "silence stupid and ignorant people" (2:15). Also, Christian women married to unbelievers have the potential, through kindness, to "win him over by what you do" (3:1).

Peter doesn't go so far as to say that Christians should seek out opportunities to play the martyr—as Christians in later centuries will do. But he does say, "Count it a blessing when you suffer for being a Christian" (4:14). In the anti-Christian climate of the mid-first century, it is inevitable that Christians will face persecution—they don't need to go looking for trouble. It will come. And when it does, Peter asks the believers to think of themselves not as victims, but as teachers with a unique opportunity to show others what Christians are really made of—and to follow in the footsteps of Jesus. ❏

Famous Lines

- Do not repay evil for evil (3:9, New Revised Standard Version).

- Love covers over a multitude of sins (4:8, New International Version). *Apostle Peter says that love helps unite people, because it provides the motivation to forgive over and over.*

- Cast all your anxiety on him because he cares for you (5:7, New International Version). *Peter's advice to Christians being persecuted because of their religion.*

Behind the Scenes of 1 Peter

⭐ Starring Role

Peter, leader among the twelve original disciples of Jesus (1:1)

📖 Plot

Christians in five Roman provinces throughout western Turkey are facing serious persecution because of their belief in Jesus. Romans no longer consider Christianity as a branch of Judaism, which is an approved faith. So Roman authorities begin pressuring Christians into accepting the Roman culture and gods, and not stirring up the Jews with their disturbing message about a messiah. Refusal to comply with Roman expectations can mean threats, confiscation of property, attack, and even execution.

Peter writes to sustain and inspire the believers. He reminds them of Christ's sacrifice, and what that means for eternity: "You were not rescued by such things as silver or gold that don't last forever. You were rescued by the precious blood of Christ" (1:18–19).

The apostle then urges Christians to live the righteous life to which God has called them. He says they should respectfully submit to those in authority, yet be prepared to gently defend the Christian faith.

🎥 What to Look For

Persecution. Notice that the people Peter writes to are clearly facing persecution for their faith. The apostle refers to their condition throughout his short letter. "You are better off to obey God and suffer for doing right," Peter says, "than to suffer for doing wrong" (3:17).

Submission. To Christians faced with severe persecution, and who are perhaps tempted to fight back, Peter urges submission at all levels of society.

He urges submission of constituents to political rulers, of slaves to masters, of wives to husbands, and of young men to elders. To support his case, Peter appeals to the example of Jesus, who submitted to insults, beating, and death, yet without retaliating in any way.

Quotes from the Old Testament. Peter is a man especially interested in taking the news of Jesus to his own people, the Jews. This shows in his use

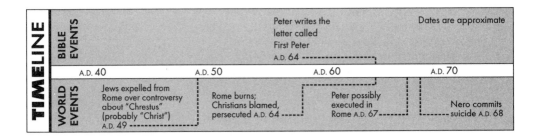

of quotes from Jewish Scripture, known among Christians today as the Old Testament or the First Testament. In urging believers to cling to their trust in the promises of God, for example, Peter quotes poetry from the prophet Isaiah:

> *"Humans wither like grass,*
> *and their glory fades like wild flowers.*
> *Grass dries up, and flowers fall to the ground.*
> *But what the Lord has said will stand forever"* (1:24–25).

Did You Know?

• The Roman Catholic Church considers Peter the first in a long line of church leaders first called bishop of Rome and later called pope. They base this on what Jesus tells Peter: "I will call you Peter, which means 'a rock.' On this rock I will build my church. . . . I will give you the keys to the kingdom of heaven, and God in heaven will allow whatever you allow on earth" (Matthew 16:18–19).

Author and Date

The letter is "from Peter, an apostle of Jesus Christ" (1:1). The writing style is refined Greek, a surprising literary style for a Jewish fisherman. But Peter admits "Silvanus helped me write this short letter" (5:12). Perhaps Peter's words were polished by Silvanus, also known as Silas—a Christian who traveled with Paul throughout the Greek-speaking world (Acts 15:22).

Peter may have written the letter during unofficial, localized outbreaks of persecution in the early 60s. Or perhaps he wrote later, after Nero blamed Christians for torching Rome in A.D. 64.

The A.D. 95 writings of Clement, a church leader in Rome, seem to reflect an awareness of 1 Peter. And Christians writing in the second century, such as Polycarp, quote the book.

On Location

Peter writes to Christians scattered throughout five Roman provinces in western Turkey. (See map in Acts, page 323.) It's uncertain where Peter is writing from. He sends greetings from "Babylon" (5:13). This could refer to cities of that name in Iraq or Egypt. But it might be a code name for Jerusalem or Rome. Jews start calling Rome "Babylon" as early as A.D. 70, when Rome destroys Jerusalem. Perhaps they used the nickname even earlier. The Jews associate these two empires because each one is wealthy and evil, and because each one levels Jerusalem and destroys the temple. ❏

Big Scene from 1 Peter

Christianity begins as a Jewish movement, led by Jews and embraced primarily by Jews. For this reason, Romans treat Christians with the same tolerance as Jews—for Judaism is an approved religion.

But as the decades pass, and violent clashes persist between Jews and Christians, it becomes obvious to everyone that Christianity is more than just another of the many branches or denominations of Judaism. It's a new religion—and a troublesome one at that. Romans shy away from new religions, and they shut down troublesome ones. That's because Romans want stability in their empire. As far as they are concerned, Christianity is just another mysterious cult with secret meetings and possibly disgusting rituals. Communion services, in which bread and wine represent the body and blood of Jesus, produce rumors of cannibalism. And the custom of greeting spiritual "brothers" and "sisters" with a kiss generates gossip about incest.

"Always be ready to give an answer when someone asks you about your hope," Peter advises. "Give a kind and respectful answer and keep your conscience clear. This way you will make people ashamed for saying bad things about your good conduct as a follower of Christ" (3:15–16).

"Dear friends," Peter adds, "don't be surprised or shocked that you are going through testing that is like walking through fire. Be glad for the chance to suffer as Christ suffered. It will prepare you for even greater happiness when he makes his glorious return" (4:12–13).

**Roman soldiers arrest Christians
(4:12–19)** •••

Reviews

Submission limited. Peter spent so much time cautioning people to be submissive—even to tormentors—that he seemed to have no backbone at all.

Nothing could be further from the truth. When he and John were arrested and appeared before the seventy-man Jewish Council, which served as the national legislature and high court, Peter was anything but submissive. The Jewish elders ordered him to stop teaching about Jesus, and Peter replied, "We cannot keep quiet about what we have seen and heard" (Acts 4:20).

When Peter and the other apostles were arrested a second time, they all faced a possible death sentence from this same council that conspired to execute Jesus. Furious, the high priest insisted on knowing why they flagrantly disregarded the high court's order.

"We don't obey people," Peter replied, respectfully but sternly. "We obey God" (Acts 5:29).

There are times to submit to leaders. But following leaders away from God is not one of those times.

Women, the weaker sex. After urging wives to submit to their husbands, Peter commendably called on husbands to show consideration for their wives. Unfortunately he did so in words that are today politically incorrect. Peter said men should be "paying honor to the woman as the weaker sex" (3:7, New Revised Standard Version).

In what way did Peter think women are weaker? He didn't explain.

Perhaps he meant physically and mentally. In his day, men provided much of the brawn and brains for the family. Women worked in the home. And as youngsters, they were denied the education that boys received in the synagogue.

Peter also may have been thinking of the social plight of women. In the courts, they were treated as minors who had no legal voice or civil rights. They were the property of their fathers and then of their husbands. When their husbands died or divorced them, they were left with nothing but the dowry they brought to the wedding, and with any compassion that extended family and friends might show them. ❑

Encore

- Second Peter is a sequel, warning against false teachers in the church.

- Some of the themes in 1 Peter seem drawn from Paul's letters to the Ephesians and the Colossians. For example, compare 1:1 - 3 with Ephesians 1:1 - 3; 3:1 - 7 with Ephesians 5:22 - 31; and 2:18 with Colossians 3:22. ❑

2 PETER

When It Happened

(dates are approximate)

Jesus born 7/6 B.C.

Jesus crucified
Pentecost A.D. 30

2 Peter written A.D. 65
Temple destroyed A.D. 70

Death of John
A.D. 100

Why Hasn't Jesus Come Back Yet?

For thirty years or more, apostles and other church leaders have been assuring first-generation Christians that Jesus is coming back soon. As far as many in Generation-Christ are concerned, he's late. And the apostles are wrong.

Perplexed believers start looking for answers. Smooth-talking spiritual guides arrive on the scene, full of answers. Peter, however, says that what they're full of is nonsense. Like the fraudulent Christians that Jude writes about, these smart-sounding teachers say it's okay for Christians to sin, since Christians have already been forgiven of sin. These teachers practice what they preach. Peter says they're immoral, greedy, and headed for trouble.

The apostle's message for all Christians confronted by questionable teachings is this: don't give up the faith.

Peter reminds us that history is filled with examples of how God deals with sin. And as far as the Second Coming is concerned, Peter says, that's in God's hands. The Day will come, he adds, and Christians should never lose hope of that. Yet "while you are waiting, you should make certain that the Lord finds you pure, spotless, and living at peace" (3:14). ❏

Famous Lines

- The day of the Lord's return will surprise us like a thief (3:10). *The Second Coming of Jesus will be perhaps as surprising as his First Coming.*

- For the Lord one day is the same as a thousand years, and a thousand years is the same as one day (3:8). *Peter begins to explain why Jesus has not yet returned.*

Behind the Scenes of 2 Peter

⭐ Starring Role

Peter, leader among the twelve original disciples of Jesus (1:1)

📖 Plot

Fraudulent Christians teaching a new and distorted gospel begin making headway in the churches throughout the Roman Empire. The apostle Peter has mysteriously received word from heaven that he will die soon. So he writes a short, final letter to warn believers not to get taken in by these false teachers. "They promise freedom to everyone," Peter says, likely referring to freedom from moral rules. "But they are merely slaves of filthy living, because people are slaves of whatever controls them" (2:19).

Peter assures the church that God will punish people who twist the gospel of Jesus Christ into a counterfeit, do-as-you-please religion: "Ungodly people will be destroyed" (3:7).

Instead of following these false teachers down the wrong path, Peter says, Christians should follow the example of Jesus and the directions given by the apostles and Paul.

🎥 What to Look For

Warnings about false teachers. This is the primary motive behind the book. Peter writes from death's doorstep to send a final, urgent message to the Christian community that has been invaded by heretical teachers.

"These teachers don't really belong to the Master," Peter says (2:1). They're smooth-talking philosophers interested in nothing more lofty than sex, money, and wild parties (2:3, 13–14).

Explanation for the delay of Christ's return. After waiting several decades for Jesus to return "soon," as the apostles have long been preaching, some believers are starting to wonder if he's ever coming back. Fraudulent teachers apparently capitalize on this impatience and start convincing people that Jesus is not returning.

Peter explains the delay this way: "For the Lord one day is the same as a thousand years, and a thousand years is the same as one day. The Lord isn't slow about keeping his promises, as some people think he is. In fact, God is

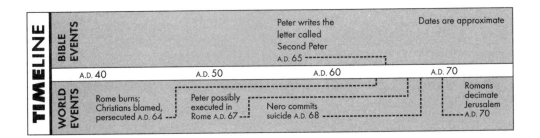

TIMELINE	BIBLE EVENTS			Peter writes the letter called Second Peter A.D. 65	Dates are approximate
		A.D. 40	A.D. 50	A.D. 60	A.D. 70
	WORLD EVENTS	Rome burns; Christians blamed, persecuted A.D. 64	Peter possibly executed in Rome A.D. 67	Nero commits suicide A.D. 68	Romans decimate Jerusalem A.D. 70

patient, because he wants everyone to turn
from sin and no one to be lost. The day of the
Lord's return will surprise us like a thief"
(3:8–10).

Author and Date

The letter is "from Simon Peter, a servant and an apostle of Jesus Christ" (1:1).
But Christian scholars from as early as the
second century have doubted this, and suspect the letter was written in Peter's name
(see "In search of an author" in the Reviews section).

If Peter wrote the letter, as many scholars believe, he likely wrote it just before he died. He said in the letter that he has been told by Jesus that he will
soon die (1:14). The Bible doesn't say anything about his death, but early Christian writers report that Peter was crucified upside down in Rome during Nero's
persecution of Christians (A.D. 64–68).

Scholars who believe the letter was written by someone other than Peter
suggest it was penned any time from A.D. 100 to 150.

On Location

The letter doesn't identify where it was written, or to whom. Peter does say
"this is the second letter I have written to encourage you" (3:1). His audience
may be the same as in 1 Peter: churches in five Roman provinces throughout
western Turkey. (See map in Acts, page 323.) ❏

Big Scene from 2 Peter

In an open letter to all Christians, Peter reveals that he expects to die soon. Because of this, his letter serves as a last will and testament. He expresses three deep desires: that Christians will continue growing in the faith (chapter 1), that they will reject false teachers (chapter 2), and that they will live in patient anticipation of the Second Coming (chapter 3).

The false teachers that Peter warns about are apparently infiltrating the church and teaching that, since Jesus has delayed his return for so long, it's obvious he's not coming back (3:4). They also seem to teach that there will be no Judgment Day and that Christians can live anyway they please, as long as they profess Jesus as Savior.

Peter describes these teachers with blunt condemnation: "They are immoral, and the meals they eat with you are spoiled by the shameful and selfish way they carry on. All they think about is having sex with someone else's husband or wife. There is no end to their wicked deeds. They trick people who are easily fooled, and their minds are filled with greedy thoughts. But they are headed for trouble!" (2:13–14).

The harvest of trouble they'll reap, Peter explains, is the judgment of God. The apostle illus-

trates his point by drawing on past judgments: the Flood, Sodom and Gomorrah, and the profiteering prophet Balaam. The Israelites killed Balaam for luring some of their people into sex rituals in worship of Baal, a Canaanite fertility god (Numbers 31:8, 16).

"My dear friends," Peter concludes, "don't let the errors of evil people lead you down the wrong path and make you lose your balance. Let the wonderful kindness and the understanding that come from our Lord and Savior Jesus Christ help you to keep on growing" (3:17–18).

**False teachers in the church
(2:1–22)** ••

Reviews

How to spot a false teacher. The fraudulent Christian teachers whom Peter writes about sound much like some of the same people Paul encountered. And Peter's advice for dealing with the religious frauds is on target with what Paul said in many of his letters.

Peter says these teachers profess to know Jesus, but they live like the devil—engaging in orgies and profiteering (2:13 - 14). Paul, writing the heresy-plagued church of Colossae, warns believers to "kill every desire for the wrong kind of sex. . . . Don't be greedy" (Colossians 3:5).

Both writers also agree that any and all teachings about Christianity need to be measured against the original teachings of Jesus and the apostles. If new teachings don't measure up, they are false. "You must remember what the apostles told you our Lord and Savior has commanded us to do," Peter writes (3:2). Teachings contrary to this, Peter says, are nothing but "stupid nonsense" (2:18).

Paul puts it this way in a letter to his friend and associate, Timothy: "Stupid talk . . . sounds smart but really isn't" (1 Timothy 6:20). Paul adds, "If anyone teaches false doctrines and does not agree to the sound instruction of our Lord Jesus Christ and to godly teaching, he is conceited and understands nothing" (6:3 - 4, New International Version).

In search of an author. The most common criticism of this letter is that the apostle Peter didn't write it, contrary to what 1:1 says. The letter is written in a less refined Greek than 1 Peter. The writer also implies that the letters of Paul have already been collected and are revered as part of Scripture: after speaking of Paul's letters, Peter refers to "other Scriptures too" (3:16). Furthermore, writing in the name of a respected teacher was a common practice among Greeks and Jews. It was the opposite of plagiarism; it was applying the master teacher's theology to current issues and then humbly giving credit to him instead of taking it.

These clues suggest to some scholars that the letter was written long after Paul and Peter died. Both men were likely killed during Nero's persecution of Christians in the mid-60s. Second Peter may not have been written until A.D. 100 or later, these scholars say, when the church clearly begins treating selected Christian writings as sacred.

Like some modern scholars, early Christian scholars also doubted Peter wrote the letter. These men include Origen (185 - 253) and Eusebius (265 - 340). On the other hand, Bishop Clement of Rome, writing in A.D. 95, may refer to the teachings of Second Peter, though stopping short of quoting the letter.

Scholars who say Peter wrote the letter argue that he admitted having help writing the first one; this could account for the difference in style (1 Peter 5:12). And by the time Peter wrote this second letter, near the end of his life, some of Paul's letters would have been in circulation for ten years or more, and increasingly regarded as authoritative. ❏

Encore

- In wording and content, Jude has striking parallels to 2 Peter. Compare Jude 4 - 13, 16 - 18 with 2 Peter 2:1 - 17; 3:1 - 3.

- For other warnings about false teachers, review Colossians, 1 Timothy, Titus. ❏

1 JOHN

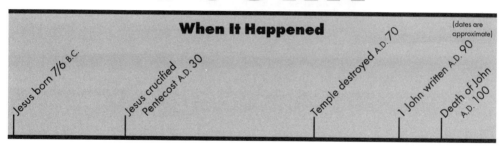

When It Happened

(dates are approximate)

Jesus born 7/6 B.C.

Jesus crucified
Pentecost A.D. 30

Temple destroyed A.D. 70

1 John written A.D. 90

Death of John A.D. 100

Battling Warped Teachings About Jesus

Pilate had a great question for Jesus, but his timing was all wrong.

This Roman governor asked, "What is truth?" (John 18:38). It was a superb question because in Pilate's day, as today, the world was full of competing religions and philosophies.

Pilate's question showed horrible timing, however, because Jesus had just given the answer: "I was born into this world to tell about the truth" (John 18:37). His teachings are the truth. In fact, he is the embodiment of Truth (John 14:6). Pilate was looking Truth in the face, and he couldn't recognize it.

More than fifty years later, Christians started having trouble recognizing the truth, too. They didn't seem sure about who Jesus was and what exactly he taught. A main problem was that some professing Christians started adding to the good news, trying to make it better. They made it worse. For example, by the time the apostle John had become an elderly man, someone came up with the idea that Jesus was just a spirit who only looked human. A religious movement started, and churches split.

> ### Famous Line
>
> • If we confess our sins, he is faithful and just to forgive us our sins, and to cleanse us from all unrighteousness (1:9, King James Version).

For perplexed believers, John wrote a sermon called 1 John. In this essay he points Christians back to the basics—to Jesus' original teachings about what to believe, how to behave, and how to know they are true children of God. John also reminds the Christians that they have the added benefit of the Holy Spirit, who teaches from the inside out. "The Spirit is truthful and teaches you everything. So stay one in your heart with Christ, just as the Spirit has taught you to do" (2:27).

What is truth?

It's in our hands when we hold the Bible, and it's in our heart when we accept Jesus. And we can know that we belong to the Truth. ❑

Behind the Scenes of 1 John

⭐ Starring Roles

Jesus, God's son who has come to earth in human form to offer eternal life to everyone who believes in him (1:3)

John, one of the twelve original disciples of Jesus, and probably the author of this letter along with 2 and 3 John, the Gospel of John, and Revelation

📖 Plot

Churches split after a group of Christians deny that Jesus was truly human. These unorthodox Christians, apparently forefathers of a heresy that explodes into full bloom during the second and third centuries, believe that everything physical is flawed and evil—including the human body. They teach that God, on the other hand, is completely spiritual and good.

Christians who embrace this premise are forced to conclude that Jesus only appeared to be physical—but was really spiritual. Furthermore, they argue that the Crucifixion plays no role in salvation, since the Son of God was not really killed. Salvation, they explain, comes from secret knowledge about how to transcend the body. This secret knowledge, apparently expressed in rituals and words, eventually gives the religious movement its name: Gnosticism, from *gnosis,* the Greek word for knowledge.

"I am writing to warn you about those people who are misleading you," John says. "You can tell God's children from the devil's children, because those who belong to the devil refuse to do right or to love each other" (2:26; 3:10).

When confronted by such false teachers, Christians should "keep thinking about the message you first heard" (2:24).

🎥 What to Look For

Antichrists. "You have heard that the antichrist is coming," John writes, "even now many antichrists have come" (2:18, New International Version). John describes these individuals as enemies of Christ who "came from our own group, yet they were not part of us. If they had been part of us, they would have stayed with us. But they left, which proves that they did not belong to our group" (2:19).

These former church members have seceded from the union of believers, formed their own congregation based on ideas blended from a variety of reli-

TIMELINE	BIBLE EVENTS									
		Jesus crucified A.D. 30	First John written A.D. 90	John writes Revelation from exile on Patmos island A.D. 95				Dates are approximate		
		A.D. 30	A.D. 40	A.D. 50	A.D. 60	A.D. 70	A.D. 80	A.D. 90	A.D. 100	
	WORLD EVENTS	Pilate begins 10-year rule as Judean governor A.D. 26	Mount Vesuvius destroys Pompeii, Italy A.D. 79		Emperor Domitian, persecutor of Christians, begins 15-year reign A.D. 81			Paper invented in China A.D. 103		

gions, and are trying to lure new members from the church.

Opposites. Notice the contrasting figures of speech that are identical to those used in John's Gospel: truth vs. lies, love vs. hate, light vs. darkness, life vs. death.

Not all religious issues are black and white. But as far as John is concerned, the heresy that apparently emerges in the Ephesus region is clearly in the wrong. He describes its advocates as liars incapable of teaching the truth. These people are enemies of Christ because, instead of loving the church, they hate it. This hatred proves they remain in spiritual darkness, which will lead to their spiritual death.

A sermon. First John reads more like a sermon or an essay than a letter. Missing are an opening and closing, commonly used in letters. Many scholars suggest John wrote this message to deal with a regional problem, and that these words become a circular letter read aloud in many churches.

Did You Know?

• As Jesus hung on the cross, he entrusted his elderly mother to the care of an unnamed disciple he loved deeply. Since at least the second century, Christian writers have identified this disciple as John.

• Jesus nicknamed John and his brother James the "sons of thunder," apparently because of their fiery temperaments. True to his nickname, John boldly calls professing Christians "liars" if they teach anything contrary to the original message about Jesus.

Author and Date

Like most New Testament books, the author is not identified. But the themes and the style of writing (simple Greek) are strikingly similar to those of John's Gospel. Early Christian writers from at least the second century have attributed both books to the apostle John, a fisherman, and one of Jesus' closest disciples. John may also have been a first cousin of Jesus.

It's uncertain when the book was written. Christian leaders in the second century said John wrote it in Ephesus late in the first century, roughly A.D. 90 or perhaps later.

On Location

John likely wrote during his old age, while living in Ephesus. The first documented use of the letter is in Ephesus. (See map in Acts, page 323.) ❏

Big Scene from 1 John

Within half a century after Jesus died and rose again, Christians are becoming increasingly confused about who he is and why he came. Some are starting to accessorize their faith with teachings from other religions and philosophies. Drawing from the insights of respected Greek philosophers who teach that divinity is a mysterious ideal that is both invisible and eternal—not physical and temporal—some Christians conclude that Jesus could not have been human. He was a spirit, they argue, who only looked human.

The church grows uncertain about what to believe.

"Don't believe everyone who claims to have the Spirit of God," John writes. "You can know which ones come from God. His Spirit says that Jesus Christ had a truly human body. But when someone doesn't say this about Jesus, you know that person has a spirit that doesn't come from God" (4:1–3).

John adds that there is yet another way to identify if professing Christians are really of God: God's children "do right" and "love each other" (3:10).

"Our love for each other proves that we have gone from death to life," John explains. "But if you don't love each other, you are still under the power of death" (3:14).

**Jesus: God in the flesh
(4:1–6)** •

Reviews

Evidence favoring John as writer. There are plenty of reasons to conclude that the apostle John wrote this letter—reasons beyond the similarities between 1 John and the Gospel of John. Irenaeus, a church leader who lived about A.D. 140 - 203, quoted extensively from the book and attributed the work to John. Other church leaders who lived about the same time attributed it to John as well: Clement of Alexandria, Tertullian, and Origen. An even earlier Christian, Polycarp of Smyrna (about A.D. 69 - 155), seems to have drawn from 1 John when he insisted that anyone who does not confess that Jesus came in the flesh is an antichrist.

The early church fathers said John wrote in Ephesus, during the final years of his life. This region, in what is now western Turkey, was a virtual stew of varied cultures and religions—an ideal location for mixing new batches of creatively blended religions, like those described in the Gospel and letters bearing John's name.

The end is near. "Children, this is the last hour," John writes (2 : 18). That was about 2,000 years ago, or 17 million hours.

"The last hour" is a phrase, like "the last days," which means more than the months or years just before the Second Coming. It also means "the age of the Messiah," fully inaugurated by the death and resurrection of Jesus. This phrase is similar to one that John uses repeatedly in his Gospel when speaking of the Crucifixion. When Jesus realizes it is nearly time for him to fulfill the reason he came to earth—to die—he says "the time has come" (John 17 : 1).

"The last hour" can refer to events immediately preceding the Second Coming, but it also marks the beginning of the end of God's long-term plan to save the world from sin. Here, John likely intends the latter meaning. In Old Testament times, God's plan involved animal sacrifices. In New Testament times, the plan features the ultimate sacrifice: God's Son. ❏

Encore

- For more of John's writings dealing with similar religious issues, read 2 and 3 John, along with John's Gospel. ❏

2 JOHN

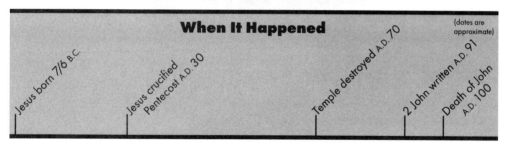

When It Happened

(dates are approximate)

Jesus born 7/6 B.C.

Jesus crucified Pentecost A.D. 30

Temple destroyed A.D. 70

2 John written A.D. 91

Death of John A.D. 100

No Welcome Mat for Heretics

Second John reads a bit like a P.S. to 1 John.

The apostle John, presumed the writer, condenses the five-chapter message of his first letter into a mere thirteen verses. In addition to repeating and abbreviating his warning against false teachers who argue that Jesus was not human, John adds that Christians should not show hospitality to these teachers.

In Bible times, Christians aren't the only ones traveling around the land and preaching. So are quasi-Christian evangelists, trying to spread the word that spiritual things are good and physical things are evil, and that because of this, Jesus was a spirit who only looked human. It is customary in early Christian days for believers to invite into their homes any traveling evangelists, and to later send them on their way with provisions for the trip.

John warns church members to be discerning about who they support. He says if people don't preach the genuine story of Jesus, "don't welcome them into your home or even greet them. Greeting them is the same as taking part in their evil deeds" (10).

This doesn't mean we should turn all sinners away from our door. Jesus came to help sinners. He even sought them out (Luke 15:2–7). But John teaches that we shouldn't encourage and support their sin. ❏

Famous Line

• Love each other (1:5).

Behind the Scenes of 2 John

⭐ Starring Roles

The church leader, identified in many translations as "the Elder," probably the apostle John, one of Jesus' twelve original disciples (1:1)
A very special woman and her children, probably a figure of speech for the church and its members (1:1)

📖 Plot

The apostle John seems to have a soft spot in his heart for an unnamed church that he identifies only as "a very special woman and her children" (1:1). So he writes a special letter to this congregation, repeating some of what he has said in 1 John. Then he adds a warning against showing hospitality to traveling evangelists who teach false doctrines.

Though 1 John reads like a sermon or essay—without an introductory greeting and a closing that are common in letters—2 John has both of these. Perhaps 1 John is a general message circulated among all the churches in John's region, and 2 John is a personal letter to an individual church—a letter that accompanies their copy of 1 John.

💻 Author and Date

The writer is identified as "the church leader" (1:1). The writing style, ideas, and testimony of Christian leaders in the second century indicate the writer was the apostle John. This close disciple of Jesus was also probably author of 1 and 3 John, along with the Gospel of John and Revelation. One central theme in 1 John is truth—an important idea in a day when the church was being bombarded with lies about Jesus. This theme is repeated in John's Gospel as well as 1 and 3 John.

Like 1 and 3 John, it's uncertain when 2 John was written. Christian leaders in the second century said John wrote it in Ephesus late in the first century, roughly A.D. 90 or perhaps later. ❏

3 JOHN

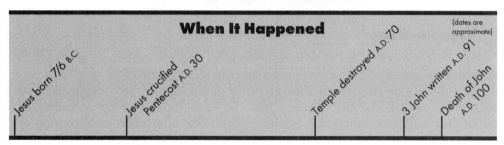

When It Happened

(dates are approximate)

Jesus born 7/6 B.C.

Jesus crucified A.D. 30
Pentecost

Temple destroyed A.D. 70

3 John written A.D. 91

Death of John A.D. 100

Showing Hospitality to Christians

The most personal of John's three letters, 3 John is the only one addressed to an individual: Gaius, a kind believer who is part of a church led by Diotrephes, a minister who runs the congregation like a rebel general runs a junta.

John commends Gaius for obeying the true teachings about Jesus, and especially for showing hospitality to Christian missionaries—possibly some John has sent into the area. John knows that Gaius might be punished for this since Diotrephes rejects all outsiders who might undermine his authority. And he boots people out of the church who refuse to do the same.

"Dear friend," John writes to Gaius, "don't copy the evil deeds of others! Follow the example of people who do kind deeds. They are God's children, but those who are always doing evil have never seen God" (11).

Even in the beginning years of Christianity, believers face stern and influential enemies within the church—fraudulent Christians who worship values cherished in the kingdom of this world: power and prestige. John's advice to believers is to keep doing what they know God wants them to do: obey the truth, love others, and support those spreading the gospel, regardless of the risk. ❏

Famous Line

• Follow the example of people who do kind deeds (11).

Behind the Scenes of 3 John

⭐ Starring Roles

The church leader, identified in many translations as "the Elder," probably the apostle John, one of Jesus' twelve original disciples (1:1)

Gaius, a Christian commended for showing kindness and hospitality to Christian travelers (1:1)

Diotrephes, a dictatorial church leader who abuses his authority by excommunicating those who disagree with his policy of refusing to welcome Christian travelers (1:9)

📖 Plot

In the early decades of Christianity, the organization is loose; local churches are guided by letters and representatives sent from leaders scattered around the Roman Empire. In one unnamed church, a minister named Diotrephes "likes to be the number-one leader" (9). He refuses to respect the authority of the apostle John, and even spreads malicious rumors about him. When John writes to this church, Diotrephes apparently refuses to even read the letters in public. And when John sends representatives, Diotrephes refuses to welcome them. Furthermore, this autocratic church leader excommunicates any members who do welcome them.

The apostle John writes to Gaius, a member in this troubled church. John commends Gaius for showing hospitality to all Christian travelers and urges him to keep doing this no matter what Diotrephes says.

John concludes his letter by saying he hopes to see Gaius soon, so they can talk in person. When John arrives, he says, he will deal with Diotrephes.

💻 Author and Date

As in 2 John, the writer is identified as "the church leader" (1:1). The writing style, ideas, and testimony of Christian leaders in the second century indicate the writer was the apostle John, who also likely wrote 1 and 2 John, along with the Gospel of John and Revelation.

As with 1 and 2 John, it's uncertain when 3 John was written. Christian leaders in the second century said John wrote it in Ephesus late in the first century, roughly A.D. 90 or perhaps later. ❏

JUDE

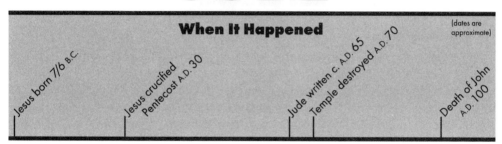

When It Happened

(dates are approximate)

Jesus born 7/6 B.C.

Jesus crucified
Pentecost A.D. 30

Jude written c. A.D. 65
Temple destroyed A.D. 70

Death of John
A.D. 100

If We're Forgiven, What's Wrong with Sin?

Christians in the first century called themselves followers of the Way, meaning the way to eternal life, through Jesus. Some, however, were followers of the Shortcut. They believed they had found an easier way to heaven, through a colossal loophole.

The loophole was this: Jesus had forgiven them of sin. Therefore, they figured, sin didn't matter anymore. They could sin all they wanted; they were forgiven. Besides, they reasoned, God's grace is greater than all our sin.

There's a place for creativity in the kingdom of God, but this is a bit much. Jude knows that professing Christians who are carriers of a light view of sin can infect and destroy an entire congregation. Sin is serious business. In Old Testament times, animals died as a reminder that sin is a matter of life and death. In New Testament times, God's Son died to save us from sin—not so we could sin all we wanted, but to free us from the power that sin has to enslave us. As Jesus once put it, "Anyone who sins is a slave of sin!" (John 8:34).

"Defend the faith," Jude writes (3).

As long as there are followers of the Shortcut, preaching the gospel of the Loophole, Jude says there needs to be knowledgeable Christians who can point to examples in Scripture—such as grumbling Israelites on the Exodus, or sex addicts in Sodom—and say, "Don't forget what happened to those people" (5). ❑

Famous Line

• To him who is able to keep you from falling and to present you before his glorious presence without fault and with great joy—to the only God our Savior be glory, majesty, power and authority, through Jesus Christ our Lord, before all ages, now and forevermore! Amen (24 – 25, New International Version).
The benediction of Jude's letter.

Behind the Scenes of Jude

⭐ Starring Role

Jude, author of this letter, and possibly a brother of Jesus (1:1)

📖 Plot

Jude writes a forceful letter to an unnamed church, warning the people about Christian imposters who have infiltrated the congregation and who are rising to positions of leadership.

These fraudulent Christians are teaching that it's okay for Christians to sin, since Christians have already been forgiven of sin. "God treats us much better than we deserve," Jude quotes them as saying, "so it is all right to be immoral" (4). These people practice what they preach. Jude describes them as filthy minded, shameful, and selfish (12).

"I really wanted to write you about God's saving power," Jude says. "But instead, I must write and ask you to defend the faith" (3).

Using a wide array of examples from the Old Testament and from revered Jewish literature not included in Scripture, Jude shows that God punishes sin. "Be warned by what happened to the cities of Sodom and Gomorrah," Jude says, citing one memorable case study. "Their people became immoral and did all sorts of sexual sins. Then God made an example of them and punished them with eternal fire" (7).

Jude asks true believers to take a stand for what they know is right.

💻 Author and Date

The writer is "Jude, a servant of Jesus Christ and the brother of James" (1). Many scholars believe Jude is also the brother of Jesus. They draw this conclusion partly because "Jude" is a form of the Hebrew name Judah, which is Judas in Greek. Jesus had brothers named Judas and James (Matthew 13:55). James rose to leadership within the Jerusalem church, which may be why Jude identified himself as the brother of James.

Another possibility is that Jude was one of the twelve disciples (Luke 6:16). This seems unlikely, however, because the writer speaks of the apostles as though he is not one of them (17–18).

There is nothing in this letter to identify when it was written. It could have been written during the lifetime of Jesus' brothers. Paul addressed some of the same issues within about thirty years of the Crucifixion. For example, he felt compelled to remind Christians that they should not take advantage of God's grace by continuing to sin (Romans 6:1–2).

Jude could have addressed his letter either to Jewish Christians or Gentile Christians. The many references to Jewish scriptures and legends, however, suggest that Jewish Christians would have found the arguments especially convincing. ❏

REVELATION

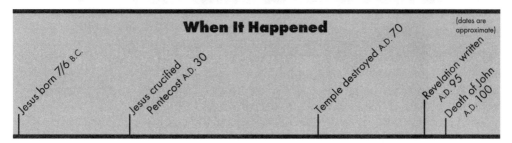

When It Happened
(dates are approximate)

Jesus born 7/6 B.C.

Jesus crucified
Pentecost A.D. 30

Temple destroyed A.D. 70

Revelation written
A.D. 95

Death of John
A.D. 100

The End Is Just the Beginning

By some the most avoided book of the Bible, while by others the most closely studied, Revelation can seem bizarre, scary, and thoroughly mystifying. What, for example, is a modern Christian to make of heavenly creatures "covered front and back with eyes" (4:6)?

Revelation is also perhaps the most misunderstood book of the Bible. When Iraq, for instance, has taken provocative, threatening action, some interpreters have turned to Revelation 18 to warn that the end is near, and Babylon is about to fall. (The ancient ruins of Babylon are near Baghdad.) Yet the first readers of this book saw the name "Babylon" but read "Rome." Jews had used Babylon as a code name for Rome ever since A.D. 70, when Rome did to Jerusalem what Babylon had done centuries earlier: burned and leveled it.

This closing book of the Bible is an encrypted message written especially for persecuted Christians near the end of the first century. Those believers have the key to interpret much of what the writer, John, says. We have only part of their ancient insight into the dramatic symbols John uses. But this is more than enough to decode the main message: Evil and its followers don't win; God and his followers do.

In the end—when the age of fallen human beings gives way to the new age of fully redeemed beings—God will restore the paradise that was lost through the sin of Adam and Eve. He will make a new creation and populate it with happy, resurrected humans who want to live with him forever. ❏

Famous Lines

- I am the Alpha and the Omega, the Beginning and the End (1:8, New King James Version). *Alpha and Omega are the first and last letters of the Greek alphabet.*

- God will wipe all tears from their eyes (7:17). *Figurative language to describe the absence of sorrow in God's heavenly kingdom.*

- I saw a new heaven and a new earth (21:1). *In a vision, John sees God restore creation to the paradise it was before sin entered.*

Behind the Scenes of Revelation

⭐ Starring Roles

John, author of the book, who describes his captivating visions of the future; possibly one of Jesus' twelve original disciples (1:1)
Jesus, Son of God, who returns to earth to judge all people and to take his followers to heaven (1:1)

📖 Plot

John, exiled to a small and rocky island apparently for refusing to worship the Roman emperor as god, experiences a long series of dramatic visions. Some visions are bizarre—even horrifying. Others are beautiful and deeply comforting. But all of them prove to John that his faith is real, and that no matter what Rome or any other power tries to do to God's church, the Lord and his people will prevail.

The writer describes his visions in stark and often disturbing detail. He speaks of international chaos, God's people martyred, world-shattering catastrophes, and cosmic upheavals. Humanity and the world cease to exist.

But in their place, God restores paradise lost. Human beings become spirit beings, fully capable of enjoying God's new creation for the rest of eternity.

🎥 What to Look For

Apocalypse, the genre. The unique style of writing in Revelation is called apocalyptic, from the Greek word *apocalypsis,* which means "reveal." That's where the book gets its name.

This writing paints a graphic picture of the present evil world, followed by a glorious future—and it does so through dramatic visions, strange symbolism, and code words. The point is to comfort persecuted readers by assuring them that their difficult circumstances won't last forever—God will punish the wicked, reward the righteous, and usher in a new and wonderful age.

One reason the writer uses extraordinary symbolism is to prevent government authorities from deciphering the message. The Roman emperor, for example, would not take kindly to someone saying that God is going to destroy both him and his empire. Yet that's what John means when he says "Babylon has fallen" (14:8). After Rome decimated Jerusalem in A.D. 70, just as Babylon did in 586 B.C., many Jews began referring to the Roman Empire as Babylon.

Though the key for decoding much of the symbolism is lost, some remains. Revelation itself reveals the code for some of the less dangerous ideas: stars are angels and lampstands are churches (1:20). The heavenly Jerusalem is the church, the bride of Jesus (21:9–10; compare with Ephesians 5:25–32).

Numbers. To secretly communicate his message, John supplements his strange symbolism and fantastic word pictures with a perplexing use of numbers.

Seven. One of John's favorite numbers is seven, which he uses more than fifty times. He talks about seven churches, seven spirits, seven golden lampstands, seven stars, seven seals, seven trumpets—and the list goes on. Throughout Jewish history, seven symbolizes completion; it was on the seventh day that God rested after finishing Creation.

So when John dictates letters to seven churches, praising their good traits and warning them of their weaknesses, he and his readers may have understood that he was addressing the entire Christian church. In fact, the church today still looks to these letters for guidance. Since the number symbolizes something that is complete, it's little wonder John uses it so much in a book about the end of human history and the fulfillment of God's plan of salvation.

Did You Know?

• Armagedon, the place where Revelation says the final battle between good and evil will take place, is a huge valley plain in northern Israel (16:16). Over the past 4,000 years there have been no less than 22 invasions into this valley. In John's time, Armagedon (Hebrew for "mountain of Megeddo") was already a name synonymous with war.

144,000. This number, which appears in Revelation 7:4, may be another one that symbolizes completeness. In Revelation it could mean "all God's people." John shows that this number comes from the twelve tribes of Israel: twelve times twelve, with multiplied thousands—suggesting the new Israel, which is the entire assembly of God's people.

666. Known as the Mark of the Beast, 666 is likely a coded reference to Nero—Rome's most vicious persecutor of Christians. John gives this clue: "You need wisdom to understand the number of the beast! But if you are smart enough, you can figure this out. Its number is six hundred sixty-six, and it stands for a person" (13:18).

Hebrew and Greek letters have numeric equivalents. When the numbers that spell the Hebrew name of Nero Caesar are combined, the total is 666.

Connections to the Old Testament. Revelation is full of allusions to the Old Testament. Nearly 300 of the approximately 400 verses have some connection to the Old Testament.

For example, the vision John has of God's throne and the song John hears the heavenly beings sing are much like those described by Ezekiel and Isaiah (compare 4:1–8 with Ezekiel 1 and Isaiah 6:3).

Also, the plague of "hail and fire mixed with blood" (8:7) is reminiscent of the thunder, hail, and fire of the seventh plague on Egypt (Exodus 9:22–26). And the plague of locusts, coming with smoke that blots out the sun (9:1–3), is based on Joel 1–2.

TIMELINE	BIBLE EVENTS				
			Paul and Peter executed in Rome A.D. 67	John writes Revelation from exile on Patmos island A.D. 95	Dates are approximate
		A.D. 60	A.D. 70	A.D. 80	A.D. 90
	WORLD EVENTS		Rome burns; Nero blames Christians, launches persecution A.D. 64	Rome destroys Jerusalem and temple A.D. 70	Emperor Domitian assassinated, ending his persecution of Christians A.D. 96

Author and Date

The writer identifies himself as John. But which John? Christian writer Justin Martyr (about A.D. 100–165) is the first person on record to identify the author as the apostle John, one of the closest disciples of Jesus, and author of the Gospel of John and the three letters of John. About 100 years later, other Christians began to challenge this. Dionysius, a theologian from Alexandria, Egypt, said the writing style is not at all like the other works of the apostle John. However, the frequent references to the Old Testament and the style of the Greek that the writer used suggest he was a Jew from Israel.

John may have written this masterpiece of mystery during the Christian persecutions late in the reign of Nero, in the mid 60s. But most scholars date the book to the final years of Emperor Domitian, who was assassinated in A.D. 96. Late in his reign, Domitian forced his subjects to address him as "Lord and God." Those who refused were harshly punished. Many Christians were exiled to penal colonies or executed.

On Location

John writes from fifty miles offshore of western Turkey, on the rocky island of Patmos, about ten miles long and five miles wide. He begins the book with letters addressed to churches in seven cities near the coast of western Turkey. The futuristic visions that John writes about involve the entire planet. He says the last battle between good and evil will take place in the Valley of Armagedon, known today as Megeddo, and that God will make a new Jerusalem. Since the genre of the book is apocalyptic, characterized by extreme symbolism, scholars debate whether John had any of these actual sites in mind. ❏

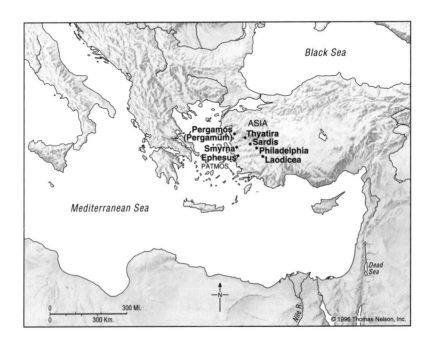

Big Scenes from Revelation

Roman authorities exile a Christian leader named John to a small and rocky island fifty miles off the coast of western Turkey. John apparently receives this punishment for refusing to worship the emperor as a god. Actually, this punishment is comparatively light, because many other Christians are executed for such insolence. Perhaps John receives a lighter sentence because of his advanced age.

On this island of Patmos, John begins to experience a long series of dramatic visions. First, he receives divine insight into seven prominent churches in western Turkey, and he dictates letters of commendation and warning to each.

Afterward, he finds his spirit standing in the very throne room of God. What he sees is much like that which the prophet Ezekiel saw hundreds of years earlier (Ezekiel 1). In the background, heavenly beings continually praise God in words and song. One such song is similar to what the prophet Isaiah once heard in a vision: "Holy, holy, holy is the Lord, the all-powerful God, who was and is and is coming!" (4:8; see Isaiah 6:3).

Suddenly John sees God holding a scroll locked with seven seals. Among all the beings in the heavenly court, only Jesus is deemed worthy to break the seals. As Jesus breaks each one, John experiences a new vision—including terrifying scenes of the four horsemen of the Apocalypse, who represent conquest, war, famine, and lethal disease.

Silence falls as Jesus breaks the seventh seal. Suddenly, seven trumpets blast, one after another, each one heralding destruction, persecution, martyrdom, or God's punishment for humanity's evil.

John sees a vision of heaven
•• **(4:1—5:14)**

As the visions progress, John sees two hideous monsters born of Satan. Some scholars interpret them as symbolizing the Roman Empire, or perhaps humanity's evil. Others see in them the Antichrist, assisted by a Satanic prophet who performs miracles that convince humanity to worship the Antichrist.

After seeing all this tragedy, John witnesses a glorious sight: a rider on a white horse, preparing to lead the army of heaven into battle against all the forces of evil—natural and supernatural. The rider wears a robe engraved with his title: KING OF KINGS AND LORD OF LORDS. The rider is Jesus Christ, coming as the warrior king that the Jews expected to see in their messiah.

John witnesses a great battle in which the heavenly forces strike a coalition army belonging to "the beast and all kings of the earth." Jesus wins. The soldiers of the evil army are annihilated, their bodies left as carrion for scavengers. The two beasts and Satan are condemned to everlasting torment in a lake of burning sulfur.

Rider on a white horse
(19:11—20:11) ••

John then sees what happens next, at the end of human history. He sees Judgment Day.

"I saw a great white throne with someone sitting on it," John writes. "I also saw all the dead people standing in front of that throne" (20:11–12).

Heavenly authorities open "the book of life." Then all the people who have ever lived are judged according to what they have done in life. The judge is none other than Jesus, of whom Paul wrote, "When Christ Jesus comes as king, he will be the judge of everyone" (2 Timothy 4:1).

"Anyone whose name wasn't written in the book of life was thrown into the lake of fire" (20:15).

Scholars debate what that means. Some interpret the description literally, arguing that sinners follow their lord and master, Satan, to his eternal fate. Others say this graphic image symbolizes separation from Christ—that people who want Jesus, and people who want nothing to do with Jesus, each are given their heart's desire.

Judgment Day (20:11–15) ••

I saw a new heaven and a new earth," John writes. This is the same new creation that Isaiah had spoken of hundreds of years earlier. Quoting God, Isaiah wrote: "I am creating new heavens and a new earth. . . . full of happy people. . . . There will be no more crying or sorrow" (Isaiah 65:17–19).

Since the dawning of human history, when Adam and Eve contaminated God's good creation with sin, God has been working his plan to remove all traces of defilement. "Everything is finished!" God now says. "I am the Alpha and Omega, the beginning and the end. I will freely give water from the life-giving fountain to everyone who is thirsty. All who win the victory will be given these blessings. I will be their God, and they will be my people" (21:6–7).

With this, God and his people settle in for an eternity. Evil is gone. Beauty, tenderness, and joy fill the realms of paradise restored.

Heaven, eternal reward of the faithful •• **(21:1—22:6)**

I am coming soon!" Jesus tells John. "And when I come, I will reward everyone for what they have done" (22:12).

"If you are thirsty, come!" Jesus adds, for all to hear. "If you want life-giving water, come and take it. It's free!" (22:17).

To all John has witnessed, both the tragic and the wondrous, he has but one, short response: "Lord Jesus, please come soon!" (22:20).

The Second Coming (22:7–20) •••

Reviews

Letters to the seven churches. Though it's unclear if the letters John addressed to seven churches were intended for them alone, or for the entire church, John carefully chose word pictures appropriate for the churches.

To the church in Laodicea, an immensely wealthy city famous for its eye ointments and medical center, John says, "You are pitiful, poor, blind. . . . Buy medicine for your eyes, so that you will be able to see" (3:17 - 18). Further, he calls them "lukewarm" (3:16), an ironic description for a people located just a few miles from hot springs, a popular attraction for tourists and the sick.

To the church in Smyrna, home of a large and militant group of Jews, John says he understands how hard it is to live there as a Christian. "I know the slander of those who say they are Jews and are not, but are a synagogue of Satan" (2:9, New International Version). Polycarp, bishop of Smyrna, was arrested for his faith and burned to death there in about A.D. 155.

Hell. Punishment for doing wrong is something most people seem to understand and accept. But eternal torture in a lake of burning sulfur is quite another thing—especially if the torturer is God, whom the Bible describes as the essence of love (1 John 4:8).

Part of the problem in understanding what God's end-time punishment for sinners will be like is that the Bible has to resort to word pictures from the physical world to describe what will take place in an entirely different, spiritual dimension. John says Satan and his followers will be thrown into "a lake of burning sulphur" (19:20) where they will suffer "in pain day and night forever and ever" (20:10, see also 20:15). Jesus confirms that sinners are "in danger of the fires of hell" (Matthew 5:22), a place outside of the kingdom of God where people "cry and grit their teeth in pain" (Matthew 8:12). Surprisingly, Jesus also describes this as a place of darkness (Matthew 8:12). Yet fire displaces darkness.

What exactly is that place of fire and darkness, which the Bible sometimes calls hell? Hell is a word that comes from the Hebrew term *gehenna*, an ever-smoldering garbage dump in a valley outside ancient Jerusalem. Here is where people threw their trash, as well as the corpses of executed criminals. The Jews in Jesus' time used this place as a figure of speech to describe God's punishment of sinners on Judgment Day.

From beginning to end, the Bible is clear that people have to suffer the consequences of their sinful choices. God honors their decision to reject him, his love, and his rescue from sin and judgment. But how those who reject him will suffer remains in the hands of God who "never does wrong" and "can always be trusted to bring justice" (Deuteronomy 32:4). ❏

Encore

• For other apocalyptic writings in the Bible, read Isaiah 24–27; Ezekiel 38–39; Daniel 7–12; Joel 2; Zechariah 9–14; Matthew 24; Mark 13; Luke 12. ❏

The Apocrypha
Books Left Out of the Old Testament

Jews wrote many revered books during the final centuries before Christ, and even up until Rome destroyed Jerusalem in A.D. 70—books eventually eliminated from their Bible but kept in some Christian Bibles.

These are books about dramatic Jewish history, romance, wise sayings, prayers, and miracles. Jews respected these books enough to include them in the Septuagint, an ever-expanding Greek translation of sacred Hebrew writings, started in the 200s B.C. Yet when Jewish scholars later decided to agree on an authoritative collection of Scripture, they eliminated these books known as the Apocrypha, a Greek word meaning "hidden." The Jews believed the books were not as reliable as those kept.

When Christian scholar Jerome translated the Jewish and Christian Scriptures into a Latin edition of the Bible in about A.D. 405, he included some of the Apocrypha. But even those he bothered translating he considered less than sacred, criticizing them as "the crazy wanderings of a man whose senses have taken leave of him."

When 16th-century Protestant reformer Martin Luther broke from the Roman Catholic Church, he decided that the Christian Bible should include only the Old Testament books in the Hebrew Bible. As a result, the Protestant Bible is shorter than both the Catholic Bible and the Eastern Orthodox Bibles (Eastern churches had split from the Catholics about the time of the Crusades, in A.D. 1054).

There's no standard list of Apocrypha books.

The Roman Catholic Church accepts seven: Tobit, Judith, 1 and 2 Maccabees, Wisdom, Sirach, and Baruch—along with additions to Esther and Daniel (in sections called the Prayer of Azariah and the Song of the Three Jews, Susanna, and Bel and the Dragon).

The Eastern Orthodox Church accepts all those in the Catholic Bible, and adds several more. The Greek Orthodox, for example, adds 1 Esdras, the Prayer of Manasseh, 3 Maccabees, and Psalm 151.

The Slavonic church adds 2 Esdras. (Slavonia is part of southern Europe that suffered in the war of Bosnia and Herzegovina, which ended in 1995.)

Other Eastern churches add 4 Maccabees.

Here's a short introduction to each of these apocryphal books and portions of books.

Tobit. This is the story of Tobit, a Jewish man who is deported with his family to Nineveh, capital of the Assyrian Empire, after Assyria conquers Israel. Against imperial law, Tobit boldly continues giving a proper burial to executed Jews. One night after doing this then sleeping outside, he is blinded by sparrow droppings that fall into his eyes. For eight years he prays that God will cure him. This prayer is answered when his son, at the instructions of the archangel Raphael, smears Tobit's eyes with bile from a fish.

Judith. A beautiful Jewish widow, Judith saves her city that is besieged by an Assyrian invasion force. She leaves her city and offers her services as an informant. The general gladly accepts, and invites her to a small party with the hope of seducing her. By party's end, the general is drunk and passed out on his bed. Judith stays with him, under the guise of spending the night with him. Instead, she cuts off his head and takes it back to her city. At her urging, the Jews launch an attack at first light. When the Assyrians try to awaken their commander, they discover his headless corpse, panic, and run for their lives.

Esther additions. The Old Testament story of Esther, a Jewish woman and Persian queen, does not mention God at all. But 107 extra verses in the Greek version mention him more than 50 times. For example, the original story written in Hebrew tells of the Persian king having a sleepless night. But the later Greek version explains why: "The Lord took sleep from the king."

Wisdom. Traditionally attributed to Solomon, this collection of wise sayings was composed in Greek, perhaps in the first century B.C. The writer speaks of righteous people receiving God's gift of immortality, an idea not taught in more ancient Jewish writings. The writer also brags that Jewish wisdom, which comes from God, is greater than the wisdom of the Greeks, who are renowned for their sages.

Sirach. Called by early Christians as Ecclesiasticus, meaning "church book," Sirach is a 51-chapter collection of maxims, sacred songs, and reflections about life—much like the books of Proverbs and Psalms. Early Christians used this book in worship rituals. The author is a respected sage and teacher named Jesus the son of Sirach, a man who lived about 200 years before Christ, when Israel was dominated by successors of Alexander the Great.

Baruch. This story is set among the Jewish exiles taken to Babylon, after the Babylonian Empire decimates Jerusalem in 586 B.C. The writer claims to be Baruch, assistant to the prophet Jeremiah—though the book of Jeremiah says both men escaped to Egypt (43:6–7). The five-chapter book includes a confession of the Jewish nation's sins, along with a prayer for deliverance, and a song of praise about the wisdom God has given Israel through his commandments.

Letter of Jeremiah. Often treated as the sixth chapter of Baruch, this claims to be a letter that the prophet Jeremiah sent to Jewish exiles in Babylon, warning them not to worship idols while they are there.

Prayer of Azariah and the Song of the Three Jews. Added to the Greek edition of Daniel, this work tells of Daniel's three friends who survive in a fiery furnace. The prayer is by Azariah—one of Daniel's three friends, better known by his Babylonian name of Abednego. The song that follows is what he and his friends—Shadrach and Meshach—sang while in the furnace.

Susanna. Also added to Daniel is this story of Susanna, a beautiful and rich young woman who is said to have launched Daniel's career as a prophet. Two respected but lustful Jewish leaders falsely accuse her of having an affair, after she refuses to have sex with them. Young Daniel publicly and separately interrogates the two men, revealing inconsistencies in their stories. Susanna is saved and the two men face the punishment they intended for her: execution.

Bel and the Dragon. In yet another addition to the Greek version of Daniel, the prophet Daniel uncovers hoaxes about two Babylonian gods: Bel and a serpent. (1) Bel: Each evening the Babylonians place food in the temple of their god, Bel. By morning, the food is gone. One evening Daniel scatters ashes on the temple floor, and the next morning points out footprints to show that priests came in through a secret passage and carried the food away. (2) Dragon: Babylonians also worship a serpent, which Daniel feeds a lethal mixture of tar, fat, and hair. The concoction expands inside the "dragon," making it explode.

1 Maccabees. This book tells about the Jewish revolt and war of independence after Syrian occupiers desecrate the Jewish temple and try forcing the Jews to abandon their religion. Leading the resistance is a priest and his five sons, known as the Maccabees. After winning the war they set up what becomes known as the Hasmonean dynasty, which rules Israel for a century—until Rome arrives.

2 Maccabees. This supplements the story of the Jewish war for independence, focusing especially on how God helped the Jews win against incredible odds.

1 Esdras. The books of 1 Esdras through 3 Maccabees are in the Bibles of Greek and Russian Orthodox churches, though not in the Roman Catholic Bible. First Esdras summarizes the fall of Jerusalem and the exile of the Jews to Babylon, then concentrates on the Jews returning to Israel and rebuilding of the temple and the capital. Much of the material is found also in the book of Ezra. In fact, Esdras is the Greek form of the Hebrew name Ezra.

Prayer of Manasseh. Manasseh was one of the most wicked kings in the history of the Jewish nation. He worshiped idols, and even sacrificed his sons in pagan offerings. The Prayer of Manasseh claims to be his prayer of repentance, perhaps written to justify his long and apparently successful reign. In ancient times, many Jews associated success with God's approval.

Psalm 151. This is a short song that David is said to have sung after defeating Goliath, the Philistine champion. A copy of the song was found among the famous Dead Sea Scrolls. It was written in Hebrew during the first century before Christ.

3 Maccabees. The title of this book is misleading; the story has nothing to do with the Maccabean heros who fought and won the Jewish war of independence in the mid-100s B.C. Instead, the story is set a half-century earlier and deals with the struggles of Egyptian Jews suffering under an oppressive king. He assembles them in an arena and tries to crush them with a herd of elephants. But God makes the animals turn and trample the armed Egyptians behind them. The king repents.

2 Esdras. This book appears in the Slavonic Bible. Most of the book tells about the visions that the prophet Ezra has concerning the last days of human history. These include the signs that the end is near, the suffering that will occur, and God's deliverance of the righteous.

4 Maccabees. This book appears in some other Eastern church Bibles, and as an appendix to the Greek Bible. Set just before the Jewish revolt and war of independence in the mid-100s B.C., this book is an emotional plea for Jews to continue obeying the laws of Moses—even though Judaism has been outlawed by Syrian occupiers, and observant Jews are being executed.

Glossary and Index

als in occupied nations. Jews hated tax collectors, and considered them traitors who were ritually unclean. Merely touching one would render Jews unfit to worship God until they cleansed themselves with purification rituals. **282, 308**

Tekoa 223

Temple, Jewish worship facility in Jerusalem. Once Solomon completed the first temple, Jews could sacrifice only there. After Babylon destroyed the temple in 586 B.C., Jews rebuilt a more modest version of it, which King Herod remodeled into a magnificent center. Rome destroyed it in A.D. 70, while crushing a Jewish rebellion. Its destruction ended the sacrificial system, since the temple has never been rebuilt. An ancient mosque now sits on the hilltop where the temple once rested. **95, 102, 104, 125, 128, 200, 202, 264, 270, 300**

Ten Commandments, ten fundamental laws on which all other laws in the Bible are based. God gave these to Moses, engraved on two stone tablets. **40**

Thaddaeus 295

Theology, study of God—of what he has revealed about himself in the Bible and of how humans have responded. **331**

Theophilus 304, 322

Thessalonians 379, 385

Thessalonica 382, 388

Thomas 313, 317

Thyatira 454

Tigris River 28, 246

Timothy 391, 392, 395, 397, 398

Tithe, a tenth of one's income, which the Israelites gave to support the temple and temple workers. **276**

Titus 348, 403, 404

Tobit 459

Tola 72

Tower of Babel 30

Transfiguration, mountaintop event in which Jesus was temporarily transformed into a being of light, and appeared talking with Moses and Elijah, who had been dead for centuries (Matthew 17:1-8). **286, 297**

Trinity, God the Father, the Son (Jesus), and the Holy Spirit—not three gods who act as one, but one God who reveals himself as three "persons." **19**

Triumphal entry 286, 298

Tyndale, William 5

Ur 28

Uz 145

Uzzah 96

Uzziah 178

Vashti 140, 142

Virgin birth, the miraculous birth of Jesus by his mother Mary, a virgin. **305, 310**

Vulgate, Latin translation of the Bible that had been written in Hebrew and Greek. Pope Damascus assigned the translation task to the foremost Latin scholar, Jerome, in A.D. 382. Vulgate means common, an appropriate name for the work since Latin was the common language of the day. **4**

Wesley, John 333

Wisdom literature, genre of writing that embraces short nuggets of sage advice, debates, and deeply probing essays—all about everyday life. Wisdom writers give practical tips for living, explore the possible reasons behind human suffering, and contemplate the meaning of life. Wisdom literature of the Bible includes Proverbs, Ecclesiastes, and Job. **145, 159, 422**

Word, a title describing Jesus. **312, 315**

Wycliffe, John 5

Xerxes 138

Yom Kippur 44, 46

Zacchaeus 308

Zechariah 267, 268, 305

Zechariah's Song 305

Zedekiah 184

Zephaniah 255, 256

Zerubbabel 262, 265

Zion, another name for Jerusalem. **155**

Zophar 144, 146

ABOUT THE AUTHOR

Stephen M. Miller is a seminary-educated journalist and a full-time freelance writer and editor who specializes in Bible-related books. A former newspaper reporter with a degree in journalism from Kent State University, Miller made the switch to Christian writing after adding a degree in biblical studies at Nazarene Theological Seminary. He has received numerous awards, including the Evangelical Press Association's highest honor, the Award of Excellence, for his editing of *Illustrated Bible Life*, a Bible-background magazine. Raised in Ohio, Miller now lives in the Kansas City area with his wife and two children.